Uni Göttingen 7
232 013 705

D1661961

VOLUME SIXTY ONE

THE PSYCHOLOGY OF LEARNING AND MOTIVATION

Series Editor
BRIAN H. ROSS
Beckman Institute and Department of Psychology
University of Illinois, Urbana, Illinois

VOLUME SIXTY ONE

THE PSYCHOLOGY OF LEARNING AND MOTIVATION

Edited by

BRIAN H. ROSS
Beckman Institute and Department of Psychology
University of Illinois, Urbana, Illinois

AMSTERDAM • BOSTON • HEIDELBERG • LONDON
NEW YORK • OXFORD • PARIS • SAN DIEGO
SAN FRANCISCO • SINGAPORE • SYDNEY • TOKYO
Academic Press is an imprint of Elsevier

Academic Press is an imprint of Elsevier
225 Wyman Street, Waltham, MA 02451, USA
525 B Street, Suite 1800, San Diego, CA 92101-4495, USA
Radarweg 29, PO Box 211, 1000 AE Amsterdam, The Netherlands
The Boulevard, Langford Lane, Kidlington, Oxford, OX5 1GB, UK
32 Jamestown Road, London, NW1 7BY, UK

Copyright © 2014, Elsevier Inc. All rights reserved.

No part of this publication may be reproduced, stored in a retrieval system or transmitted in any form or by any means electronic, mechanical, photocopying, recording or otherwise without the prior written permission of the publisher

Permissions may be sought directly from Elsevier's Science & Technology Rights Department in Oxford, UK: phone (+44) (0) 1865 843830; fax (+44) (0) 1865 853333; email: permissions@elsevier.com. Alternatively you can submit your request online by visiting the Elsevier web site at http://elsevier.com/locate/permissions, and selecting *Obtaining permission to use Elsevier material*

Notice
No responsibility is assumed by the publisher for any injury and/or damage to persons or property as a matter of products liability, negligence or otherwise, or from any use or operation of any methods, products, instructions or ideas contained in the material herein. Because of rapid advances in the medical sciences, in particular, independent verification of diagnoses and drug dosages should be made

ISBN: 978-0-12-800283-4
ISSN: 0079-7421

> For information on all Academic Press publications
> visit our website at store.elsevier.com

14 15 16   10 9 8 7 6 5 4 3 2 1

CONTENTS

Contributors ix

1. **Descriptive and Inferential Problems of Induction: Toward a Common Framework**   1
   Charles W. Kalish and Jordan T. Thevenow-Harrison
   1. Introduction   2
   2. Theory-Based and Similarity-Based Inductive Inference   3
   3. Induction as Statistical Inference: Descriptive and Inferential Problems   6
   4. Inductive and Transductive Inference: Sample and Population Statistics   9
   5. Using Transductive Inference   12
   6. Summary: Transductive and Evidential Theories of Inference   16
   7. Distinguishing Transductive and Evidential Inferences   17
   8. Developing Solutions to Descriptive Problems   21
   9. Solutions to Inferential Problems   27
   10. Summary and Conclusions   32
   References   34

2. **What Does It Mean to be Biased: Motivated Reasoning and Rationality**   41
   Ulrike Hahn and Adam J.L. Harris
   1. The Notion of Bias   42
   2. When is a Bias a Bias?   69
   3. Measuring Bias: The Importance of Optimal Models   76
   4. Conclusions   91
   Acknowledgment   93
   References   93

3. **Probability Matching, Fast and Slow**   103
   Derek J. Koehler and Greta James
   1. Introduction   103
   2. Dumb Matching   107
   3. Smart Maximizing   113
   4. Smart Matching   118
   5. Dumb Maximizing   124
   6. Conclusion   129

Acknowledgments 129
References 129

4. Cognition in the Attention Economy 133
Paul Atchley and Sean Lane

1. Introduction 134
2. What are the Consequences of an Attention Debt? 145
3. Why do We Overspend our Attention Budget? 156
4. Can we Expand the Attention Economy? 163
5. Conclusion 169
References 171

5. Memory Recruitment: A Backward Idea About Masked Priming 179
Glen E. Bodner and Michael E.J. Masson

1. Masked Priming 180
2. Three Accounts of Masked Priming 182
3. Four Masked Priming Phenomena 185
4. The Status of the Memory-Recruitment Account 205
5. Moving Accounts of Masked Priming Forward 208
References 209

6. Role of Knowledge in Motion Extrapolation: The Relevance of an Approach Contrasting Experts and Novices 215
André Didierjean, Vincent Ferrari, and Colin Blättler

1. Introduction 216
2. Representational Momentum 217
3. Understanding the Impact of observers' Knowledge of Objects 221
4. RM Is Modulated by Expert Knowledge 225
5. Conclusion 232
References 233

7. Retrieval-Based Learning: An Episodic Context Account 237
Jeffrey D. Karpicke, Melissa Lehman, and William R. Aue

1. Introduction 238
2. Current Status of Retrieval Practice Research 239
3. Analysis of Existing Explanations of Retrieval Practice 247
4. An Episodic Context Account of Retrieval-Based Learning 258
5. Evidence Supporting an Episodic Context Account 263

6. General Discussion and Final Comments 275
  Acknowledgments 278
  References 278

8. **Consequences of Testing Memory** **285**

   Kenneth J. Malmberg, Melissa Lehman, Jeffrey Annis, Amy H. Criss, and Richard M. Shiffrin

   1. Introduction 285
   2. Benefits of Memory Testing 287
   3. Costs of Testing Memory: Output Interference 298
   4. The Influence of One Test on the Next: Sequential Dependencies 302
   5. Past Decisions Influence Future Decisions: Shifts in Bias 306
   6. Conclusions 308
   References 308

Index *315*
Contents of Previous Volumes *323*

CONTRIBUTORS

Jeffrey Annis
Department of Psychology, University of South Florida, Tampa, Florida, USA

Paul Atchley
Department of Psychology, University of Kansas, Lawrence, Kansas, USA

William R. Aue
Department of Psychological Sciences, Purdue University, West Lafayette, Indiana, and Department of Psychology, Syracuse University, Syracuse, New York, USA

Colin Blättler
Research Center of the French Air Force (CReA), Salon-de-Provence, France

Glen E. Bodner
Department of Psychology, University of Calgary, Calgary, Alberta, Canada

Amy H. Criss
Department of Psychology, Syracuse University, Syracuse, New York, USA

André Didierjean
University of Franche-Comté & Institut Universitaire de France, Besançon, France

Vincent Ferrari
Research Center of the French Air Force (CReA), Salon-de-Provence, France

Ulrike Hahn
Department of Psychological Sciences, Birkbeck, University of London, London, United Kingdom

Adam J.L. Harris
Department of Cognitive, Perceptual & Brain Sciences, University College London, London, United Kingdom

Greta James
Department of Psychology, University of Waterloo, Waterloo, Ontario, Canada

Charles W. Kalish
Department of Educational Psychology, University of Wisconsin-Madison, Madison, Wisconsin, USA

Jeffrey D. Karpicke
Department of Psychological Sciences, Purdue University, West Lafayette, Indiana, USA

Derek J. Koehler
Department of Psychology, University of Waterloo, Waterloo, Ontario, Canada

Sean Lane
Department of Psychology, Louisiana State University, Baton Rouge, Louisiana, USA

Melissa Lehman
Department of Psychological Sciences, Purdue University, West Lafayette, Indiana, USA

Kenneth J. Malmberg
Department of Psychology, University of South Florida, Tampa, Florida, USA

Michael E.J. Masson
Department of Psychology, University of Victoria, Victoria, British Columbia, Canada

Richard M. Shiffrin
Department of Brain and Psychological Sciences, Indiana University, Bloomington, Indiana, USA

Jordan T. Thevenow-Harrison
Department of Educational Psychology, University of Wisconsin-Madison, Madison, Wisconsin, USA

CHAPTER ONE

Descriptive and Inferential Problems of Induction: Toward a Common Framework

Charles W. Kalish[1], Jordan T. Thevenow-Harrison

Department of Educational Psychology, University of Wisconsin-Madison, Madison, Wisconsin, USA
[1]Corresponding author: e-mail address: cwkalish@wisc.edu

Contents

1. Introduction	2
2. Theory-Based and Similarity-Based Inductive Inference	3
3. Induction as Statistical Inference: Descriptive and Inferential Problems	6
4. Inductive and Transductive Inference: Sample and Population Statistics	9
5. Using Transductive Inference	12
6. Summary: Transductive and Evidential Theories of Inference	16
7. Distinguishing Transductive and Evidential Inferences	17
7.1 People and Statistics	20
8. Developing Solutions to Descriptive Problems	21
8.1 Correlations and Associations	22
8.2 Componential Analysis	22
8.3 Transition Probabilities	23
8.4 Absolute to Relational Statistics	24
8.5 Global to Specific Relations	25
8.6 Simple to Complex	26
8.7 Summary of Solutions to Descriptive Problems	27
9. Solutions to Inferential Problems	27
9.1 Transductive Inference	28
9.2 Bayesian Inference	28
9.3 Between Transductive and Evidential Inference	29
9.4 Communicative Bias	30
9.5 Intentional Versus Incidental Learning	31
9.6 Summary of Solutions to Inferential Problems	31
10. Summary and Conclusions	32
References	34

Abstract

There are many accounts of how humans make inductive inferences. Two broad classes of accounts are characterized as "theory based" or "similarity based." This distinction has organized a substantial amount of empirical work in the field, but the exact dimensions of contrast between the accounts are not always clear. Recently, both accounts have used concepts from formal statistics and theories of statistical learning to characterize human inductive inference. We extend these links to provide a unified perspective on induction based on the relation between descriptive and inferential statistics. Most work in Psychology has focused on descriptive problems: Which patterns do people notice or represent in experience? We suggest that it is solutions to the inferential problem of generalizing or applying those patterns that reveals the more fundamental distinction between accounts of human induction. Specifically, similarity-based accounts imply that people make *transductive* inferences, while theory-based accounts imply that people make *evidential* inferences. In characterizing claims about descriptive and inferential components of induction, we highlight points of agreement and disagreement between alternative accounts. Adopting the common framework of statistical inference also motivates a set of empirical hypotheses about inductive inference and its development across age and experience. The common perspective of statistical inference reframes debates between theory-based and similarity-based accounts: These are not conflicting theoretical perspectives, but rather different predictions about empirical results.

1. INTRODUCTION

Induction is a fundamental cognitive process. Broadly construed, any prediction or expectation about empirical phenomena represents an inductive inference. Within Psychology, learning, categorization, probability judgments, and decision-making are all central forms of inductive inference. Other psychological processes may be treated as involving induction (e.g., perception, language comprehension). There are likely many different psychological mechanisms involved in making inductive inferences, many ways people make predictions and form expectations. This chapter focuses on a paradigm case: Learning from examples. Based on experience with a limited set of examples, people generalize to new examples. Not all inductive inferences need take this form (though by being generous about what counts as an "example" and an "expectation" almost any induction may). However, learning from examples captures an important set of phenomena, and covers a broad enough range that characterizations may apply to other forms of inductive inference.

This chapter further focuses on developmental questions. How do infants and young children learn from examples, and what changes across the lifespan? The development of inductive inference is a particularly important question because induction is both (potentially) a subject of development and a mechanism or source of developmental change. Many of the changes that occur over the lifespan may reflect learning from experience: Children learn more about their world and culture and so become more adult-like in their inferences (e.g., Carey, 1985).

Infants clearly learn from experience (e.g., Rovee-Collier & Barr, 2001). At the same time, there are many developmental processes that likely affect the nature of such learning. As children acquire language, develop abstract representations, and are exposed to formal instruction, what and how they learn from examples changes. Whether there is continuity in processes of inductive inference, or whether development involves the acquisition of new forms of inference is a major source of debate. Debates about the nature of inductive inference have a long history in cognitive development. Alternative positions have been clearly articulated and defended with empirical results. One of the primary goals of this chapter is to provide a unified account of these alternatives.

2. THEORY-BASED AND SIMILARITY-BASED INDUCTIVE INFERENCE

There are two primary approaches to inductive inference, similarity based and theory based. This basic dichotomy appears in many forms, with alternatives characterized in slightly different ways (e.g., "emergent" vs. "structured probability," Griffiths, Chater, Kemp, Perfors, & Tenenbaum, 2010; McClelland et al., 2010). In similarity theories, learning from examples involves forming associations or other representations of patterns of co-occurrence (e.g., Hampton, 2006, see papers in Hahn & Ramscar, 2001). Such accounts typically posit continuity in inductive inference, both phylogenetically and ontogenetically. They tend to invoke domain-general mechanisms and emphasize internalizing structure from environment. Changes in inductive inference are a result of changing experience: As the child forms different associations, comes to represent more or more complex patterns in experience, their thinking changes. Alternative, theory-based approaches treat learning from examples as a form of hypothesis testing (Chater, 2010; Gelman & Koenig, 2003; Gopnik et al., 2004; Murphy & Medin, 1985). Such accounts often emphasize domain-specificity (in the hypotheses available) and are congenial to nativists (e.g., innate sources of hypotheses). Theory-based views involve some developmental discontinuities, at least phylogenetically (it is unlikely that simple organisms test hypotheses). As hypothesis-testing seems to be a more complex cognitive process than association formation, a natural developmental hypothesis is that infants may start making similarity-based inductions but acquire theory-based induction at some point.

As the descriptions offered above illustrate, similarity-based and theory-based views differ on a number of dimensions. While distinctions between the two approaches have organized much of contemporary research (see Feeney & Wilburn, 2008; Gelman & Medin, 1993; Pothos, 2005; Sloutsky & Fisher, 2008; Smith, Jones, & Landau, 1996), it is not always clear just where the critical differences lie. For example, similarity-based approaches tend to emphasize domain generality and continuity across development, but need not do so. In motivating our proposal for a unifying framework, we first consider some alternative ways of characterizing the two approaches to inductive inference.

Similarity-based theories are often characterized by "bottom-up" building of associations from basic, perceptual, experience (Smith et al., 1996). Theory-based accounts emphasize "top-down" application of conceptual structures or constraints to organize experience (Wellman & Gelman, 1992). In the developmental literature, similarity-based theories are often associated with the view that young children's inductive inferences are based on apparent, perceptual features (see Keil, Smith, Simons, & Levin, 1998; Springer, 2001). Children learn from examples by forming associations between perceptual features. Theory-based views hold that even young children organize experience using abstract, theoretical, concepts, such as "cause" or "belief" (Carey, 1995; Wellman & Gelman, 1992). Children can learn not just perceptual associations in experience, but relations involving nonperceptual properties as well (Mandler, 2004). This framing of the alternatives has led to substantial research about children's representations of nonperceptual information (e.g., Gelman & Markman, 1986; Kalish, 1996; Wellman & Estes, 1986; but see Sloutsky & Fisher, 2008). However, we suggest that the perceptual versus abstract features distinction is largely orthogonal to whether induction is best characterized as similarity or theory based. For example, it is quite possible to learn similarity relations among abstract features.

A second dimension of distinction is rules versus graded representations. Theory-based inferences are characterized as all-or-none judgments based on rules or criterial features (Sloutsky, Lo, & Fisher, 2001). For example, in determining the category membership (and thus the basis for future predictions) of an animal, its parentage is particularly informative and other information (e.g., location) is largely irrelevant. The critical features may be unknown: An underlying "essence" determines category membership and forms the basis for inductive inferences (Gelman, 2003). The point is that a distinction is made between those features that truly determine category membership, or cause objects to have the properties they do, and those features that are merely associated with other features. Theory-based inductive inference depends on identifying the critical (causal, essential) features. In contrast, similarity-based theories emphasize patterns of associations across a number of features. Any pattern of association can be useful for prediction and inference: There is no distinction between "really" and "merely" associated. Features are useful for prediction because of their informational value: Does observing one feature affect the probability of observing another? This perspective tends to emphasize graded or probabilistic judgments (Yurovsky, Fricker, Yu, & Smith, 2013). Multiple features or patterns of association can be present at any one time (e.g., an animal looks like a dog but had bear parents). Inference involves combining these features (e.g., weighting by past diagnosticity; see Younger, 2003). Research motivated by this contrast addresses selectivity in inductive judgments (Kloos & Sloutsky, 2008; Sloutsky et al., 2001). Do children privilege some features over others when making inductive inferences? Can such preferences be traced back to patterns of association or do they involve beliefs about causes and essences (Gelman & Wellman, 1991; Kalish & Gelman, 1992)? For example, when a child judges that an animal that looks like a dog but has bear parents will have internal organs of a bear rather than a dog, are they using a rule or principle that "parents matter" or are they basing their judgment on the past reliability of parentage over appearance? The question of the graded versus criterial basis of children's inferences has motivated significant research but is also largely orthogonal to the distinction we wish to draw.

There are a number of other ways of distinguishing between theory-based and similarity-based inductive inference. For example, theories may involve conscious deliberate judgment, while similarity is unconscious and automatic (see Smith & Grossman, 2008). We suggest that all these distinctions are symptoms or consequences of a more fundamental difference. Theory-based accounts treat examples as evidential; similarity-based accounts treat examples as constitutive. In theory-based inference, the examples a person has encountered provide evidence for a relation (Gelman, 2003; Gopnik & Wellman, 1994; Murphy & Medin, 1985). That all the dogs one has seen so far have barked provides evidence that the next dog observed will also bark. In contrast, for similarity-based views, the prediction about the next dog is a kind of report of that past experience. The characterizations of theory-based inference discussed above are a consequence of attempts to explicate evidential inferences in terms of scientific theories (see Gopnik & Wellman, 1992, 1994). Scientists use theories to interpret evidence, and evidence is used to develop and refine theories. To assert that young children treat examples as evidence is to assert that they do what scientists do. There is also a tradition of formal approaches to evidence evaluation in the statistical and philosophical literature. As psychologists have adopted these formal approaches, a new characterization of theory-based inference has been developed (Gopnik et al., 2004; see Oaksford & Chater, 2007; Tenenbaum & Griffiths, 2001; Xu & Tenenbaum, 2007a). Theory-based inference is a type of statistical inference. Similarity-based inference is also a type of statistical inference. This common grounding in statistical theory, induction as statistical inference, provides a unified perspective on theory-based and similarity-based accounts. We develop this unified perspective below and use it to identify just what is at issue in the debate between theory-based and similarity-based views. This perspective leads directly to empirical tests of the two views.

3. INDUCTION AS STATISTICAL INFERENCE: DESCRIPTIVE AND INFERENTIAL PROBLEMS

Making a statistical inference involves two steps: describing the available data and then generalizing. For example, after conducting an experiment, a researcher needs to describe her results. She may compute the mean and standard deviations of observations in the various conditions. Those descriptive statistics convey information about patterns in the sample, in the observed data. The researcher's next step is to make some general claims based on those descriptive statistics. She wants to estimate a population parameter or identify the generative process that produced the observations. This step involves computing inferential statistics (e.g., a t-test). In a nutshell, similarity-based approaches to inductive inference focus on the first step: The descriptive problem of characterizing patterns in the data. Theory-based approaches focus on the second step: The inferential problem of estimating a generative process. In fleshing out this characterization of inductive inference, we introduce a number terms and distinctions, many of which are illustrated in Fig. 1.1.

The descriptive problem in inductive inference is noticing patterns in experience. Some patterns may be obvious, some less so. Children may

Descriptive and Inferential Problems 7

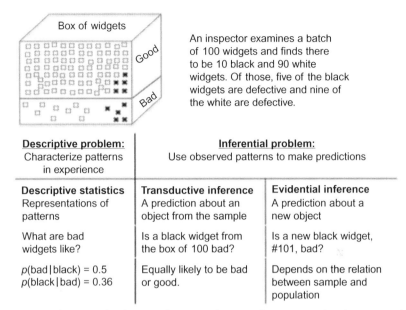

Figure 1.1 *Elements of inductive inference.* Inductive inference may be characterized in many ways. Researchers in Cognitive Science are increasingly framing empirical theories in terms drawn from statistics and statistical learning theory. Many of these terms can be illustrated with respect to a simple example.

to notice certain kinds of patterns, adults others. For example, a classic question in the developmental literature was whether children classify based on holistic or family resemblance structure rather than single-criterion rules (Bonthoux, Lautrey, & Pacteau, 1995; Kemler & Smith, 1978). Given a set of examples would children tend to form groups characterized by one or the other structure (unsupervised classification)? Would children find it more difficult to learn one kind of structure than the other (supervised classification)? A single-criterion rule (e.g., beard vs. clean-shaven) is one way to organize or describe a set of examples. Similarity to prototypes (e.g., the Smith family vs. the Jones family) is another. The psychological literature contains a number of proposals about the kinds of patterns that people tend to use to describe their experience (see Murphy, 2002). There are also different accounts of how these patterns are formed or represented. For example, prototype theory involves abstract representations of patterns (the prototypes) stored in memory. There are no fixed or abstract patterns in exemplar theories (Nosofsky, 2011). Rather the organization of a set of examples is established during elicitation. When people are asked to make an inference they compute patterns in observed (or remembered) examples on the fly (see Rouder & Ratcliff, 2006; Smith, 2005). We will return to the question of how descriptive statistics (patterns) are used to make inductive inferences below. The point here is that inductive inference requires some way of describing past experience: Certain patterns have been observed and others have not.

The inferential problem of induction is using past observations to make a prediction or generalization about new cases. In formal statistical hypothesis testing, it is the inferential problem that is the difficult one. Developing and justifying normative procedures for making predictions from samples is what statistical theory is all about. Calculating a sample mean (descriptive statistic) is relatively straightforward. Deciding what a particular sample mean implies about a new case is much less so. In part, the inferential problem involves understanding bias and precision in estimators. This problem also involves understanding relations between samples and populations (or between two samples). Statistical theory provides a particular account of the inferential problem: the "evidential" account. We can use past observations to make new predictions because those past observations provide evidence. Statistics is a theory of evidence for inductive inference.

Psychological accounts of inductive inference have tended to suggest that people adopt a different solution. The alternative solution involves computation of match. The prediction about a new or unknown example depends on how that example resembles the description of known examples. For example, if one has organized past experience in terms of two prototypes, dogs and cats, then predictions about a new case, a new animal, depends on its match to those two prototypes. Psychological theories specify the procedures used to assess match (e.g., similarity to prototype, Hampton, 2006) and to generate a prediction (e.g., Luce's (1959) choice rule for selecting among alternative matches). Old examples do not provide evidence for an inference about a new one; they provide a foundation for assessing degree of resemblance between new and old.

Not surprisingly, we argue that similarity-based approaches to induction are characterized by a "matching" solution to the inferential problem. Theory-based approaches are characterized by an "evidential" solution to the inferential problem. Similarity-based approaches suggest that people assess the match between new examples and old; theory-based approaches suggest that people use old examples as evidence about new. One immediate consequence of this claim is that facts about description are not the central point of disagreement. Whether children and adults are understood to think in terms of observable or abstract features, for example, does not immediately bear on whether they are making similarity-based or theory-based inductive inferences. It is not how experience is described or represented that distinguishes the two approaches, but rather how that is experience is used to generate predictions. This point, that it is the inferential problem that separates the accounts, is not really novel: Presentations of theory-based accounts often emphasize that people treat examples as evidence (e.g., perceptual features are evidence for underlying essences, Gelman, 2003; see Murphy & Medin, 1985). Recent Bayesian accounts of theory-based inductive inference make explicit the link to formal statistical theory (Chater, 2010; Xu & Tenenbaum, 2007b). What is missing, or at least underemphasized, is the degree to which a shared commitment to statistical inference as a model for human inference provides a basis for contrasting theory-based and similarity-based theories. To develop this comparison further, we need to say a bit more about the similarity-based solution to the inferential problem: How do we understand inferences based on matching from a statistical perspective?

4. INDUCTIVE AND TRANSDUCTIVE INFERENCE: SAMPLE AND POPULATION STATISTICS

Inferential statistics is a way of making inferences about populations based on samples. Given information about a subset of examples, how do we draw conclusions about the full set (including other specific examples in that full set)? Inferences based on principles of evidence use sample statistics. We suggest that matching and similarity-based inferences are based on population statistics. That is, if one has sample statistics then the inferential problem is to treat those statistics as evidence. If one has population statistics then the inferential problem is to assess a degree of match. Psychologists are very familiar with inferential statistics and evidence evaluation: Our studies tend to draw conclusions about populations based on samples. Rarely, if ever, do we have information about the whole population. What are inferences based on population statistics? Fortunately, there is an account of population-statistical inferences, and even a label for such inferences: Transductive.

Developmental psychologists are familiar with the term "transductive inference" from Piaget (1959). Piaget used "transductive" to describe a preoperational form of reasoning that connects specific cases with no general rule or underlying mechanism. Events that are experienced together are taken to be causally related. A car horn honks and the lights go off: The horn caused the darkness. The inference goes from one particular event (honking) to another (darkness) with no notion of a general mechanism. That is, how can honking horns cause darkness? How could this relation be generally sustained? Piaget's transductive inference seems to be a version of the "principle of association" in sympathetic magic (Frazer, 1894; events perceived together are taken to be causally related). Such a principle is also characteristic of a Humean or associative view of causation and causal inference: A causal relation just is the perception of association. Once a person associates horns and darkness, they will come to expect one given the other. Transductive inference (horn → darkness), therefore, seems to be familiar associative learning and similarity-based induction. Perhaps, Piaget was illustrating some special characteristics of young children's similarity-based inferences (e.g., "one-trial" associations) but the general process of inference is familiar. In particular, it is not clear how Piaget's transductive inference addresses the point that similarity-based inferences rely on population statistics. There is another account of transductive inference that does, however.

Apparently independent of Piaget, the term "transductive inference" was introduced into the machine learning/statistical learning theory literatures by Vladimir Vapnik (1998). Vapnik also uses "transductive" to refer to inferences from particular examples to particular examples. For Vapnik, though, transductive inferences are a kind of simplifying assumption, a way of approaching complex learning problems. Vapnik argues that (standard, evidential) statistical inference is an attempt to solve a general problem: From experience with a set of examples how can the learner construct a rule or pattern that can then be applied to new examples? The key feature of evidential inference is that the class of potential new examples is infinite. The point of transductive inference is that often the class of potential new examples is finite. For example, an inspector might encounter the problem of predicting which widgets in a batch of 100 are defective (see Fig. 1.1). Solving the problem for the particular batch will usually be much simpler than solving the problem of identifying defective widgets in general. For Vapnik, transductive inference is the strategy of limiting focus to the specific examples that the learner will actually encounter. Here is the link to Piaget's transductive inference. If the child's conclusion (horns cause darkness) is restricted just to that particular observed situation, then it seems less problematic: It is only when generalized that it falls apart. Similarly, the link to sample and population statistics becomes more apparent. In (standard, evidential) statistical inference, the 100 widgets are a sample. The learner's task is to use this sample to form representation of the class or population of widgets. In transductive inference, the 100 widgets are the population. The learner's task is to learn and use statistics to make predictions about this population.

An example will help illustrate the relation between transductive-population and evidential-sample inferences. Consider the 100 widgets. Suppose an inspector has examined all 100 and discovered the following: There are 10 black widgets and 90 white widgets moreover 5 of the black widgets are defective and 9 of the white are defective. These are descriptive statistics. The inspector's challenge is to use these descriptive statistics to make some inferences. We distinguish two kinds of inferences the inspector could be called upon to make: transductive or evidential (what we have been calling "standard statistical inference"). If the inference concerns the 100 widgets, the statistics observed are population statistics. For example, suppose the inspector is shown one of the widgets and told that it is white. The inspector recalls that only 10% of white widgets were defective and predicts that it will be fine. This is clearly a kind of inductive inference in that it is not guaranteed to be correct: The inspector's past experience makes the conclusion probable but not certain. But it is a special kind of inductive inference, a transductive inference. The inspector's problem is relatively simple. After having calculated the descriptive statistic, $p(\text{defective}|\text{white}) = 0.1$, there is really very little work to be done. The inspector can be confident using the descriptive statistic to guide his inferences because the statistic was calculated based on the examples he is making inferences about. In a certain respect, the inspector is not even making an inference, just reporting a description of the population. To move from "9 of these 90 white widgets are defective" to "one of these white widgets has a 10% chance of being defective" to "a white widget selected at random is probably not defective" hardly seems like much of an inductive leap at all. Put slightly differently, once the inspector has solved the descriptive problem (what is $p(\text{defective}|\text{white})$ among the 100 widgets?) the inferential problem of making a prediction about a randomly selected widget is easy.

The inspector faces a more difficult problem when making inferences about a widget not in the "training" set, widget 101. In this case, the descriptive statistics (e.g., $p(\text{defective}|\text{white}) = 0.1$) are characteristics of a sample and the inspector must calculate inferential statistics to make predictions. In this case, the inspector must consider the evidential relation between his sample (of 100 widgets) and the general population (from which the new widget was drawn). Is the sample biased? Recognizing and adjusting for sample bias is a specific problem of evidential inference. It is this inferential problem that distinguishes transductive inference from evidential inference. Sample bias does not matter when making a transductive inference to one of the 100 original widgets.

Consider the problem of predicting the color of a widget identified as defective. If the defective widget was one of the 100, the prediction is clear: It is probably white. Nine of the 14 defective widgets encountered were white. If the defective widget is new, widget 101, the prediction is less clear. The 100 original widgets were mostly white. Is that true of the general population widgets or is that a bias in the sample? Unless the inspector knows about the relation between his sample and the population he cannot use the former to make predictions about the latter. However, figuring out that relation, solving this inferential problem, is irrelevant for a transductive inference. If the 100 widgets are considered the population, there is no sampling bias. In this way, transductive inference can be used as a kind of simplifying assumption for inductive inference. Transductive inference is inductive inference where sample-population relations are ignored, where sample statistics are treated as population statistics. The challenge of transductive inference is limited to developing useful descriptions (characterizing the patterns in the available data).

5. USING TRANSDUCTIVE INFERENCE

Transductive inference is useful as a model of human inference. It focuses on the question of how people describe their experience. People may be disposed toward certain kinds of descriptions. They may be more successful at noticing and representing some patterns than others. In the example, the "hard" work is deciding to calculate the probability of defectiveness conditional on color. It is possible to imagine using a different conditional probability (e.g., $p(color|defectiveness)$) or a predictive system that uses descriptions other than conditional probabilities. In the second half of this chapter, we consider developmental changes in the kinds of descriptions formed. An important part of the psychology of human inference is understanding the kinds of descriptions people form and use.

Once the inspector has selected the relevant description of the widgets he is almost, but not quite, done with the predictive work. There is still the problem of applying the descriptive statistic.[1] In the example, the inspector is given color information about a widget (it is white). The inspector has to match that information to one of his descriptions. Should he make a prediction based on $p(\text{defective}|\text{white})$ or $p(\text{defective}|\text{black})$? Which description is a better match for the example in question? Here, the matching problem is simple: The target widget is white. In multidimensional problems, the match can be more challenging. The target widget might partially match many descriptions. If the inspector has learned a set of single-feature conditional probabilities, he faces the challenge of deciding which probability to use (or how to combine them). For example, does the widget's color, shape, or size best predict? The inspector might have very partial information about the target widget (e.g., know its color but not shape or size). The inspector may have to make decisions about how to weight various features in determining how to use information about the known widgets to make his prediction. Within Psychology, exemplar theories are particularly focused on this matching problem (see Nosofsky, 2011). The description of the examples is relatively unproblematic (in the extreme, a veridical representation of each individual encountered). The substance of the theory concerns how people match targets of inference to those descriptions (i.e., the nature of the similarity computation). Transductive inference need not be easy. Understanding how people accomplish the difficult task of forming and using descriptions, even with full-population information, would be valuable contribution to the Psychology of inductive inference.

From the description of transduction, however, it is not immediately clear how this is a generally useful account of inductive inference. It is very rare that people have access to the entire population or want to limit their inferences to the set of examples already encountered. Vapnik's proposal is that transductive inference can be applied in a fairly wide variety of situations: Transductive inference is more useful than it might appear.

Transductive inference is useful when there is only partial information available about the population. Suppose the inspector has his 100 widgets but only knows about the quality (defective or not) of a few of them. One of the virtues of transductive inference is that the widgets of unknown

---

[1] The distinction between descriptive and inferential problems is a bit arbitrary at this point. Deciding which description to use to solve a particular prediction problem could be characterized as part of the inferential problem. However, on our account this same problem is faced when using sample descriptions to make population inferences (though the inspector might use different statistics in the sample and population cases). Because we are interested in distinguishing transductive and evidential approaches, we define "inferential" to best make this distinction.

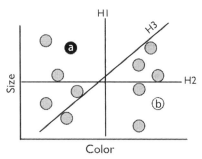

Figure 1.2 *Example of a partial information problem.* The inspector has 12 widgets but only knows the quality of two of them: (a) is defective and (b) is sound. The two known or labeled cases (a and b) support a large number of hypothesis about how to label the other cases. H1, H2, and H3 are all plausible decisions boundaries for distinguishing defective from sound widgets. Transductive inference and semi-supervised learning use information about the unlabeled widgets to constrain hypotheses. In this case, there is an obvious cluster structure or discontinuity along the color dimension. This structure in the unlabeled cases makes H1 preferred over H2 or H3.

quality can be used to generate a description. This same idea underlies "semi-supervised" learning (Zhu & Goldberg, 2009). Structure in the partial examples can be informative. Consider the problem in Fig. 1.2. Widgets vary along two dimensions, color and size. The inspector knows the quality of only two widgets (a and b) (Fig. 1.2). A large number of descriptions are compatible with the two known examples (e.g., decision boundaries or hypotheses, H1–H3). By taking the distribution of the unknown widgets as informative, the learner is able to select among the descriptions, is able to prefer one hypothesis over others.

The point of this example is that partial examples can be used to develop descriptive statistics. This has important practical consequences for speeding learning in complex data sets where complete information is costly (Zhu & Goldberg, 2009). The example also illustrates a way that transductive inference can be extended to new instances. Transductive inference is characterized by restriction to the sample of examples used to develop the descriptive statistics: The sample is treated as the population. In theory, a transductive inference based on 100 widgets would make no prediction about widget 101. However, it is always possible to iterate transductive inference. When the inspector is confronted with widget 101, he can redo his transductive inference process. He can compute new statistics for a population of 101 widgets. Some of those widgets (including widget 101) will be of unknown quality. The descriptive statistics provide a basis for imputing any missing features. Thus transductive inference can be extended to cover each new example that appears.

In practice, a single new example is unlikely to change the descriptive statistics very much. The best way to predict the quality of an unknown widget will likely be the same for the sample of 101 as it was for the sample of 100. That is, transductive inference can do the same work as evidential inference. Transductive inference can make predictions about new examples, by "acting as if" the new examples were part of the original training set. If the new example had been an old one, what would it have been expected to be like? The transductive strategy is to treat new examples as if they were old ones.

Almost all psychological models of classification and inference can be characterized as transductive. These models generally make predictions based on what would be expected of the new item were it a member of the original set. Based on a training set, the learner arrives at some policy for predicting features of interest. When new examples are encountered that same policy is applied. This is, effectively, what is happening when learners are understood to compute the match between old examples (or descriptions of old examples) and new. What prediction would be made about an old example with the features of the new one? Consider that psychological models of induction and classification do not distinguish between old (in the training set) and new examples.[2] Exemplar, prototype, and connectionist models (to name a few) operate by matching partial examples to descriptions.

In contrast to transductive inference, evidential inference based on inferential statistics requires more than a match between new and old examples. A prediction about an old example may be different than the prediction about a new example, even if the old and new examples have exactly the same known features. The reason for this difference is that the descriptions developed from old examples provide a different sort of evidence for old than for new examples. Descriptive statistics are calculated from old examples: Had the old examples been different, the descriptive statistics would have been different as well. The old example is partially constitutive of the description. The link between descriptive statistics and new examples is less direct. It is less clear how or when descriptive statistics computed

---

[2] This is not necessarily true in that a new example can have a novel feature, "is a new example," that distinguishes it from all old examples. Exactly how inductive and transductive models can be expected to differ is the subject of the next section.

for one set of examples warrant predictions for new sets of examples. Coming up with these warrants, the how and when, is the job for a theory of evidence or inferential statistics. To make an inductive inference based on evidence requires considering relations between samples and populations. The features that define the relation of a sample to a population can be called "inferential features" (see Thevenow-Harrison & Kalish, 2013). Inferential features of samples include the size of the sample, the process used to generate the sample, and the distinction between old and new examples.

In the context of machine learning and statistical learning theory, transduction is a simplifying assumption: Certain problems may be solved more easily by ignoring inferential features. The question is whether it is a useful assumption. Under what conditions is the gain in ease of learning/computation worth the cost in failures of prediction? Transduction is the strategy of overfitting. Overfitting may often be a good idea. In the context of Psychology, transduction is a hypothesis about how people make inductive inferences. The transductive hypothesis is that people do not attend to inferential features. The question is whether this is a good hypothesis. When people make an inductive inference based on experience with a sample of examples, do they consider the relation between the sample and the population? Do people worry about overfitting?

6. SUMMARY: TRANSDUCTIVE AND EVIDENTIAL THEORIES OF INFERENCE

We began by offering statistics as a model or illustration of inductive inference. Statistics is formal and normative approach to inference that has been widely influential in shaping psychological theories. Within this approach, there is a major distinction between descriptive and inferential statistics. Descriptive statistics characterize samples. Inferential statistics indicate what can be inferred about a population based on a sample. This suggests there are two "problems" involved in inductive inference: a descriptive problem and an inferential problem. Making an inductive inference requires some description of past examples, and a procedure for using that description to make an inference about new examples. Psychological theories of inference are claims about how people solve these descriptive and inferential problems. By and large theories have focused on the descriptive problem. Different psychological theories make different claims about the kinds of descriptions people form: prototypes versus exemplars, similarity versus rules, perceptual versus abstract features, propositional versus nonpropositional representations, innate versus learned.

Many psychological theories share a commitment to a single solution to inferential problems: They imply that people make transductive inferences. Transductive inference proceeds by treating the available sample as the full population. The inferential problem in transductive inference is to compute a match between descriptions of a sample and a target example. The inference "fills in" some missing features of the target example. The implicit assumption is that the target example is a member of the sample that was used to compute the descriptions, or at least that the descriptions used were computed from the union of the original sample and the target. In contrast, theory-based and Bayesian accounts adopt a different solution to inferential problems, one modeled more closely on formal inferential statistics (see Oaksford & Chater, 2007; Tenenbaum & Griffiths, 2001). The key point to this approach is that samples provide evidence for inductive inferences to new examples and populations. The inferential problem lies in evaluating this evidence; theory-based approaches require attending to relations between samples and populations, or between different samples. The features that describe those relations we call "inferential features." Inferential features include how the original sample was selected, and whether the target of inference comes from that original sample or not. We argue that the major distinction between similarity-based and theory-based accounts of inference is that the former are transductive and the latter are evidential.

7. DISTINGUISHING TRANSDUCTIVE AND EVIDENTIAL INFERENCES

As discussed above, the contrast between theory-based and similarity-based accounts of inductive inference has been drawn along many dimensions. In our terms, there are contrasting claims concerning the descriptions people form in the course of learning from examples. For example, are descriptions built from patterns in the observable features, or do descriptions include abstract or invisible features? Similarity-based and theory-based approaches also contrast in their accounts of the ways descriptions are used to generate predictions about new examples, in how inferences are made. Similarity-based approaches are transductive; theory-based approaches are evidential. We have argued the different accounts of inference are more central to characterizing the two approaches than are descriptive differences. Thus an important goal for research on the psychology of induction is determining whether people make transductive or evidential inferences. How do people solve the inferential problem?

That inferential processes are central does not mean that descriptive processes are irrelevant. It may be that transductive and evidential inference use different kinds of descriptions. For example, descriptions that involve imputing hidden features, latent variables, or causal models, seem more consistent with evidential inference (e.g., Gelman, 2003; Gopnik et al., 2004). The learner forms a representation of the structure underlying the observed examples. That structure can be understood as a generative or population model. After observing 100 widgets, the inspector might describe his experience as involving "essentially faulty widgets" and "essentially sound widgets." The observable features correlated with defectiveness (e.g., color) serve as indicators for some underlying construct. When making an inference about a new widget the inspector assesses the evidence that the new widget has one or the other essences. Thus describing the examples in terms of hidden features or causal models is useful for later evidential inference.

However, that is not the only way that hidden features can be used. A construct like "essentially faulty widget" could be understood as a summary description of a complex set of component relations. There is a pattern in the examples that predicts defectiveness. That pattern defines what it is to be "essentially faulty." When the inspector encounters another widget, he matches it to patterns developed from his past experience. The key similarity/transductive point is that the construct, "essentially faulty," is nothing more than the pattern. The construct itself "does not work," it is just a shorthand for a complex pattern. This is the sense in which emergentist approaches (e.g., connectionist, dynamic systems, and even exemplar) argue that concepts do not exist or are epiphenomenal (McClelland et al., 2010; Smith, 2000). Both theory-based and similarity-based approaches can characterize people as forming abstract representations or models of their experience. The difference is how those models work inferentially. For similarity-based accounts, there are only descriptions. For theory-based accounts, there are descriptions (the patterns) and inferences (what the patterns provide evidence for). The difference between the two approaches is not whether they involve hidden features and abstract representations, but rather how they explain the inferential processes involving those representations.

We suggest that theory-based and similarity-based theories are distinguished by their claims about how people use descriptions to make inductive inferences. Similarity-based approaches can be relatively neutral about the kinds of descriptions people tend to form. Any description can be used to determine the match between old and new examples. Theory-based approaches, however, are committed to some more specific claims about the nature of descriptions. While any description can be assessed for match to a new example, only certain descriptions can be assessed as evidence regarding a new example. At a minimum, the description must distinguish between new and old examples. To assess evidence a reasoner would also want information about the relation between the original sample and the population. Those features of samples and examples that are used to assess evidential relations are inferential features. Theory-based accounts imply that people's inductive inferences are sensitive to inferential features. For example, people will distinguish between old and new examples. Similarity-based theories are not committed to a particular role for inferential features. They do not need to deny that people attend to such features, but do not assign those features any special significance. In this way, theory-based accounts make stronger claims about the nature of inductive inference than to similarity-based accounts.

Theory-based accounts are also stronger in making particular claims about how inferential features should affect induction. For example, a similarity-based inductive system could distinguish between old and new examples, but assign higher confidence to predictions about new than old. In the sample of widgets described above, an old black widget had a 50% chance of being defective. If all the new black widgets encountered are defective, the system may conclude it can make more confident predictions about new than old examples. This system has picked up on a predictive regularity involving new–old examples, but it does not seem to be using old examples as evidence. Treating examples as evidence seems to imply that inferences to a population are always less secure than inferences within a sample.[3] However, exactly just what constitutes an evidential inference is not at all clear. Is an inference evidential only if it conforms to some normative standard? Must it conform completely? If people use inferential features of examples in way that differ from formal statistics (e.g., Bayesian inference) are they not making evidential inferences?

---

[3] One could be 100% confident that a black widget from the sample has a 50% chance of being defective: certain one cannot be certain. Distinguishing the probability that something is the case from the precision of that probability judgment is part of an evidential understanding of data. Note the claim is not that similarity-based accounts must act as described, just that they may do so.

7.1. People and Statistics

To this point, we have been using statistics as a model for evidential inference. But statistics as a normative theory of evidence, of just what information is needed and how it is to be used, is both complex and a matter of continuing debate. For Psychology, statistics is a computational level model—it is an idealized account (see Chater, Tenenbaum, & Yuille, 2006; Oaksford & Chater, 1998). A computational model serves as an example of the kinds of processes and information that are involved in accomplishing some goal (Marr, 1982). Such models suggest hypotheses about processes and information that humans use to accomplish the same goals. For example, a computational level account of inductive inference (e.g., statistics) distinguishes between biased and unbiased samples. Do humans also make such distinctions, and if so how and when? Computational level models provide standards against which human performance can be measured and understood.

We have offered an account of transductive inference that is clearly distinguished from evidential inference. Transductive inference does not represent relations between samples and populations: It operates with population statistics. In these terms, any consideration of the relation between samples and populations, such as distinguishing old examples from the sample from new examples from the population, would render an inference process "non-transductive." We have also offered an account of evidential inference based on formal statistics. In these terms, any deviation from formal statistical inference would render a process "non-evidential." We suspect that human inductive inference is both non-transductive and non-evidential. That is, people do attend to sample-population relations but do not do so in exactly the ways formal statistical approaches do. Recall that inferential features are those elements of inductive problems that concern the relation between samples and populations. Transductive inference is insensitive to inferential features; these features do not affect predictions. Evidential inference is sensitive to inferential features in a very particular way (established by formal statistics). Our hypothesis is that human inductive inference is sensitive to inferential features but does not, or does not always, accord with formal statistical principles. The empirical challenge is documenting just how and when people are sensitive to inferential features of inductive problems.

Taking statistics as a computational level model of inductive inference, similarity-based transductive account and theory-based evidential accounts of human performance differ in degree, not in kind. Both accounts suggest that human inductive inference approaches formal statistical inference to some degree, and that human performance can be productively understood in comparison with formal statistics. The two approaches have often been distinguished by their claims about the descriptions people form during the course of learning from examples (e.g., perceptual vs. conceptual features). We have argued that they are also distinguished by the ways descriptions are used to make inferences (transductive vs. evidential). Ultimately, the labels "similarity based" and "theory based" should be replaced by specific hypotheses about descriptive and inferential processes. In the remainder of this chapter, we consider some of these specific hypotheses. How do people solve the descriptive and inferential problems of induction? We focus particularly on developmental research, as it is in this field that alternatives have been most clearly articulated. In the course of development, people might adopt different solutions to these two problems.

We have argued that account of inductive inference can be divided into those focusing on descriptive problems and those focusing on inferential problems. The former address the kinds of patterns people learn from experience; the latter address the ways people generalize learned patterns. While these approaches have generally been understood as alternatives, we suggest that they are complementary. Any account of inductive inference needs to explain both the patterns people learn and the ways those patterns are generalized. Below we very briefly review some of the main strands of research on descriptive and inferential problems. In each case, where possible, we focus on developmental claims. What might constitute relatively simple or early emerging inductive inferences and how would inferences be expected to change with age and experience?

8. DEVELOPING SOLUTIONS TO DESCRIPTIVE PROBLEMS

In this section, we focus on theories of description. Much of this work is framed in terms of statistical learning. Theories about statistical learning, broadly construed, explore how people track associations in data and become sensitive to the statistical structure of the world. The challenge is to identify just which statistical patterns people track. Within this literature, we focus on a few illustrative accounts about what develops as children make inductive inferences.

8.1. Correlations and Associations

A longstanding hypothesis about statistical learning is that people attend to correlated attributes (e.g., Rosch, 1975) or patterns of association between events (Hull, 1932). Work in connectionist and dynamic systems frameworks focuses on the emergence of higher-order associations, patterns of patterns. One claim about what develops is that experience leads to abstraction: First-order regularities give rise to higher order regularities. If a child sees a series of round or container-like objects and is told that each one is a "ball" or a "cup," then the ability to categorize balls and cups is a result of the associations between those experiences. If encounters with round things are associated with the sound "ball," then a first first-order generalization may result: "ball" is associated with round shape (Colunga & Smith, 2003). Higher-order generalizations result from the associations and regularities between first-order processes: balls and cups are both solid things defined primarily by their shape or function (Smith, Colunga, & Yoshida, 2003). This is not an explicit rule; it is knowledge "inseparable from the real-time processes of perceiving, remembering, and attending" (Colunga & Smith, 2008). This second-order knowledge enables learners to quickly learn and generalize from a single example. These higher-order correlations are the result of further exposure to regular data over time. This developmental claim is a claim about exposure to regular statistical structure in the world; the development happens *through* exposure; the processes themselves remain fundamentally unchanged, but operate on more and more abstract structures. In general, we should expect people to encode patterns of correlation. As children develop, as they gain more experience and more practice making inductive inferences, they become sensitive to higher order correlations.

8.2. Componential Analysis

Related work in connectionist models of knowledge and inference emphasizes learning increasingly fine-grained discriminations (Rogers & McClelland, 2004). A relatively novice learner, or model early in training, will represent the most broadly predictive discriminations. A collection of objects may be divided into "animates" and "inanimates" as this provides the greatest predictive utility. Animacy may be the first principle component. With experience, further training, people begin to represent finer-grained predictive structure: additional principle components, sub-type structures, and contextual filters. As above, these statistical patterns are not explicitly represented, but are rather consequences of changes in the ways experience is encoded in distributed (sub-featural) representations. For example, fruits and vegetables might be initially represented as very similar; the learner would make the same inferences about fruits and vegetables. With further experience patterns discriminating the two classes would be encoded. In the context of "agriculture," fruits and vegetables are similar, but in the context of "cooking" they are distinct. A developmental hypothesis is that children will initially make inductive inferences based on a single most effective discrimination (e.g., animate vs. inanimate). With experience inference will become sensitive to finer-grained and more contextualized statistical patterns.

8.3. Transition Probabilities

Research on statistical learning explores a number of statistical relations children may use to identify structure in their environment (see Aslin & Newport, 2008; Lany & Saffran, 2013 for reviews). One specific proposal concerns transition probabilities (Saffran, Aslin, & Newport, 1996). Transition probabilities are patterns in the orderings of experiences. For example, element B might always follow when element A is encountered. Transition probabilities are particularly useful statistics for identifying structure in temporally extended events, like speech. Adults are able to determine the boundaries of "words" in a continuous stream of artificial speech using only the distributions of phonemes (Hayes & Clark, 1970). Differences in transition probabilities between phonemes cue learners about word boundaries (Saffran et al., 1996). Critically, children and adults can segment using transition probabilities even when segments are not indicated by co-occurrence statistics, which merely describe events that occurred together (e.g., the frequency of AB pairings). Even newborns seem to be sensitive to these transitional probabilities: neonates show differences in event-related potentials at word onset and offset when exposed to a syllable stream with queues to three-syllable word boundaries embedded in transition probabilities between phonemes (Teinonen, Fellman, Näätänen, Alku, & Huotilainen, 2009). Learners seem to represent transition probabilities in contexts besides speech, including event perception (Baldwin, Andersson, Saffran, & Meyer, 2008) and visual sequences (Fiser & Aslin, 2002; Kirkham, Slemmer, & Johnson, 2002). This perspective suggests some developmental hypothesis. Learners might begin representing individual event frequencies and then move to representing co-occurrence statistics or transition probabilities. However, the data seem to argue against this as infants are sensitive to transition probabilities. An alternative is that young learners may form representations based on immediate transitional probabilities, while more skilled learners (those with greater processing capacity or those with more exposure to these transitional probabilities in the world) track more long-ranged transition probabilities with intervening elements (Romberg & Saffran, 2013; Santelmann & Jusczyk, 1998).

8.4. Absolute to Relational Statistics

A common feature of the preceding accounts is that they emphasize relations between elements: People are representing patterns across features and events. In some ways, the simplest descriptions of experience would seem to involve absolute or unconditional frequencies, such as how many red things one has seen. However, absolute frequencies may be less useful than relative (e.g., more red than green) or conditional (e.g., red is more likely after seeing green). This idea that relational information is more important or useful than absolute has also been extended to the kinds of elements over which statistics are calculated. In particular, Gentner and colleagues (Gentner, 1988, 2003; Goldstone, Medin, & Gentner, 1991) have distinguished between patterns in absolute and relational features. An absolute feature is an intrinsic feature, true of an object in isolation, such as shape. A relational feature is something true of an object compared to others, such as being to the left of, or being part of. Learners may represent patterns in absolute or relational features, or both. A developmental hypothesis is that children initially focus on absolute features, with patterns of relational features playing a larger role in later inference. If a child is trying to learn that red trucks pick up garbage and blue trucks deliver filtered water, discriminating the trucks based on patterns of absolute features (red vs. blue) is easier than learning the color of the trucks based on their behavior. As children gain experience with trucks that do things, the large amount of overlap between the more immediate and perceptual features of redness and blueness will begin to coalesce into categories of trucks. As these comparisons progress the small differences between the features and behaviors of trucks become more salient, allowing "marginally more abstract representations that can then participate in more distant comparisons" (Gentner, 2003). Taxis cease to be yellow cars and become hirable transportation. As knowledge about categories increases from progressive exposure during development, alongside the acquisition of relational language, absolute feature comparison subsides and gives rise to relational similarity. Relational patterns become the basis for inference and analogy.

8.5. Global to Specific Relations

One of the perennial questions, especially within the developmental literature, is whether people first learn very general patterns in experience and then refine or whether they learn very specific patterns and then integrate (see Gibson, 1979, 1982; Kemler & Smith, 1978; Ward, 1980). Connectionist (Rogers & McClelland, 2004) and dynamic systems (Smith, 2000) models tend to suggest a differentiation process: People first notice global patterns and then refine representations to account for specific contexts and features. Statistical learning and, perhaps, relational similarity views suggest that people may first notice very specific or local patterns and then build more comprehensive representations. Sloutsky and colleagues (Kloos & Sloutsky, 2008; Sloutsky, 2010; Sloutsky & Fisher, 2004) have argued for a global to specific shift. Children's early representations of patterns rely on a high degree of redundancy. They notice regularities instantiated across many correlated features but have difficulty noticing single-feature regularities. Thus, for example, the large number of obvious physical and behavioral features that whales share with fish overwhelms the small number of features whales share with other mammals. The pattern children notice is that whales are like fish. In contrast, older children and adults can restrict their attention to single criterial features when the context demands it. Linguistic labels are one important "focusing" context (Gelman & Markman, 1986; Waxman, Lynch, Casey, & Baer, 1997).

A slightly different perspective on the question of global versus focused patterns concerns the specificity of the statistical relations represented. One way to characterize a global pattern is as one that involves many, rather than few, features. A global pattern could also be more abstract, less specific. For example, association is a bidirectional relation: A is associated with B in the same way that B is associated with A. Conditional probability is a unidirectional relation: $p(A|B)$ need not equal $p(B|A)$. Association is a more global representation of the relation between two variables than is conditional probability; indeed association can be understood to be composed of conditional probabilities. It has been suggested that association may be a more basic way of describing experience than conditional probability (Vadillo & Matute, 2007). For example, young children find it easier to learn symmetric patterns of association than asymmetric patterns of conditional probability and often interpret the latter as the former. When show a set of objects where all the red things were square, but some squares were also blue, preschool-aged children learned an imperfect correlation between color and shape, rather than a set of distinct conditional probabilities (e.g., $p(\text{Square}|\text{Red}) = 1$, $p(\text{Red}|\text{Square}) < 1$, Kalish, 2010). A similar tendency to represent more general patterns may underlie the inverse fallacy (taking $p(A|B) = p(B|A)$, Dawes, Mirels, Gold, & Donahue, 1993; Villejoubert & Mandel, 2002) and illusory correlations (see Villejoubert & Mandel, 2002).

8.6. Simple to Complex

In addition to global to specific changes in descriptions, there is also evidence of the reverse pattern. People may start with relatively simple, rule-like representations and move to more integrative, complex representations. A classic statement of this position was the hypothesis that children tend to see categories as defined by one or a small number of features (Clark, 1973). Such representations would tend to lead to overextensions or overgeneralizations such as the inference that any older man is an "uncle" (neglecting to consider the relatedness features). More recent statements of this position have originated from dual-process accounts of learning and inference (Ashby, Alfonso-Reese, Turken, & Waldron, 1998). There is a linguistically mediated system of learning relations that develops simple rule-like descriptions. There is also an implicit system that develops more complex descriptions integrating across multiple stimulus dimensions. Rule-like representations emerge early in learning and can be formed on the basis of just a few examples. Implicit, integrative, representations emerge with increasing experience. Thus early in learning people may form simple descriptions that provide partial predictive success. With experience, they form more complex descriptions that capture more of the predictive structure of the environment. Several studies have shown this kind of rule to integration shift in categorization and description. Interestingly, young children may be more prone to stick with their initial, simple, representations. On a task requiring integration across stimulus dimensions (e.g., Category A = "large and square" or "small and circle"), people first learn a simple rule (e.g., Category A = "large") that is partially successful. Adults improve with trials as they come to use a more implicit, exemplar-based approach, integrating the two dimensions into a representation that is not easily specified as a verbalizable rule, but is sensitive to and can integrate covariances across multiple dimensions (Ashby et al., 1998). Young children who learn a partially successful single-condition rule do not show improvement across trials, they stick with the simple rule (Huang-Pollock, Maddox, & Karalunas, 2011). This result is consistent with the perspective that gist representations are characteristic of expertise (Reyna & Brainerd, 1994). Novices rely on verbatim rules, while experts use complex implicit descriptions.

8.7. Summary of Solutions to Descriptive Problems

This brief review has illustrated a few proposals about the kinds of descriptions people form based on experience with examples. These proposals are especially useful as they involve developmental hypotheses. How might the patterns that people notice change with development and/or experience? We focused on proposals regarding the structure of descriptions. There are also a number of other proposals about the content of descriptions. For example, do people represent patterns of observable, perceptual features or more abstract, conceptual features (see Mandler, 2004; Springer, 2001)? Similarly, there may be differences across domains in the types of features included in descriptions (e.g., a "whole object-bias" for word learning, Markman, 1989; Smith et al., 2003) and in the structure of descriptions (e.g., taxonomic hierarchies in representations of living things, Atran, 1995). However, rather than attempting a comprehensive review of these alternatives (see Hayes, 2007; Lany & Saffran, 2013; Sloutsky, 2010 for recent reviews), we now turn to the other half of inductive inference: the inferential problem.

9. SOLUTIONS TO INFERENTIAL PROBLEMS

Understanding how people describe or represent their experiences with examples is certainly a critical component of a theory of inductive inference, but this aspect has tended to dominate. Considerably less attention has been paid to the equally critical problem of how people use descriptions to generate predictions and to make inductive inferences. As above, we frame this discussion in terms of sensitivity to "inferential features." Inferential features are those aspect of an inductive problem that are relevant to evidential inference, features such as the bias in a sample or whether the target of an inference is a member of the observed sample or the unobserved population.

9.1. Transductive Inference

As noted above, most psychological accounts of inference are implicitly transductive. The descriptions that people form function as population statistics, and matching procedures do not consider inferential features. Although typically implicit, this position represents a plausible empirical hypothesis: Human inductive inference is transductive rather than evidential. A developmental version might hold that children's, or novices', inferences are transductive and insensitive to sample-population relations. Fiedler (2000) offers precisely this hypothesis in arguing that people are "myopic." When drawing inferences from experience, people tend to focus on that which is close at hand: the examples they have encountered. Sampling considerations, how one came to encounter those particular examples, are remote and tend to be overlooked. Fiedler argues that myopia can account for a number of empirical results in the judgment and decision-making literature. For example, people have difficulty ignoring repeated information (Unkelbach, Fiedler, & Freytag, 2007). They seem not to distinguish between the same example sampled twice and two identical elements sampled separately. Base-rate neglect (e.g., in medical diagnosis problems, see Sweets, Dawes, & Monahan, 2000) and the inverse fallacy (Dawes, Mirels, Gold, & Donahue, 1993; Villejoubert & Mandel, 2002) both stem from failing to consider the larger populations from which examples were drawn. Fiedler (2008) notes that different sampling procedures introduce complex biases into the sets of examples encountered. Appropriately adjusting for this bias, according to Fiedler, is a difficult cognitive problem requiring deliberate meta-cognitive control. People are generally unwilling, or unable, to make such adjustments and instead rely on myopic intuitions.

9.2. Bayesian Inference

In contrast to viewing people as transductive reasoners, many researchers now argue that people are actually very good evidential reasoners. This work adopts Bayesian inference as a rational model of human performance (see Oaksford & Chater, 2001, 2007). By and large, people evaluate the evidential significance of examples they have encountered: People are sensitive to inferential features. Among the most striking empirical demonstrations inferences are findings that even infants attend to the relations between samples and populations. When 11-month-old infants see an experimenter selecting five red balls and one white ball from an occluded box, they look longer when the distribution in the full box is revealed to be incongruous with the sample (e.g., many white balls but only a few red) than when the full box matches the sample (mostly red with a few white). This only occurs when the experimenter is blindfolded during the sampling procedure or samples randomly; infants seem not to expect samples and populations to match when the experimenter looked into the box while sampling, or if the infants previously learned that the experimenter liked the color red (Xu & Denison, 2009). The interpretation is that infants are surprised that random (blindfolded) selection would yield a non-representative sample (see also Teglas, Girotto, Gonzalez, & Bonatti, 2007; Xu & Garcia, 2008). Preschool-aged children can use observed or inferred bias in samples to learn word meanings and people's preferences (Kushnir, Xu, & Wellman, 2010; Xu & Tenenbaum, 2007b). In contrast to Fiedler's myopia, young children seem to perceive the inferential features of samples quite clearly. Bayesian approaches represent a clear alternative to transductive claims. Although often framed as a rational model (i.e., a way to understand what inductive inference is and how it can be evaluated), Bayesian inference can be used as an empirical hypothesis. Perhaps people, even infants, do make evidential inferences on much the same basis as normative statistical theory.

9.3. Between Transductive and Evidential Inference

Most discussion has focused on whether people make evidential inferences (e.g., "are Bayesians") or not, with relatively less attention to questions of how or to what degree people are sensitive to inferential features. To conclude this section, we offer some hypotheses regarding intermediate positions between fully transductive and fully evidential inference. One of the most basic intermediate positions is just recognizing that these are two different cases. That is, people may distinguish between sample and population inferences without a full (normative) appreciation of the implications. In practice, this might involve a distinction between predictions about old and new examples. Sample versus population may be a very basic inferential feature. Some evidence that young children make this distinction comes from a belief revision task (Kalish, Kim, & Young, 2012). Participants first learned a perfect correlation between two attributes from a set of examples (e.g., all and only red fish are large). They then encountered another set of examples that undermined one of the component conditional relations (e.g., all red fish are large, but some blue fish are large as well). The question was whether children would abandon both conditionals (e.g., come to believe that color and size are uncorrelated) or would maintain one but not the other. When the identity of a test item (e.g., a red fish) was unspecified, or it was described as being a new example (a new fish from the pond), 7- to 8-year-old children made no consistent predictions. However, when the test item was described as one of the test set (one of the fish that we caught) children made accurate predictions based on the combined samples (all but not only red fish are large). Preschool-aged children did not show this effect because they had difficulty even representing the simple conditional probabilities (just tracked overall correlation). The suggestion is that older children succeeded in representing the statistics of the sample (making predictions only about encountered fish) but refused to generalize to the population. This may have been because the two samples of fish differed so much that it was unclear they were drawn from the same population (e.g., a nonstationary process). This is not to say that young children understood bias or nonstationarity, but rather that they had some intuitions to be suspicious—that sampling mattered. In a similar demonstration with younger children, Thevenow-Harrison and Kalish (2013) found that preschool-aged children would make accurate predictions about the distribution of features in a biased sample (produced by a deceptive informant) but would not apply those predictions to new instances. One basic form of evidential inference may be simply to distinguish cases where sample-population relations matter from those where they do not. Such a distinction may not involve any sophisticated ways to deal with sample bias, but just suspicion or reluctance to generalize in such cases.

9.4. Communicative Bias

Most of the demonstrations of young children's sensitivity to sampling and other inferential features of inductive problems come in social contexts (though see Teglas et al., 2007). Shafto, Goodman, and Frank (2012) interpret pedagogical and communicative effects on learning in terms of sample selection. One reason it helps to have a teacher is that the learner can understand the teacher's examples as having been purposefully selected, and therefore as having particular implications for the larger population. We are suggesting something like the converse: Children may find it particularly easy to evaluate evidential relations in the context of communication or inferring another person's goals and motives. For example, young children are often insensitive to the diversity of the examples they encounter (e.g., generalizing from three examples of the same breed of dog vs. three examples of different breeds, see Gelman, 2003 for discussion). However, when learning from another or generating examples for someone else to learn from, young children reliably prefer diverse sets (Rhodes, Gelman, & Brickman, 2010). Rhodes and colleagues suggest that young children may find it easier to think of sample selection in terms of the messages being conveyed (e.g., "What is she trying to tell me?") rather than as purely statistical features.

9.5. Intentional Versus Incidental Learning

Another way of framing the fact that children seem more sensitive to inferential features in pedagogical contexts is that they are consciously learning in such contexts. Perhaps, children (and adults) make evidential inferences when consciously learning and predicting: In implicit contexts, people may rely on transductive inference. This hypothesis is consistent with Fiedler's (2012) view of myopia as a meta-cognitive failure. Accounting for sample-population relations requires focused attention. People may be able to attend to inferential features (especially basic ones like sample vs. population inferences), but tend not to. This perspective provides a natural developmental hypothesis: As children are generally more likely to rely on automatic processes, they should tend to make more transductive inferences. Evidential inferences are a more complicated and mature form of reasoning. Some evidence consistent with this hypothesis comes from the Thevenow-Harrison and Kalish (under review) study. They found that young children were more likely to use a regular relation in a biased sample to make predictions about members of the sample than about new examples. This pattern held only for relations that children explicitly focused on learning during a practice phase. During practice, children were taught to predict the color of an object from its shape. Because the correlation was perfect, it was also possible to predict shape from color, an implicit pattern. Children did learn and use the implicit pattern to make predictions, but did not distinguish between old and new examples or biased and representative samples. It may be that more automatic or procedural forms of learning produce transductive inference. Sensitivity to inferential features may be a feature of more explicit, problem-solving processes.

9.6. Summary of Solutions to Inferential Problems

In this section, we briefly reviewed some hypotheses about the descriptive and inferential aspects of inductive inference. Clearly, there are many more options than we have been able to address. One notable omission is work on causal inference or learning (see Gopnik et al., 2004; Gopnik & Schulz, 2007; Sobel & Kushnir, 2006). The idea that people form causal models of experience that serve as the basis for future inference seems most consistent with evidential inference. In particular, people are understood to be learning generative models, representations that abstract away from the particular examples encountered and function as a kind of population model (a generative process that produces specific samples). Procedures for learning causal models that focus on interventions are designed to distinguish real patterns that would occur in future samples from spurious patterns that occur in samples because of biased or incomplete sampling (e.g., only certain combination of variables will be naturally observed). However, explicating the relation between this kind of causal inference and evidential inference as described is beyond the scope of this brief review.

10. SUMMARY AND CONCLUSIONS

Our main goal has been to understand the relations between theories of transductive inference (e.g., associative or similarity-based models) and theories of evidential inference (e.g., Bayesian or theory-based models). These accounts are competing alternatives (see Chater et al., 2006; McClelland et al., 2010), but there are many dimensions of difference not all equally central. In many respects, similarity-based and theory-based approaches are talking past each other: They focus on different aspects of inductive inference. Similarity-based approaches focus mainly on the descriptive problem of representing statistical patterns in the set of encountered examples. Theory-based approaches focus mainly on the inferential problem of using an observed pattern to make predictions about future examples.

Any account of inductive inference must address both descriptive and inferential problems so there are various ways to compare and contrast. For example, theory-based accounts may hold that descriptions will be domain-specific, reflect some innate biases, involve conceptual/abstract features, and be propositional and relatively rule-like (see Gelman & Kalish, 2006; Gelman & Wellman, 1991). Similarity-based accounts may favor exactly the opposite forms of descriptions (see Rogers & McClelland, 2004). It is certainly a valuable project to empirically assess each of these alternatives. We will not have a complete theory of the psychology of inductive inference without understanding how people solve the descriptive problem. But, positions on description do not necessarily distinguish theory-based and similarity-based approaches: A similarity theory could involve innate, abstract, rule-like descriptions, for example. In characterizations of the inferential problem, the approaches are more sharply distinguished. We suggest that what characterizes a similarity-based approach is a commitment to transductive inference. Theory-based approaches are characterized by a commitment to evidential inference. One of the major challenges in distinguishing theory-based and similarity-based theories, then, is developing a clear account of transductive and evidential inference. We have relied on statistics and statistical learning to provide this account. In so doing, we have attempted to draw out empirical hypotheses and motivate some proposals for how human inference may be (more or less) transductive or evidential.

In presenting this account of inductive inference, we have proceeded as if the descriptive and inferential problems were independent. This is likely not the case. The descriptions developed from experience will be used to draw inferences: Different descriptions may be suited for different inferential procedures. In particular, evidential inference involves models of populations or generative processes. The goal in describing experience is to form a representation of an abstract entity. For instance, after encounters with several dogs, an evidential inference would form a representation of the kind or class of dog. The information extracted from encounters with individual dogs, the pattern noticed, contributes to this organized representation. It is possible to conduct evidential inference in a more piecemeal way. Someone could learn just the average size of dogs or the distribution of colors of dogs. In this case, the result is a model of a single parameter (e.g., size) rather than an organized concept. Put slightly differently, a model of a population or generative process will presumably be useful in many inductive problems: A representation of dogs can be used to predict size, color, sound, etc. There is no reason that transductive inference could not also form organized, conceptual, representations. However, because there is no sense of building representation of abstract entities (populations, processes, and kinds), there is no particular reason to do so. Transductive inference may be more consistent with special purpose, single feature, descriptions of experience.

The relation between descriptive and inferential problems is just one of the empirical questions motivated by our account of inductive inference. We believe a strength of this approach is that it provides a framework for casting theoretical debates into empirical hypotheses. In the second section of this chapter, we illustrated a number of empirical questions that both similarity-based and theory-based approaches might address.

Ultimately, our goal is to dissolve the distinction between similarity- and theory-based accounts of inductive inference. There are different empirical predictions, particularly about how people solve inferential problems, but there is a common framework. The great virtue of statistics and statistical learning as models of human inference is that they provide this common framework.

REFERENCES

Ashby, F. G., Alfonso-Reese, L. A., Turken, A. U., & Waldron, E. M. (1998). A neuropsychological theory of multiple systems in category learning. *Psychological Review, 105*(3), 442–481. http://dx.doi.org/10.1037/0033-295X.105.3.442.

Aslin, R. N., & Newport, E. L. (2008). What statistical learning can and can't tell us about language acquisition. In J. Colombo, P. McCardle, & L. Freund (Eds.), *Infant pathways to language: Methods, models, and reearch disorders* (pp. 15–29). New York, NY: Psychology Press.

Atran, S. (1995). Causal constraints on categories and categorical constraints on biological reasoning across cultures. In D. Sperber & D. Premack (Eds.), *Causal cognition: A multidisciplinary debate. Symposia of the Fyssen Foundation* (pp. 205–233). New York, NY: Clarendon Press/Oxford University Press.

Baldwin, D., Andersson, A., Saffran, J., & Meyer, M. (2008). Segmenting dynamic human action via statistical structure. *Cognition, 106*(3), 1382–1407. http://dx.doi.org/10.1016/j.cognition.2007.07.005.

Bonthoux, F., Lautrey, J., & Pacteau, C. (1995). Processing modes of schematic faces in 5-year-old and 10-year-old children. *British Journal of Developmental Psychology, 13*(1), 31–44. http://dx.doi.org/10.1111/j.2044-835X.1995.tb00662.x.

Carey, S. (1985). Are children fundamentally different kinds of thinkers and learners than adults? In S. F. Chipman, J. W. Segal, & R. Glaser (Eds.), *Thinking and learning skills*: Vol. 2. (pp. 485–517). Hillsdale, NJ: Lawrence Erlbaum Associates, Inc.

Carey, S. (1995). On the origin of causal understanding. In D. Sperber, D. Premack, & A. J. Premack (Eds.), *Causal cognition: A multidisciplinary debate* (pp. xiv–350). New York, NY: Oxford University Press.

Chater, N. (2010). Probabilistic models of cognition: Exploring the laws of thought. *Trends in Cognitive Sciences, 14,* 357–364.

Chater, N., Tenenbaum, J. B., & Yuille, A. (2006). Probabilistic models of cognition: Conceptual foundations. *Trends in Cognitive Sciences, 10*(7), 287–291. http://dx.doi.org/10.1016/j.tics.2006.05.007.

Clark, E. V. (1973). What's in a word? On the child's acquisition of semantics in his first language. In T. E. Moore (Ed.), *Cognitive development and the acquisition of language.* New York, NY: Academic Press.

Colunga, E., & Smith, L. B. (2003). The emergence of abstract ideas: evidence from networks and babies. *Philosophical Transactions of the Royal Society of London. Series B: Biological Sciences, 358*(1435), 1205–1214. http://dx.doi.org/10.1098/rstb.2003.1306.

Colunga, E., & Smith, L. B. (2008). Knowledge embedded in process: the self-organization of skilled noun learning. *Developmental Science, 11*(2), 195–203. http://dx.doi.org/10.1111/j.1467-7687.2007.00665.x.

Dawes, R. M., Mirels, H. L., Gold, E., & Donahue, E. (1993). Equating inverse probabilities in implicit personality judgments. *Psychological Science, 4*(6), 396–400. http://dx.doi.org/10.1111/j.1467-9280.1993.tb00588.x.

Feeney, A., & Wilburn, C. (2008). Deciding between theories of how reasoning develops is hard. *Cognition, 108*(2), 507–511. http://dx.doi.org/10.1016/J.Cognition.2008.04.010.

Fiedler, K. (2000). Beware of samples! A cognitive-ecological sampling approach to judgment biases. *Psychological Review, 107*(4), 659–676. http://dx.doi.org/10.1037/0033-295X.107.4.659

Fiedler, K. (2008). The ultimate sampling dilemma in experience-based decision making. *Journal of Experimental Psychology Learning, Memory, and Cognition, 34*(1), 186–203. http://dx.doi.org/10.1037/0278-7393.34.1.186.

Fiedler, K. (2012). Meta-cognitive myopia and the dilemmas of inductive-statistical inference. In B. H. Ross (Ed.), *57* (pp. 1–55). San Diego, CA US: Elsevier Academic Press.

Fiser, J., & Aslin, R. N. (2002). Statistical learning of higher order temporal structure from visual shape-sequences. *Journal of Experimental Psychology Learning, Memory, and Cognition, 28*, 458–467.

Frazer, S. J. G. (1894). *The golden bough: A study in comparative religion*. New York, NY: Macmillan & Co.

Gelman, S. A. (2003). *The essential child: Origins of essentialism in everyday thought*. Oxford, New York: Oxford University Press.

Gelman, S. A., & Kalish, C. W. (2006). Conceptual development. In D. Kuhn & R. S. Siegler (Eds.), *Handbook of child psychology: Cognition, perception, and language* (6th ed., pp. 687–733). Vol. 2. Hoboken, NJ: Wiley.

Gelman, S. A., & Koenig, M. A. (2003). Theory-based categorization in early childhood. In D. H. Rakison & L. M. Oakes (Eds.), *Early category and concept development: Making sense of the blooming, buzzing confusion* (pp. 330–359). New York, NY: Oxford University Press.

Gelman, S. A., & Markman, E. M. (1986). Categories and induction in young children. *Cognition, 23*(3), 183–209.

Gelman, S. A., & Medin, D. L. (1993). What's so essential about essentialism? A different perspective on the interaction of perception, language, and conceptual knowledge. *Cognitive Development, 8*(2), 157–167.

Gelman, S. A., & Wellman, H. M. (1991). Insides and essence: Early understandings of the non-obvious. *Cognition, 38*(3), 213–244.

Gentner, D. (1988). Metaphor as structure mapping: The relational shift. *Child Development, 59*(1), 47–59. http://dx.doi.org/10.2307/1130388.

Gentner, D. (2003). Why we're so smart. In D. Gentner & S. Goldin-Meadow (Eds.), *Language in mind: Advances in the study of language and thought* (pp. 195–235). Cambridge, MA: MIT Press.

Gibson, J. J. (1979). *The ecological approach to visual perception*. Hillsdale, NJ: Erlbaum.

Gibson, E. J. (1982). The concept of affordances in development: The renascence of functionalism. In W. A. Collins (Ed.), *The minnesota symposia on child psychology: The concept of development*: Vol. 15. (pp. 55–81). Mahwah, NJ: Erlbaum.

Goldstone, R. L., Medin, D. L., & Gentner, D. (1991). Relational similarity and the non-independence of features in similarity judgments. *Cognitive Psychology, 23*(2), 222–262. http://dx.doi.org/10.1016/0010-0285(91)90010-L.

Gopnik, A., Glymour, C., Sobel, D. M., Schulz, L. E., Kushnir, T., & Danks, D. (2004). A theory of causal learning in children: Causal maps and Bayes nets. *Psychological Review, 111*(1), 3–32. http://dx.doi.org/10.1037/0033-295X.111.1.3.

Gopnik, A., & Schulz, L. E. (2007). *Causal learning: Psychology, philosophy, and computation*. New York, NY: Oxford University Press.

Gopnik, A., & Wellman, H. M. (1992). Why the child's theory of mind really is a theory. *Mind & Language, 7*(1 and 2 Spring/Summer), 145–171.

Gopnik, A., & Wellman, H. M. (1994). The theory theory. In L. A. Hirschfeld & S. A. Gelman (Eds.), *Mapping the mind: Domain specificity in cognition and culture* (pp. 257–293). New York, NY: Cambridge University Press.

Griffiths, T. L., Chater, N., Kemp, C., Perfors, A., & Tenenbaum, J. B. (2010). Probabilistic models of cognition: Exploring representations and inductive biases. *Trends in Cognitive Sciences*, *14*(8), 357–364. http://dx.doi.org/10.1016/j.tics.2010.05.004.

Hahn, U., & Ramscar, M. (2001). *Similarity and categorization*. New York, NY: Oxford University Press.

Hampton, J. A. (2006). Concepts as prototypes. In B. Ross (Ed.), *The psychology of learning and motivation. Advances in research and theory*. Vol. 46. (pp. 79–113). San Diego, CA: Elsevier Academic Press.

Hayes, B. K. (2007). The development of inductive reasoning. In A. Feeney & E. Heit (Eds.), *Inductive reasoning* (pp. 25–54). New York, NY: Cambridge University Press.

Hayes, J. R., & Clark, H. H. (1970). Experiments in the segmentation of an artificial speech analog. In J. R. Hayes (Ed.), *Cognition and the development of language* (pp. 221–234). New York, NY: Wiley.

Huang-Pollock, C. L., Maddox, W. T., & Karalunas, S. L. (2011). Development of implicit and explicit category learning. *Journal of Experimental Child Psychology*, *109*(3), 321–335. http://dx.doi.org/10.1016/j.jecp.2011.02.002.

Hull, C. L. (1932). The goal-gradient hypothesis and maze learning. *Psychological Review*, *39*(1), 25–43. http://dx.doi.org/10.1037/h0072640.

Kalish, C. W. (1996). Preschoolers' understanding of germs as invisible mechanisms. *Cognitive Development*, *11*(1), 83–106. http://dx.doi.org/10.1016/S0885-2014(96)90029-5.

Kalish, C. W. (2010). How children use examples to make conditional predictions. *Cognition*, *116*(1), 1–14. http://dx.doi.org/10.1016/j.cognition.2010.03.008.

Kalish, C. W., & Gelman, S. A. (1992). On wooden pillows—Multiple classification and childrens category-based inductions. *Child Development*, *63*(6), 1536–1557. http://dx.doi.org/10.1111/J.1467-8624.1992.Tb01713.X.

Kalish, C. W., Kim, S., & Young, A. G. (2012). How young children learn from examples: Descriptive and inferential problems. *Cognitive Science*, *36*(8), 1427–1448. http://dx.doi.org/10.1111/j.1551-6709.2012.01257.x.

Keil, F. C., Smith, W. C., Simons, D. J., & Levin, D. T. (1998). Two dogmas of conceptual empiricism: Implications for hybrid models of the structure of knowledge. *Cognition*, *65*(2–3), 103–135.

Kemler, D. G., & Smith, L. B. (1978). Is there a developmental trend from integrality to separability in perception? *Journal of Experimental Child Psychology*, *26*(3), 498–507. http://dx.doi.org/10.1016/0022-0965(78)90128-5.

Kirkham, N. Z., Slemmer, J. A., & Johnson, S. P. (2002). Visual statistical learning in infancy: Evidence for a domain general learning mechanism. *Cognition*, *83*(2), B35–B42. http://dx.doi.org/10.1016/S0010-0277(02)00004-5.

Kloos, H., & Sloutsky, V. M. (2008). What's behind different kinds of kinds: Effects of statistical density on learning and representation of categories. *Journal of Experimental Psychology. General*, *137*(1), 52–72. http://dx.doi.org/10.1037/0096-3445.137.1.52.

Kushnir, T., Xu, F., & Wellman, H. M. (2010). Young children use statistical sampling to infer the preferences of other people. *Psychological Science*, *21*(8), 1134–1140. http://dx.doi.org/10.1177/0956797610376652.

Lany, J., & Saffran, J. R. (2013). Statistical learning mechanisms in infancy. In J. L. R. Rubenstein & P. Rakic (Eds.), *Comprehensive developmental neuroscience: Neural circuit development and function in the brain*, Vol. 3. Amsterdam: Elsevier.

Luce, R. D. (1959). *Individual choice behavior: A theoretical analysis*. New York, NY: Wiley.

Mandler, G. (2004). *The foundations of mind: Origins of conceptual thought*. New York, NY: Oxford University Press.

Markman, E. (1989). *Categorization and naming in children*. Cambridge, MA: MIT Press.

Marr, D. (1982). *Vision: A computational investigation into the human representation and processing of visual information*. New York, NY: Henry Holt and Co. Inc.

McClelland, J. L., Botvinick, M. M., Noelle, D. C., Plaut, D. C., Rogers, T. T., Seidenberg, M. S., et al. (2010). Letting structure emerge: Connectionist and dynamical systems approaches to cognition. *Trends in Cognitive Sciences*, *14*(8), 348–356.

Murphy, G. L. (2002). *The big book of concepts*. Cambridge, MA: MIT Press.

Murphy, G. L., & Medin, D. L. (1985). The role of theories in conceptual coherence. *Psychological Review*, *92*(3), 289–316. http://dx.doi.org/10.1037/0033-295X.92.3.289.

Nosofsky, R. M. (2011). The generalized context model: An exemplar model of classification. In E. M. Pothos & A. J. Wills (Eds.), *Formal approaches in categorization*. New York, NY: Cambridge University Press.

Oaksford, M., & Chater, N. (1998). *Rational models of cognition*. Oxford: Oxford University Press.

Oaksford, M., & Chater, N. (2001). The probabilistic approach to human reasoning. *Trends in Cognitive Sciences*, *5*(8), 349–357.

Oaksford, M., & Chater, N. (2007). *Bayesian rationality: The probabilistic approach to human reasoning*. New York, NY: Oxford University Press.

Piaget, J. (1959). *The language and thought of the child*. New York, NY: Humanities Press.

Pothos, E. M. (2005). The rules versus similarity distinction. *Behavioral and Brain Sciences*, *28*, 1–49.

Reyna, V. F., & Brainerd, C. J. (1994). The origins of probability judgment: A review of data and theories. In G. Wright & P. Ayton (Eds.), *Subjective probability* (pp. 239–272). Oxford: John Wiley & Sons.

Rhodes, M., Gelman, S. A., & Brickman, D. (2010). Children's attention to sample composition in learning, teaching and discovery. *Developmental Science*, *13*(3), 421–429. http://dx.doi.org/10.1111/j.1467-7687.2009.00896.x.

Rogers, T. T., & McClelland, J. L. (2004). *Semantic cognition: A parallel distributed processing approach*. Cambridge, MA: MIT Press.

Romberg, A. R., & Saffran, J. R. (2013). All together now: Concurrent learning of multiple structures in an artificial language. *Cognitive Science*, *37*(7), 1290–1320. http://dx.doi.org/10.1111/cogs.12050.

Rosch, E. (1975). Cognitive representations of semantic categories. *Journal of Experimental Psychology General*, *104*(3), 192–233.

Rouder, J. N., & Ratcliff, R. (2006). Comparing exemplar- and rule-based theories of categorization. *Current Directions in Psychological Science*, *15*(1), 9–13. http://dx.doi.org/10.1111/j.0963-7214.2006.00397.x.

Rovee-Collier, C., & Barr, R. (2001). Infant learning and memory. In G. Bremner & A. Fogel (Eds.), *Blackwell handbook of infant development* (pp. 139–168). Malden: Blackwell Publishing.

Saffran, J. R., Aslin, R. N., & Newport, E. L. (1996). Statistical learning by 8-month-old infants. *Science*, *274*(5294), 1926–1928.

Santelmann, L. M., & Jusczyk, P. W. (1998). Sensitivity to discontinuous dependencies in language learners: Evidence for limitations in processing space. *Cognition*, *69*(2), 105–134. http://dx.doi.org/10.1016/S0010-0277(98)00060-2.

Shafto, P., Goodman, N. D., & Frank, M. C. (2012). Learning from others: The consequences of psychological reasoning for human learning. *Perspectives on Psychological Science*, *7*(4), 341–351. http://dx.doi.org/10.1177/1745691612448481.

Sloutsky, V. M. (2010). From perceptual categories to concepts: What develops? *Cognitive Science*, *34*(7), 1244–1286. http://dx.doi.org/10.1111/j.1551-6709.2010.01129.x.

Sloutsky, V. M., & Fisher, A. V. (2004). Induction and categorization in young children: A similarity-based model. *Journal of Experimental Psychology. General*, *133*(2), 166–188.

Sloutsky, V. M., & Fisher, A. V. (2008). Attentional learning and flexible induction: How mundane mechanisms give rise to smart behaviors. *Child Development*, *79*(3), 639–651. http://dx.doi.org/10.1111/j.1467-8624.2008.01148.x.

Sloutsky, V. M., Lo, Y. F., & Fisher, A. V. (2001). How much does a shared name make things similar? Linguistic labels, similarity, and the development of inductive inference. *Child Development*, *72*(6), 1695–1709.

Smith, L. B. (2000). Learning how to learn words. In R. M. Golinkoff (Ed.), *Becoming a word learner: A debate on lexical acquisition*. Oxford, NY: Oxford University Press.

Smith, J. D. (2005). Wanted: A new psychology of exemplars. *Canadian Journal of Experimental Psychology/Revue Canadienne de Psychologie Expérimentale*, *59*(1), 47–53. http://dx.doi.org/10.1037/h0087460.

Smith, L. B., Colunga, E., & Yoshida, H. (2003). Making an ontology: Cross-linguistic evidence. *Cognitie Creier Comportament*, *7*(1), 61–90.

Smith, E. E., & Grossman, M. (2008). Multiple systems of category learning. *Neuroscience and Biobehavioral Reviews*, *32*(2), 249–264. http://dx.doi.org/10.1016/j.neubiorev.2007.07.009.

Smith, L. B., Jones, S. S., & Landau, B. (1996). Naming in young children: A dumb attentional mechanism? *Cognition*, *60*(2), 143–171.

Sobel, D. M., & Kushnir, T. (2006). The importance of decision making in causal learning from interventions. *Memory & Cognition*, *34*(2), 411–419. http://dx.doi.org/10.3758/BF03193418.

Springer, K. (2001). Perceptual boundedness and perceptual support in conceptual development. *Psychological Review*, *108*(4), 691–708. http://dx.doi.org/10.1037/0033-295X.108.4.691.

Sweets, J., Dawes, R., & Monahan, J. (2000). Better decisions through science. *Scientific American*, *283*(4), 82–87.

Teglas, E., Girotto, V., Gonzalez, M., & Bonatti, L. L. (2007). Intuitions of probabilities shape expectations about the future at 12 months and beyond. *Proceedings of the National Academy of Sciences of the United States of America*, *104*(48), 19156–19159. http://dx.doi.org/10.1073/pnas.0700271104.

Teinonen, T., Fellman, V., Näätänen, R., Alku, P., & Huotilainen, M. (2009). Statistical language learning in neonates revealed by event-related brain potentials. *BMC Neuroscience*. 10. , http://dx.doi.org/10.1186/1471-2202-10-21.

Tenenbaum, J. B., & Griffiths, T. L. (2001). Generalization, similarity, and Bayesian inference. *Behavioral and Brain Sciences*, *24*(4), 629–640. http://dx.doi.org/10.1017/S0140525X01000061discussion 652–791.

Thevenow-Harrison, J. T. & Kalish, C. W. (2013). What do children learn from an unrepresentative sample? *Submitted to Cognitive Science*, 2013–11.

Unkelbach, C., Fiedler, K., & Freytag, P. (2007). Information repetition in evaluative judgments: Easy to monitor, hard to control. *Organizational Behavior and Human Decision Processes*, *103*(1), 37–52. http://dx.doi.org/10.1016/j.obhdp.2006.12.002.

Vadillo, M. A., & Matute, H. (2007). Predictions and causal estimations are not supported by the same associative structure. *The Quarterly Journal of Experimental Psychology*, *60*(3), 433–447.

Vapnik, V. N. (1998). *Statistical learning theory*. New York, NY: Wiley.

Villejoubert, G., & Mandel, D. R. (2002). The inverse fallacy: An account of deviations from Bayes's theorem and the additivity principle. *Memory & Cognition*, *30*(2), 171–178.

Ward, T. B. (1980). Separable and integral responding by children and adults to the dimensions of length and density. *Child Development*, *51*(3), 676–684. http://dx.doi.org/10.2307/1129452.

Waxman, S. R., Lynch, E. B., Casey, K. L., & Baer, L. (1997). Setters and samoyeds: The emergence of subordinate level categories as a basis for inductive inference in preschool-age children. *Developmental Psychology*, *33*(6), 1074–1090.

Wellman, H. M., & Estes, D. (1986). Early understanding of mental entities: A reexamination of childhood realism. *Child Development*, *57*(4), 910–923.

Wellman, H. M., & Gelman, S. A. (1992). Cognitive development: Foundational theories of core domains. *Annual Review of Psychology, 43*, 337–375. http://dx.doi.org/10.1146/annurev.ps.43.020192.002005.

Xu, F., & Denison, S. (2009). Statistical inference and sensitivity to sampling in 11-month-old infants. *Cognition, 112*(1), 97–104. http://dx.doi.org/10.1016/j.cognition.2009.04.006.

Xu, F., & Garcia, V. (2008). Intuitive statistics by 8-month-old infants. *Proceedings of the National Academy of Sciences of the United States of America, 105*(50), 5012–5015.

Xu, F., & Tenenbaum, J. B. (2007a). Sensitivity to sampling in Bayesian word learning. *Developmental Science, 10*(3), 288–297. http://dx.doi.org/10.1111/j.1467-7687.2007.00590.x.

Xu, F., & Tenenbaum, J. B. (2007b). Word learning as Bayesian inference. *Psychological Review, 114*(2), 245–272.

Younger, B. A. (2003). Parsing objects into categories: Infants' perception and use of correlated attributes. In D. H. Rakison & L. M. Oakes (Eds.), *Early category and concept development: Making sense of the blooming, buzzing confusion* (pp. 77–102). New York, NY: Oxford University Press.

Yurovsky, D., Fricker, D. C., Yu, C., & Smith, L. B. (2013). The role of partial knowledge in statistical word learning. *Psychonomic Bulletin & Review, 21*(1). http://dx.doi.org/10.3758/s13423-013-0443-y.

Zhu, X., & Goldberg, A. B. (2009). *Introduction to semi-supervised learning*. San Rafael, CA: Morgan & Claypool.

CHAPTER TWO

What Does It Mean to be Biased: Motivated Reasoning and Rationality

Ulrike Hahn[*,1], **Adam J.L. Harris**[†]
[*]Department of Psychological Sciences, Birkbeck, University of London, London, United Kingdom
[†]Department of Cognitive, Perceptual & Brain Sciences, University College London, London, United Kingdom
[1]Corresponding author: e-mail address: u.hahn@bbk.ac.uk

Contents

1. The Notion of Bias — 42
   1.1 "Bias" in Psychology — 42
   1.2 The Notion of Bias in Statistics — 59
   1.3 Implications — 68
2. When is a Bias a Bias? — 69
   2.1 Understanding Bias: Scope, Sources, and Systematicity — 69
3. Measuring Bias: The Importance of Optimal Models — 76
   3.1 Bayesian Belief Revision — 77
   3.2 Divergence of Normative Predictions and Experimenter Intuition — 79
   3.3 Bayes and Experimental Demonstrations of Motivated Reasoning — 85
4. Conclusions — 91
Acknowledgment — 93
References — 93

Abstract

In this chapter, we provide a historical overview of research on bias in human cognition, ranging from early work in psychology through the detailed, quantitative examinations of belief revision in the 1960s, the Heuristic and Biases program initiated by Kahneman and Tversky, and bias focused research in personality and social psychology. Different notions of "bias" are identified and compared with the notion of bias in statistics, machine learning, and signal detection theory. Comparison with normative models then forms the basis for a critical look at the evidence that people succumb to motivated reasoning aimed at enabling them "to believe what they want to believe."

1. THE NOTION OF BIAS

A reader venturing into the psychological literature about human biases soon realizes that the word "bias" means many things to many people. This holds not just for its wider connotations, but even its immediate meaning. Consequently, it seems necessary to start with a survey of the term's usage.

In everyday use, the term "bias" refers to a lack of impartiality or an undue preference: bias is "an inclination or prejudice for or against one person or group, especially in a way considered to be unfair" (Oxford English Dictionary), or "a tendency to believe that some people, ideas, etc., are better than others that usually results in treating some people unfairly" (Merriam Webster). However, even dictionary definitions contain related meanings that lack the negative connotation, with "bias" being described also as "a strong interest in something or ability to do something" (Merriam Webster).

Already apparent in these definitions of everyday use are a number of fundamental distinctions: whether bias is a property of beliefs or of decisions, and whether or not it is inherently negative or "wrong."

However, these are not the only dimensions of variation that may structure the debate within the psychological literature. The word "bias" also has sharpened, more technical, meanings—in particular in statistics—that are also sometimes intended in research on bias. Statistical treatments also provide very balanced consideration of when being "biased" might be good, so we will introduce these technical meanings in more detail. We start, however, by an overview of the concept of "bias" within psychological research.

1.1. "Bias" in Psychology

Without a more thorough historical analysis than we are willing (or able) to conduct, any overview of the enormous wealth of research on biases and its reception within cognitive and social psychology will necessarily remain subjective and incomplete. Our main goal is to identify broad contrasts and key dimensions of variation thus setting the stage for a more detailed look at a particular class of biases—indicative of "motivated reasoning"—in the second half of this chapter.

1.1.1 Origins

Interest in biases within human cognition developed early in psychology. Vaughan's (1936) book "General Psychology" contains a chapter titled "The Importance of Bias." On the definition of bias, Vaughan writes:

A bias is a slant or bent, a pointing of the mental life toward certain views and reactions. Consciously, a bias is a point of view; behavioristically, it is a posture, a set, a preparedness for acting, thinking, or judging, in a definite manner. A bias is an attitude—an anticipation—a prejudice which may manifest itself in overt behavior or in thoughts and feelings about behavior. Very often the determining tendency operates unconsciously, that is, without the individual's being aware of the motive fundamentally responsible for his thinking or action. (p. 211)

Vaughan speaks of biases in perception, memory, judgment, belief, and choice. Some of his evidence is informal and anecdotal; however, psychological research at that time already possessed empirical demonstrations of judgment biases (e.g., Macdougall, 1906—savor the hand drawn graphs!), attitudinal biases and their impact on memory (e.g., Levine & Murphy, 1943), attentional biases in perception (e.g., Wolff, 1933), response biases (see e.g., Landahl, 1939), and a sizeable literature on perceptual illusions (see e.g., Pierce, 1901).

One also already finds in this literature both an interest in studying biases with a view to allowing human beings to overcome them and with a view to studying biases as a means of coming to understand underlying mechanisms—two motivations that are reiterated in the literature on biases time and again (e.g., Gregg & Sedikides, 2004; Kahneman, 2000; Kahneman & Tversky, 1996; Kunda, 1990). Finally, the early literature already distinguishes between a notion of bias as filtering or selectivity in a very general sense and a more specific sense of bias as a distortion. Macdougall (1906) writes:

. . .selective attention working under the guidance of our organic interests operates upon the materials and processes of the external world, adding accentuation and emphasis, seizing upon and preserving certain elements which we call pleasing or important, and relegating the rest to obscurity or oblivion. Often the account in which this recasting results is unrecognizable by a fellow-observer of the event. The existence of subjective bias is thus not an incidental error in our observations but is fundamental to the very character of the human mind. We can conceive its elimination only in an absolutely dispassionate consciousness devoid of feeling and purpose.

This universal bias roots in the fact that at each moment of our experience some one interest is for the time being paramount, and determines both the objects which shall be attended to and the interpretation which they shall receive. (p. 99)

MacDougall considers such subjective selection and emphasis "to pervade all mental activities, perceptive, imaginative, and rationalizing," but also, once acknowledged in its existence, not to be a concern. Indeed, he considers it "the basis of intelligibility in the world and of a rational adjustment to its changes" that "the apprehension of that world varies from moment to moment in dependence upon transitions in the point of view and present purpose of the beholder" (p. 100).

An altogether different matter, however, is what he calls "bias of the second order," namely *distorted evaluations* of our necessarily selective perceptions of the world. These too he considers to be ubiquitous ("as pervasive as gravity," in fact), but of considerable practical consequence, because the distortions arise through "factors of evaluation of whose presence we are unaware at the moment of judgment" (p. 100).

He takes such evaluative distortions to arise at all levels of the system, from sensation through perception to memory and judgment, through to evaluation of complex conceptual objects. And in an assessment that could not have foreseen better the course of future research on this topic, he notes the ever-increasing difficulty of study as one moves through this list.

1.1.2 The 1960s: Wason's Confirmation Bias in Rule Induction

Given the range of different types of bias suggested by early psychological research, it may seem somewhat surprising that one of the most famous of all cognitive biases does not fit neatly into any of the categories mentioned so far. Peter Wason's (1960) paper "On the failure to eliminate hypotheses in a conceptual task" introduced the bias that has probably attracted the most enduring interest of all cognitive biases: the so-called confirmation bias. In his study, participants' task was to correctly infer a rule governing triplets of numbers (e.g., 2 4 6, and the underlying rule "increasing in magnitude") by generating query-triplets for which the experimenter indicated whether or not they conform to the rule. Wason's finding was that a proportion (though by no means all) of his participants sought to obtain evidence for what, if confirmed, would be positive instances, as opposed to negative instances. This tendency to "seek evidence that would confirm" violates the (then dominant) Popperian prescription of the need to seek falsification in the testing of scientific hypotheses (Popper, 1959), and was thus taken to fail the standard for "rational inference."

Given that it is about evidence selection, this "confirmation bias" seems closest to an attentional bias. It is not about suppression of particular content or information (e.g., attending to color as opposed to shape), but about strategy (i.e., deciding where to look): What kinds of questions should we ask of the world in order to determine the accuracy of our beliefs? The actual outcome of that query may turn out to confirm or to disconfirm our beliefs; hence, a "positive test strategy" must be distinguished from confirmation or disconfirmation of the hypothesis itself. Nor need participants have any actual psychological desire to confirm the hypothesis for which they seek evidence (Wason, 1962; Wetherick, 1962), and the majority in Wason's study ultimately managed to infer the correct rule.

Nevertheless, "confirmation bias" has come to provide an umbrella term for a number of distinct ways in which beliefs and/or expectations influence both the selection, retention, and evaluation of evidence (see Nickerson, 1998, for a review). Nickerson (1998) lists under the banner of "confirmation" bias a wealth of distinct phenomena, drawn from both cognitive and social psychology, which we have collated here in Table 2.1.

In fact, these "subbiases" constitute the majority of phenomena listed by Baron (2008) under the header of "motivated bias," that is, biases reflecting "myside bias" or "wishful thinking." Confirmation bias has thus expanded from a particular type of search strategy to a concept considerably overlapping with the notion of "motivated reasoning," even though the original phenomenon contains no scrutiny of "motivation" whatsoever.

For the moment, it suffices to note that gathering evidence via search (like the retention of "evidence" in memory) necessarily has quite different standards for evaluation than does a distorting evaluation of evidence (or "secondary bias," in MacDougall's terms). In fact, such standards are not at all trivial to specify, and it is by no means enough to demonstrate merely that on occasion "something goes wrong."

1.1.3 The 1960s: Conservatism
Clear evaluative standards were, however, present in a wealth of research in the 1960s that examined carefully people's belief revision in light of new evidence. This line of research typically used "bookbags" and "pokerchips," that is, bags with varying compositions of colored chips (e.g., 60% red and 40% blue for one bag, and 40% red and 60% blue for the other). Participants then saw samples drawn from one of these bags and indicated their new, revised, degree of belief in the composition of that bag (e.g., that the bag was the one with predominantly blue chips). This paradigm allowed for careful quantitative evaluation of the extent to which participants' belief revision matched the prescriptions of Bayes' rule as a norm for updating beliefs (e.g., Peterson & Miller, 1965; Peterson & Uleha, 1964; Peterson, Schnieder, & Miller, 1965; Peterson, Uleha, Miller, & Bourne, 1965; Phillips & Edwards, 1966; see Peterson & Beach, 1967; Slovic & Lichtenstein, 1971, for reviews).

Table 2.1 Phenomena That Have Been Brought Under the Header of "Confirmation Bias"

1. Hypothesis-determined information seeking and interpretation	1.1 *Restriction of attention to a favored hypothesis.*	Considering only $P(D|H)$ and not $p(D|notH)$, for example, Doherty, Mynatt, Tweney, and Schiavo (1979)—sometimes referred to as *pseudodiagnosticity-bias*; but see Crupi, Tentori, and Lombardi (2009)
	1.2 *Preferential treatment of evidence supporting existing beliefs.*	*My-side bias*: tendency to produce reasons for favored side, for example, Baron (1995)
	1.3 *Looking only or primarily for positive cases.*	Tendency to ask questions for which answer would be "yes" if hypothesis were true: Wason (1960)
	1.4 *Overweighting positive confirmatory instances.*	For example, Gilovich (1983)
	1.5 *Seeing what one is looking for.*	For example, effects of expectations on social perception Kelley (1950); but Lenski and Leggett (1960) general tendency to respond to questions in acquiescence to interrogator hypothesis.
	1.6 *Remembering what one expects*	Eagly, Chen, Chaiken, and Shaw-Barnes (1999)
	1.7 *Illusory correlation*	Chapman and Chapman (1967), but see Fiedler and Krueger (2011)
2. *Wason selection task and formal reasoning*		Failure to pursue falsificationist strategy in context of conditional reasoning, Wason (1968); but see Oaksford and Chater (1994)
3. *The primacy effect and belief persistence*		*Resistance of* a belief or opinion to change once formed Pitz, Downing, and Reinhold's (1967) inertia effect; Lord, Ross, and Lepper (1979) "biased assimilation"
4. *Overconfidence and the illusion of validity*		For example, Lichtenstein and Fischhoff (1977); but see also Erev, Wallsten, and Budescu (1994)

Categories follow Nickerson's (1998) as do most of the examples, though newer references have been given in some cases.

The main finding of this research was that people responded in qualitatively appropriate ways to evidence, but—quantitatively—changed their beliefs less than the normative prescription of Bayes' rule mandated. In other words, their belief revision was what researchers called "*conservative*": people extracted less certainty from the evidence than it justified. Conservatism was found not just in relation to the diagnosticity of evidence but also to manipulations of the prior probability of the hypothesis in advance of the data, and affected not just belief revision but also the extent to which response criteria were shifted in normatively appropriate ways in signal detection tasks (which we discuss in more detail below; see e.g., Peterson & Beach, 1967; Ulehla, 1966 for further references).

These systematic deviations from optimal responding did not, however, lead researchers to form a negative conclusion of human rationality. In fact, the conclusion was that probability theory, which provides optimal models for making inferences under conditions of uncertainty, provides "a good first approximation for a psychological theory of inference" (Peterson & Beach, 1967, p. 42).

It is worth mentioning two sets of studies within the "bookbag and pokerchip" tradition that figure in discussions of motivated reasoning. First, after sequences of conflicting evidence that should have "cancelled out," participants' judgements did not necessarily return fully to the point of origin (see e.g., Pitz, 1969b; Peterson & DuCharme, 1967; Pitz et al., 1967; but see also Peterson et al., 1968), a phenomena dubbed the "inertia effect."

Second, under conditions where participants need to "purchase" information in order to reach a judgment, they purchased less information than they "should" (if they were maximizing expected value) and, hence, in a sense "jump to conclusions" (e.g., Green, Halbert, & Minas, 1964; Pitz, 1969a; though the reverse has also been found, see Tversky & Edwards, 1966; Wendt, 1969). This tendency to "under-sample" has been replicated many times since (see e.g., Fiedler & Kareev, 2006; Hertwig, Barron, Weber, & Erev, 2004). At first glance, it stands in seeming conflict with conservatism in belief revision, with people seeming simultaneously both too cautious and too decisive in their information evaluation. Such findings, in which people seem prone simultaneously to "opposing" biases have been a regular feature of the literature on biases ever since (see e.g., Table 1 in Krueger & Funder, 2004).

Though undersampling, like the inertia effect, has been assimilated into confirmation bias and motivated reasoning, cognitive psychologists have recently argued that the tendency to select small samples reflects that sample proportions in small samples are exaggerated and may thus be easier to "read-off," an advantage that potentially comes at little cost (e.g., Fiedler & Kareev, 2006; Hertwig & Pleskac, 2008, 2010; on the wider role of small samples in judgment and decision see also, Hahn, 2014). Moreover, these benefits should be even more pronounced if evaluation of larger samples is conservative.

Despite a wealth of evidence, the causes of the pervasive conservatism observed in participants' judgments have never been fully resolved (see Erev et al., 1994). Edwards (1968) distinguished two possibilities: misaggregation and misperception. Participants could be misaggregating in their calculations of revised (posterior) degrees of belief; in keeping with this it was found that inference often seemed close to optimal with a single datum, deviating more strongly only as the amount of evidence increased (see e.g., DuCharme & Peterson, 1968; but see also DuCharme, 1970). Alternatively, participants could be misperceiving the diagnostic value of evidence. In keeping with this, participants (mis)perceived the sampling distributions from which their evidence was drawn to be flatter than they actually were (see e.g., Peterson, DuCharme, & Edwards, 1968; Wheeler & Beach, 1968). Training people to provide more veridical estimates of the underlying sampling distributions decreased conservatism. Furthermore, people's belief revision in general was typically found to be better predicted by their own subjective estimates of data characteristics, than by objective values; in other words, the internal consistency of people's probability judgments exceeded the correspondence of those judgments with objective, environmental values (see e.g., Peterson & Beach, 1967; Peterson, Schnieder, et al., 1965; Peterson, Uleha, et al., 1965, for further references); subjectively, people were "more Bayesian" than the degree of match between their judgments and the evidence suggested.

While there is thus both evidence in favor of misaggregation and in favor of misperception, neither factor explains all aspects of the data. Hence, other factors seem to play a role, including response bias. DuCharme (1970) found participants' responses to be optimal within a limited range either side of the initial, experimenter defined odds (i.e., the ratio between the probabilities of the two competing hypotheses under consideration).[1] Beyond this range, responses became increasingly conservative indicating a reluctance to move too far beyond whatever initial odds the experimenter provided (a reluctance which may reflect an everyday world in which very diagnostic evidence is rare). Within that range, however, responses showed neither misaggregation nor misperception.

---

[1] DuCharme (1970) found this range to correspond to log-odds of +/−1.

This fact argues against an explanation whereby conservatism is simply an artifactual result of a failure by participants to understand a complex experimental task (but see, e.g., Slovic & Lichtenstein, 1971). However, it has been demonstrated that the addition of random error to judgments may be one source of conservatism (e.g., Erev et al., 1994), and, in keeping with this, several of the studies that provided manipulations that reduced conservatism (e.g., Phillips & Edwards, 1966; Wheeler & Beach, 1968) reported reductions in variability.

In the 1970s, research in this area briefly turned to simple features of the evidence (such as sample proportion within the evidence seen) that participants might be tracking (see e.g., Manz, 1970; Slovic & Lichtenstein, 1971), before interest in the paradigm eventually waned.

This may to a good part be attributed to the fact that the optimistic assessment of human rationality soon gave way to a more dire assessment in the wake of Tversky and Kahneman's so-called Heuristics and Biases program.

Where authors such as Peterson and Beach (1967) were not only positive about the descriptive utility of probability and decision theory (and, in fact, anticipated the extension of their application to other aspects of human cognition), the project of "statistical man" or "man as an intuitive statistician" received a severe blow with Kahneman and Tversky's "Heuristics and Biases program" (e.g., Gilovich, Griffin, & Kahneman, 2002; Kahneman, Slovic, & Tversky, 1982; Tversky & Kahneman, 1974).

1.1.4 Heuristics and Biases

This research tradition soon came to dominate cognitive psychological research on bias. It focused on (probability) judgment and decision-making, and "bias" in this context means systematic deviation from the (putative) normative standards of probability and expected utility theory. Systematic violations of these standards should give rise to outcomes that are inferior, either in terms of judgmental accuracy or goal attainment. The overarching interest in such systematic violations was motivated by a desire to find descriptively accurate characterizations of human judgment and decision-making that give insight into underlying mechanisms and processes. It has been much repeated within this tradition that biases may serve the same role of guiding the development of process theories as visual illusions had in the study of perception (see e.g., Kahneman & Tversky, 1982, 1996; Tversky & Kahneman, 1974).

Unlike in the study of perception, however, that promise has, to date, remained largely unfulfilled, and critics maintain that the paradigm has provided little more than a fairly haphazard list of supposed cognitive frailties (see e.g., Krueger & Funder, 2004). Not only has the study of judgment and decision-making reached nowhere near the maturity of perception, but also both the empirical adequacy and explanatory power of the heuristics that supposedly underlie these biases have been severely doubted (see e.g., Gigerenzer, 1991, 2006).

Heuristics are procedures that are not guaranteed to succeed (see e.g., Newell, Shaw, & Simon, 1958) but that provide often highly effective shortcuts—in effect "rules of thumb." Consequently, heuristics, by definition, will occasionally—and systematically—be wrong. Heuristics thus bring with them "bias" (in the sense of systematic inaccuracy) by definition (see also, Kahneman, 2000).

More specifically, heuristics will be only partially correlated with true values. Where and when deviations occur depends on the nature of the heuristic. Substituting an easy to track property such as "availability" or "recognition" for the true determinants of some environmental frequency, for example, will overweight that property and neglect other, genuinely predictive, sources of information. This means the glass is half full: one may stress the fact of deviation; alternatively one may stress the fact that the heuristic often leads to the correct response given the actual environment in which the agent operates and that it does so in a computationally simple fashion, thus providing some measure of "adaptive rationality" (see e.g., Gigerenzer, Todd, & The ABC Research Group, 1999). What are in many ways otherwise closely related programs concerned with heuristics—the Heuristics and Biases program on the one hand, and Gigerenzer and colleagues subsequent search for "simple heuristics that make us smart" (e.g., Todd & Gigerenzer, 2000) on the other—can thus, through a difference in emphasis, come to seemingly strongly conflicting perspectives (see e.g., the exchange Gigerenzer, 1996; Kahneman & Tversky, 1996).

While the later adaptive rationality tradition avoids the term "bias," the words "bias," "error," and "fallacy" figure centrally in the Heuristics and Biases program, and the overwhelming reception of its findings (whatever the original intention) has been as an indictment of human rationality. In the words of Kahneman and Tversky themselves:

> "...it soon became apparent that "although errors of judgments are but a method by which some cognitive processes are studied, the method has become a significant part of the message"
> **(Kahneman & Tversky, 1982, p. 124, and requoted in Kahneman & Tversky, 1996, p. 582)**

In particular, the spectacular success of the program in reaching adjacent disciplines has done much to propagate the notion of human cognition as littered with bias. At the time of writing, Tversky and Kahneman's (1974) Science paper "Judgment under uncertainty: Heuristics and biases" has over 19,000 citations on Google Scholar, and their (1979) paper on decision-making over 28,000, with the majority of these outside of psychology.

This negative assessment of human rationality was perhaps an inevitable side effect of the program's concern with documenting violations of probability theory and decision theory, which themselves have widespread currency as standards of rationality in adjacent disciplines from philosophy to economics. Tversky and Kahneman decidedly took issue with the notion that utility maximization, in particular, provides an empirically adequate descriptive theory of human behavior (e.g., Kahneman & Tversky, 1979). Given that maximization of expected utility effectively defined the "rational man" of economics (see e.g., Simon, 1978), it is unsurprising that a view of people as irrational was the result.

Unlike the 1960s program concerned with "statistical man" just discussed, Tversky and Kahneman focused not on quantitative assessments that sought to identify how closely (or not) human performance matched that of an optimal agent (e.g., measuring degree of conservatism), but rather on *qualitative* violations of probability and decision theory. In many ways, the particular genius of Tversky and Kahneman as experimenters lay in their ability to derive simple problems on which particular patterns of responding would directly indicate normative violations without the need for quantitative modeling.

On the one hand, this makes for simple and compelling demonstrations; on the other hand, however, it does not allow assessment of *how costly* such violations might actually be to people going about their everyday lives. This undoubtedly makes it more tempting to equate "bias" with "irrationality," even though one does not imply the other. As a simple example, consider the conjunction fallacy: assigning a higher probability to the conjunction of two events than to the least probable of the two conjuncts is a simple logical error. The conjunct can be no more probable because, by necessity, the least probable conjunct occurs whenever both events (i.e., the conjunction) occur. One of the most famous fallacies identified by Tversky and Kahneman (see e.g., Tversky & Kahneman, 1983), it implies error by design. Nevertheless, of the many rival explanations for the fallacy (and there are likely many contributing factors, see e.g., Jarvstad & Hahn, 2011 and references therein for a review), a leading one is that it is the result of a (weighted) averaging strategy for deriving probability estimates (see e.g., Nilsson, Winman, Juslin, & Hansson, 2009). As shown via computer simulation by Juslin, Nilsson, and Winman (2009), such a strategy can provide a remarkably effective combination rule in circumstances where knowledge of the component probabilities is only approximate. Where component estimates are noisy, the multiplicative nature of Bayes' rule means that noise too has a multiplicative effect, an effect that is dampened by additive combination. An additive combination strategy, though normatively incorrect, may thus lead to comparable levels of performance on average, given such noise.

One other well-known bias deserves mention in this context: the tendency for participants to underweight base rates in deriving estimates, a phenomenon labeled "base rate neglect" (Kahneman & Tversky, 1973). It has generated considerable controversy, with literally hundreds of studies investigating the extent to which base rates are underweighted and which circumstances moderate their use (see e.g., Bar-Hillel, 1980; Koehler, 1996).

Not only does an underweighting of base rates fit with an additive combination strategy, and may thus be connected with both the conjunction fallacy and the fact that additive combination may often be a "good" strategy in practical terms (see Juslin et al., 2009), but it also resonates directly with earlier findings discussed under Section 1.1.3 above. In fact, underweighting of base rates replicates earlier findings in bookbag- and pokerchip-like paradigms whereby participants showed sensitivity to the prior probability of hypotheses, but were less sensitive than normatively desirable (see e.g., Green et al., 1964; Wendt, 1969; and for an estimation-only context, e.g., Green, Halbert, & Robinson, 1965). Unlike many studies, those earlier paradigms also allowed assessment of the cost to the participant of deviation from optimal—a cost that in those studies tended to be small (see e.g., Wendt, 1969).

More generally, the case of base rate neglect highlights the need to examine putative biases (as deviations from accuracy) over a broad range of values. This is essential not just for understanding the cost of that deviation but also for the bias' proper scope and interpretation. In the case of low prior probability (e.g., the presence of serious illness such as AIDS, which in the general population has a base rate that is low), underweighting of the base rate means effectively "jumping to conclusions" on the basis of a diagnostic test (such as an AIDS test). Normatively, the actual likelihood of illness given even a high-quality test remains fairly low in light of the low prior probability.

At the other end of the scale, for high prior probabilities, underweighting of base rates means that judgments are not extreme enough. Examining only high *or* low prior probabilities in isolation would lead one to conclude erroneously that people were either too extreme or too hesitant in their judgments, when, in fact, the pattern of responding is indicative of a more general "conservatism," that is, sensitivity to normatively relevant factors, but by not enough.

In the decades since, judgment and decision-making research has chipped away at the discrepancies between normative and descriptive highlighted by the Heuristics and Biases program in a number of distinct ways (though typically with considerably lower profile than the original negative news, see e.g., Christensen-Szalinski & Beach, 1984). In particular, it has been argued that seeming errors may stem from divergent construals of the task by experimenters and participants (e.g., Hilton, 1995; Schwarz, 1996). There have also been arguments over normative evaluations of the tasks (e.g., Gigerenzer, 1991; Koehler, 1996), both in judgment and decision-making and in the context of investigations of human rationality in adjacent fields such as logical reasoning (e.g., Oaksford & Chater, 1994, 2007; Wason, 1968).

It has also been demonstrated that the biases in question are far from universal (e.g., Stanovich & West, 2000). In studies of the conjunction fallacy, for example, there is typically a proportion of participants who do not commit the fallacy (see e.g., Jarvstad & Hahn, 2011). This may be taken to be indicative of interesting facts about cognitive architecture (such as the existence of multiple cognitive "systems" capable of generating responses, see e.g., Kahneman, 2000). However, it may also be taken to undermine the very project. Rather than providing evidence of systematic and pervasive irrationality, the existence of stable individual differences in susceptibility to bias could be taken to imply "that the vast literature on heuristics and biases may embody little more than a collection of brain teasers that most people get wrong but that a few people—without tutoring and despite everything—manage to get right" (Funder, 2000, p. 674). Viewed from that perspective, this tradition of research does not reveal systematic irrationality, but "variations in the ability to answer difficult questions," where "some questions are so difficult that only very smart people get them right"—a state of affairs that is intrinsically no more interesting and no more informative of the nature of human cognition than that SATs (scholastic aptitude tests administered to students in the US) contain questions that most students will get wrong (Funder, 2000).

1.1.5 Social Psychology

While the Heuristics and Biases program came to dominate cognitive psychology (more specifically, judgment and decision-making research), its impact in social psychology was less strong. There too, it is perceived to have become increasingly influential (see e.g., Krueger & Funder, 2004 for discussion of this point), but social psychology contains much distinct work of its own concerned with bias and error (with often seemingly little distinction between the two, see also Kruglanski & Ajzen, 1983). In fact, it has attracted high-profile critiques of its unduly "negative" focus. Krueger and Funder (2004) lament that

> ...social psychology is badly out of balance, that research on misbehavior has crowded out research on positive behaviors, that research on cognitive errors has crowded out research on the sources of cognitive accomplishment, and that the theoretical development of social psychology has become self-limiting.
>
> **(Krueger & Funder, 2004, p. 322)**

As a consequence, social psychology, in Krueger and Funder's perception, has accumulated a long list of putative, often contradictory, biases (e.g., false consensus effect and false uniqueness effect, see e.g., Table 1 of Krueger & Funder, 2004), a list that continues to grow as variants of old biases are rediscovered with new names. This, in their view, has led to a warped, unduly negative, overall assessment of human competence, while providing little insight into underlying mental processes.

The wave of research into errors and biases (according to e.g., Funder, 1987; Kenny & Albright, 1987) is seen in part as a response to the demise of early research into the accuracy of interpersonal perception within social and personality psychology that was brought about by devastating methodological critiques of standard methods (in particular, critiques by Cronbach, 1955; Gage & Cronbach, 1955; Gage, Leavitt, & Stone, 1956). In the context of social judgment, "truth" is hard to come by: if someone perceives someone to be "friendly" on the basis of their interactions thus far, it is hard to establish the criterion value against which their accuracy might be assessed. In light of these difficulties, the preferred method in early research on the accuracy of interpersonal judgments was to get members of a group to provide judgments about each other and then to evaluate their accuracy in terms of how well they agreed (see e.g., Dymond, 1949, 1950). Cronbach and Gage's critiques demonstrated exactly how difficult such data were to interpret, more or less bringing research in this tradition to a halt. Subsequent research on social judgment sought to "bypass the accuracy problem" by turning to the study of errors and biases brought about by the use of heuristics, by (unwarranted) implicit assumptions, and by "egocentric orientation" (Kenny & Albright, 1987).

In so doing, the error and bias tradition within social judgment proceeded by making "normative standards" inherent in the experimental manipulation itself. For example, an (erroneous) judgmental tendency to overascribe behavior to enduring dispositions (as opposed to situational factors) was inferred from experimental paradigms in which dispositional information is (supposedly) rendered irrelevant by experimental design. In Jones and Harris (1967) classic study of attribution, participants were shown essays favoring Fidel Castro that were purportedly written by people who had no choice in writing a pro-Castro piece. Participants nevertheless showed a tendency to view pro-Castro essays as reflecting "true" pro-Castro positions on the part of the authors.

In this way, differential responses to experimental materials become evidence of error and bias. In particular, evidence for motivated distortions of evidence have been sought in this way. For example, Lord et al. (1979) famously demonstrated "biased assimilation" in this manner. In their study, participants were presented with mixed evidence on the effectiveness of capital punishment in deterring crime. Each participant read two (experimenter designed) journal articles, one purporting to show effectiveness and the other purporting to show ineffectiveness. Participants rated the report that agreed with their prior opinion as "more convincing," and more readily found flaws in the reports that went against it. Moreover, the effect of each report on the participant's subsequent beliefs was stronger when the report agreed with their prior self-assessment as proponents or opponents of capital punishment. In other words, participants' beliefs became more polarized by conflicting evidence that, if anything, should have made them less sure of their beliefs.

To the extent that there is a general rationality principle that might be articulated for such cases, it is what Baron (2008) calls the "neutral evidence principle": "Neutral evidence should not strengthen belief," that is evidence that is equally consistent with a belief and its converse, such as mixed evidence, should not alter our beliefs. This neutral evidence principle is violated when ambiguous evidence is interpreted as supporting a favored belief.

In many ways, the notion of "bias" operative here is thus close to the lay meaning of bias as "lack of impartiality." However, it is typically assumed that such a bias will also have systematic negative effects on the accuracy of our beliefs (see e.g., Baron, 2008).

Other methods for examining bias in social judgment make use of comparative ratings. In the many studies concerned with self-enhancement biases, for example, the true level of a participant's skill (e.g., Svenson, 1981), or risk of experiencing an adverse life event (e.g., Weinstein, 1980), etc., is unknown. In these circumstances, bias is ascertained via a comparison between multiple quantities, such as self versus other perception, or self versus average and so on. The logic here is that while it may be impossible to say whether a given individual is a "better-than-average" driver or not, (sufficiently large) groups of individuals rating their driving skills should come to match average values. Intuitive as that may seem, the application of formal models has shown such reference point dependent evaluations to be prone to statistical artifacts, in particular regression artifacts (see e.g., Fiedler & Krueger, 2011).

In general, it may be said that the types of bias observed within social psychology are, if anything, seen as even more "irrational" than those observed by cognitive psychologists in the context of judgment and decision-making:

> *Motivational biases are characterized by a tendency to form and hold beliefs that serve the individual's needs and desires. Individuals are said to avoid drawing inferences they would find distasteful, and to prefer inferences that are pleasing or need-congruent. Being dependent on the momentary salience of different needs, such motivational influences could presumably yield judgmental biases and errors. Even in the absence of motivated distortions, human judgments are assumed subject to biases of a more cognitive nature. Unlike motivational biases that are presumed to constitute largely irrational tendencies, cognitive biases are said to originate in the limitations of otherwise reasonable information-processing strategies.*
> **(Kruglanski & Ajzen, 1983, p. 4)**

In other words, putative motivational biases stem from a tendency to engage in "wishful thinking" in order to maintain self-serving motives such as the need for "self-enhancement" or "effective control," whereas cognitive biases are mere side effects from the use of suboptimal judgment heuristics or strategy. From the perspective of the biased agent, motivational and cognitive biases thus differ in fundamental ways: for the former, the bias is, in a sense, the goal; for the latter, it is an (undesirable) by-product of a system that is otherwise striving for accuracy.

Both types of bias should violate normative models of judgment such as Bayes' rule but, unlike the Heuristics and Biases tradition, social psychological research typically examined bias (and error) independently of normative framework. Kruglanski and Ajzen (1983) noted that

> *Contemporary research on bias and error in human judgment is decidedly empirical in character. It lacks a clearly articulated theory and even the central concepts of 'error' and 'bias' are not explicitly defined. Nor is it easy to find a clear characterization of the objective, or unbiased inference process from which lay judgments are presumed to deviate.*
>
> *(Kruglanski & Ajzen, 1983 p. 2)*

This state of affairs has largely remained, and means that in many social psychological studies concerned with bias, there is simply no clearly articulated standard of rationality (see also, Griffin, Gonzalez, & Varey, 2001; Krueger & Funder, 2004).

Earlier research in social psychology had seen some reference to Bayesian belief revision; for example, Ajzen and Fishbein (1975) argued that a wealth of different findings on causal attribution might be understood (and thus unified) from a Bayesian perspective. In other words, experimental variations probing factors influencing causal attribution can typically be recast as manipulations that affect the diagnosticity (and hence evidential value) of the information given to participants. So their responses may be understood as tracking that information in a process of subjective belief revision that approximates the Bayesian norm in the same way that participants respond in broadly qualitatively appropriate ways to probabilistically relevant factors in bookbag and pokerchip paradigms. Such reference to the Bayesian framework, however, is the exception rather than the rule.

Moreover, even those social psychologists who have taken issue with bias focused research (e.g., Funder, 1995; Kruglanski, 1989; Kruglanski & Ajzen, 1983; Krueger & Funder, 2004) and have argued strongly for a research focus on accuracy using tasks where accuracy can be meaningfully defined, have tended to express some skepticism towards the use of normative models on the grounds that there is debate about normative standards of rationality, and there may thus be rival "norms" (see also, Elqayam & Evans, 2011).

Such debate has several sources. Even for tasks such as probability judgment for which there is considerable consensus about norms, applying these to particular experimental tasks and questions may be less than straightforward and much of the critical debate surrounding the heuristics and biases tradition originates here (see e.g., Gigerenzer, 1991; Koehler, 1996). In other cases, debate about normative standards is more fundamental, with ongoing debate about how best to conduct the inference in question, that is, norms themselves. For example, much research on causal attribution was closely related to particular, classical (frequentist) statistics such as analysis of variance (see e.g., Kelley & Michela, 1980), for which there are now rival statistics. In other cases, general assumptions about how science should proceed provided the role model. Neither the philosophy of science nor epistemology, however, are "completed," and both have been subject to considerable development and debate, in particular a move from an emphasis on deduction as found in Popperian falsification (Popper, 1959) to a more recent emphasis on Bayesian probability (see e.g., Howson & Urbach, 1996). In the meantime, social psychologists themselves have sought to formulate their own perspectives of "lay epistemology" (e.g., Kruglanski & Ajzen, 1983).

At the same time, researchers within social (and personality) psychology, have considered broader conceptions of "truth" and consequently "accuracy" (see e.g., Funder, 1995; Kruglanski, 1989). These encompass not just accuracy as "correspondence between a judgment and a criterion" (in parallel to correspondence theories of truth, see e.g., Funder, 1987; Hastie & Rasinski, 1988; Kenny & Albright, 1987), but also a constructivist perspective that views "accuracy as interpersonal agreement between judges" (e.g., Kruglanski, 1989) and a conceptualization of the accuracy of a judgment in terms of its adaptive value (in keeping with a pragmatic notion of truth, see e.g., McArthur & Baron, 1983; Swann, 1984).

There are thus multiple reasons why social psychologists have not always viewed biases as ultimately "bad." Self-enhancement biases have been taken to provide "cognitive illusion" that promote well-being and mental health (e.g., Taylor & Brown, 1988), biases have been argued to (sometimes) promote accuracy in person perception (e.g., Funder, 1995), and they have been argued to reflect evolutionary adaptations to asymmetric costs of errors (e.g., "error management theory," Haselton & Buss, 2000; Haselton & Funder, 2006). More generally, a focus on adaptive consequences may give rise to a terminological distinction between error and bias itself. McArthur and Baron's (1983) ecological perspective suggests that

> ...bias is different from error: Bias is simply a matter of selective attention and action, and whether a given bias leads to error in adaptive behavior is an empirical, not a logical, problem. (p. 230)

Likewise, a focus on real-world outcomes led Funder (1987) to distinguish between "errors" and "mistakes":

> ...An error is a judgment of an experimental stimulus that departs from a model of the judgment process. If this model is normative, then the error can be said to represent an incorrect judgment. A mistake, by contrast, is an incorrect judgment of a real-world stimulus and therefore more difficult to determine.

> Although errors can be highly informative about the process of judgment in general, they are not necessarily relevant to the content or accuracy of particular judgments, because errors in a laboratory may not be mistakes with respect to a broader, more realistic frame of reference and the processes that produce such errors might lead to correct decisions and adaptive outcomes in real life. (p. 75)

From here, it no longer seems surprising that a recent methodological proposal for the study of social judgment by West and Kenny (2011) employs a notion of "bias" that encompasses *any evidence* (other than simply the truth itself) that may be used by an agent to infer some quantity to be judged.

1.1.6 Summary
It seems fair to describe the use of the term "bias" within psychological research as varied, at times encompassing almost polar opposites: the term has been used to denote both systematic deviations from accuracy and mere error, it has been taken to reflect both "outcome" and process, a side effect and a goal, and bias has been viewed variously as obviously irrational, as rational, or neither.

In a sense, any terminology is fine as long as it is clear. However, terminological confusion tends to obscure important empirical issues. Our goal in this chapter is to lend some precision particularly to what has and has not been shown in the domain of "motivated cognitions." For this, it is useful to provide some indication of more formal notions of "bias" within statistics. We discuss these next, before returning to a more in depth look at wishful thinking and motivated reasoning.

1.2. The Notion of Bias in Statistics
1.2.1 Bias as Expected Deviation
In statistics (and related disciplines such as machine learning) the term "bias" refers to (expected) systematic deviation (see e.g., Bolstad, 2004). If, for example, we are trying to estimate a proportion, such as the proportion of the population who will contract a particular disease, on the basis of a sample, then the bias of an estimator (a statistic for estimating that proportion) is the difference between the expected value of that estimator and the true population proportion:

$$\text{bias}(\text{estimator}) = E(\text{estimator}) - \text{True Population Value}$$

in other words, the difference between the true proportion and the average value of the estimator (over samples).

Similarly, consider a case in which we try to estimate a function on the basis of a (finite) sample of data, so that we may generalise to other, as yet unseen, values. Our predictor is said to be "biased" if the average value of our predictor is different from the true value (or where there is noise, from its expectation).

"Bias" may thus intuitively seem like a "bad thing." However, the situation is more complicated. If, as is common, we evaluate our accuracy in terms of mean squared error (the average squared distance of the estimator from the "true value") then

$$\text{MSE} = \text{bias}(\text{estimator})^2 + \text{variance}(\text{estimator})$$

Thus, if it has smaller variance, a biased estimator may be more accurate, on average, than an unbiased estimator and provide a value that is closer to the truth.

As an illustration, we consider an example from the current debate in psychology on whether to use classical, frequentist statistics or "Bayesian" counterparts (e.g., Kruschke, 2010; but see also already Edwards, Lindman, & Savage, 1963). The standard frequentist measure for estimating a population proportion, such as those who contract a particular disease, is the sample mean: the proportion of diseased within our sample. The sample mean is an unbiased estimator.

Alternatively one might seek to estimate that same proportion in a different way. We think of the true proportion as a particular value from a distribution of possible values (ranging from 0 to 1) and calculate a posterior distribution in light of our sample, taking the mean of that posterior to be our estimator. In this case, we need to choose a prior distribution that is combined with our evidence via Bayes' theorem to calculate that posterior. A standard choice (but it is a choice!) would be a beta distribution as a prior with values that give a uniform distribution over all values between 0 and 1 (i.e., beta(1,1)), reflecting a lack of any knowledge that would make some proportions more or less likely *a priori*. This measure is not unbiased (and typically Bayesian statistics are not), yet its average mean squared error (over the range of possible true values of the population proportion) is lower than that of the unbiased sample mean. As seen in Fig. 2.1, which shows both bias and variance components and resulting MSE (for formulae used in calculation, see e.g., Bolstad, 2004) for sample sizes of 5, 10, and 20, the posterior mean outperforms the sample mean not just in particular "lucky" cases, but does better for most (though not all) possible population

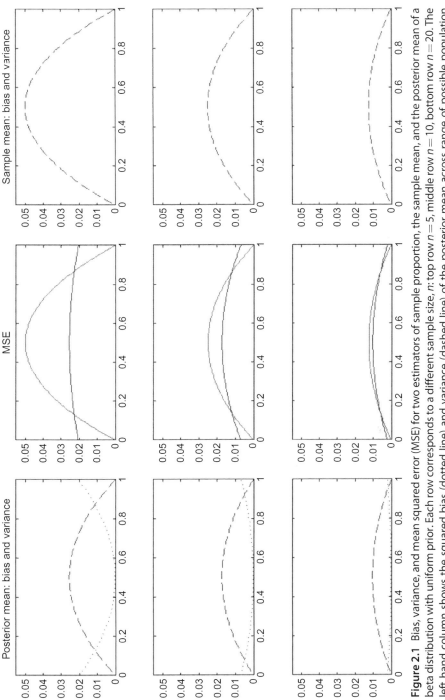

Figure 2.1 Bias, variance, and mean squared error (MSE) for two estimators of sample proportion, the sample mean, and the posterior mean of a beta distribution with uniform prior. Each row corresponds to a different sample size, n: top row $n = 5$, middle row $n = 10$, bottom row $n = 20$. The left hand column shows the squared bias (dotted line) and variance (dashed line) of the posterior mean across range of possible population proportions (x-axis). The right hand column shows bias (always 0) and variance for the sample mean. The middle column shows the MSE error of both predictors (sample mean, grey line (red in online version); posterior mean, black line (blue in online version)) which is the sum of squared bias and variance. As can be seen, MSE is lower for the posterior mean across most of the range, and always lower on average.

proportions, and does better on average. If accuracy is our goal (as seems reasonable in this context), we may consequently be better off with a "biased" estimator.

Moreover, it may not be possible to minimize *both* bias and variance. As Geman, Bienenstock, and Doursat (1992) show for the case of generalization, decreasing bias may come at the expense of increasing variance, and vice versa—a phenomenon they refer to as the "bias/variance dilemma."

Consider the case of a feed-forward neural network trained by back-propagation (e.g., Ripley, 1996). Such networks perform a type of (nonparametric) regression. A small network with a very limited number of hidden units is likely to be quite biased, as the range of functions that can be captured exactly over the possible hidden unit weights will be restricted. Increasing the number of hidden units will reduce bias, but increasing the number of parameters means that the variance increases: the network will (over)fit the training data meaning that generalization predictions will be tied too closely to the specific characteristics of the training sample and will vary widely with variation in that sample as opposed to robustly approximating the underlying function. Figure 2.2 shows an example reproduced from Geman et al. (1992) involving neural networks learning to classify handwritten digits. The figure shows total error on a test set of 600 images of handwritten digits, after training on an independent set of 200 images. Bias and variance are approximated by averaging over repeated simulations of networks with different numbers of hidden units. As can be seen, small networks show high bias and low variance, large networks, low bias and high variance.

At the one extreme, a completely biased learner is oblivious to the data; at the other, the learner is so sensitive to the characteristics of the particular sample that no meaningful generalization to new instances occurs. For fixed samples, optimal learning requires a balance between constraints on the learner, which introduce bias, and variance that arises as a result of sensitivity to the data. The best performance will be obtained by a learner that has a bias suitable to the problem at hand.[2]

It should be noted that the exact relationship between bias and variance depends on the type of problem and the measure of success that is appropriate (i.e., the loss function or scoring rule, see e.g., Domingos, 2000; Wolpert, 1997). However, the above examples suffice to show that, in the context of statistics and machine learning, "bias" does not equal "bad."

---

[2] This trade-off also underlies Gigerenzer and colleagues arguments for adaptive heuristics (see e.g., Gigerenzer, 2008).

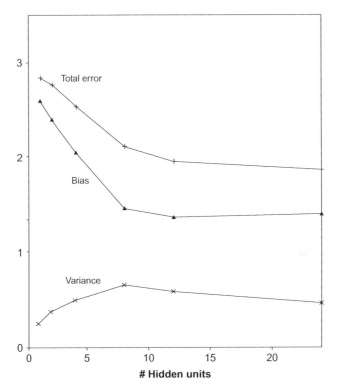

Figure 2.2 Reproduced from Geman et al. (1992). The x-axis displays the number of hidden units in the network, the y-axis the mean squared error across the test set. Each entry is the result of 50 network trials except for the last entry (24 hidden units) which is based on 10 trials only. In each case, network learning (i.e., the number of sweeps through the training set) was continued to the optimal point, that is, the point that minimized total error.

1.2.2 Signal Detection Theory

The discussion of bias in statistics so far has focused on generating estimates, but we often also need to make decisions. Indeed, even assigning an item to a discrete category on the basis of the evidence involves a decision of sorts. In the context of decisions, "bias" corresponds to a preference for one of several decision outcomes. As we saw in the everyday use of the word, a bias in the context of choices is manifest in selections that are based on something above and beyond "intrinsic merits" of the options.

A familiar use of the term bias in this decision-based sense arises in signal detection theory (SDT), a popular technique for modeling empirical decision processes. SDT was originally derived from statistical decision theory (Berger, 1985; Wald, 1950) in order to relate choice behavior to a psychological decision space for a wide range of underlying tasks such as discrimination, recognition, or classification (see e.g., Green & Swets, 1966; Swets, 1964; see also Pastore, Crawley, Berens, & Skelly, 2003, for a history). SDT has found application in psychology not just for the study of perceptual processes, but also memory, or medical diagnosis, and has also seen increasing application in adjacent fields such as forecasting (see e.g., Swets, Dawes, & Monahan, 2000, for references).

Statistical decision theory, in general, seeks to define optimal decision strategies in situations where evidence itself is noisy or uncertain. An optimal approach involves evaluating the likelihood that an observed value of that evidence has arisen from each of a range of alternative hypotheses that are being considered. Optimal decisions should reflect those likelihoods, but should also take into account potential asymmetries in costs and benefits (where they exist).

SDT is an application of statistical decision theory to the modeling of human decision behavior, providing a set of measures that allow the decomposition of performance into distinct contributing components. Specifically, it is assumed that the decision-maker aggregates evidence and evaluates the likelihood of obtaining that evidence under each of two alternative hypotheses (e.g., "signal present, no signal present," "word/nonword," "old item/new item," though generalizations to multiple hypotheses have also been derived, see e.g., DeCarlo, 2012). The likelihood comparisons can be represented along a single underlying dimension representing, for example, the ratio of the contrasted likelihoods—the so-called likelihood ratio (LHR)[3]—that is, the probability of the evidence obtained given that Hypothesis 1 is true, $P(e|H1)$, divided by the probability of obtaining that evidence if Hypothesis 2 were true, $P(e|H2)$ (see Pastore et al., 2003). This provides an underlying measure of "accumulated evidence."

In order to select a response ("*H*1" or "*H*2," "old item," or "new item," etc.), the decision-maker must select a threshold on this underlying continuous dimension, whereby values above the threshold receive one response, and values below receive the other response. There are thus two factors that will affect overall performance: (1) how well the evidence evaluation discriminates between the two alternative hypotheses and (2) where the decision threshold is placed. The literature contains a wealth of terms to

---

[3] The underlying dimension may also be a monotonic transformation of the LHR (see Pastore et al., 2003). By contrast, the widespread characterization of the underlying dimension as reflecting "a single sensory continuum" as opposed to a measure of accumulated evidence is incorrect (see Pastore et al., 2003).

refer to each of these. To avoid confusion with other concepts in this chapter, we will refer to (1) as "discrimination ability" and (2) as the "decision criterion."[4]

The relationship between these two components in determining overall performance is illustrated by the so-called receiver operating curve (ROC), see Fig. 2.3 for an example. An ROC plot shows the impact of shifting the

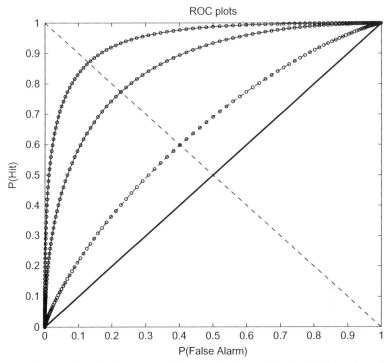

Figure 2.3 Illustrative ROC curves. On the x-axis is the probability of a false alarm (false positive), on the y-axis is the probability of a "hit." The positive diagonal (full line) represents inability to discriminate between the two alternatives. The different curves represent different levels of discrimination ability, with discrimination ability increasing with the area under the curve. The negative diagonal (dashed line) indicates an unbiased decision criterion. The intersection of that diagonal with each of the ROC curves indicates the hit rate and false-positive rate for an unbiased response selection at that level of discrimination ability. Alternative (biased) decision criteria are represented by circles along a given curve. In other words, picking different decision criteria on the part of the responder corresponds to moving along a given curve, and thus systematically shifting the hit and false alarm rates.

---

[4] Discrimination ability is also referred to as "accuracy" (see e.g., Pastore et al., 2003) or "sensitivity" (see e.g., Stanislaw & Todorov, 1999), the criterion is also referred to as "response bias," or "bias" (see e.g., Pastore et al., 2003).

decision criterion on patterns of responding. On the *y*-axis is plotted the probability of a "hit" (a correct identification of hypothesis *H*1), and on the *y*-axis the "false alarms" (the probability of incorrectly responding *H*1, when it is *H*2 that is true). A given level of discrimination ability marks out a curve in this space, and different points along this curve correspond to different values of the decision criterion that could be chosen (i.e., the slope of the curve at that point is equal to the LHR, see Swets et al., 2000). Because discrimination ability is imperfect, adopting a more liberal decision criterion—that is, requiring less compelling evidence in favor of hypothesis *H*1—will not only affect the hit rate but also the false-positive rate. Setting a less stringent criterion in evaluating a mammogram will lead to more referrals for further examination. This will not only increase the hit rate (detecting cancer) but also generate more false positives (giving rise to what turns out to be needless intervention). Where a decision-maker best sets the criterion will consequently depend in part on overall goals.

The decision criterion that simply always selects the hypothesis with the higher likelihood[5] is *unbiased*. In Fig. 2.3, it is represented by the negative diagonal indicated by the dotted line. However, once again "bias" does not equal "bad." The unbiased decision criterion only maximizes accuracy (i.e., the proportion of correct responses[6]), when the prior probabilities of both hypotheses are the same, that is, the base rates of the two alternatives are equal. If cancer is rare, then an unbiased decision criterion will lead to many false positives.

Moreover, the unbiased decision criterion does not factor in costs and benefits that might be associated with the selection of different alternatives. The benefits of the correct decision outcome(s) may far outweigh the costs of the incorrect selections, or vice versa.

Given that the decision-maker does not know the true state of the world, the optimal decision criterion must be based on expectations. As with other decisions involving uncertainty, the optimal decision policy should maximize the *expected value* of the response selection. According to Swets et al. (2000) it was first derived by Peterson, Birdsall, and Fox (1954) what the exact relationship between base rates, costs, and benefits for this is. The expected value for choosing one of the two response alternatives is defined as follows. The decision-maker is seeking to determine which of two hypotheses, *H*1 or *H*2, is correct (e.g., a medical condition is present or

---

[5] That is, the decision criterion = 1, and the hypothesis in the numerator is chosen whenever the LHR is >1, and the hypothesis in the denominator when it is less than 1.

[6] Accuracy in this sense is equal to (Hits + Correct Rejections)/(Hits + Correct Rejections + False Positives + Incorrect Rejections), where a correct rejection is a response of "not *H*1" (i.e., *H*2) when *H*2 is true.

absent, the word on a given memory trial is "old" or "new," etc.). D_{H1} represents the selection of $H1$ as the chosen response, and the same for D_{H2}; C and B represent "costs" and "benefits" so that $B(D_{H1}\ \&\ H1)$ represents the benefits of choosing $H1$ as the response when in fact $H1$ turns out to be true (i.e., a "hit"), and $C(D_{H1}\ \&\ H2)$ represents the costs of a "false positive," that is, responding $H1$ when $H2$ is in fact the case. $P(H1)$ and $P(H2)$ represent the prior probabilities (base rates) of $H1$ and $H2$. The optimal decision criterion C(optimal) is then given as[7]:

$$C(\text{optimal}) = \frac{P(H1)}{P(H2)} \times \frac{B(D_{H2}\ \&\ H2) + C(D_{H1}\ \&\ H2)}{B(D_{H1}\ \&\ H1) + C(D_{H2}\ \&\ H1)} \quad (2.1)$$

As can be seen from this formula, if all benefits and costs are considered equal (i.e., their ratio is 1.0), they play no role in determining the expected value of a selected response; in this case, it is the prior probabilities alone that determine the optimal threshold (Swets et al., 2000).

In summary, according to the normative prescriptions of decision theory, it *is rational to be biased* in responding whenever the base rates of the two alternatives are not equal and/or the relevant cost/benefit ratios are unequal. In these cases, which will be numerous in the real world, it would be irrational to adopt an unbiased decision criterion in the sense that it would lead, on average, to less good outcomes for the decision-maker. Ignoring base rates will reduce accuracy, and ignoring costs and benefits will mean missing out in terms of overall consequences (see Harris & Osman, 2012, on the importance of such parameters in understanding the status of the illusion of control as an (ir)rational bias).

For a decision criterion to be irrational, the bias of the decision-maker must deviate from Eq. (2.1). It is, of course, entirely possible that people's biases do deviate and that they are both irrational and maladaptive in this sense. However, base rates (and beliefs about them), costs, and benefits are rarely explicitly assessed in actual experiments. In fact, much of the appeal of SDT stems from the fact that it provides statistical procedures for estimating discrimination ability and decision criterion from empirical data in circumstances where underlying probability distributions governing the decision are not known (see Pastore et al., 2003). Experiments may seek to control base rates and costs and benefits associated with correct and

---

[7] For C as the slope at any given point along the ROC curve when the underlying continuum represents the LHR see Swets et al. (2000). For other conceptualizations of the underlying "evidence" dimension in the SDT model, other relationships may apply.

incorrect responding by experimental design; however, this still requires that the participant's perceptions of the situation match those of the experimenter and this cannot simply be taken for granted. It has been a recurring theme of critiques of experiments supposedly highlighting human irrationality that their results depend on systematic (and misleading) violations of participant expectations and that when discrepancies are reduced, so are the deviations from normative, rational responding (see e.g., Hilton, 1996; Schwarz, 1996 for discussion and specific examples).

1.3. Implications

Several general points emerge from the preceding general overview of research concerned with "bias." The first of these is that "bias" is neither necessarily irrational nor bad in any wider sense. "Bias" in the sense of response bias may be *optimal* when costs of hits, false positives and correct and incorrect rejections are unequal (as is capitalized on in e.g., error management theory; Haselton & Buss, 2000). In the remainder of this chapter, we concern ourselves only with accuracy goals. When a bias compromises accuracy goals, it makes sense to consider whether there may be secondary justifications for it. Where a bias does not compromise accuracy, there is no need to look for further justification (and, in fact, that further justification will be baseless), nor need one look for adaptive rationales where the mere existence of bias is not even clearly established. A focus on accuracy thus seems a necessary first step. Here, a bias may be desirable even where it is only accuracy one cares about because "response bias" (a biased decision criterion) is a consequence of optimal responding in the case of unequal priors. Moreover, the desirability of bias in estimators is generally subject to trade-offs.

This has several implications for establishing the presence of costly "bias." In order to show that an estimation process is biased in a way that will compromise the accuracy of people's belief systems, one needs to show more than that it is sometimes wrong. Rather,

1. "bias" must be understood as a property of an estimator that holds for an *expectation*, that is on average
2. this expectation must be calculated over a broad range of values in order to allow meaningful evaluation, that is, it needs to be shown that the estimator is *systematically wrong* across different contexts
3. and, finally it needs to be shown that it is wrong *at a cost* (in first instance an accuracy cost, though other costs are of course relevant in principle)

It may be argued that most research on "bias" falls short in one or more of these respects. Research on conservatism in the bookbag and pokerchip tradition has gone furthest at meeting these requirements. In Kahneman and Tversky's Heuristics and Biases program, the issue of accuracy costs (3) is typically unaddressed. In fact, it may be argued that many of their violations of decision-theoretic norms, for example, have been obtained in contexts where the two options presented for choice differ so minimally in expected value that such violations come at virtually no cost (see for recent examples, Jarvstad, Hahn, Rushton, & Warren, 2013; Jarvstad, Hahn, Warren, & Rushton, 2014; the general issue is discussed in detail by Winterfeldt and Edwards (1982) under the header of "flat maxima"). Furthermore, accuracy costs may also have implications for (2), that is the systematicity and scope of the bias, because it seems possible that the application of heuristics may be confined to cases where there is little cost in getting things wrong and that optimal strategies are applied elsewhere (for evidence to this effect see also, Brandstätter, Gigerenzer, & Hertwig, 2006).

It should be equally clear that much of the social psychological research discussed above already fails to meet requirement (1): a demonstration that participants process a few pieces of information in what, by experimental design, seems like a "biased" way does not even allow evaluation of the average impact of such behavior (if indeed it generalizes beyond the confines of that experiment). In this case, it is simply assumed that the behavior in question extends in ways that (1)–(3) are met. Such extrapolation, however, is perilous and we seek to demonstrate the frailties of such inference in the remainder, drawing on examples from research findings that have been taken as evidence of "motivated reasoning." In so doing, we show why such extrapolation invariably requires reference to optimal (normative) models.

Specifically, the remainder of the chapter will provide detailed examination of criteria (1)–(3) in motivated reasoning research, in particular in the context of wishful thinking, confirmation bias in evidence selection, biased assimilation of evidence, and the evidence neutrality principle.

2. WHEN IS A BIAS A BIAS?
2.1. Understanding Bias: Scope, Sources, and Systematicity

We begin our example-based discussion with a very general bias which, if robust, would provide direct evidence of motivated reasoning, namely "wishful thinking." Under this header, researchers (mostly in the field of judgment and decision-making) group evidence for systematic overestimation in the perceived probability of outcomes that are somehow viewed as desirable, as opposed to undesirable.

In actual fact, robust evidence for such a biasing effect of utilities or values on judgments of probability has been hard to come by, despite decades of interest, and the phenomenon has been the dubbed "the elusive wishful thinking effect" (Bar-Hillel & Budescu, 1995). Research on wishful thinking in probability judgment has generally failed to find evidence of wishful thinking under well-controlled laboratory conditions (see for results and critical discussion of previous research, e.g., Bar-Hillel & Budescu, 1995; Bar-Hillel, Budescu, & Amar, 2008; Harris, Corner, & Hahn, 2009). There have been observations of the "wishful thinking effect" outside the laboratory (e.g., Babad & Katz, 1991; Simmons & Massey, 2012). These, however, seem well explained as "an unbiased evaluation of a biased body of evidence" (Bar-Hillel & Budescu, 1995, p. 100, see also Gordon, Franklin, & Beck, 2005; Kunda, 1990; Morlock, 1967; Radzevick & Moore, 2008; Slovic, 1966). For example, Bar-Hillel et al. (2008) observed potential evidence of wishful thinking in the prediction of results in the 2002 and 2006 football World Cups. However, further investigation showed that these results were more parsimoniously explained as resulting from a salience effect than from a "magical wishful thinking effect" (Bar-Hillel et al., 2008, p. 282). Specifically, they seemed to stem from a shift in focus that biases information accumulation and not from any direct biasing effect of desirability. Hence, there is little evidence for a general "I wish for, therefore I believe..." relationship (Bar-Hillel et al., 2008, p. 283) between desirability and estimates of probability. Krizan and Windschitl's (2007) review concludes that while there are circumstances that can lead to desirability indirectly influencing probability estimates through a number of potential mediators, there is little evidence that desirability directly biases estimates of probability.

What is at issue here is the systematicity of the putative bias—the difficulty of establishing the presence of the bias across a range circumstances. The range of contexts in which a systematic deviation between true and estimated value will be observed depends directly on the underlying process that gives rise to that mismatch. Bar-Hillel and Budescu's (1995) contrast between "an unbiased evaluation of a biased body of evidence" and a "magical wishful thinking effect" reflects Macdougall's (1906) distinction between "primary" and "secondary bias," namely a contrast between selective information uptake and a judgmental distortion of information so acquired.

Both may, in principle, give rise to systematic deviations between (expected) estimate and true value; however, judgmental distortion is more pernicious in that it will produce the expected deviation much more reliably. This follows readily from the fact that selective uptake of information cannot, by definition, guarantee the *content* of that information. Selectivity in where to look may have some degree of correlation with content, and hence lead to a selective (and truth distorting) evidential basis. However, that relationship must be less than perfect, simply because information uptake on the basis of the content of the evidence itself would require processing of that content, and thus fall under "judgmental distortion" (as a decision to neglect information already "acquired").

In fact, selective attention to some sources over others can have a systematic effect on information content *only* where sources and content are systematically aligned and can be identified in advance.

Nevertheless, selectivity in search may lead to measurable decrements in accuracy if it means that information search does not maximize the expected value of information. In other words, even though a search strategy cannot guarantee the content of my beliefs (because there is no way of knowing whether the evidence, once obtained, will actually favor or disfavor my preferred hypothesis), my beliefs may systematically be less accurate because I have not obtained the evidence that could be expected to be most informative.

This is the idea behind Wason's (1960) confirmation bias. Though the term "confirmation bias," as noted, now includes phenomena that do not concern information search (see earlier, Fischhoff & Beyth-Marom, 1983), but rather information evaluation (e.g., a potential tendency to reinterpret or discredit information that goes against a current belief, e.g., Lord et al., 1979; Nisbett & Ross, 1980; Ross & Lepper, 1980), Wason's original meaning concerns information acquisition. In that context, Klayman and Ha (1989) point out that it is essential to distinguish two notions of "seeking confirmation":

1. examining instances most expected to verify, rather than falsify, the (currently) preferred hypothesis.
2. examining instances that—if the currently preferred hypothesis is true—will fall under its scope.

Concerning the first sense, "disconfirmation" is more powerful in deterministic environments, because a single counter-example will rule out a hypothesis, whereas confirming evidence is not sufficient to establish the truth of an inductively derived hypothesis. This logic, which underlies Popper's (1959) call for falsificationist strategies in science, however, does not apply in probabilistic environments where feedback is noisy. Here, the optimal strategy is to select information so as to maximize its expected value (see e.g., Edwards, 1965; and on the general issue in the context of science, see e.g., Howson & Urbach, 1996). In neither the deterministic nor the probabilistic case, however, is it necessarily wrong to seek confirmation in the second sense—that is, in the form of a positive test strategy. Though such a strategy led to poorer performance in Wason's (1960) study this is not generally the case and, for many (and realistic) hypotheses and environments, a positive test strategy is, in fact, more effective (see also, Oaksford & Chater, 1994).[8] This both limits the accuracy costs of any "confirmation bias"[9] and makes a link with "motivated reasoning" questionable.

Consideration of systematicity and scope of a putative bias consequently necessitates a clear distinction between the different component processes that go into the formation of a judgment and its subsequent report (whether in an experiment or in the real world). Figure 2.4 distinguishes the three main components of a judgment: evidence accumulation; aggregation, and evaluation of that evidence to form an internal estimate; and report of that estimate. In the context of wishful thinking, biasing effects of outcome utility (the desirability/undesirability of an outcome) can arise at each of these stages (readers familiar with Funder's (1995), realistic accuracy model of person perception will detect the parallels; likewise, motivated reasoning research distinguishes between motivational effects on information accumulation and memory as opposed to effects of processing, see e.g., Kunda, 1990). Figure 2.4 provides examples of studies concerned with biasing effects of outcome desirability on judgment for each of these component processes. For instance, demonstrations that participants' use information about real-world base rate (Dai et al., 2008) or real world "representativeness" (Mandel, 2008) in judging the probability of events exemplify effects of outcome utility on the information available for the judgment: events that are extremely bad or extremely good are less likely in the real world than ones of moderate desirability, so that outcome utility provides information about frequency of occurrence which can be used to supplement judgments where participants are uncertain about their estimates.

---

[8] As a reminder, the target rule governing triples of numbers in Wason's study was "increasing numbers." A positive test strategy means testing triples that would be instances of the currently preferred rule. This cannot lead to success when the true rule is less general than the current hypothesis (e.g., "increasing by two" vs. "increasing numbers").

[9] Though people may still, and most likely do, do less well than an optimal model by overreliance on positive test strategies even in circumstances where its expectation is lower than that of a negative test strategy (see for some examples, Klayman & Ha, 1989).

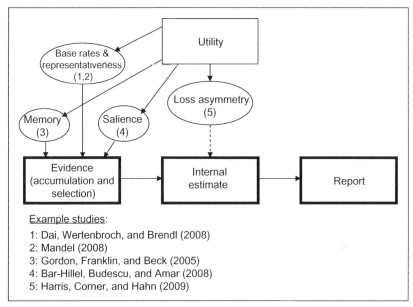

Figure 2.4 Locating indirect effects of utility (outcome desirability/undesirability) in the probability estimation process. Framed boxes indicate the distinct stages of the judgment formation process. Ovals indicate factors influencing those stages via which outcome utility can come to exert an effect on judgment. Numbers indicate experimental studies providing evidence for a biasing influence of that factor. Note that Dai, Wertenbroch, and Brendl (2008), Mandel (2008), and Harris et al. (2009) all find higher estimates for undesirable outcomes (i.e., "pessimism"). *Figure adapted from Harris et al. (2009).*

Confirming our observations about the relative reliability of primary and secondary bias in generating systematic deviations, the different components of the judgment process vary in the extent to which they generally produce "wishful thinking" and several of the studies listed (see Fig. 2.3) have actually found "anti" wishful thinking effects, whereby undesirable events were perceived to be more likely.

Such mixed, seemingly conflicting, findings are, as we have noted repeatedly, a typical feature of research on biases (see e.g., Table 1 in Krueger & Funder, 2004). However, only when research has established that a deviation is systematic has the existence of a bias been confirmed and only then can the nature of that bias be examined. The example of base rate neglect above illustrated how examination of only a selective range of base rates (just low prior probabilities or just high prior probabilities) would have led to directly conflicting "biases." The same applies to other putative biases.

In general, names of biases typically imply a putative scope: "wishful thinking" implies that, across a broad range of circumstances, thinking is "wishful." Likewise, "optimistic bias" (a particular type of wishful thinking, see Sharot, 2012) implies that individuals' assessments of their future are *generally* "optimistic." Researchers have been keen to posit broad scope biases that subsequently do not seem to hold over the full range of contexts implied by their name. This suggests, first and foremost that no such bias exists.

To qualify as optimistically biased for example, participants should demonstrate a tendency to be optimistic across a gamut of judgments or at least across a particular class of judgments such as probability judgments about future life events (e.g., Weinstein, 1980; in keeping with Weinstein's original work we restrict the term "optimistic bias" to judgments about future life events in the remainder). However, while people typically seem optimistic for rare negative events and common positive events, the same measures show pessimism for common negative events and rare common events (Chambers et al., 2003; Kruger & Burrus, 2004). Likewise, for the better-than-average effect (e.g., Dunning, Heath, & Suls, 2004; Svenson, 1981), people typically think that they are better than their peers at easy tasks, but worse than their peers at difficult tasks (Kruger, 1999; Moore, 2007), and the false consensus effect (whereby people overestimate the extent to which others share their opinions, Ross, Greene, & House, 1977) is mirrored by the false uniqueness effect (Frable, 1993; Mullen, Dovidio, Johnson, & Copper, 1992; Suls, Wan, & Sanders, 1988).

One (popular) strategy for responding to such conflicting findings is to retain the generality of the bias but to consider it to manifest only in exactly those situations in which it occurs. Circumstances of seemingly contradictory findings then become "moderators," which require understanding before one can have a full appreciation of the phenomenon under investigation (e.g., Kruger & Savitsky, 2004): in the case of the better-than-average effect therefore that moderator would be the difficulty of the task.

2.1.1 The Pitfalls of Moderators

Moderators can clearly be very influential in theory development, but they must be theoretically derived. *Post hoc* moderation claims ensure the unfalsifiability of science, or at least can make findings pitifully trivial. Consider the result—reported in the Dutch Daily News (August 30th, 2011)—that thinking about meat results in more selfish behavior. As this study has since been retracted—its author Stapel admitting that the data were fabricated—it is likely that this result would not have replicated. After (say) 50 replication attempts, what is the most parsimonious conclusion?

One can either conclude that the effect does not truly exist or posit moderators. After enough replication attempts across multiple situations, the latter strategy will come down to specifying moderators such as "the date, time and experimenter," none of which could be predicted on the basis of an "interesting" underlying theory.

This example is clearly an extreme one. The moderators proposed for the optimism bias and better-than-average effects are clearly more sensible and more general. It is still, however, the case that these moderators must be theoretically justified. If not, "moderators" may prop up a bias that does not exist, thus obscuring the true underlying explanation (much as in the toy example above). In a recent review of the literature, Shepperd, Klein, Waters, and Weinstein (2013) argue for the general ubiquitousness of unrealistic optimism defined as "a favorable difference between the risk estimate a person makes for him- or herself and the risk estimate suggested by a relevant, objective standard...Unrealistic optimism also includes comparing oneself to others in an unduly favorable manner," but state that this definition makes "no assumption about why the difference exists. The difference may originate from motivational forces...or from cognitive sources, such as...egocentric thinking" (Shepperd et al., 2013, p. 396).

However, the question of why the difference exists is critical for understanding what is meant by the term unrealistic optimism especially in the presence of findings that clearly appear inconsistent with certain accounts. The finding that rare negative events invoke comparative optimism, while common negative events invoke comparative pessimism seems entirely inconsistent with a motivational account. If people are motivated to see their futures as "rosy," why should this not be the case for common negative events (or rare positive events) (Chambers, Windschitl, & Suls, 2003; Kruger & Burrus, 2004)? One can say that comparative optimism is moderated by the interaction of event rarity and valence, such that for half the space of possible events pessimism is in fact observed, but would one really want to call this "unrealistic optimism" or an "optimistic bias"? Rather, it seems that a more appropriate explanation is that people focus overly on the self when making comparative judgments (e.g., Chambers et al., 2003; Kruger & Burrus, 2004; see Harris & Hahn, 2009 for an alternative account which can likewise predict this complete pattern of data)—a process that simply has the by-product of optimism under certain situations. It might be that such overfocus on the self gives rise to bias, but through a correct understanding of it one can better predict its implications. Likewise, one is in a better position to judge the potential costs of it.

In summary, when bias is understood in a statistical sense as a property of an expectation, demonstration of deviation across a range of values is essential to establishing the existence of a bias in the first place, let alone understanding its nature. Conflicting findings across a range of values (e.g., rare vs. common events in the case of optimism) suggest an initial misconception of the bias, and any search for moderators must take care to avoid perpetuating that misconception by—unjustifiedly—splitting up into distinct circumstances one common underlying phenomenon (i.e., one bias) which has different effects in different circumstances (for other examples, see on the better-than-average/worse-than-average effect, see e.g., Benoit & Dubra, 2011; Galesic, Olsson, & Rieskamp, 2012; Kruger, 1999; Kruger, Windschitl, Burrus, Fessel, & Chambers, 2008; Moore & Healy, 2008; Moore & Small, 2007; Roy, Liersch, & Broomell, 2013; on the false uniqueness/false consensus effect see Galesic, Olsson, & Rieskamp, 2013; more generally, see also, Hilbert, 2012).

3. MEASURING BIAS: THE IMPORTANCE OF OPTIMAL MODELS

Having stressed the importance of viewing bias as an expected deviation from accuracy, and the attendant need to examine the performance of inferential procedures across a range, we next highlight the difficulties of establishing a deviation from accuracy in the first place.

In some cases, the true value is known and can be compared directly with a participant's estimate, but as we saw earlier, in social psychological studies the true value is typically not known and researchers resort to other, less direct ways of ascertaining bias. Here, comparison with normative models that specify how to perform the task "optimally" is essential.

Given the unease with normative models in social psychology, we not only provide some examples of where common-sense intuition may be misled, but also outline why the normative standard—in this case Bayesian probability—is appropriate to the task.

Our first example carries on with the "wishful thinking" theme by examining unrealistic optimism about future life events.

Here, people's actual risk is not known directly to the participant or the experimenter, rather it must be inferred from available evidence. "Rationality" in such circumstances is thus necessarily about inferential procedures, not about whether particular answers derived by such a procedure are right or wrong as such—simply because it is in the nature of induction as an ampliative inference that goes beyond the data given—that sometimes even one's "best guess" will be wrong (see e.g., Baron, 2008).

3.1. Bayesian Belief Revision

The common standard for such inductive inference is Bayesian belief revision. Within the Bayesian framework, probabilities are conceptualized as subjective degrees of belief, rather than as objective frequencies existing in the external environment. Bayesian inference is thus concerned with the consistency and coherence of those probabilities. Most importantly in the present context, it can be shown that "being Bayesian" (that is adherence to the axioms of the probability calculus and the use of Bayes' rule in incorporating evidence for the revision of ones beliefs) has lawful connections with accuracy. Accuracy-based justifications of Bayesianism invoke scoring rules as are used to measure the accuracy of probabilistic forecasts (e.g., in meteorology). As shown by de Finetti (1974), given a scoring rule by which a person incurs a penalty of $(1-p)^2$ if an event is found to be true and p^2 if an event is found to be false (where p denotes a numerical value previously assigned by the person to the likelihood of the event in question), a person will *necessarily* incur a larger penalty if their likelihood estimates do not obey the probability axioms. Lindley (1982, 1994) argues that if other scoring rules are used then either people should provide responses that are, in reality, only transformations of probability (e.g., odds), or people should only estimate 0 or 1 (demonstrating the inadequacy of such a scoring rule). Hence, "all sensible rules lead back, via a possible transformation, to probability. Probability is inevitable" (Lindley, 1994, p. 6; see also, e.g., Cox, 1946; Horvitz, Heckerman, & Langlotz, 1986; Snow, 1998).

Furthermore, Rosenkrantz (1992) shows that updating by Bayes' rule maximizes the expected score after sampling; in other words, other updating rules will be less efficient in the sense that they will require larger samples, on average, to be as accurate. Leitgeb and Pettigrew (2010b) demonstrate that for a suitable measure of accuracy (justified in Leitgeb & Pettigrew, 2010a; but see Levinstein, 2012), Bayesianism follows from the simple premise that an agent ought to approximate the truth, and hence seek to minimize inaccuracy.

Being Bayesian thus provides a route for realistic beliefs about future life events as studied within the unrealistic optimism literature. How then does a Bayesian form their beliefs about whether or not they will at some point in their lives experience a negative life event? Bayes' rule provides normative guidance on how beliefs should be updated upon receipt of new information:

$$P(h|e) = \frac{P(h)P(e|h)}{P(e)} \qquad (2.2)$$

Equation (2.2) mandates that one evaluate the likelihood of a hypothesis, h, in light of some evidence, e, by multiplicatively combining one's prior degree of belief in that hypothesis, $P(h)$ (i.e., one's degree of belief before receiving the present evidence), with the likelihood of obtaining that evidence in the case that the hypothesis is true, $P(e|h)$, and then normalize by dividing by the likelihood of obtaining that piece of evidence regardless of the truth or falsity of the evidence, $P(e)$.

The base rate of an event (let us use a disease as an example) in a population can be defined as a frequentist percentage—for example, the number of people per 100 who will contract the disease. This is the most appropriate information to use as one's prior degree of belief that the disease will be contracted, $P(h)$. Consequently, if no individuals within the population have any information with which to differentiate their chance of experiencing a disease from the average person's, all individuals should state that their chance of experiencing the disease is equal to the base rate. It is easy to see in this instance that the population's probability judgments are coherent and well calibrated: each individual states their chance of contracting the disease as being the base rate; thus, the average-risk rating of the population is the base rate, which in turn is the same as the true proportion of people who will actually experience the disease.

However, this relationship will also hold in instances in which different individuals have information to differentiate their own chance from the average person's. Consider a simple situation in which a disease is known to be predictable, in part, by family history (as is the case for many serious illnesses, e.g., Walter & Emery, 2006). We further assume that everyone in the population knows whether or not they have a family history of the disease and that this is the only information that is known about the etiology of the disease. Those with a family history will estimate their own risk using Eq. (2.2), while those without will be estimating the likelihood that they will contract the disease knowing they have no family history of it, $P(h|\neg e)$ (Eq. 2.3):

$$P(h|\neg e) = \frac{P(h)P(\neg e|h)}{P(\neg e)} \qquad (2.3)$$

The average of people's estimates of self-risk is obtained by adding together those estimates and dividing by the number of individuals. This is functionally equivalent to multiplying each of the two risk estimates (Eqs. 2.2 and 2.3) by the proportion of people expressing them and summing across the two distinct (average) estimates; the result will once again equal the base rate (Harris & Hahn, 2011). Thus, the average risk estimate of a population of Bayesians who use the base rate to estimate their prior degree of belief will result in average risk estimates that are calibrated (at the population level) to the base rate statistic.

This guaranteed population level calibration demonstrates why Bayesian belief revision is normatively appropriate in this context and it confirms researchers' intuition that optimism can be assessed at the group level even in the absence of knowledge about a given individual's personal likelihood of experiencing an event.

3.2. Divergence of Normative Predictions and Experimenter Intuition

3.2.1 Unrealistic Comparative Optimism

At a group level, average estimates of personal risk should equal average estimates of the average person's risk, or base rate, $P(h)$, whether we know the individual's risk and the true base rate or not. Consequently, if the population's estimate of self-risk is *lower* than their estimate of the base rate then their estimates can be said to be biased in an optimistic direction—the classic phenomenon of unrealistic comparative optimism (e.g., Weinstein, 1980).

While the basic logic of this is sound, its application in standard experimental methods is not. Harris and Hahn (2011) demonstrated that optimal Bayesian agents completing standard questionnaires for studying optimism (following Weinstein's classic, 1980, method) would show patterns taken to indicate unrealistic optimism, even though they are entirely rational and in no way optimistic. This stems from three independent sources whose effects will combine and amplify one another in any given study: (1) scale attenuation, because participants provide their responses on a limited, noncontinuous, scale (e.g., -3 to $+3$, see e.g., Covey & Davies, 2004; Klar, Medding, & Sarel, 1996; Price, Pentecost, & Voth, 2002; Weinstein, 1982, 1984, 1987; Weinstein & Klein, 1995) which does not allow faithful conversion of underlying probability estimates; (2) minority undersampling, arising from the fact that estimates are elicited from only a sample taken from the population so that calibration at the group level is no longer guaranteed; and (3) base rate regression. The base rate regression mechanism derives from the fact that people's actual estimates of probabilities are likely to be regressive; that is, due to random error small probabilities will, on average, be overestimated and large probabilities will be underestimated (because of the bounded nature of the probability scale). This will bias population results because base rates assumed by agents in the calculation of their individual risk will no longer match the impact of diagnostic evidence. Bayes' rule no longer guarantees that the appropriate incorporation of diagnostic evidence results in population level calibration if the base rate estimates going into the agents' estimates are regressive. Specifically, their mean will no longer equal the average individual risk, because that is based not just on base rate estimates but also on the diagnostic evidence each individual has received, and this diagnostic evidence is dispensed "by the world," as it were.[10] It is thus governed by the true base rate, not by its regressive subjective estimate. Put simply, the number of people who will have a family history of a disease as opposed to the number who will not depends on the "true" distribution of the disease, not one's beliefs about it. Harris and Hahn (2011) demonstrate that the resultant mismatch will yield comparative optimism for rare negative events (i.e., mean estimates of self-risk are lower than the perceived "average person's risk") and absolute optimism (i.e., the mean estimated self-risk is higher than the true population mean), as is indeed observed in the empirical literature (Chambers et al., 2003; Kruger & Burrus, 2004; Moore & Small, 2008).

The same underlying issue of a clash between the diagnostic information dispensed "by the world" and the base rates that are assumed (by participants or experimenters) plagues research that has sought to provide evidence of unrealistic optimism by studying belief updating directly, as opposed to examining its results.

3.2.2 Optimistic Belief Updating

Lench and colleagues' "automatic optimism" (Lench, 2009; Lench & Bench, 2012; Lench & Ditto, 2008) provides a motivational account of optimism bias based on an "optimism heuristic." As a default reaction, people "simply decide that events that elicit positive affective reactions are likely to occur and events that elicit negative affective reactions are unlikely to occur" (Lench & Bench, 2012, p. 351), when they experience approach or avoidance reactions to future events. In support, Lench and Ditto (2008) provided participants with matched positive and negative future life events, for which participants were given equal base rates. Participants then

---

[10] Shepperd et al. (2013) appear to misunderstand this base rate regression mechanism, confusing it with accounts of other self-enhancement phenomena in terms of differentially regressive estimates for self and other (e.g., Moore & Small, 2008). Differential regression concerns the relationship between two estimates, one of which is more regressive than the other. Other than that "regressiveness" of ratings are involved in both differential regression and the base rate regression mechanism, they have nothing to do with one another and are not only conceptually but also empirically distinct.

rated their own chance of experiencing that event. In a direct comparison, the mean estimates for negative events were lower than for the matched positive events, suggesting optimism.

The problem lies in the fact that Lench and Ditto's (2008) used negation to generate corresponding negative ("will get cancer") and positive ("will not get cancer") events. However, complementary events can be equiprobable only if their base rate is exactly 50%. This is not the case for events such as "getting cancer," "owning one's own home," "at some point being unemployed," or "developing asthma" as used by Lench and Ditto (2008). That participants are told equivalent base rates does not make things equal, because the distribution of participants' individual diagnostic knowledge will be governed by the true base rate (i.e., "the way the world is"), precisely because that knowledge is diagnostic.

To illustrate, cancer has a life-time prevalence of about 40%, so most people will genuinely not get cancer. By the same token, more people will possess diagnostic knowledge indicating lower risk than there will be people with knowledge indicating greater risk. This means that averages across estimates of individual risk will deviate from the experimenter provided base rate even if participants fully believe that base rate and incorporate it into their own prediction. Moreover, because the negative event in question is rare, it will necessarily deviate in the direction of seeming "optimism," even if people's estimates are otherwise fully rational and Bayesian.

The same issue plagues Sharot and colleagues demonstrations of seemingly optimistic belief updating and its moderators (Chowdhury, Sharot, Wolfe, Düzel, & Dolan, 2013; Korn, Sharot, Walter, Heekeren, & Dolan, 2014; Moutsiana et al., 2013; Sharot, Guitart-Masip, Korn, Chowdhury, & Dolan, 2012; Sharot, Kanai, et al., 2012; Sharot, Korn, & Dolan, 2011). In these studies, participants seemingly display motivated reasoning by virtue of the fact that they are selective in their use of desirable and undesirable information, revising their beliefs to a greater extent in response to "good news" than to "bad."

Participants are required to estimate their chance of experiencing a series of negative events. As in Lench and Ditto's (2008) study, they are then provided with the base rate statistic for each event, in this case, a genuine estimate of the true base rate.[11] Participants then provide a second estimate of their personal risk. Rather than comparing the means of those estimates with

---

[11] This "true base rate" is a base rate sourced from real-world statistics about people from the same sociocultural environment as the participants, although given that sources for these statistics include the Office for National Statistics, it is unlikely that University College London research participants (e.g., Sharot et al., 2011) constitute a representative sample of the general population from which that estimate was devised.

the base rate, Sharot and colleagues examine the amount of belief change from first to second estimate. The typical finding is a seemingly optimistic asymmetry in belief updating. Specifically, when the chance of experiencing a negative event is higher than participants initially thought (undesirable information), they revise their personal risk estimates less than when it is lower (desirable information).

This result seems a particularly strong form of motivated reasoning, since it is difficult to envisage how participants could maintain any "illusion of objectivity" given they receive *only* the base rate (e.g., Kunda, 1990). Motivated reasoning research has typically come to the conclusion that, psychologically, people do not seem at liberty to distort their beliefs however they desire; rather, their motivational distortions must have at least some basis in the evidence allowing them to maintain the "illusion of objectivity" by selectively focusing on particular aspects in order to reach a desired conclusion. Recent demonstrations that participants updating are asymmetrically optimistic in their judgments about their attractiveness (Eil & Rao, 2011) and their intelligence (Eil & Rao, 2011; Mobius, Niederle, Niehaus, & Rosenblat, 2011), seem more in line with this typical view; attractiveness is a highly subjective attribute, and intelligence is a multidimensional construct, of which different intelligence tests typically measure different aspects, giving participants ample room for selective focus that seems unavailable in Sharot et al.'s paradigm.

However, Sharot et al.'s paradigm also differs methodologically from these recent studies of belief revision about intelligence or attractiveness. Whereas Eil and Rao (2011) and Mobius et al. (2011) compare actual updating with explicitly calculated Bayesian prescriptions, Sharot et al. simply measure belief change. Unfortunately, this is a good example in which intuition and normative standards clash, and again, the distribution of events in the world (and with them diagnostic information) relative to perceived base rates is key to where intuition goes wrong.

Given that the only "new information" participants receive in Sharot et al.'s paradigm is the "true" base rate, this is also the only quantity they should modify in calculating their own best estimates. Rational agents updating their beliefs in accordance with Bayes' rule should replace their own base rate estimate with the true base rate and recalculate their estimate of individual risk (Eq. 2.3). If their initial base rate estimate was lower than the true base rate, then their new estimate of self-risk will be higher; if their initial self-estimate was based on an overestimate of the base rate, then their new estimate of self-risk will be lower; and finally, if the two base rates match, their estimate remains unchanged.

It seems plausible that given equal amounts of deviation from the base rate for both over- and underestimates, the change scores (that is the absolute value of the first self-estimate–second self-estimate) should be equal between those receiving "good news" (a lower base rate than they had assumed) and those receiving "bad news" (a higher base rate than assumed). However, this is *not* the case. Equal (average) error in base rate estimate does not translate directly into equal average error in self-estimates (and hence "change" on correction), because—once again—the distribution of diagnostic information follows the true base rate, not the perceived base rates. Consequently, even for unbiased error about the base rate (i.e., mean = 0) average change for entirely rational agents can differ between base rate over- and under-estimators (see Shah, Harris, Bird, Catmur, & Hahn, 2013, Appendix B for demonstration). "Equal change in self-estimate" across good and bad news about the base rate is thus *not* normatively mandated, and can fail in entirely rational, Bayesian, agents.

Sharot and colleagues' actual studies further compound this methodological error by failing to ascertain participants' initial base rate estimates in order to determine whether they are, in fact, receiving good or bad news about the base rate. Rather they identify "good news" and "bad news" relative to the participants' estimate of *individual* risk, but that estimate, of course, rightfully also contains individual, diagnostic information. Rational agents in possession of diagnostic information indicating lower risk (e.g., those who do not have a family history of cancer) legitimately consider themselves to be at less risk than the "average person" (see also Weinstein & Klein, 1996), and the only "news" they have received concerns the base rate. "Good" and "bad" news must consequently be defined relative to that base rate, not relative to perceived self-risk.

Analytic examples and simulations demonstrate that classification of entirely rational Bayesian agents on the basis of the relationship between self-estimate and base rate yields considerable misclassification, and is sufficient to generate data indicative of "optimistic updating" even for a population of simulated rational Bayesian agents (Harris, Shah, Catmur, Bird, & Hahn, 2013).

It is worth emphasising that nothing in the preceding analyses requires that participants actually be Bayesian. Rather the point is that an experimental measure that yields "optimism" with rational agents who are, by design, rational and not optimistic, can provide neither evidence of optimism nor of irrationality.

In summary, intuitions about accuracy can go badly wrong, making consideration of normative, optimal models essential. In reference to debates and concerns about normative status, it is important to acknowledge that such debates exist and that the theoretical understanding of norms of rationality is incomplete and still developing. This makes it important to articulate in a given context why something is considered a norm and what relationship its justification bears to the problem at hand (see also Corner & Hahn, 2013).

One issue that has been subject to debate is the interpretation of probability (and hence risk) itself. On a Bayesian, subjectivist interpretation, probabilities reflect subjective degrees of belief, whereas on a frequentist, objectivist interpretation of probability, they reflect proportions (see e.g., von Mises, 1957/1981). The two are not mutually exclusive to the extent that Bayesians also wish to adopt "objective probabilities" (such as the proportion of balls of a given color in an urn from which random draws are taken) as subjective degrees of belief, where such probabilities are available (the so-called Principal principle, Lewis, 1986; Meacham, 2010), and this is what we have assumed in our examples of populations and adverse events such as diseases. However, where Bayesians and frequentists differ is in probabilities for unique events, such as whether or not I will contract a particular disease at some point in my life. For frequentists, there is no sample from which proportions could be inferred, so questions about the probability of singular future events are meaningless (an issue that has figured prominently in critiques of the Heuristics and Biases program, see e.g., Gigerenzer et al., 1989; Cosmides & Tooby, 1996). They can be understood only as questions about individuals as members of a reference class (e.g., "women," "women who smoke," "women who are overweight and smoke," etc.). From this perspective, questions about self- and average risks in unrealistic optimism studies involve different reference classes, where self-risk may be taken from a more specific reference class ("men with no family history of the disease who exercise regularly") than the average person (i.e., the target population). Again, ratings of self-risk may legitimately be lower than average-risk ratings. Moreover, due to what is known as the "reference class problem" there is no unique answer for self-risk: any given individual will belong to many different references classes (i.e., "woman who are overweight and smoke" are also "woman who smoke" and "woman," see e.g., Cosmides & Tooby, 1996). As a consequence, there is also no reason why self-ratings should average out and equal ratings of average risk,[12] so, from a purely frequentist perspective, optimism research, whether it be comparative ratings or belief updating, is a nonstarter. In short,

---

[12] Specifically, average self-risk would average out to the population mean only if all reference classes used by raters formed a partition, that is, were mutually exclusive and jointly exhaustive of the population as a whole. There is no way to ensure in standard test that they ever would.

competing strands of the normative debate concur in leading to a negative assessment of these methods.

In conclusion, we could not agree more with "norm sceptics" that simply claiming that something is normative is not enough. However, as the present examples hopefully illustrate, the fact that there can be legitimate debate about normativity does not preclude that, in a specific context, the issues may be clear enough, and that it would be detrimental to ignore putatively normative considerations: an incomplete map of the terrain is likely to still be better than no map at all.

3.3. Bayes and Experimental Demonstrations of Motivated Reasoning

Our critical evaluation of biased focused research in the context of motivated reasoning thus far has focused on only a subset of what is a vast and sprawling literature. Wishful thinking in the context of judgments of probability or risk constitutes only a small portion of the relevant research literature; at the same time, however, it is a part which, in principle, affords rigorous research with respect to bias. Systematicity of deviation from expected values can, and has been, evaluated in that researchers have examined many kinds of outcomes over a broad range of probabilities where criteria for accuracy exist at least in principle.

It is our contention that the majority of the remaining research on motivated reasoning has not done enough to establish "bias" in the sense of systematic deviation from accuracy—let alone establish that participants' reasoning is irrational or flawed. This is obviously a contentious statement, but it follows rather directly from the fact that most studies of motivated reasoning that fall outside the paradigms already discussed rely on the impact of what are perceived to be normatively irrelevant experimental manipulations on participants' beliefs as their methodology. Not only does that bring with it evaluations of performance that lack systematic variations of context, but it also means that the purported impact of participant sensitivity to such manipulations stands and falls with experimenter intuitions, which are typically not given any robust justification. Consideration of fundamental aspects of Bayesian belief revision, in many cases, suggests that these experimenter intuitions are hard to defend.

In this context, it is qualitative properties of Bayesian belief revision that are relevant, simply because most of the experimental studies show only that responses are "different" across the conditions. Matching broad qualitative prescriptions of Bayes' rule is obviously a good deal easier than matching quantitatively the precise degree to which beliefs should change. Thus, our analysis in this section leaves open the possibility that people may fail more exacting quantitative tests. Indeed, this is to be expected in light of the detailed findings of less than optimal sensitivity to probabilistically relevant variables ("conservatism") within the 1960s tradition of bookbags and pokerchips. We are thus by no means out to proclaim complete rationality of participants; rather, the purpose is to point out that, if responding is in keeping with broad qualitative trends, then establishing bias must by necessity go down more specific and detailed routes. At the same time, however, qualitative sensitivity to "the right factors" will serve to bound participants' inaccuracy in practice.

Finally, in keeping with earlier emphasis on the need to be explicit about one's normative justifications, it seems relevant to point out (in addition to the reasons given for adherence to the Bayesian calculus so far) that the Bayesian framework has come to take a central role in current epistemology and philosophy of science as a standard for rationality (see e.g., Bovens & Hartmann, 2004; Howson & Urbach, 1996). This, in and of itself, seems enough to support the perception that patterns of inference that are in qualitative agreement with Bayesian prescriptions are not obviously *irrational* whatever experimenters may have assumed!

With these introductory words in place, what can be concluded about bias on the basis of the motivated reasoning literature?

Clearly, a systematic review of that literature is beyond the scope of this chapter. So our examples will necessarily be selective (though hopefully with broader implications). In this case, it seems appropriate to take as our point of departure key reviews of that literature; thus, whatever general picture is drawn in those, it will at least not be driven by our own perspective. The standard point of departure here is Kunda's classic (1990) review.

Kunda's review is set in the historical context of long-standing debate between cognitive and motivational explanations of findings, in particular in the context of attribution that seemed to indicate motives affecting reasoning in such a way as "to allow people to believe what they want to believe because they want to believe it" (Kunda, p. 480). Critiques of motivated explanations of such findings maintained that early findings could be understood entirely in nonmotivational, cognitive terms (e.g., Dawes, 1976; Miller & Ross, 1975; Tetlock & Levi, 1982). Kunda's own conclusion, a decade later, was that whereas these earlier critiques rejected the case for motivational forces on parsimony grounds (as findings were explicable in cognitive terms alone), the situation had now reversed in that "a single motivational process for which unequivocal independent evidence now exists may be used to account for a wide diversity of phenomena (p. 493)," many of which could not be accounted for in nonmotivational, cognitive terms, or would require ad hoc assumptions without independent support.

Our focus is on accuracy and bias (in the sense of systematic deviations from accuracy); consequently, the distinction between cognitive and motivational factors is of interest, here, only to the extent that it might reliably be associated with differential outcomes with regard to accuracy.

Kunda's main conclusions are that people's inferential processes are subject to two motivational influences: (1) a motivation to be accurate and (2) a motivation to reach a desired conclusion. Moreover, on the available evidence, even directionally motivated reasoning does not constitute a carte blanche to believe whatever one desires; the desired conclusion is only drawn if it can be supported by evidence—indeed, if that evidence could "persuade a dispassionate observer" (Kunda, 1990, pp. 482–483). Kunda provides only very limited evidence of judgmental distortions, and what evidence is listed is quite weak (e.g., purported evidence of direct biasing influences of desirability on probability judgement, which subsequent research on "wishful thinking" as discussed above has discredited). Rather, in her view, the key mechanism that past research points to is accumulation and selection of evidence that is biased in such a way that the resulting inferential process might lead to an outcome that seems biased from an external perspective (i.e., viewed in terms of correspondence), but which is subjectively rational given the evidence considered at that time (i.e., viewed in terms of coherence, at least in terms of the selected evidential base). In fact, she acknowledges that present evidence is entirely compatible with the idea that the impact of motivation on reasoning is exhausted by the setting of a directional query or hypothesis (e.g., "Am I healthy?" as opposed to "Am I ill?") without further effect on the processes through which these questions are answered.

We are thus led back to the issue of the extent to which biases at the information accumulation stage may reliably support a *systematic* deviation from accuracy, as opposed to occasional error.

However, it also remains less than clear to what extent biases at these stages, in fact, exist. With regard to evidence accumulation, Hart et al. (2009) conducted an extensive meta-analysis of 67 experimental studies examining "selective exposure," that is, the extent to which people choose to examine information they have been told will be congenial to a prior attitude or belief they hold, as opposed to information that runs counter to it. As discussed above, this perfect (or near perfect) correlation between an information source and its content is not typically found in the real world. In the real world, we do not have this much control over the content of the information we receive, but such paradigms may nevertheless be indicative of selectivity. The 67 studies provide both evidence of a congeniality bias and evidence for its opposite, an anticongeniality bias. This not only raises the now familiar question about the existence of a congeniality bias, but it also, in itself, lessens the probability of systematic impact on the accuracy of beliefs.

Hart et al. (2009) do go on to examine both the shape of the distribution of effect sizes and to calculate an average effect size (which they find to be positive and indicative of participants, on average, being almost twice as likely to select congenial over uncongenial information). However, with regard to bias in the sense of expected deviation from a true value, the analysis makes no distinctions between studies examining beliefs about facts, for which truth, and hence accuracy as correspondence with the truth is well defined, and attitudes, for which no objective standards may be available. This makes sense in the wider context of motivated reasoning research which has not distinguished between beliefs and attitudes, but it is essential to the question of rationality and quantifying deviations from true values for establishing bias.[13] Moreover, it is important not just at the point of trying to calculate such values, but also at the point of examining behavior: it cannot be assumed that people's information acquisition and evaluation strategies are the same whether the target concerns a fact or the degree to which someone or something is "liked," and there is much reason, both normative and empirical, to assume that they are not. Consequently, including in the calculation of effect sizes studies for which a correct answer may not be defined clouds the extent to which "congeniality bias" exists in a form that could negatively affect accuracy even in principle.

The same applies to studies of congeniality bias in memory in the context of attitudes. Here, too, the meta-analysis by Eagly et al. (1999) reveals considerable inconsistency in the literature, with an overall meta-analytic effect size of the congeniality effect in memory of zero (with 40% of studies showing the opposite bias, an uncongeniality effect). This latter result led Eagly

---

[13] To be clear, the congeniality question in the context of valuation is of course of central importance to "bias" in the sense of impartiality or fairness, but the focus of the present chapter is on whether people are rational, not on whether people are nice.

et al. to propose that people engage in "active" defense strategies. That is, attitude inconsistent information is attended to at least as much as attitude inconsistent information, and processed more deeply to enable counter-arguments (support for which was obtained in Eagly, Kulesa, Brannon, Shaw, & Hutson-Comeaux, 2000, Eagly, Kulesa, Chen, & Chaiken, 2001; see also, Ditto, Scepansky, Munro, Apanovitch, & Lockhart, 1998; Edwards & Smith, 1996). More recently, Waldum and Sahakyan (2012) found that both directed memory and directed forgetting were enhanced for incongruent versus congruent political statements, which seemed based on more episodic contextual information being encoded in the memory trace for incongruent versus congruent information.

In either case, whether or not the true effect size for congeniality bias for beliefs in exposure or memory is zero or not, the fact that it is so strongly subject to "moderating factors," again, weakens the extent to which it could have *systematic directional* effects on our beliefs, as opposed to promoting occasional error.

A final question, however, remains, and that is the question of what, from a normative perspective, would actually promote accuracy goals and hence what should count as criteria for "defensive" or "accuracy" orientation, whether in the selection or the subsequent judgmental evaluation of evidence. The standard view in the literature on motivated reasoning is this:

> *Accuracy motivation should promote tendencies to process information in an objective, open-minded fashion that fosters un-covering the truth*
> **(Chaiken et al., 1989; Kunda, 1990) (quoted from Hart et al., 2009, p. 558).**

The assumption, here, is that it is some kind of even-handedness or objectivity that is critical to accuracy in our inferences. The same intuition is present in the "neutral evidence principle." Mixed evidence in the context of biased assimilation paradigms, such as in Lord et al.'s (1979) study, should not change our beliefs, because positive and negative evidence should balance each other out; that is, regardless of our prior beliefs, the diagnostic impact of a piece of evidence should be the same.

Following the discussion of bias in statistics above, in particular the comparisons between a Bayesian and a classical estimator of proportion, it should already be apparent that this is too simplistic. The impact of a piece of evidence is not constant across the range of priors, and Bayesian inference has its relationship with accuracy not just in spite of the fact that judgment is influenced by priors, but also because of it. Where information is received sequentially, that is bit by bit, as is typical in the world, priors summarize past evidence.

One may argue, however, that even though the actual effect on our beliefs of a piece of evidence may, from a Bayesian perspective, vary, its diagnosticity, as measured by the LHR, should at least stay the same. That is, wherever a piece of positive information takes us to, an equally diagnostic piece of negative information should take us back to where we started—in keeping with the neutral evidence principle.

However, even this may—and has been—disputed from a normative perspective. In particular, it is questionable whenever source reliability comes into play. Much of our knowledge comes from the testimony of others. We have, for example, typically not observed the outcome of scientific or medical tests directly, but rather have access to them only through reports. Moreover, this is exactly the situation in which experimental participants in motivated reasoning experiments find themselves.

After a long history of neglect, philosophical interest has recently turned to testimony (e.g., Coady, 1992) and a crucial aspect of testimony is trust. Unless, we believe a source to be perfectly reliable—a condition unlikely to be met by even the most well-intentioned informants—the impact of testimonial evidence should be somewhat less than had we observed the evidence directly (see e.g., Hahn, Harris, & Corner, 2009; Hahn, Oaksford, & Harris, 2012; Schum, 1981, 1994). From a Bayesian, epistemological perspective, source, and evidence characteristics combine to determine the overall diagnostic value of the evidence. Furthermore, the content of the testimony itself may provide one indicator (and in many contexts our only indicator) of the source's reliability. Recent work in epistemology has thus endorsed the position that message content should impact our beliefs about the source (see e.g., Bovens & Hartmann, 2004; Olsson, 2013).

Evidence that is surprising (i.e., conflicts with our prior beliefs) may lower our degree of belief, but it will also lower our degree of trust in the reliability of the source. Although this question has received little attention in psychology, there is some recent evidence to suggest that people naturally draw inferences about the reliability of the source from the degree to which message content is expected (Jarvstad & Hahn, 2011).

This conflicts directly with Baron's neutral evidence principle: once there is no normative requirement for people with opposing views on the content of the message perceive its source as equally reliable, there is also no longer a requirement that they perceive the overall diagnostic value to be the same. What, to an experimenter, may seem equally strong evidence for and against need not be for other observers once source reliability is taken into account.

"Biased assimilation" is indeed a consequence of this, and on occasion, this can lead us to go badly wrong: we end up believing a falsehood while, wrongly, viewing sources who conflict with our opinion as unreliable. However, as we have stressed throughout this chapter, this must distinguished from whether or not this is detrimental to our beliefs *on average*. The fact that an inductive procedure fails occasionally does not mean it is undesirable in general.

The question of the global impact of such sensitivity to source reliability can be examined through simulation. Olsson (2013) simulates a population of Bayesian agents who receive both information "from the world" and from the testimony of others, updating their beliefs about the content of the report and about other's reliability as a function of that content. In the simulation, a proportion of the population ends up believing the wrong thing and distrusting all non-like-minded agents. The majority, however, converge on the truth. The simulation thus shows both "belief polarization" and that such polarization need not undermine our overall accuracy goals (see also, Olsson & Vallinder, 2013). There is much more to be said here than present space permits. Intuitively, the reader may consider that in Lord et al. (1979) study, biased assimilation means that some participants are now "more wrong" than before (depending on which view is actually correct), but those with the opposing view will have moved their beliefs in the direction of "the truth." On average, accuracy may thus readily increase. In summary, it is neither clear that the "neutral evidence principle" is indeed a normative principle, nor that it serves our accuracy goals to be "objective" in the sense that Hart et al. (2009) suggest.

What holds for the judgmental impact of our beliefs, however, also carries through to information selection, and hence, "exposure paradigms." Choosing what information to sample is a *decision*, and thus, normatively subject to expected value. Where the impact of evidence, once obtained, differs, so does its expected value. Source reliability considerations thus affect both "biased" evaluation and selective exposure, and, it would seem that what counts in both contexts as "defensive" as opposed to "accuracy seeking" needs reevaluation.

In summary, consideration of qualitative aspects of Bayesian belief revision indicates that present evidence for motivated reasoning is considerably less good than presumed.

4. CONCLUSIONS

Our "tour" of bias research has, in some ways, come full circle. Source considerations were mentioned as one possible explanation of the "inertia effect" within 1960s conservatism studies (Peterson & DuCharme, 1967), in that participants may "disbelieve" later evidence (see also, Slovic & Lichtenstein, 1971). Source reliability also provides a potential factor in conservatism more generally (see Corner, Harris, & Hahn, 2010).

It should be clear from the preceding evidence indicating the importance of normative models in studying bias that we think the 1960s studies within the bookbag and pokerchip tradition have much to recommend them. Last but not least, their quantitative nature allows simultaneous assessment both of how bad and how good human judgment is (cf. Funder, 1995; Krueger & Funder, 2004) and affords insight into bias in the all-important sense of systematic deviation from accuracy, alongside assessment of its costs.

The bookbag and pokerchip paradigm has been criticized both on grounds that it is confusing for participants and that it is typically quite artificial and unnatural (e.g., Manz, 1970; Slovic & Lichtenstein, 1971). However, the artificiality does, in fact, make it informative for the study of motivated reasoning. While phenomena such as undersampling and "inertia" (Pitz et al., 1967) are typically cited as evidence in favor of motivated cognition (see e.g., Baron, 2008; Nickerson, 1998), it seems in many ways hard to imagine testing beliefs in which participants could be *less* invested in in any genuine sense, than whether the experimenter-selected bag on this trial contains predominantly red or blue chips. If anything, we thus take the parallels to motivated reasoning phenomena observed in these studies to be evidence *against* motivational accounts. Or to put it differently, if attachments to hypotheses (and with that directional questions) are so readily formed, it, once again, becomes hard to see how motivated cognition could exert any systematic effects on the accuracy of our beliefs. It should also be stressed that it is entirely possible to conduct quantitative studies of belief revision with more naturalistic materials (see e.g., Harris & Hahn, 2009; Harris, Hsu, & Madsen, 2012). Such research, we think, will be necessary, because although some cognitive and social psychologists have recognized and stressed the need to examine global accuracy when studying bias, the majority of this research has not.

The main thing to take away from our critical survey of research on bias is that with respect to the question of human rationality, an interesting notion of bias is established only once it has been shown that there is systematic deviation, that is deviation *on average* across a broad range of instances, and that deviation comes at an accuracy cost, in that there exist actual procedures that could do better. Common-sense intuition, time and again, provides an unreliable guide to when that might be.

Consequently, the rather surprising conclusion from a century of research purporting to show humans as poor at judgment and decision-making, prone to motivational distortions, and inherently irrational is that it is far from clear to what extent human cognition exhibits systematic bias that comes with a genuine accuracy cost.

ACKNOWLEDGMENT
The first author was supported by the Swedish Research Council's Hesselgren Professorship.

REFERENCES
Ajzen, I., & Fishbein, M. (1975). A Bayesian analysis of attribution processes. *Psychological Bulletin, 82*, 261–277.
Babad, E., & Katz, Y. (1991). Wishful thinking—Against all odds. *Journal of Applied Social Psychology, 21*, 1921–1938.
Bar-Hillel, M. (1980). The base-rate fallacy in probability judgments. *Acta Psychologica, 44*, 211–233.
Bar-Hillel, M., & Budescu, D. (1995). The elusive wishful thinking effect. *Thinking and Reasoning, 1*, 71–103.
Bar-Hillel, M., Budescu, D. V., & Amar, M. (2008). Predicting World Cup results: Do goals seem more likely when they pay off? *Psychonomic Bulletin & Review, 15*, 278–283.
Baron, J. (1995). Myside bias in thinking about abortion. *Thinking and Reasoning, 7*, 221–235.
Baron, J. (2008). *Thinking and deciding*. Cambridge: Cambridge University Press.
Benoit, J.-P., & Dubra, J. (2011). Apparent overconfidence. *Econometrica, 79*, 1591–1625.
Berger, J. O. (1985). *Statistical decision theory and Bayesian analysis*. New York: Springer.
Bolstad, W. M. (2004). *Introduction to Bayesian statistics*. Hoboken, NJ: Wiley.
Bovens, L., & Hartmann, S. (2004). *Bayesian epistemology*. Oxford: Oxford University Press.
Brandstätter, E., Gigerenzer, G., & Hertwig, R. (2006). The priority heuristic: Making choices without trade-offs. *Psychological Review, 113*, 409–432.
Chambers, J. R., Windschitl, P. D., & Suls, J. (2003). Egocentrism, event frequency, and comparative optimism: When what happens frequently is "more likely to happen to me" *Personality and Social Psychology Bulletin, 29*, 1343–1356.
Chapman, L. J., & Chapman, J. P. (1967). Genesis of popular but erroneous psychodiagnostic observations. *Journal of Abnormal Psychology, 72*, 193–204.
Chowdhury, R., Sharot, T., Wolfe, T., Düzel, E., & Dolan, R. J. (2013). Optimistic update bias increases in older age. *Psychological Medicine, 4*, 1-10. [Epub ahead of print].
Christensen-Szalinski, J. J., & Beach, L. R. (1984). The citation bias: Fad and fashion in the judgment and decision literature. *American Psychologist, 39*, 75–78.
Coady, C. A. J. (1992). *Testimony: A philosophical study*. Oxford: Oxford University Press.
Corner, A., & Hahn, U. (2013). Normative theories of argumentation: Are some norms better than others? *Synthese, 190*, 3579–3610.
Corner, A., Harris, A., & Hahn, U. (2010). Conservatism in belief revision and participant skepticism. In S. Ohlsson, & R. Catrambone (Eds.), *Proceedings of the 32nd annual conference of the cognitive science society* (pp. 1625–1630). Austin, TX: Cognitive Science Society.
Cosmides, L., & Tooby, J. (1996). Are humans good intuitive statisticians after all? Rethinking some conclusions from the literature on judgment under uncertainty. *Cognition, 58*, 1–73.
Covey, J. A., & Davies, A. D. M. (2004). Are people unrealistically optimistic? It depends how you ask them. *British Journal of Health Psychology, 9*, 39–49.

Cox, R. (1946). Probability frequency and reasonable expectation. *American Journal of Physics*, *14*, 1–13.
Cronbach, L. J. (1955). Processes affecting scores on "understanding of others" and "assumed similarity". *Psychological Bulletin*, *52*, 177–193.
Crupi, V., Tentori, K., & Lombardi, L. (2009). Pseudodiagnosticity revisited. *Psychological Review*, *116*, 971–985.
Dai, X., Wertenbroch, K., & Brendl, C. M. (2008). The value heuristic in judgments of relative frequency. *Psychological Science*, *19*, 18–20.
Dawes, R. M. (1976). Shallow psychology. In J. S. Carroll, & J. W. Payne (Eds.), *Cognition and social behavior*. Oxford, UK: Lawrence Erlbaum.
DeCarlo, L. T. (2012). On a signal detection approach to m-alternative forced choice with bias, with maximum likelihood and Bayesian approaches to estimation. *Journal of Mathematical Psychology*, *56*, 196–207.
De Finetti, B. (1974). *Theory of Probability*, (Vol. 1). NewYork: Wiley.
Ditto, P. H., Scepansky, J. A., Munro, G. D., Apanovitch, A. M., & Lockhart, L. K. (1998). Motivated sensitivity to preference-inconsistent information. *Journal of Personality and Social Psychology*, *75*, 53–69.
Doherty, M., Mynatt, C., Tweney, R., & Schiavo, M. (1979). Pseudodiagnosticity. *Acta Psychologica*, *43*, 111–121.
Domingos, P. (2000). A unified bias-variance decomposition and its applications. In *Proceedings of the seventeenth international conference on machine learning* (pp. 231–238). Stanford, CA: Morgan Kaufmann.
DuCharme, W. M. (1970). Response bias explanation of conservative human inference. *Journal of Experimental Psychology*, *85*, 66–74.
DuCharme, W., & Peterson, C. (1968). Intuitive inference about normally distributed populations. *Journal of Experimental Psychology*, *78*, 269–275.
Dunning, D., Heath, C., & Suls, J. M. (2004). Flawed self-assessment: Implications for health, education, and the workplace. *Psychological Science in the Public Interest*, *5*, 69–106.
Dymond, R. F. (1949). A scale for the measurement of empathic ability. *Journal of Consulting Psychology*, *13*, 127–133.
Dymond, R. F. (1950). Personality and empathy. *Journal of Consulting Psychology*, *14*, 343–350.
Eagly, A. H., Chen, S., Chaiken, S., & Shaw-Barnes, K. (1999). The impact of attitudes on memory: An affair to remember. *Psychological Bulletin*, *125*, 64–89.
Eagly, A. H., Kulesa, P., Brannon, L. A., Shaw, K., & Hutson-Comeaux, S. (2000). Why counterattitudinal messages are as memorable as proattitudinal messages: The importance of active defense against attack. *Personality and Social Psychology Bulletin*, *26*, 1392–1408.
Eagly, A. H., Kulesa, P., Chen, S., & Chaiken, S. (2001). Do attitudes affect memory? Tests of the congeniality hypothesis. *Current Directions in Psychological Science*, *10*, 5–9.
Edwards, W. (1965). Optimal strategies for seeking information: Models for statistics, choice reaction times, and human information processes. *Journal of Mathematical Psychology*, *2*, 312–329.
Edwards, W. (1968). Conservatism in human information processing. In B. Kleinmuntz (Ed.), *Formal representation of human judgment* (pp. 17–52). New York: Wiley.
Edwards, W., Lindman, H., & Savage, L. J. (1963). Bayesian statistical inference for psychological research. *Psychological Review*, *70*, 193–242.
Edwards, K., & Smith, E. E. (1996). A disconfirmation bias in the evaluation of arguments. *Journal of Personality and Social Psychology*, *71*, 5–24.
Eil, D., & Rao, J. M. (2011). The good news-bad news effect: Asymmetric processing of objective information about yourself. *American Economic Journal: Microeconomics*, *3*, 114–138.
Elqayam, S., & Evans, J. St. B. T. (2011). Subtracting 'ought' from 'is': Descriptivism versus normativism in the study of human thinking. *Behavioral and Brain Sciences*, *34*, 233–248.

Erev, I., Wallsten, T. S., & Budescu, D. V. (1994). Simultaneous over- and underconfidence: The role of error in judgement processes. *Psychological Review, 101*, 519–527.

Fiedler, K., & Kareev, Y. (2006). Does decision quality (always) increase with the size of information samples? Some vicissitudes in applying the law of large numbers. *Journal of Experimental Psychology, Learning, Memory, and Cognition, 32*, 883–903.

Fiedler, K., & Krueger, J. I. (2011). More than an artifact: Regression as a theoretical construct. In J. I. Krueger (Ed.), *Social judgment and decision making*. New York, Taylor and Francis: Psychology Press.

Fischhoff, B., & Beyth-Marom, R. (1983). Hypothesis evaluation from a Bayesian perspective. *Psychological Review, 90*, 239–260.

Frable, D. E. S. (1993). Being and feeling unique: Statistical deviance and psychological marginality. *Journal of Personality, 61*, 85–110.

Funder (2000). Gone with the wind: Individual differences in heuristics and biases undermine the implication of systematic irrationality. *Behavioral and Brain Sciences, 23*, 673–674.

Funder, D. C. (1987). Errors and mistakes: Evaluating the accuracy of social judgment. *Psychological Bulletin, 101*, 75–90.

Funder, D. C. (1995). On the accuracy of personality judgment: A realistic approach. *Psychological Review, 102*, 652–670.

Gage, N. L., & Cronbach, L. J. (1955). Conceptual and methodological problems in interpersonal perception. *Psychological Review, 62*, 411–422.

Gage, N. L., Leavitt, G. S., & Stone, G. C. (1956). The intermediary key in the analysis of interpersonal perception. *Psychological Bulletin, 53*, 258–266.

Galesic, M., Olsson, H., & Rieskamp, J. (2012). Social sampling explains apparent biases in judgments of social environments. *Psychological Science, 23*, 1515–1523.

Galesic, M., Olsson, H., & Rieskamp, J. (2013). False consensus about false consensus. In M. Knauff, M. Pauen, N. Sebanz, & I. Wachsmuth (Eds.), *Proceedings of the 35th annual conference of the cognitive science society* (pp. 472–476). Austin, TX: Cognitive Science Society.

Geman, S., Bienenstock, E., & Doursat, R. (1992). Neural networks and the bias/variance dilemma. *Neural Computation, 4*, 1–58.

Gigerenzer, G. (1991). How to make cognitive illusions disappear: Beyond "heuristics and biases" In W. Stroebe, & M. Hewstone (Eds.), *European review of social psychology: Vol. 2*, (pp. 83–115). Chichester, England: Wiley.

Gigerenzer, G. (1996). On narrow norms and vague heuristics: A reply to Kahneman and Tversky. *Psychological Review, 103*, 592–596.

Gigerenzer, G. (2006). Surrogates for theories. *Theory & Psychology, 8*, 195–204.

Gigerenzer, G. (2008). Why heuristics work. *Perspectives on Psychological Science, 3*(1), 20–29.

Gigerenzer, G., Swijtink, Z., Porter, T., Daston, L., Beatty, J., & Kruger, L. (1989). *The empire of chance: How probability changed science and everyday life*. Cambridge, UK: Cambridge University Press.

Gigerenzer, G., Todd, P. M., & The ABC Research Group (1999). *Simple heuristics that make us smart*. Oxford: Oxford University Press.

Gilovich, T. (1983). Biased evaluation and persistence in gambling. *Journal of Personality and Social Psychology, 44*, 1110.

Gilovich, T., Griffin, D., & Kahneman, D. (Eds.). (2002). *Heuristics and biases: The psychology of intuitive judgment*. Cambridge: Cambridge University Press.

Gordon, R., Franklin, N., & Beck, J. (2005). Wishful thinking and source monitoring. *Memory and Cognition, 33*, 418–429.

Green, P. W., Halbert, M. H., & Minas, J. S. (1964). An experiment in information buying. *Advertising Research, 4*, 17–23.

Green, P. E., Halbert, M. H., & Robinson, P. J. (1965). An experiment in probability estimation. *Journal of Marketing Research, 2*, 266–273.

Green, D. M., & Swets, J. A. (1966). *Signal detection theory and psychophysics.* New York: Wiley.

Gregg, A. P., & Sedikides, C. (2004). Is social psychological research really so negatively biased? *Behavioral and Brain Sciences, 27*, 340.

Griffin, D., Gonzalez, R., & Varey, C. (2001). The heuristics and biases approach to judgment under uncertainty. *Blackwell Handbook of Social Psychology: Intra-Individual Processes*: Vol. 1, (pp. 207–235).

Hahn, U. (2014). Experiential limitation in judgment and decision. *Topics in Cognitive Science.* http://dx.doi.org/10.1111/tops.12083. [Epub ahead of print].

Hahn, U., Harris, A. J. L., & Corner, A. J. (2009). Argument content and argument source: An exploration. *Informal Logic, 29*, 337–367.

Hahn, U., Oaksford, M., & Harris, A. J. (2012). Testimony and argument: A Bayesian perspective. In F. Zenker (Ed.), *Bayesian argumentation* (pp. 15–38). Netherlands: Springer.

Harris, A. J. L., Corner, A., & Hahn, U. (2009). Estimating the probability of negative events. *Cognition, 110*, 51–64.

Harris, A. J. L., & Hahn, U. (2009). Bayesian rationality in evaluating multiple testimonies: Incorporating the role of coherence. *Journal of Experimental Psychology. Learning, Memory, and Cognition, 35*, 1366–1373.

Harris, A. J. L., & Hahn, U. (2011). Unrealistic optimism about future life events: A cautionary note. *Psychological Review, 118*, 135–154.

Harris, A. J. L., Hsu, A. S., & Madsen, J. K. (2012). Because Hitler did it! Quantitative tests of Bayesian argumentation using ad hominem. *Thinking and Reasoning, 18*, 311–343.

Harris, A. J. L., & Osman, M. (2012). The illusion of control: A Bayesian perspective. *Synthese, 189*(1, Suppl. 1), 29–38.

Harris, A. J. L., Shah, P., Catmur, C., Bird, G., & Hahn, U. (2013). Autism, optimism and positive events: Evidence against a general optimistic bias. In M. Knauff, M. Pauen, N. Sebanz, & I. Wachsmuth (Eds.), *Proceedings of the 35th annual conference of the cognitive science society* (pp. 555–560). Austin, TX: Cognitive Science Society.

Hart, W., Albarracín, D., Eagly, A. H., Brechan, I., Lindberg, M. J., & Merrill, L. (2009). Feeling validated versus being correct: A meta-analysis of selective exposure to information. *Psychological Bulletin, 135*, 555–588.

Haselton, M. G., & Buss, D. M. (2000). Error management theory: A new perspective on biases in cross-sex mind reading. *Journal of Personality and Social Psychology, 78*, 81–91.

Haselton, M. G., & Funder, D. C. (2006). The evolution of accuracy and bias in social judgment. In M. Schaller, et al. (Eds.), *Evolution and social psychology* (pp. 15–37). New York: Psychology Press.

Hastie, R., & Rasinski, K. A. (1988). The concept of accuracy in social judgment. In D. Bar-Tal & A. W. Kruglanski (Eds.), *The social psychology of knowledge* (pp. 193–208). Cambridge, England: Cambridge University Press.

Hertwig, R., Barron, G., Weber, E. U., & Erev, I. (2004). Decisions from experience and the effect of rare events in risky choice. *Psychological Science, 15*, 534–539.

Hertwig, R., & Pleskac, T. J. (2008). The game of life: How small samples render choice simpler. In N. Chater, & M. Oaksford (Eds.), *The probabilistic mind: Prospects for Bayesian cognitive science* (pp. 209–235). Oxford, England: Oxford University Press.

Hertwig, R., & Pleskac, T. J. (2010). Decisions from experience: Why small samples? *Cognition, 115*, 225–237.

Hilbert, M. (2012). Toward a synthesis of cognitive biases: How noisy information processing can bias human decision making. *Psychological Bulletin, 138*, 211–237.

Hilton, D. (1995). The social context of reasoning: Conversational inference and rational judgment. *Psychological Bulletin*, *118*, 248–271.

Horvitz, E. J., Heckerman, D., & Langlotz, C. P. (1986). A framework for comparing alternative formalisms for plausible reasoning. In *Proceedings of the 5th national conference on AI (AAAI 1986)* (pp. 210–214).

Howson, C., & Urbach, P. (1996). *Scientific reasoning: The Bayesian approach* (2nd edition). Chicago, IL: Open Court.

Jarvstad, A., & Hahn, U. (2011). Source reliability and the conjunction fallacy. *Cognitive Science*, *35*(4), 682–711. http://dx.doi.org/10.1111/j.1551-6709.2011.01170.x.

Jarvstad, A., Hahn, U., Rushton, S., & Warren, P. (2013). Perceptuo-motor, cognitive and description-based decisions seem equally good. *Proceedings of the National Academy of Sciences of the United States of America*, *110*, 16271–16276.

Jarvstad, A., Hahn, U., Warren, P., & Rushton, S. (2014). Are perceptuo-motor decisions really more optimal than cognitive decisions? *Cognition*, *130*, 397–416.

Jones, E. E., & Harris, V. A. (1967). The attribution of attitudes. *Journal of Experimental Social Psychology*, *3*, 1–24.

Juslin, P., Nilsson, H., & Winman, A. (2009). Probability theory, not the very guide of life. *Psychological Review*, *116*, 856–874.

Kahneman, D. (2000). A psychological point of view: Violations of rational rules as a diagnostic of mental processes. *Behavioral and Brain Sciences*, *23*, 681–683.

Kahneman, D., Slovic, P., & Tversky, A. (Eds.). (1982). *Judgment under uncertainty: Heuristics and biases*: Cambridge: Cambridge University Press.

Kahneman, D., & Tversky, A. (1973). On the psychology of prediction. *Psychological Review*, *80*, 237–251.

Kahneman, D., & Tversky, A. (1979). Prospect theory: An analysis of decision under risk. *Econometrica*, *47*, 263–291.

Kahneman, D., & Tversky, A. (1982). On the study of statistical intuitions. *Cognition*, *11*, 123–141.

Kahneman, D., & Tversky, A. (1996). On the reality of cognitive illusions. *Psychological Review*, *103*, 582–591.

Kelley, H. H. (1950). The warm-cold variable in first impressions of persons. *Journal of Personality*, *18*, 431–439.

Kelley, H. H., & Michela, J. L. (1980). Attribution theory and research. *Annual Review of Psychology*, *31*, 457–501.

Kenny, D. A., & Albright, L. (1987). Accuracy in interpersonal perception: A social relations analysis. *Psychological Bulletin*, *102*, 390–402.

Klar, Y., Medding, A., & Sarel, D. (1996). Nonunique invulnerability: Singular versus distributional probabilities and unrealistic optimism in comparative risk judgments. *Organizational Behavior and Human Decision Processes*, *67*, 229–245.

Klayman, J., & Ha, Y. (1989). Confirmation, disconfirmation, and information in hypothesis testing. *Psychological Review*, *94*, 211–228.

Koehler, J. J. (1996). The base rate fallacy reconsidered: Descriptive, normative and methodological challenges. *Behavioral and Brain Sciences*, *19*, 1–53.

Korn, C., Sharot, T., Walter, H., Heekeren, H. R., & Dolan, R. J. (2014). Depression is related to an absence of optimistically biased belief updating about future life events. *Psychological Medicine*, *44*, 579–592.

Krizan, Z., & Windschitl, P. D. (2007). The influence of outcome desirability on optimism. *Psychological Bulletin*, *133*, 95–121.

Krueger, J. I., & Funder, D. C. (2004). Towards a balanced social psychology: Causes, consequences, and cures for the problem-seeking approach to social behavior and cognition. *Behavioral and Brain Sciences*, *27*, 313–327.

Kruger, J. (1999). Lake Wobegon be gone! The "below-average effect" and the egocentric nature of comparative ability judgments. *Journal of Personality and Social Psychology, 77,* 221–232.

Kruger, J., & Burrus, J. (2004). Egocentrism and focalism in unrealistic optimism (and pessimism). *Journal of Experimental Social Psychology, 40,* 332–340.

Kruger, J., & Savitsky, K. (2004). The "reign of error" in social psychology: On the real versus imagined consequences of problem-focused research. *Behavioral and Brain Sciences, 27,* 349–350.

Kruger, J., Windschitl, P. D., Burrus, J., Fessel, F., & Chambers, J. R. (2008). The rational side of egocentrism in social comparisons. *Journal of Experimental Social Psychology, 44,* 220–232.

Kruglanski, A. W. (1989). The psychology of being "right": The problem of accuracy in social perception and cognition. *Psychological Bulletin, 106,* 395–409.

Kruglanski, A. W., & Ajzen, I. (1983). Bias and error in human judgment. *European Journal of Social Psychology, 13,* 1–44.

Kruschke, J. K. (2010). What to believe: Bayesian methods for data analysis. *Trends in Cognitive Sciences, 14,* 293–300.

Kunda, Z. (1990). The case for motivated reasoning. *Psychological Bulletin, 108,* 480–498.

Landahl, H. D. (1939). A contribution to the mathematical biophysics of psychophysical discrimination II. *The Bulletin of Mathematical Biophysics, 1,* 159–176.

Leitgeb, H., & Pettigrew, R. (2010a). An objective justification of Bayesianism I: Measuring inaccuracy. *Philosophy of Science, 77,* 201–235.

Leitgeb, H., & Pettigrew, R. (2010b). An objective justification of Bayesianism II: The consequences of minimizing inaccuracy. *Philosophy of Science, 77,* 236–272.

Lench, H. C. (2009). Automatic optimism: The affective basis of judgments about the likelihood of future events. *Journal of Experimental Psychology. General, 138,* 187–200.

Lench, H. C., & Bench, S. W. (2012). Automatic optimism: Why people assume their futures will be bright. *Social and Personality Psychology Compass, 6,* 347–360.

Lench, H. C., & Ditto, P. H. (2008). Automatic optimism: Biased use of base rate information for positive and negative events. *Journal of Experimental Social Psychology, 44,* 631–639.

Lenski, G. E., & Leggett, J. C. (1960). Caste, class, and deference in the research interview. *American Journal of Sociology, 65,* 463–467.

Levine, J. M., & Murphy, G. (1943). The learning and forgetting of controversial material. *The Journal of Abnormal and Social Psychology, 38*(4), 507–517.

Levinstein, B. A. (2012). Leitgeb and Pettigrew on accuracy and updating. *Philosophy of Science, 79,* 413–424.

Lewis, D. (1986). A subjectivist's guide to objective chance. In *Philosophical papers: Vol. 2.* (pp. 83–132). London: Oxford University Press.

Lichtenstein, S., & Fischhoff, B. (1977). Do those who know more also know more about how much they know? *Organizational Behavior and Human Performance, 20,* 159–183.

Lindley, D. V. (1982). Scoring rules and the inevitability of probability. *International Statistical Review, 50,* 1–26.

Lindley, D. (1994). Foundations. In G. Wright, & P. Ayton (Eds.), *Subjective probability* (pp. 3–15). Chichester, UK: John Wiley & Sons.

Lord, C., Ross, L., & Lepper, M. R. (1979). Biased assimilation and attitude polarization: The effects of prior theories on subsequently considered evidence. *Journal of Personality and Social Psychology, 37,* 2098–2109.

Macdougall, R. (1906). On secondary bias in objective judgments. *Psychological Review, 13,* 97–120.

Mandel, D. R. (2008). Violations of coherence in subjective probability: A representational and assessment processes account. *Cognition, 106,* 130–156.

Manz, W. (1970). Experiments on probabilistic information processing. *Acta Psychologica*, *34*, 184–200.
McArthur, L. Z., & Baron, R. M. (1983). Toward an ecological theory of social perception. *Psychological Review*, *90*, 215–238.
Meacham, C. J. G. (2010). Two mistakes regarding the principal principle. *The British Journal for the Philosophy of Science*, *61*, 407–431.
Miller, D. T., & Ross, M. (1975). Self-serving biases in the attribution of causality: Fact or fiction? *Psychological Bulletin*, *82*, 213–225.
Mobius, M. M., Niederle, M., Niehaus, P., & Rosenblat, T. S. (2011). *Managing self-confidence: Theory and experimental evidence*. Working paper.
Moore, D. A. (2007). Not so above average after all: When people believe they are worse than average and its implications for theories of bias in social comparison. *Organizational Behavior and Human Decision Processes*, *102*, 42–58.
Moore, D. A., & Healy, P. J. (2008). The trouble with overconfidence. *Psychological Review*, *115*, 502–517.
Moore, D. A., & Small, D. A. (2007). Error and bias in comparative judgment: on being both better and worse than we think we are. *Journal of Personality and Social Psychology*, *92*(6), 972–989. http://dx.doi.org/10.1037/0022-3514.92.6.972.
Moore, D., & Small, D. (2008). When it is rational for the majority to believe that they are better than average. In J. I. Krueger (Ed.), *Rationality and social responsibility: Essays in honor of Robyn Mason Dawes* (pp. 141–174). New York, NY: Psychology Press.
Morlock, H. (1967). The effect of outcome desirability on information required for decisions. *Behavioral Science*, *12*, 296–300.
Moutsiana, C., Garrett, N., Clarke, R. C., Lotto, R. B., Blakemore, S. J., & Sharot, T. (2013). Human development of the ability to learn from bad news. *Proceedings of the National Academy of Sciences of the United States of America*, *110*(41), 16396–16401.
Mullen, B., Dovidio, J. F., Johnson, C., & Copper, C. (1992). In-group-out-group differences in social projection. *Journal of Experimental Social Psychology*, *28*, 422–440.
Newell, A., Shaw, J. C., & Simon, H. A. (1958). Elements of a theory of human problem solving. *Psychological Review*, *65*, 151–166.
Nickerson, R. S. (1998). Confirmation bias: A ubiquitous phenomenon in many guises. *Review of General Psychology*, *2*, 175–220.
Nilsson, H., Winman, A., Juslin, P., & Hansson, G. (2009). Linda is not a bearded lady: Configural weighting and adding as the cause of extension errors. *Journal of Experimental Psychology. General*, *138*, 517–534.
Nisbett, R., & Ross, L. (1980). *Human inference: Strategies and short-comings of social judgment*. Englewood Cliffs, NJ: Prentice-Hall.
Oaksford, M., & Chater, N. (1994). A rational analysis of the selection task as optimal data selection. *Psychological Review*, *101*, 608–631.
Oaksford, M., & Chater, N. (2007). *Bayesian rationality: The probabilistic approach to human reasoning*. Oxford: Oxford University Press.
Olsson, E. J. (2013). A Bayesian simulation model of group deliberation and polarization. In *Bayesian argumentation* (pp. 113–133). Netherlands: Springer.
Olsson, E. J., & Vallinder, A. (2013). Norms of assertion and communication in social networks. *Synthese*, *190*, 2557–2571.
Pastore, R. E., Crawley, E. J., Berens, M. S., & Skelly, M. A. (2003). "Nonparametric" A' and other modern misconceptions about signal detection theory. *Psychonomic Bulletin and Review*, *10*, 556–569.
Peterson, C. R., & Beach, L. R. (1967). Man as an intuitive statistician. *Psychological Bulletin*, *68*, 29–46.
Peterson, W. W., Birdsall, T. G., & Fox, W. C. (1954). The theory of signal detectability. *IRE Professional Group on Information Theory*, *PGIT-4*, 171–212.

Peterson, C. R., & DuCharme, W. M. (1967). A primacy effect in subjective probability revision. *Journal of Experimental Psychology, 73,* 61–65.

Peterson, C. R., DuCharme, W. M., & Edwards, W. (1968). Sampling distributions and probability revisions. *Journal of Experimental Psychology, 76*(2 pt. 1), 236–243.

Peterson, C., & Miller, A. (1965). Sensitivity of subjective probability revision. *Journal of Experimental Psychology, 70,* 117–121.

Peterson, C., Schnieder, R., & Miller, A. (1965). Sample size and the revision of subjective probabilities. *Journal of Experimental Psychology, 69,* 522–527.

Peterson, C., & Uleha, Z. (1964). Uncertainty, inference difficulty and probability learning. *Journal of Experimental Psychology, 67,* 523–530.

Peterson, C., Uleha, Z., Miller, A., & Bourne, L. (1965). Internal consistency of subjective probabilities. *Journal of Experimental Psychology, 70,* 526–533.

Phillips, L., & Edwards, W. (1966). Conservatism in a simple probability inference task. *Journal of Experimental Psychology, 72,* 346–354.

Pierce, A. H. (1901). *Studies in auditory and visual space perception.* New York: Longmans.

Pitz, G. F. (1969a). The influence of prior probabilities on information seeking and decision-making. *Organizational Behavior and Human Performance, 4,* 213–226.

Pitz, G. F. (1969b). An inertia effect (resistance to change) in the revision of opinion. *Canadian Journal of Psychology/Revue Canadienne de Psychologie, 23,* 24–33.

Pitz, G. F., Downing, L., & Reinhold, H. (1967). Sequential effects in the revision of subjective probabilities. *Canadian Journal of Psychology/Revue Canadienne de Psychologie, 21,* 381–393.

Popper, K. R. (1959). *The logic of scientific discovery.* London: Hutchinson.

Price, P. C., Pentecost, H. C., & Voth, R. D. (2002). Perceived event frequency and the optimistic bias: Evidence for a two-process model of personal risk judgments. *Journal of Experimental Social Psychology, 38,* 242–252.

Radzevick, J. R., & Moore, D. A. (2008). Mypoic biases in competitions. *Organizational Behavior and Human Decision Processes, 107,* 206–218.

Ripley, B. D. (1996). *Pattern recognition and neural networks.* Cambridge: Cambridge University Press.

Rosenkrantz, R. D. (1992). The justification of induction. *Philosophy of Science, 59,* 527–539.

Ross, L., Greene, D., & House, P. (1977). The "false consensus effect": An egocentric bias in social perception and attribution processes. *Journal of Experimental Social Psychology, 13,* 279–301.

Ross, L., & Lepper, M. R. (1980). The perseverance of beliefs: Empirical and normative considerations. In R. A. Shweder (Ed.), *New directions for methodology of behavioral science fallible judgment in behavioral research* (pp. 17–36). San Francisco: Jossey-Bass.

Roy, M. M., Liersch, M. J., & Broomell, S. (2013). People believe that they are prototypically good or bad. *Organizational Behavior and Human Decision Processes, 122,* 200–213.

Schum, D. A. (1981). Sorting out the effects of witness sensitivity and response-criterion placement upon the inferential value of testimonial evidence. *Organizational Behavior and Human Performance, 27,* 153–196.

Schum, D. A. (1994). *The evidential foundations of probabilistic reasoning.* Evanston, IL: Northwestern University Press.

Schwarz, N. (1996). *Cognition and communication: Judgmental biases, research methods, and the logic of conversation.* New York, London: Psychology Press.

Shah, P., Harris, A. J. L., Bird, G., Catmur, C., & Hahn, U. (2013). *A pessimistic view of optimistic belief updating.* Manuscript under revision.

Sharot, T. (2012). *The optimism bias: Why we're wired to look on the bright side.* London, UK: Constable & Robinson Limited.

Sharot, T., Guitart-Masip, M., Korn, C. W., Chowdhury, R., & Dolan, R. J. (2012). How dopamine enhances an optimism bias in humans. *Current Biology, 22*, 1477–1481.

Sharot, T., Kanai, R., Marston, D., Korn, C. W., Rees, G., & Dolan, R. J. (2012). Selectively altering belief formation in the human brain. *Proceedings of the National Academy of Sciences of the United States of America, 109*, 17058–17062.

Sharot, T., Korn, C. W., & Dolan, R. J. (2011). How unrealistic optimism is maintained in the face of reality. *Nature Neuroscience, 14*, 1475–1479.

Shepperd, J. A., Klein, W. M. P., Waters, E. A., & Weinstein, N. D. (2013). Taking stock of unrealistic optimism. *Perspectives on Psychological Science, 8*, 395–411.

Simmons, J. P., & Massey, C. (2012). Is optimism real? *Journal of Experimental Psychology. General, 141*, 630–634.

Simon, H. A. (1978). Rationality as process and as product of thought. *The American Economic Review, 68*, 1–16.

Slovic, P. (1966). Value as a determiner of subjective probability. *IEEE Transactions on Human Factors in Electronics, HFE-7*, 22–28.

Slovic, P., & Lichtenstein, S. (1971). Comparison of Bayesian and regression approaches to the study of information processing in judgment. *Organizational Behavior and Human Performance, 6*, 649–744.

Snow, P. (1998). On the correctness and reasonableness of Cox's Theorem for finite domains. *Computational Intelligence, 14*, 452–459.

Stanislaw, H., & Todorov, N. (1999). Calculation of signal detection theory measures. *Behavior Research Methods, Instruments, & Computers, 31*, 137–149.

Stanovich, K., & West, R. (2000). Individual differences in reasoning: Implications for the rationality debate? *Behavioral and Brain Sciences, 23*, 645–726.

Suls, J., Wan, C. K., & Sanders, G. S. (1988). False consensus and false uniqueness in estimating the prevalence of health-protective behaviors. *Journal of Applied Social Psychology, 18*, 66–79.

Svenson, O. (1981). Are we all less risky and more skillful than our fellow drivers? *Acta Psychologica, 47*, 143–148.

Swann, W. B., Jr. (1984). Quest for accuracy in person perception: A matter of pragmatics. *Psychological Review, 91*, 457–477.

Swets, J. A. (Ed.). (1964). *Signal detection and recognition by human observers: Contemporary readings.* New York: Wiley.

Swets, J. A., Dawes, R. M., & Monahan, J. (2000). Psychological science can improve diagnostic decisions. *Psychological Science in the Public Interest, 1*, 1–26.

Taylor, S. E., & Brown, J. D. (1988). Illusion and well-being: A social psychological perspective on mental health. *Psychological Bulletin, 103*, 193–201.

Tetlock, P. E., & Levi, A. (1982). Attribution bias: On the inconclusiveness of the cognition-motivation debate. *Journal of Experimental Social Psychology, 18*, 68–88.

Todd, P. M., & Gigerenzer, G. (2000). Précis of simple heuristics that make us smart. *Behavioral and Brain Sciences, 23*, 727–741.

Tversky, A., & Edwards, W. (1966). Information versus reward in binary choices. *Journal of Experimental Psychology, 71*, 680–683.

Tversky, A., & Kahneman, D. (1974). Judgment under uncertainty: Heuristics and biases. *Science, 185*, 1124–1131.

Tversky, A., & Kahneman, D. (1983). Extensional versus intuitive reasoning: The conjunction fallacy in probability judgment. *Psychological Review, 90*, 293–315.

Ulehla, Z. J. (1966). Optimality of perceptual decision criteria. *Journal of Experimental Psychology, 71*, 564–569.

Vaughan, Wayland F. (1936). In: *General psychology* (pp. 211–237). Garden City, NY, USA: Doubleday, Doran & Company. http://dx.doi.org/10.1037/11466-007.? xxi, 634 pp.

von Mises, R. (1957/1981). *Probability, statistics and truth* (2nd rev. English ed.). New York: Dover.
Wald, A. (1950). *Statistical decision functions*. New York: Wiley.
Waldum, E. R., & Sahakyan, L. (2012). Putting congeniality effects into context: Investigating the role of context in attitude memory using multiple paradigms. *Journal of memory and language, 66*(4), 717–730.
Walter, F. M., & Emery, J. (2006). Perceptions of family history across common diseases: A qualitative study in primary care. *Family Practice, 23*, 472–480.
Wason, P. C. (1960). On the failure to eliminate hypotheses in a conceptual task. *Quarterly Journal of Experimental Psychology, 12*, 129–140.
Wason, P. C. (1962). Reply to Wetherick. *Quarterly Journal of Experimental Psychology, 14*, 250.
Wason, P. (1968). Reasoning about a rule. *Quarterly Journal of Experimental Psychology, 20*, 273–281.
Weinstein, N. D. (1980). Unrealistic optimism about future life events. *Journal of Personality and Social Psychology, 39*, 806–820.
Weinstein, N. D. (1982). Unrealistic optimism about susceptibility to health problems. *Journal of Behavioral Medicine, 5*, 441–460.
Weinstein, N. D. (1984). Why it won't happen to me: Perceptions of risk factors and susceptibility. *Health Psychology, 3*, 431–457.
Weinstein, N. D. (1987). Unrealistic optimism about susceptibility to health problems: Conclusions from a community-wide sample. *Journal of Behavioral Medicine, 10*, 481–500.
Weinstein, N. D., & Klein, W. M. (1995). Resistance of personal risk perceptions to debiasing interventions. *Health Psychology, 14*, 132–140.
Weinstein, N. D., & Klein, W. M. (1996). Unrealistic optimism: Present and future. *Journal of Social and Clinical Psychology, 15*, 1–8.
Wendt, D. (1969). Value of information for decisions. *Journal of Mathematical Psychology, 6*, 430–443.
West, T. V., & Kenny, D. A. (2011). The truth and bias model of judgment. *Psychological Review, 118*, 357–378.
Wetherick, N. E. (1962). Eliminative and enumerative behaviour in a conceptual task. *Quarterly Journal of Experimental Psychology, 14*(4), 246–249.
Wheeler, G., & Beach, L. R. (1968). Subjective sampling distributions and conservatism. *Organizational Behavior and Human Performance, 3*, 36–46.
Winterfeldt, von D., & Edwards, W. (1982). Costs and payoffs in perceptual research. *Psychological Bulletin, 91*, 609–622.
Wolff, W. (1933). The experimental study of forms of expression. *Journal of Personality, 2*, 168–176.
Wolpert, D. H. (1997). On bias plus variance. *Neural Computation, 9*, 1211–1243.

CHAPTER THREE

Probability Matching, Fast and Slow

Derek J. Koehler[1], Greta James
Department of Psychology, University of Waterloo, Waterloo, Ontario, Canada
[1]Corresponding author: e-mail address: dkoehler@uwaterloo.ca

Contents

1. Introduction 103
2. Dumb Matching 107
3. Smart Maximizing 113
4. Smart Matching 118
5. Dumb Maximizing 124
6. Conclusion 129
Acknowledgments 129
References 129

Abstract

A prominent point of contention among researchers regarding the interpretation of probability-matching behavior is whether it represents a cognitively sophisticated, adaptive response to the inherent uncertainty of the tasks or settings in which it is observed, or whether instead it represents a fundamental shortcoming in the heuristics that support and guide human decision making. Put crudely, researchers disagree on whether probability matching is "smart" or "dumb." Here, we consider evidence for both "smart" and "dumb" variants of probability-matching behavior, as well as its alternative, maximizing. We rely on the influential and often-cited distinction between two "systems" of thinking to organize the research and competing interpretations of probability-matching behavior as "smart" or "dumb."

1. INTRODUCTION

Consider a simple computer game in which, on each trial, either a green or a red light appears. Your task is to predict which color will appear, and you will be paid a small amount of money for each correct prediction. What should you do, assuming your goal is to earn as much money as possible? Much of the challenge in this task arises from uncertainty regarding the process that determines whether the green or the red light appears on each trial (e.g., Green, Benson, Kersten, & Schrater, 2010). Does one light appear more frequently than the other? Is there a predictable pattern in the sequence of red and green outcomes? Does the probability of the green light illuminating change over the course of the game? Is it affected by your own actions, that is, the guesses that you have made on previous trials?

In the first experiments that investigated this type of task, one particular regularity in people's responses became the focus of researchers' attention: people tended to make their predictions in a manner that matched the relevant outcome probabilities (Goodnow, 1955; Grant, Hake, & Hornseth, 1951). For instance, if the green light was illuminated on 70% of trials and the red light on the remaining 30%, people tended to predict green on 70% of the trials and red on the remaining 30%. This phenomenon is referred to as *probability matching*, which can be defined more generally as the tendency to match choice proportions to outcome proportions in a binary prediction task.

In the experiments investigating probability matching that are of interest here, the outcomes being predicted (e.g., green vs. red light) are determined by a random process that is serially independent and stationary, which means that the probability of, say, the green light illuminating is the same on every trial, regardless of what occurred on the previous trial or how many trials have elapsed. Under such circumstances, it is easy to show that, if one's goal is to maximize the number of correct predictions, probability matching is inferior to an alternative strategy in which the higher probability outcome is predicted on every trial. This superior strategy is referred to as *maximizing*. For example, when the probability of a green outcome is 70%, maximizing (predicting green on every trial) yields an average predictive accuracy of 70%, while matching (predicting green on 70% of trials and red on the other 30%) yields an average predictive accuracy of $(0.70 \times 0.70) + (0.30 \times 0.30) = 58\%$.

Probability matching has attracted interest because it represents a violation of a cornerstone principle of rational choice theory, referred to as stochastic dominance. According to this principle, a gamble offering a probability P of some desired outcome should always be preferred to an otherwise equivalent gamble offering a lower probability P^* of obtaining that same outcome. Under conditions where payment is received for each correct prediction, a probability matcher violates the principle of stochastic dominance every time he or she predicts the lower probability outcome (e.g., red in the example above in which red occurs on only 30% of trials). In other words, he or she is choosing a gamble with a lower probability P^* of receiving a payment over one that offers a higher probability P of receiving the same payment. Probability matching, in short, appears anomalous from the perspective of rational choice models and for that reason demands explanation.

What causes probability matching? Who does it, and under what circumstances is it more or less likely to occur? In this chapter, we review some possible answers to these questions that have been offered in recent research on the topic. Our intent is not to systematically and exhaustively review every article that has been published on probability matching. Our review is highly selective and focuses almost exclusively on what might be referred as a "second wave" of research on probability matching that has taken place over the past decade or so. The voluminous original work on the topic in the 1950s and 1960s is not reviewed here; instead, the reader is directed to a helpful review by Vulkan (2000). It is worth noting, however, that several features of that early work, rooted almost exclusively in the then-predominant probability-learning paradigm, have proved unnecessary to observe probability-matching behavior. For instance, as is elaborated later in this chapter, probability matching is observed even in tasks in which the relevant outcome probabilities are known to participants from the outset, rather than having to be learned via trial-by-trial outcome feedback (e.g., Gal & Baron, 1996). In other words, even when many of the questions a person might have about the binary prediction task, such as those in our opening paragraph, are circumvented, probability matching is still regularly observed.

The most prominent point of contention among researchers regarding the interpretation of probability-matching behavior is whether it represents a cognitively sophisticated, adaptive response to the inherent uncertainty of the tasks or settings in which it is observed, or whether instead it represents a fundamental shortcoming in the heuristics that support and guide human decision making. Put bluntly, researchers disagree on whether probability matching is "smart" or "dumb." Our use of these terms is not intended to be entirely pejorative. Rather, they can be used to characterize, for instance, a person's own response—after having engaged in probability matching—to the argument that maximizing is a superior strategy. The person might explain, based on their understanding of the task, why it might have been reasonable to engage in matching (i.e., that it was a "smart" response to the task); alternatively, the person might do a forehead slap and acknowledge that they made a mistake (i.e., that matching was a "dumb" response to the task). Researchers themselves have disagreed as to whether or not probability matching should be viewed as a mistake. One of our main goals in this chapter is to organize the theoretical depictions of probability matching that have been offered around this admittedly crude distinction between "smart matching" and "dumb matching" accounts.

We rely on the influential and often-cited distinction between two "systems" of thinking (e.g., Kahneman & Frederick, 2002; Sloman, 1996; Stanovich & West, 2000; for a review, see Evans, 2008) to organize the research and competing interpretations of probability-matching behavior. One category of cognitive and affective processes shares the characteristics of being fast, effortless, unintentional, and unavailable to conscious awareness; the other category is relatively slow, effortful, intentional, and available to conscious awareness. We refer to the former as constituting the "intuitive" system and the latter as the "deliberative" system. We also adopt Kahneman's (2011; Kahneman & Frederick, 2002) characterization of the relation between the two systems as one in which the output of the intuitive system is imperfectly monitored and sometimes corrected or overridden by the deliberative system. In particular, Kahneman's account identifies well-known judgmental heuristics with the operations of the intuitive system and attributes many biases of judgment to a substitution process in which a person faced with a particular question receives from the intuitive system the answer to a different question but fails to recognize the discrepancy, and instead "endorses" that answer. This process of "attribute substitution" is discussed further below as it pertains to probability matching.

From a dual-system perspective, then, probability matching is "dumb" when it emerges from an intuitive response to the prediction task that goes uncorrected by the deliberative system. Maximizing, by this account, is "smart" when it results from the deliberative system correcting or overriding the intuition that makes matching compelling. Conversely, there may be circumstances under which maximizing represents the intuitive system's initial response to the task, giving rise to "dumb" maximizing. By contrast, probability matching under certain circumstances may emerge as the product of effortful deliberation (e.g., in which maximizing is considered but rejected as a possible strategy), which would be a case of "smart" matching. The remainder of the chapter organizes the recent findings of studies on probability matching in terms of evidence supporting smart and dumb variants of probability-matching and -maximizing behavior.

2. DUMB MATCHING

We will use a task, developed by Koehler and James (2010), as a running example of the characterization of probability matching as a "dumb" or intuitive response. As shown in Fig. 3.1, participants were presented with 10 pairs of cups, placed upside down on a table. Each pair consisted of one green and one red cup. Participants were told that, before they had entered the room, a dollar coin had been hidden under one member of each pair of cups. Which cup in the pair, green or red, the coin had been placed under had been determined by the roll of a 10-sided die with seven green faces and three red faces.[1] Participants were instructed to guess, for each pair, under which cup the coin was hidden by dropping a black ring over the cup. Participants were informed that once all 10 guesses had been made, the cups would be turned over and the participant could keep all the coins whose location had been correctly predicted.

Probability matching in this task would entail making seven green and three red predictions. Maximizing would entail making 10 green predictions. Of course, participants did not limit themselves to these two strategies, but matching and maximizing did represent the two modal responses to the task, as is shown in Fig. 3.2. In this particular study, fewer participants engaged in matching than in maximizing; in other studies, we have found the opposite. For present purposes, the important observation is that matching and maximizing emerged as two commonly used strategies in the cups task.

Figure 3.1 Schematic illustration of the cups task developed by Koehler and James (2010). In this example, the participant's predictions (indicated by black rings) follow a probability-matching strategy.

---

[1] For ease of discussion, we will refer to green as being the more probable color. In fact, this variable was counterbalanced such that, for half of the participants, red was the more likely outcome.

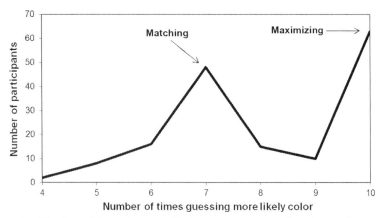

Figure 3.2 Number of times the more likely outcome was predicted, out of a possible 10, in Koehler and James (2010; collapsed across Study 1 and the no-hint condition of Study 2) made by each participant; probability matching should result in 7 such predictions and maximizing 10.

What evidence is there to suggest that, of the two strategies commonly used in this task, matching is the more intuitive, "dumb" response? As alluded to above, one benchmark involves asking the participants themselves which strategy is superior.

After they had played the cups game, but before the cups were turned over and they learned their payoff, participants were presented with two alternative strategies that could have been used in the game, one ascribed to a character named "Mike," who had guessed green for all 10 pairs of cups, and the other to "John," who had guessed green for 7 pairs and red for the remaining 3 pairs. Thus, Mike and John's strategies corresponded to maximizing and matching, respectively. When asked whose strategy most closely resembled their own, participants tended to answer in accord with the choices they had just made during the cups task. But, when asked whose strategy would be expected to earn more money, and whose strategy they would use if they were to play again, a substantial proportion (over 40%) of participants who had matched on the cups task nonetheless selected maximizing as the superior strategy. A substantially larger proportion of participants was able to identify maximizing as the superior strategy in a direct comparison to matching than had actually engaged in strict maximizing on the cups task itself. A similar finding was reported by Koehler and James (2009). In effect, many participants who engaged in probability matching in the binary prediction task later acknowledged that they would have been better off using a maximizing strategy instead.

We take this as evidence that many participants themselves would categorize probability matching as a "dumb" or inferior strategy. In fact, it is possible that the results above underestimate the proportion of participants who agreed with this categorization upon being presented with the direct comparison of the matching and maximizing strategies, as some participants who had engaged in matching on the cups task might have been reluctant to acknowledge their mistake to the experimenter. On the other hand, it is also possible that participants' responses to the strategy questions, such as the one asking which strategy they would use if they were to play again, do not accurately reflect what they would actually do if given such an opportunity. In a second study, Koehler and James (2010) provided a more direct test by presenting a strategy comparison question to some participants before they completed the binary prediction (cups) task. That is, these participants were presented with the two strategies that could be used on the cups task (7 green and 3 red, or 10 green and 0 red) and asked which would be expected to earn more money, prior to completing the cups task for themselves. Compared to a control group that did not first complete the strategy question, those who had compared the two strategies directly in terms of expected earnings were more likely to engage in strict maximizing and less likely to engage in strict matching on the subsequent cups task.

The results of Koehler and James (2010) suggest that one reason why people engage in probability matching rather than maximizing, at least on the cups task, is that matching is a more highly available strategy than maximizing: When confronted with the prediction task, matching tends to spring to mind more readily as a possible response than does maximizing. When the two strategies are equated for availability, as in the strategy comparison questions that describe both strategies, the relative appeal of matching diminishes. As researchers, many of us find probability matching intriguing because we are puzzled by why people choose to match rather than to maximize. From the participant's perspective, however, it seems that they are not really choosing between matching and maximizing strategies, as maximizing may simply not have come to mind as an alternative strategy to matching. Instead, perhaps, if matching is the only strategy that comes readily to mind as a response to the prediction task, specific alternatives to matching (such as maximizing) need to be effortfully "unpacked" from the generic "do something other than matching" category of strategies. For many people, apparently, matching springs to mind as a response and it seems "good enough" that the effort that would have to be expended to generate alternative strategies does not seem worthwhile. (The effortfulness of generating the maximizing strategy is discussed further in the next section.)

We take the results above to suggest that the matching strategy comes to mind more quickly and effortlessly than does the maximizing strategy as a possible response to the binary prediction task. In other words, probability matching may be characterized as an intuitive response. The idea that probability matching reflects an intuitive response, that may or may not be overridden by effortful deliberation, has been suggested by other researchers as well (Kogler & Kuhberger, 2007; West & Stanovich, 2003). But this characterization begs the question of *why* probability matching might be generated by the intuitive system as a response to prediction tasks such as the cups task described above. We recently conducted some studies to answer this question, in which we attempted to connect probability matching to an important function of the intuitive system: the generation of expectations.

To illustrate, imagine a 10-sided die with 7 green sides and 3 red sides. The die is going to be rolled 10 times. For most people, we suggest, simply providing this description is enough to trigger the expectation that the die roll will come up green seven times and red three times.[2] Much of our mental machinery is dedicated to the generation of expectations and predictions (e.g., Bar, 2007). For instance, most adults can readily translate outcome probabilities (e.g., that there is a 70% chance of a green outcome on each roll) into expected frequencies over a repeated sequence (e.g., that in 10 rolls of the die, 7 green and 3 red outcomes are expected). In fact, previous research has documented people's tendency to expect, even for very short sequences, outcome relative frequencies to correspond to the long-run probabilities governing the random generation process (Kahneman & Tversky, 1972; Tversky & Kahneman, 1971). We characterize this expectation generation process as an operation of the intuitive system. As with other such operations, its adaptive benefits are obvious. In the case of the 10-sided die, for example, if participants were asked to predict how many greens and how many reds would be rolled, then this expectation is exactly what is called for by the task. Precisely because of its usefulness in many predictive tasks, we suggest that expectation generation is the type of operation one might assume would migrate, with practice or experience, to the

---

[2] Here, we focus on the case of "described" prediction tasks in which participants are informed from the outset of the relevant outcome probabilities. It seems plausible that people would generate similar expectations in the case in which outcome probabilities are learned through observation, but it should be noted that the research we review in the remainder of this section involved described prediction tasks only.

intuitive system, such that expectations of this sort can be generated quickly, effortlessly, and without prompting from the deliberative system (e.g., Kahneman & Klein, 2009).

For the binary prediction task, however, expectation generation may not be entirely helpful. In the 10-sided die example, for instance, if one's task is simply to predict, prior to each of the 10 rolls, whether it will come up green or red, the best course of action is to maximize. Maximizing, in turn, requires only that the more likely outcome be predicted on every roll. As long as green is the more likely outcome, from the perspective of maximizing its precise probability does not matter, nor does the expected frequency of its occurrence over the sequence (i.e., 7 out of 10 rolls). But suppose the intuitive system nonetheless generates expected frequencies, quickly and effortlessly, such that they come to mind whether or not they are needed for the particular task at hand. Kahneman and Frederick (2002) describe a process of *attribute substitution* in which a heuristic attribute is rapidly evaluated via operations of the intuitive system and then—due to lax monitoring of the deliberative system—is substituted for the evaluation of the target attribute that is the intended focus of judgment. We use the notion of attribute substitution to explain the intuitive appeal of probability matching: expected frequencies generated by the intuitive system (e.g., expect seven greens and three reds) are in turn used to guide selection of a congruent prediction strategy (e.g., predict seven greens and three reds).

An important feature of this account, which we have referred to as *expectation matching*, is its focus on expected outcome frequencies over a sequence of events. In the 10-sided die example, the expectation that is evoked regards the sequence of 10 rolls as a whole: Over that sequence, we expect to see seven green rolls and three red rolls. A testable prediction of the expectation matching account, then, is that manipulations that disrupt or block the generation of sequence-wide expectations should reduce the rate of probability-matching behavior.

We conducted three experiments to test this prediction (James & Koehler, 2011). Each involved a sequence of 10 outcomes in a binary prediction task, in which the probability of one outcome was always 70% and the other was always 30%, as in the 10-sided die example we have been using here. We reasoned that when a single event (or "game") was played 10 times, as in the example of repeatedly rolling the 10-sided die, people would readily generate a sequence-wide expectation (e.g., 7 greens and 3 reds), which in turn was expected to foster probability matching in the prediction task. By contrast, if the 10 events or games were more individuated or distinct from one another, we reasoned, people would be less prone to generate (or apply) a sequence-wide expectation over the diverse collection of events or games, even if the outcome probabilities were the same, and therefore would be less likely to engage in probability matching.

In our first experiment, a unique games condition was created by asking participants to make binary predictions of the outcomes of 10 different games, which involved such activities as drawing ping-pong balls from a bingo cage, spinning a wheel of fortune and rolling a 10-sided die. In each game, as participants were informed in advance of making their predictions, one of the outcomes had a 70% probability of occurring and the other had a 30% probability. In the repeated games condition, 1 of the 10 games from the unique games condition was randomly selected for each participant and presented to him or her 10 times. Participants faced mathematically equivalent prediction tasks in the two conditions, which differed only in the superficial features that individuated the games in the unique-games but not in the repeated-games condition. Nonetheless, the rates of matching and maximizing in the two tasks differed significantly, as predicted: Participants in the unique games condition were less likely than those in the repeated games condition to engage in strict matching (3% vs. 38% of participants), and more likely to engage in strict maximizing (70% vs. 44% of participants).

A similar result was obtained in a second experiment (James & Koehler, 2011, Experiment 2), in which a 10-roll die game either involved the same die (with red and green sides) rolled 10 times or 10 different dice with unique markings (triangles vs. squares, hearts vs. flowers, etc.) which were each rolled once. In both experiments, apparently, individuating the sequence of outcomes made it less likely that participants generated or applied a sequence-wide expectation in making their predictions, reducing the rate of probability matching as a consequence. A third experiment presented an identically described prediction sequence to all participants, but preceded it by a priming manipulation designed to focus attention either on the sequence as a whole or on the individual outcomes within the sequence. This was accomplished by asking participants, after the prediction task involving the 10-sided die had been described to them, either to indicate in how many of the 10 rolls they expected each outcome (global focus condition) or to indicate, on any individual roll of the die, which outcome was more likely (local focus condition). We assumed that the global focus condition encourages generation of a sequence-wide expectation and the local focus condition does not. As hypothesized on this assumption, participants in the global focus condition were more likely to match and less likely to maximize on the prediction task than were those in the local focus condition.

In summary, the characterization of probability matching as "dumb" depicts it as arising from a fast intuitive process that is not reliably overridden by subsequent deliberation. Two lines of evidence support this characterization. First, matching occurs less frequently when the alternative maximizing strategy is brought explicitly to participants' attention, consistent with the claim that matching comes to mind quickly and spontaneously while maximizing does not. Second, consistent with the idea that matching results from an intuitive process that generates sequence-wide expectations, manipulations that individuate the sequence or otherwise encourage a focus on single outcomes decrease the rate of matching and increase the rate of maximizing.

3. SMART MAXIMIZING

On an account that characterizes probability matching as "dumb" in the sense of being a mistake rooted in the operations of the intuitive system, maximizing must be characterized as "smart" in the sense of representing avoidance or correction of that mistake through operations of the deliberative system. What evidence is there that maximizing is "smart" in this sense?

One strand of evidence suggesting that maximizing requires effortful deliberation comes from a study by Shanks, Tunney, and McCarthy (2002). Their participants made binary predictions in a standard probability-learning task and were paid for each correct prediction. After every 50-trial block, participants received a summary of their proportion of correct predictions on the block, and also the proportion correct that could have been obtained using an "optimal strategy." The number of participants who engaged in strict maximizing, which was defined as predicting the higher probability outcome on at least 50 consecutive trials, was examined as a function of the number of prediction blocks completed. In their Experiment 1, which consisted of 300 trials, only 6 of 16 participants were categorized as having engaged in strict maximizing. In their Experiment 2, in which the number of trials was increased to 1800 trials, 8 out of 12 participants eventually engaged in strict maximizing. What is striking to us about this result is how difficult it is, apparently, for participants to generate and consistently use the maximizing strategy despite repeated suggestions that a better strategy than matching is available and provision of hundreds of trials to identify it.

A natural starting point for discussing "smart maximizing" is the observation that not everybody engages in probability matching in binary prediction. As illustrated in Fig. 3.2, the typical finding is that some people match while others maximize. What individual difference variables distinguish these two groups? Broadly speaking, probability matching is more likely to be overridden in favor of maximizing when the individual is willing to engage in deliberation (i.e., has the appropriate motivation or thinking disposition) and has mastery of the basic normative principles (e.g., the calculation of expected value) needed to identify maximizing as the superior strategy. The distinction between these two components of deliberation has recently moved to the forefront of theoretical development of the idea of distinct thinking systems (e.g., Evans & Stanovich, 2013; Stanovich, 2009), but for our purpose, we largely gloss over this distinction and focus broadly on variables related to either facet of deliberative ability. On the smart maximizing account, we would expect variables that measure the propensity to rely on deliberation, or the effectiveness of deliberation, to positively correlate with the use of maximizing in prediction.

West and Stanovich (2003) found, in three studies, that maximizers tended to score higher than probability matchers on a measure of cognitive ability (self-reported total scores on the SAT Reasoning Test). This result, which was replicated in two subsequent studies by Stanovich and West (2008), is consistent with the idea that maximizing is fostered by processes of deliberation that are executed more reliably and efficiently by those of greater cognitive ability. Interestingly, in their studies, West and Stanovich did not find an association between the tendency to maximize (vs. match) and the number of math or statistics courses the participants reported having taken. This result could be taken to suggest that it is general deliberative ability, rather than specific mathematical knowledge, that promotes the use of maximization over matching. West and Stanovich did find, however, that matchers and maximizers differed in some important respects with regard to their perceptions or beliefs about the probabilities governing the outcomes in the prediction task. Specifically, matchers were significantly more likely than maximizers to endorse the gambler's fallacy that a long streak of one outcome made the alternative outcome more likely, while maximizers were more likely to endorse the notion of serial independence of outcomes (see also Gal & Baron, 1996).

Cognitive ability, then, which might be thought of as a measure of a person's ability to engage in effective deliberation, is associated with the tendency to maximize rather than to match, supporting the notion of "smart maximizing." Another, possibly related measure concerns *cognitive reflection*, or a person's tendency to scrutinize rather than unreservedly accept their initial, intuitive response to a problem or decision. In a highly influential paper, Frederick (2005) developed a brief cognitive reflection test (CRT) that can be taken as a measure of individual differences in proneness toward cognitive reflection (vs. reliance on intuition). The CRT consists of three mathematical problems, each of which has an "intuitive" but incorrect answer that many people report comes readily to mind. Correct responding, therefore, requires the person to override or correct that initial intuitive response. Toplak, West, and Stanovich (2011) report that CRT scores are independently, and more strongly, predictive of scores on a battery of "heuristics and biases" tasks (which included two probability-matching tasks) than is a measure of cognitive ability. On an account in which probability matching is the intuitive response, which must be overridden via deliberation to arrive at a maximizing strategy instead, higher CRT scores would be expected to be associated with a tendency to maximize rather than to match.

In the study involving the cups task described previously, we subsequently administered the CRT to all participants. Figure 3.3 relates performance on the prediction task to CRT scores in Study 1 of Koehler and

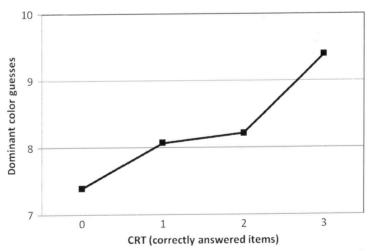

Figure 3.3 Mean number of predictions of the more probable outcome, out of a possible 10, on the cups task of Koehler and James (2010, Study 1), by CRT score.

James (2010). The mean number of times the dominant color (green in the example we have been using) was chosen is compared for those scoring 0, 1, 2, and 3 correct answers on the CRT. The figure reflects the substantial positive correlation between the two variables ($r=0.40$): Those scoring higher on the CRT were more likely to maximize, and less likely to match, than those scoring lower on the CRT. Indeed, the mean number of green guesses for those scoring 3 out of 3 correct on the CRT is approaching that expected under strict maximizing, while the mean number of green guesses among those scoring 0 out of 3 on the CRT approaches that expected under strict matching. The relation between CRT score and maximizing remained statistically significant even after controlling for mathematical ability, as measured either by self-reported proficiency or by the number of math courses taken.

In one study involving the cups task (Koehler & James, 2010, Study 2), we also subsequently administered another task designed to measure proneness to reliance on intuition in decision making, namely, a variant of Epstein's jelly beans task (see, e.g., Denes-Raj & Epstein, 1994). Epstein and colleagues have depicted the jelly beans task as putting the intuitive and deliberative systems into conflict. Pacini and Epstein (1999) found that performance on the jelly beans task related to scores on the rational thinking component of the Rational–Experiential Inventory, a measure of individual differences in thinking dispositions. In our version of the task, participants were asked to consider two urns, one containing 1 gold ball and 9 white balls and the other containing 9 gold balls and 91 white balls. Participants were instructed to imagine that they are to make a single draw, at random, from one of the urns and that if a gold ball is drawn, they would win a free vacation. Although the urn with only a single gold ball offers the higher probability of winning, many people experience and even express a preference for the urn that offers the larger absolute number of gold balls (a phenomenon commonly referred to as "ratio bias"). Participants were asked to give ratings on which urn (1) offered the higher probability of drawing a gold ball, (2) they felt would be easier to win with when they drew from it, (3) would be more exciting to draw from, (4) they would choose to draw from, and (5) they would pay more to draw from. A composite sum of these ratings correlated significantly with choices on the cups task, such that higher ratings in favor of the inferior urn (greater absolute number but smaller proportion of gold balls) were associated with a tendency to match rather than maximize on the cups task. Along with the results from the CRT, these findings support the idea that individual differences in the tendency to rely on (vs. override) an initial intuition are predictive of probability-matching behavior, as would be expected on a "smart maximizing" (or "dumb matching") account.

The "smart maximizing" account further predicts that experimental manipulations that foster deliberation ought to decrease the rate of probability matching in favor of maximizing. Surprisingly, few studies have tested this prediction directly. As is discussed further below, manipulations of cognitive load or working memory capacity could reasonably be expected to *reduce* the activity or involvement of the deliberative system. Therefore, on the smart maximizing account, they would be expected to increase the rate of matching. Unfortunately, interpretation of such studies is complicated—particularly when studied in the probability-learning paradigm—because such manipulations may also have effects on other mental operations such as those involved in detecting patterns or in monitoring and responding on the basis of observed outcome frequencies, and not just on the extent to which deliberation is used in selecting a prediction strategy. Here, we focus instead on manipulations intended to *increase* the general level of involvement of the deliberative system in overseeing and potentially correcting the output of the intuitive system.

The most direct evidence we know of comes from a study by Kogler and Kuhberger (2007), who studied probability matching in a task developed by Rubinstein (2002) that involves selecting 5 cards at random from a deck with known composition (36 green cards, 25 blue, 22 yellow, and 17 red), placing them in 5 envelopes, and asking participants to guess the color of the card contained in each envelope. Note that, even when selecting without replacement from the deck, the green card is the most likely outcome for each draw and therefore constitutes the maximizing response. Matching involves a representative selection of guesses that more closely reproduces the proportion of cards of each color in the deck. Previous work by the authors, and by Rubinstein (2002), showed that many people failed to maximize on this task and instead engaged in something more closely resembling a matching strategy. Kogler and Kuhberger (2007) compared responses from a control group, in which the task was likened to a lottery, to those assigned to a "corrective" condition in which the task was described as a statistical test designed to assess their level of statistical competence. Participants in the corrective condition were also advised to take their time in responding and to "carefully reconsider" their initial predictions before making a final response. The rate of maximizing was nearly three times higher among participants in the corrective condition (43%) than among those in the control condition (15%). Matching, by contrast, was more prevalent in the control (61%) than in the corrective (37%) condition. We take this result as supportive evidence for the claim that maximizing is a "smart" response that is fostered by enhanced deliberation, though of course other interpretations are also possible. In another strand of potentially supportive evidence, Fantino and Esfandiari (2002) found that telling participants that they would be asked, following the prediction task, to recommend a strategy to another participant—which arguably would motivate participants to think harder about the rationale for their predictions on the task—also increased the rate of maximizing. More recently, Taylor, Landy, and Ross (2012) found that providing a causal explanation for why one probabilistic outcome is more likely than another reduced the rate of probability matching in favor of a more optimal prediction strategy (though typically not strict maximizing), which could have resulted from the causal explanation triggering more extensive or rule-based deliberation.

In summary, the "smart maximizing" strategy depicts maximizing behavior as the product of a deliberative process that overrides the initial, intuitive tendency to engage in probability matching. Evidence supporting this characterization comes from correlational studies showing a positive association between maximizing and individual difference measures of cognitive ability and thinking disposition, and from experiments demonstrating increased maximizing as the result of manipulations designed to encourage greater deliberation.

4. SMART MATCHING

In the dual-systems account we have provided thus far, maximizing has been construed as resulting from deliberation and probability matching the result of a fast effortless heuristic, which we have labeled expectation matching. We have argued, therefore, that probability matching is essentially "dumb," but this view is not shared by all researchers who have studied the phenomenon. Indeed, probability-matching behavior has also been characterized as a sophisticated and adaptive response to an uncertainty about the true random nature of the binary prediction task (e.g., Gaissmaier & Schooler, 2008; Green et al., 2010). Evidence provided for this argument rests on two basic lines of research: (A) That probability matching tends to occur less in situations that tax cognitive resources and (B) that probability matching seems to be related to an effortful exploration of the environment (in this case, the sequence of outcomes observed in the binary prediction task). We will review both of these lines of evidence and evaluate how strongly they support the claim that probability matching is smart.

Return for a minute to our earlier argument that probability matching is intuitive. Typically, within a dual-systems framework, system 2 (deliberative) responses are considered to be more effortful or the result of more complex cognition and more easily disrupted by conditions that tax cognitive resources (e.g., Masicampo & Baumeister, 2008). By contrast, system 1 (intuitive) responses tend to be relatively effortless and less dependent on availability of cognitive resources. Given this, we could reasonably predict that probability matching should require less cognitive effort and resources. But research, reviewed below, has reached the opposite conclusion. This research suggests instead that probability matching is the result of effortful cognition and that maximizing occurs when cognitive resources are taxed.

For example, a number of studies have demonstrated that probability matching is associated with more effort or cognitive complexity than maximizing. Unturbe and Corominas (2007) and McMahon and Scheel (2010) both asked participants to report any strategies they used during the binary prediction task and found that the complexity of the patterns or rules reported by participants were inversely correlated with their tendency to choose the more probable option. In other words, probability matchers reported using more complex rules or strategies than did maximizers, a finding that appears to be at odds with the notion that probability matching is "dumb" and maximizing is "smart." Instead, it would seem to support the notion of "smart matching."

In addition, studies have also demonstrated that probability matching *decreases* under conditions of increasing cognitive load. (Recall that if probability matching is intuitive we would predict the opposite.) Wolford, Newman, Miller, and Wig (2004) demonstrated that giving participants a dual task that competed for left-hemisphere resources resulted in a decrease in probability matching. This result, however, was not replicated by Otto, Taylor, and Markman (2011) who failed to find any difference between rates of probability matching and maximizing under conditions of load versus no load. Nevertheless, even this result is potentially problematic for a dual-system account of probability matching (in which probability matching is "dumb"), because this account implies that probability matching ought to *increase* under load, which was not observed in Wolford et al. or in Otto et al.

As an alternative to manipulating working memory or cognitive load, researchers have recently attempted to reduce the engagement of the deliberative system through manipulations that decrease the supply of glucose available to the brain (e.g., Donohoe & Benton, 1999; Masicampo &

Baumeister, 2008). If probability matching is "dumb," we would predict that a lower supply of glucose, on which deliberation is claimed to be dependent, should lead to more matching, but in a study by McMahon and Scheel (2010), it was found that depleting glucose led to more maximizing and less probability matching. Again, this result could be taken to imply that probability matching is "smart" after all.

However, there are two ways to interpret the results of the studies presented above. One interpretation is that probability matching is *not* "dumb" (the product of effortless intuition), but "smart" (the product of effortful deliberation). While this is a viable interpretation, if adopted, we have to reconcile it with the evidence provided earlier that suggests that matching is "dumb." Another possibility is that probability matching is intuitively generated as a response strategy, but it is effortful to implement in the standard binary prediction task. That is, concluding that you should allocate outcome predictions in proportion to their probability may be intuitive, but actually implementing a matching strategy is relatively effortful (e.g., because it requires monitoring the relative frequency with which predictions are made over a series of trials). By contrast, once you have decided to maximize (even if arriving at that strategy was effortful), all you have to do to implement it is to predict the same outcome over and over again. Currently, we know of no research that directly tests these two possible interpretations of why the prevalence of probability matching decreases under load, so we cannot yet definitively answer whether or not the findings described above challenge the notion that probability matching is "dumb."

Some researchers do argue, however, for the "smart" interpretation of probability matching, suggesting specifically that it represents misapplication or overgeneralization of the usually adaptive tendency to seek patterns or predictability in outcomes observed over time. This account rests on the notion that people tend to have misconceptions and misperceptions of randomness (see Falk & Konold, 1997 for review). Proponents of the "smart" account of probability matching argue that participants do not believe that the sequence they are exposed to in the binary prediction task is truly random, and they attempt to outperform the optimal maximizing strategy by finding a predictable outcome pattern that can be exploited to achieve better predictive accuracy (Gaissmaier & Schooler, 2008; Peterson & Ulehla, 1965). By this account (henceforth called the pattern-search hypothesis), probability matching is seen as a by-product of pattern search, in the sense that, if there actually was a predictable outcome pattern, exploiting it would produce predictions that are made in proportion to the relevant outcome probabilities. Because pattern search seems to require effortful deliberation, any resulting probability matching could be viewed as "smart" in comparison to the relatively "dumb" maximizing strategy of simply predicting the more likely outcome on every trial.

In support of the pattern-search hypothesis, several researchers have demonstrated that increasing the perceived randomness of the sequence, either by emphasizing its randomness (Morse & Runquist, 1960) or by making it appear more random[3] by increasing the frequency of alternations between different outcomes (Wolford et al., 2004), leads to more maximizing behavior. They argue that this is because the increase in apparent randomness of the outcome sequence disrupts participants' initial assumption that the sequence is nonrandom, leading participants to abandon their pattern search.

Further support for the pattern-search account comes from probability matchers' superior ability to detect patterns when they do exist. Gaissmaier and Schooler (2008) divided a typical binary prediction task into two halves. In the first half, participants were presented with a truly random sequence. From these predictions, Gaissmaier and Schooler classified participants as either probability matchers or maximizers. In the second half of the experiment, participants continued the binary prediction task, but this time, there was a nonrandom pattern in the outcome sequence. Probability matchers were significantly more likely to detect and exploit this pattern (as measured by increased prediction accuracy) than were maximizers. Gaissmaier and Schooler's work provides evidence that a probability-matching strategy, hypothesized to be grounded in pattern search, can convey an advantage in situations where patterns exist and is in this sense smart. But their results do not provide evidence that pattern search necessarily causes probability matching.

In fact, we provide evidence in Koehler and James (2009) against such a causal relationship. We asked participants to complete a computer-based binary prediction task in which they were to guess the color of marbles drawn from a bag. The bag consisted of a mix of 30 green marbles and 10 red marbles.[4] Both groups participated in a learning phase in which they

---

[3] Ironically, this actually makes it less random, but the important aspect is how it appears to participants.
[4] For ease of discussion, we will always refer to green as being the more probable colour. In fact, this was counterbalanced so that for half of the participants, the contingencies were reversed and there were 30 red marbles and 10 green marbles.

were told that 40 marbles had been drawn randomly with replacement from the bag. Participants learned about the results of this set of draws in one of two ways: they were either told that result was 30 green marbles and 10 red marbles (the aggregate learning phase), or each marble was displayed serially as it was drawn (the serial learning phase). Note that those in the serial learning phase had the opportunity to search for patterns in the sequence of draw outcomes, but those in the aggregate learning phase did not.

After completing the learning phase, participants advanced to the testing phase in which they were asked to predict the colors of 20 more marbles that would be drawn from the bag (again with replacement). For each correct prediction participants could earn $0.50. Participants either made their guesses one at a time with no feedback on their accuracy (the serial testing phase), or they indicated in aggregate how many times they intended to guess green and how many times they intended to guess red (the aggregate testing phase). Again, those in the serial testing phase had the opportunity to include pattern information in their response if they chose to, while those in the aggregate condition did not.

If probability matching is the result of a pattern search, then we would expect those given the opportunity to observe (serial learning) and exploit (serial testing) pattern information to exhibit more probability matching. In fact, we found no difference between those with access to pattern information at learning or test and those without it in terms of their prediction strategies. All conditions showed an equal and high degree of probability-matching behavior.

The results of Koehler and James (2009) suggest that, while pattern search may indeed be associated with probability matching as Gaissmaier and Schooler demonstrated, it does not (at least explicitly) appear to cause participants to probability match. More generally, it is not clear why searching for patterns itself would lead participants to probability match, assuming that they have not been successful in finding a pattern. Why couldn't a participant implement a maximizing strategy (once the outcome with the higher probability has been identified) while also keeping an eye out for patterns that, if discovered, could be exploited for greater predictive accuracy? In fact, as maximizing seems relatively effortless to implement, it would seem like the ideal candidate strategy to use while devoting the bulk of one's cognitive resources to searching for patterns.

Given that pattern information is not necessary for probability matching, and that searching for patterns does not actually require the use of a probability-matching strategy, it seems premature to conclude that pattern search causes probability matching. Indeed, the alternative interpretation (that probability matching leads to pattern search) seems equally plausible. One could argue that, having decided to probability match (arising from expectation matching by the intuitive system), participants realize that they are only part way to perfectly predicting the outcome. The vital piece of information they are missing is how to order their predictions. To fill the gap, participants begin searching for patterns. This is, of course, an ad hoc explanation that requires testing. But it does illustrate that we should be cautious in concluding that pattern search causes probability matching.

Along similar lines, if we assume that probability matching causes pattern search (instead of the other way around), we can also offer an alternative explanation of the work investigating the role of perceived randomness in dual choice tasks. Recall that when outcomes were constructed so that they appeared more random (i.e., by introducing a higher rate of alternation), it led to more maximizing behavior. Currently, this is the strongest evidence for a pattern search account (even though it is not a direct test of it), largely because it establishes causation. Assuming that pattern search does not cause probability matching requires some alternative explanation of this data. For illustrative purposes, imagine that you are engaged in a search for patterns because you have decided to probability match. As it becomes obvious through search that you will not find any pattern information, you may revisit (deliberate on) your initial strategy choice, which may cause you to switch to maximizing. Thus, if the sequence appears to have no patterns, you abandon your pattern search sooner. This interpretation is not all that different from that of the original researchers investigating perceived randomness and matching, except that it assumes that abandoning pattern search leads participants to deliberate. Indeed, in the original research, it is not clear why or how participants are said to arrive at a maximizing strategy after they abandon their matching approach. Apparently, it is assumed that maximizing is what participants would have done if they had not chosen to match instead, but this assumption remains unelaborated in the original work.

In summary, is there any conclusive evidence to suggest that probability matching is smart? The short answer, we argue, is not yet. Manipulations designed to tax cognitive resources have not been shown to increase probability-matching behavior, which we would definitely expect on the "dumb matching" account. But more work needs to be done to determine whether the results from concurrent load and depletion manipulations come about because probability matching is actually "smart," or simply because it takes more effort to implement. Those arguing that probability matching represents an overgeneralization of a usually intelligent search for patterns in outcome sequences might have a good case, but they still need to establish a solid causal relationship. However "smart" the mechanism that produces it, probability matching that arises from a fruitless search for patterns in a truly random sequence is at least "dumb" in the sense of being suboptimal and costly in that particular setting.

5. DUMB MAXIMIZING

Arguments that probability matching is the result of a deliberative search for patterns have largely neglected to discuss where maximizing comes from. It remains unclear why a strategy that is the result of a calculated analysis, according to those who think maximizing is smart, is also the default that people revert to when they are too taxed to search for patterns. In this case, it seems that maximizing is taking on the role of the dumb strategy, but this begs the question, is there a "dumb" mechanism by which maximizing can be produced?

There is, in fact, substantial evidence, suggesting that maximizing can arise from system 1 mechanisms. Although little work has investigated the issue directly, many studies have demonstrated maximizing (rather than matching) in populations that are not prone to, or efficient at carrying out, extensive deliberation. For example, children have been found to maximize when they are very young and do so even when they cannot report explicitly which event is more likely (Derks & Paclisanu, 1967). Furthermore, maximizing has been reported in a number of nonhuman species (Parducci & Polt, 1958; Wilson, 1960), who presumably do not possess the deliberative ability required to identify maximizing as the superior strategy in terms of expected value. Aside from these findings, there is also the work presented earlier demonstrating that when under cognitive load (Wolford et al., 2004) or when deprived of glucose (McMahon & Scheel, 2010), maximizing behavior also increases. Under these situations, we would expect intuitive responding, so this lends further support to the notion that there may be a "dumb" variant of maximizing.

What is the mechanism behind this intuitive, dumb maximizing? As discussed earlier, it could arise from the relative simplicity of implementing the maximizing strategy, but it could also be the result of basic operant conditioning. In situations with outcome (or reward) feedback, predicting the more probable outcome will be rewarded more frequently than will predicting the less likely outcome. Given this asymmetry of reward, operant conditioning eventually should produce maximizing behavior. Indeed, it was the assumption of the early animal literature investigating binary prediction problems that maximizing should be the default (Parducci & Polt, 1958; Wilson, 1960).

Despite the clear opportunity of a role for operant conditioning in producing maximizing behavior, little attention has been paid to it in recent work on human probability matching. McMahon and Scheel allude to it in arguing that glucose depletion should lead to maximizing because "predicting the most frequent outcome produces the highest rate of reinforcement" (McMahon & Scheel, 2010, p. 450). The general assumption in the recent literature, however, is that maximizing should prevail because it is the (deliberatively) rational solution to the binary prediction task. From a dual-system perspective, operant conditioning represents an intuitive operation of system 1, as opposed to deliberative strategy generation and comparison processes arising from system 2. But operant conditioning is quite distinct from the intuitive process (expectation matching) we argued gave rise to probability matching. Although they are both intuitive, the processes differ in two key ways: (a) the effects of operant conditioning are bottom-up (data driven) and potentially unavailable to awareness, whereas expectation matching produces a top-down (theory driven) solution that is highly available to awareness; and (b) operant conditioning can foster maximizing only in situations where outcome or reward feedback is present, while this limitation does not pertain to expectation matching. Each of these points has important ramifications for the predictions of a "dumb maximizing" account and also for how we can understand dumb maximizing within the context of dual systems, so we will discuss each of these points in turn.

To our knowledge, little research currently exists on how or when operant conditioning might influence strategy in a binary prediction task. The only available evidence that we know of comes in the form of response times. Participants are generally slower to choose the less probable option than they are to choose the more probable option in the binary prediction task (Otto et al., 2011; Unturbe & Corominas, 2007).[5] One interpretation of this finding is that participants are slower when making a prediction of the

---

[5] One initial problem with this finding is that we would expect participants to be faster if they are choosing the same response twice in a row, which they would do more often with the more probable option. More careful analysis is needed to ensure that reaction time is slower for low probability outcome predictions independent of whether it is a repeated choice or not.

lower probability outcome because operant conditioning is pushing them to choose the more probable option, and the conflict takes time to resolve.

This interpretation suggests the two strategies (top-down matching and bottom-up maximizing) can jointly influence execution of participants' predictions (Newell, Koehler, James, Rakow, & van Ravenzwaaij, 2013), but this interaction has not been extensively studied. For instance, it is not clear to what extent operant conditioning impacts strategy choice, or whether its operations are available to conscious awareness. To illustrate, consider a participant who has chosen, via a top-down strategy selection process (e.g., guided by expectation matching), to probability match. How will operant conditioning impact this participant's choices? It is possible that the impact will be small or inconsequential in comparison to their explicitly adopted strategy to probability match and will therefore have little effect. Alternatively, if the effects of operant conditioning are available to awareness, it might cause the participant to deliberate and thereby increase the incidence of top-down maximizing. Finally, operant conditioning could have an unconscious and subtle influence on choices leading the participant to blend maximizing and matching without being explicitly aware of taking that approach.[6]

Unfortunately, the current literature does not provide much basis for differentiating between these alternative accounts. If operant conditioning is having some effect on choices, we would expect to see more maximizing over time, in tasks that involve many trials and outcome or reward feedback. There is substantial evidence that the rate of maximizing increases over trials (Bereby-Meyer & Erev, 1998; Edwards, 1961), but there has been little controlled work done to investigate whether operant conditioning is the cause of this trend. In addition, the data do not allow determination of whether the effects of operant conditioning might be conscious or unconscious. If, for example, this trending is the result of operant conditioning encouraging deliberation, we might expect some individuals to switch abruptly from another strategy (e.g., matching) to strict maximizing. But, if operant conditioning is providing an unconscious nudge, the change may be more gradual and incomplete; that is, it may never reach strict maximizing, but might instead exhibit what has been referred to as overmatching (Friedman & Massaro, 1998; see also Vulkan's, 2000 review). When looking at group

---

[6] This list of potential influences of operant conditioning is intended to be illustrative rather than exhaustive.

means, however, as is typically reported in the literature, it is difficult to distinguish these two possibilities.

It has not been established that overmatching is the result of operant conditioning (let alone whether or not the effect of that conditioning is conscious, unconscious or both), but there are a variety of ways to test whether effects of operant conditioning on binary prediction are (a) conscious and (b) contributing to overmatching. If operant conditioning fosters overmatching, for example, we should see overmatching occurring more frequently in situations with feedback and many trials. It should be a less common finding in studies with few trials, no feedback, and "described" contingencies (i.e., in which the relevant outcome probabilities are explicitly provided to participants rather than having to be estimated from trial-by-trial observation of outcomes). If operant conditioning is leading to probability matching unconsciously then, when queried, overmatchers should still report that probability matching is the optimal strategy. Such a finding would provide stronger evidence that a strategy approaching maximizing (such as overmatching) need not be coupled with explicit endorsement of a maximizing strategy. In fact, it could coexist with the actual intent to probability match! We hope to investigate this possibility in future research.

The second important feature of "dumb maximizing" worth discussion is that it can only operate in situations that include feedback (or, more specifically, administration of reward). This feature suggests some promising ways to test, in future research, whether operant conditioning is at work in dumb maximizing. For example, by varying whether or not participants receive feedback, we can also vary whether or not it is possible for operant conditioning to influence responses. Thus, manipulations that encourage reliance on system 1 operations (such as the cognitive load and glucose manipulations discussed earlier) should only lead to more maximizing behavior in situations with feedback, as under those circumstances greater reliance on processes of operant conditioning should foster maximizing. If feedback is not provided, we would expect these manipulations to increase probability matching (assuming that matching and maximizing are equated on implementation effort), as the only remaining intuition, when operant conditioning is not at work, is the expectation generation process that we have argued produces "dumb" matching.

It is also worth noting that feedback is only useful for producing operant conditioning that will influence binary prediction if it serves as a reward or punishment that is contingent on predictions. For this to be the case, reward administration must follow a prediction of some sort. To use the die problem, we have referenced throughout this chapter as an example, if you predicted green and the die comes up green, you receive a reward and that response is reinforced. If the die comes up red, you fail to receive a reward and that response is negatively reinforced. But if you made no guess, there is no possibility of reward or of reinforcement. Indeed, research shows that feedback improves performance on the binary prediction task, but only if it follows a prediction made by the participant. Observation-only trials do not improve performance (Newell & Rakow, 2007; Tversky & Edwards, 1966), consistent with the operant-conditioning account.

One final piece of evidence supporting the notion that operant conditioning encourages maximizing behavior even when probability matching is the explicitly selected strategy comes from work by Newell and Rakow (2007). In their version of the binary prediction task, outcome probabilities were fully described to participants before they made any guesses. Following this description, participants made a series of predictions with or without feedback. Newell and Rakow found that performance drifted toward maximizing over time to a significantly greater extent in the feedback condition than in the no-feedback condition. This result can be seen as something of a puzzle as the explicit system already had all the necessary information (i.e., the relevant outcome probabilities) to make an optimal choice before any predictions were made or any outcomes observed. From a rational choice perspective, the information provided by feedback was completely extraneous. One way of making sense of these data is to argue that the trend toward maximizing was brought on by operant conditioning, which is necessarily inactive in conditions without feedback, but in conditions with feedback, it is able to slowly push choices toward maximizing. While many interpretations of this finding are possible, it is consistent with the notion that feedback encourages optimal responding through operant conditioning.

In summary, it is highly plausible that maximizing may arise, over the course of trial-by-trial experience, as the consequence of bottom-up processes (e.g., through mechanisms of operant conditioning) that might be characterized as relatively "dumb" (e.g., in comparison with "smart" deliberative processes that lead to top-down identification of maximizing as the superior predictive strategy). Some supportive evidence for dumb maximizing comes from studies demonstrating (a) the importance of active prediction in increasing maximizing rates over trials and (b) an increase in maximizing rates over trials with feedback even in fully described prediction tasks, as well as from response time data.

6. CONCLUSION

An overarching theme of this chapter is that probability matching, and maximizing, behavior should not necessarily be taken as the product of a single process. Instead, there may be different processes, some relatively "smart" and others relatively "dumb," that give rise to either type of behavior depending on the circumstances in which it is observed. We are not the first to note that there might be different variants of probability matching (see, e.g., Gaissmaier & Schooler, 2008; Otto et al., 2011). This chapter highlights the possibility that there might be more than one variant of maximizing, as well.

We find the dual-system approach to be helpful in organizing discussion of variants of probability matching and maximizing in terms of the mental operations that produce them. The dual-system approach, as it has been applied to date to the phenomenon of probability matching, has largely drawn attention to the "dumb" (intuitive, fast, effortless) variant of matching and to the "smart" (effortful, slow, deliberative) variant of maximizing, both in our own work and in that of other researchers (Kogler & Kuhberger, 2007; West & Stanovich, 2003). Our goal in this chapter was to expand the dual-system approach to encompass the complementary possibilities of "smart" matching and "dumb" maximizing. Without a more complete picture, we are left with the riddle of why children and nonhuman animals sometimes conform more closely in their predictions and decisions than do otherwise more sophisticated adult humans to the prevailing model of rational choice.

ACKNOWLEDGMENTS

Preparation of this chapter was supported by a grant from the Natural Sciences and Engineering Research Council of Canada to the first author. We are grateful to Ben Newell for helpful comments.

REFERENCES

Bar, M. (2007). The proactive brain: Using analogies and associations to generate predictions. *Trends in Cognitive Sciences*, *11*(7), 280–289.

Bereby-Meyer, Y., & Erev, I. (1998). On learning to become a successful loser: A comparison of alternative abstractions of learning processes in the loss domain. *Journal of Mathematical Psychology*, *42*(2–3), 266–286.

Denes-Raj, V., & Epstein, S. (1994). Conflict between intuitive and rational processing: When people behave against their better judgment. *Journal of Personality and Social Psychology*, *66*(5), 819–829.

Derks, P. L., & Paclisanu, M. I. (1967). Simple strategies in binary prediction by children and adults. *Journal of Experimental Psychology, 73*(2), 278–285.

Donohoe, R. T., & Benton, D. (1999). Cognitive functioning is susceptible to the level of blood glucose. *Psychopharmacology, 145*(4), 378–385.

Edwards, W. (1961). Probability learning in 1000 trials. *Journal of Experimental Psychology, 62*(4), 385–394.

Evans, J. S. B. T. (2008). Dual-processing accounts of reasoning, judgment, and social cognition. *Annual Review of Psychology, 59*, 255–278.

Evans, J. S. B. T., & Stanovich, K. E. (2013). Dual-process theories of higher cognition: Advancing the debate. *Perspectives on Psychological Science, 8*(3), 223–241.

Falk, R., & Konold, C. (1997). Making sense of randomness: Implicit encoding as a basis for judgment. *Psychological Review, 104*(2), 301–318.

Fantino, E., & Esfandiari, A. (2002). Probability matching: Encouraging optimal responding in humans. *Canadian Journal of Experimental Psychology/Revue Canadienne De Psychologie Expérimentale, 56*(1), 58–63.

Frederick, S. (2005). Cognitive reflection and decision making. *Journal of Economic Perspectives, 19*, 24–42.

Friedman, D., & Massaro, D. W. (1998). Understanding variability in binary and continuous choice. *Psychonomic Bulletin & Review, 5*(3), 370–389.

Gaissmaier, W., & Schooler, L. J. (2008). The smart potential behind probability matching. *Cognition, 109*, 416–422.

Gal, I., & Baron, J. (1996). Understanding repeated simple choices. *Thinking & Reasoning, 2*(1), 81–98.

Goodnow, J. J. (1955). Response sequences in a pair of two-choice probability situations. *American Journal of Psychology, 68*, 624–630.

Grant, D. A., Hake, H. W., & Hornseth, J. P. (1951). Acquisition and extinction of a verbal conditioned response with differing percentages of reinforcement. *Journal of Experimental Psychology, 42*(1), 1–5.

Green, C. S., Benson, C., Kersten, D., & Schrater, P. (2010). Alterations in choice behavior by manipulations of world model. *Proceedings of the National Academy of Sciences of the United States of America, 107*(37), 16401–16406.

James, G., & Koehler, D. J. (2011). Banking on a bad bet: Probability matching in risky choice is linked to expectation generation. *Psychological Science, 22*(6), 707–711.

Kahneman, D. (2011). *Thinking, fast and slow.* New York, NY: Farrar, Straus and Giroux.

Kahneman, D., & Frederick, S. (2002). Representativeness revisited: Attribute substitution in intuitive judgment. In T. Gilovich, D. Griffin, & D. Kahneman (Eds.), *Heuristics and Biases: The Psychology of Intuitive Judgment* (pp. 49–81). NewYork, NY: Cambridge University Press.

Kahneman, D., & Klein, G. (2009). Conditions for intuitive expertise: A failure to disagree. *American Psychologist, 64*(6), 515–526.

Kahneman, D., & Tversky, A. (1972). Subjective probability: A judgment of representativeness. *Cognitive Psychology, 3*(3), 430–454.

Koehler, D. J., & James, G. (2009). Probability matching in choice under uncertainty: Intuition versus deliberation. *Cognition, 113*(1), 123–127.

Koehler, D. J., & James, G. (2010). Probability matching and strategy availability. *Memory & Cognition, 38*(6), 667–676.

Kogler, C., & Kuhberger, A. (2007). Dual process theories: A key for understanding diversification bias? *Journal of Risk and Uncertainty, 34*, 145–154.

Masicampo, E. J., & Baumeister, R. F. (2008). Toward a physiology of dual-process reasoning and judgment: Lemonade, willpower, and expensive rule-based analysis. *Psychological Science, 19*(3), 255–260.

McMahon, A. J., & Scheel, M. H. (2010). Glucose promotes controlled processing: Matching, maximizing, and root beer. *Judgment and Decision Making, 5*(6), 450–457.

Morse, E. B., & Runquist, W. N. (1960). Probability-matching with an unscheduled random sequence. *American Journal of Psychology, 73*, 603–607.
Newell, B. R., Koehler, D. J., James, G., Rakow, T., & van Ravenzwaaij, D. (2013). Probability matching in risky choice: The interplay of feedback and strategy availability. *Memory & Cognition, 41*, 329–338.
Newell, B. R., & Rakow, T. (2007). The role of experience in decisions from description. *Psychonomic Bulletin & Review, 14*(6), 1133–1139.
Otto, A. R., Taylor, E. G., & Markman, A. B. (2011). There are at least two kinds of probability matching: Evidence from a secondary task. *Cognition, 118*(2), 274–279.
Pacini, R., & Epstein, S. (1999). The relation of rational and experiential information processing styles to personality, basic beliefs, and the ratio-bias phenomenon. *Journal of Personality and Social Psychology, 76*(6), 972–987.
Parducci, A., & Polt, J. (1958). Correction vs. noncorrection with changing reinforcement schedules. *Journal of Comparative and Physiological Psychology, 51*(4), 492–495.
Peterson, C. R., & Ulehla, Z. J. (1965). Sequential patterns and maximizing. *Journal of Experimental Psychology, 69*(1), 1–4.
Rubinstein, A. (2002). Irrational diversification in multiple decision problems. *European Economic Review, 46*, 1369–1378.
Shanks, D. R., Tunney, R. J., & McCarthy, J. D. (2002). A re-examination of probability matching and rational choice. *Journal of Behavioral Decision Making, 15*(3), 233–250.
Sloman, S. A. (1996). The empirical case for two systems of reasoning. *Psychological Bulletin, 119*(1), 3–22.
Stanovich, K. E. (2009). Is it time for a tri-process theory? Distinguishing the reflective and algorithmic mind. In J. St. B. T. Evans & K. Frankish (Eds.), *In two minds: Dual processes and beyond* (pp. 55–88). Oxford, UK: Oxford University Press.
Stanovich, K. E., & West, R. F. (2000). Individual differences in reasoning: Implications for the rationality debate? *Behavioral and Brain Sciences, 23*(5), 645–665.
Stanovich, K. E., & West, R. F. (2008). On the relative independence of thinking biases and cognitive ability. *Journal of Personality and Social Psychology, 94*(4), 672–695.
Taylor, E. G., Landy, D. H., & Ross, B. H. (2012). The effect of explanation in simple binary decision tasks. *The Quarterly Journal of Experimental Psychology, 65*(7), 1361–1375.
Toplak, M. E., West, R. F., & Stanovich, K. E. (2011). The cognitive reflection test as a predictor of performance on heuristics-and-biases tasks. *Memory & Cognition, 39*(7), 1275–1289.
Tversky, A., & Edwards, W. (1966). Information versus reward in binary choices. *Journal of Experimental Psychology, 71*(5), 680–683.
Tversky, A., & Kahneman, D. (1971). Belief in the law of small numbers. *Psychological Bulletin, 76*(2), 105–110.
Unturbe, J., & Corominas, J. (2007). Probability matching involves rule-generating ability: A neuropsychological mechanism dealing with probabilities. *Neuropsychology, 21*(5), 621–630.
Vulkan, N. (2000). An economist's perspective on probability matching. *Journal of Economic Surveys, 14*(1), 101–118.
West, R. F., & Stanovich, K. E. (2003). Is probability matching smart? Associations between probabilistic choices and cognitive ability. *Memory & Cognition, 31*(2), 243–251.
Wilson, W. A., Jr. (1960). Supplementary report: Two-choice behavior of monkeys. *Journal of Experimental Psychology, 59*(3), 207–208.
Wolford, G., Newman, S. E., Miller, M. B., & Wig, G. S. (2004). Searching for patterns in random sequences. *Canadian Journal of Experimental Psychology/Revue Canadienne De Psychologie Expérimentale, 58*(4), 221–228.

CHAPTER FOUR

Cognition in the Attention Economy

Paul Atchley[*,1], **Sean Lane**[†]

[*]Department of Psychology, University of Kansas, Lawrence, Kansas, USA
[†]Department of Psychology, Louisiana State University, Baton Rouge, Louisiana, USA
[1]Corresponding author: e-mail address: patchley@ku.edu

Contents

1. Introduction	134
1.1 The Current Problem	135
1.2 Resources and Bottlenecks	137
1.3 Automatic and Controlled Processing	138
1.4 Information Processing and a Model of the Effect of the Attention Economy on Cognition	141
2. What are the Consequences of an Attention Debt?	145
2.1 Safety	145
2.2 Aesthetics and Creativity	149
2.3 The Experience and Regulation of Emotion	153
3. Why do We Overspend our Attention Budget?	156
3.1 Our Social Brain	156
3.2 The Value of Immediate Information	158
3.3 Self-Control and Willpower	161
4. Can We Expand the Attention Economy?	163
4.1 Mental and Behavioral Prosthetics	163
4.2 Cautionary Tales on the Costs and Benefits of Automation	167
5. Conclusion	169
5.1 Toward the Study of Optimal Cognition	170
References	171

Abstract

Cognitive science studies the basic processes of cognition, often mirroring the simple informational environments for which our brain is adapted. Though our brain is adapted for simple environments, we live in an era in which we have access to more information and are surrounded by multiple distractions vying for our attention. This "attention economy" has redefined critical questions in cognitive science. The work of cognitive science must be translated to the current environment. This chapter examines how cognition works or fails to work in an attention economy across a range of phenomena from safety and willpower to the appreciation of art and the ability to think creatively. The costs of a divided cognition and how cognitive science may help us understand what has gone wrong are offered, with a look to the future to examine how the technology underlying an attention economy may help improve cognitive function. The chapter concludes with a discussion of the increasing relevance of cognitive science and a call for cognitive science to study and understand the problems of our distraction-rich world.

1. INTRODUCTION

We fool ourselves. One of the most consistent stories from psychological research over the last half-century is that many of the most important psychological processes are ones that spare us from understanding our own inconsistencies and limitations. The field of social psychology, for instance, is full of descriptions of how our attitudes and actions are often wildly at odds and the ways in which our brains try to reconcile these differences. One example known to most introductory psychology students is cognitive dissonance (Brehm & Cohen, 1962; Festinger, 1962). Though most of us feel that when faced with a mismatch between attitudes and actions we would change our actions to match our attitudes, reconciliation actually comes from a subtle change in attitudes to match the behavior.

For example, though participants in one study (Atchley, Atwood, & Boulton, 2011) rated texting and driving as one of the most dangerous things they could do, almost all of them reported doing it themselves. The nature of the disconnect between attitude and action is partially explained by dissonance theory. In the same study, participants were asked to imagine reading a text message, replying to a text that they received, or initiating a text under a variety of conditions including driving in intense weather, on the highway, or on calm city streets. They were then asked to rate how risky driving was under those conditions. A diagram of their ratings of relative risks for different road conditions is shown in Table 4.1. When

Table 4.1 Distribution of Perceived Similar Road Conditions as a Function of Texting Behavior

Read	Reply	Initiate
Intense	Intense	Intense
Highway	Highway	Highway
Normal/calm	Normal/calm	Normal/calm

Highway conditions load with both intense and nonhighway conditions when participants consider replying to a text.

thinking about reading a text, the "safest" of the three behaviors, participants rated driving in intense weather and on the highway as similarly risky, and driving under "normal" conditions or on calm streets as equivalent. When they thought about replying to a text message while driving, an unsafe behavior that they did not "choose" to engage in but was compelled to by a message from someone else, highway driving was seen as risky as driving under intense and calm conditions. Finally, when they considered initiating a text while driving, a behavior they rated as very dangerous, participants rated driving on a highway as risky as driving on a calm city street.

The brain of each of these drivers was being asked to reconcile engaging in a behavior they think is moderately risky, one that they know is very risky but they did not "choose" to start, and one of great risk but that they made the choice to perform. The key finding here is that when they felt responsible for the choice to do something risky, they rated the driving conditions as safer than they actually are. Their brains were attempting to reconcile the disconnect between their attitudes and actions by changing their attitudes about risk. We fool ourselves by downplaying risk, even known risk, when we regularly engage in risky behavior (e.g., see the work of McMaster & Lee, 1991 with smokers) or downplay its potential consequences (for an example with distracted driving, see Atchley, Hadlock, & Lane, 2012). In this chapter, we examine other risks to cognition when we interact with technology.

1.1. The Current Problem

In this chapter, we will examine the ways in which cognitive processes might be degraded by the wealth of information our new digital world brings us and suggest a framing of problems and avenues for research on the important question of how our cognitive abilities are being challenged by technology. The goal is not to just focus on the obvious problems, such as driving while distracted by technologies that encourage social connection and communication, but to also examine the effects of these technologies on higher order cognitive processes such as willpower, creativity, and emotional processing. The goal is to be broad in scope and to promote thinking about new lines of research by framing problems using classic concepts in cognitive psychology.

We have chosen the title "Cognition in the attention economy" to frame a broad discussion with the simple idea that higher order cognitive processes go through a bottleneck of attention, that attention is a limited resource and that there are many tasks vying for that resource. As Herbert Simon (1971) noted following the birth of cognitive science and on the cusp of the computer era, "a wealth of information creates a poverty of attention" (p. 41), a sentiment echoed more recently by business strategists Davenport and Beck (2001) who coined the term "attention economy." In a time when the average age of cell phone adopters is trending downward and texting is used twice as often as face-to-face contact among teens (Lenhart, Ling, Campbell, & Purcell, 2010), there are powerful forces vying for our limited attentional resources. The term "attention economy" suggests our cognitive capacity is a valuable resource but one that is limited. Further, decisions must be made about how to "spend" it, and poor decisions come with consequences.

This chapter is divided into five sections. In Section 1, we develop the general conceptual framework that will be used to consider how various cognitive processes might be affected within an attention economy. This framework will rely on classic concepts in cognitive science including resource theory and bottlenecks, the information processing (IP) approach, and the idea of automatic versus controlled processes. In Section 2, we will examine the consequences of an "attention debt." What happens when we fail to effectively coordinate multiple tasks that require attention, from the well-known issues such as distracted driving to possible higher order consequences to creativity and social connectedness? Section 3 will examine why we run an "attention debt" by looking at the brain as a social organ desiring the connectivity and immediate information technology can grant us, and that simultaneously leaves us bereft of the self-regulatory resources necessary to exert behavioral control over those temptations. Section 4 will give time to the contrary case with a review of ways that the attention economy might be expanded. The conclusion will offer some thoughts on where cognitive science might look next to help us understand, and perhaps adapt to, the attention economy. By Section 5, we hope the reader will have a broad view of how deeply technology may impact our limited cognitive systems. We hope to encourage thinking about new issues of study of this important area, and the development of connections between core principles in cognitive science and the new problems that an attention economy creates. And, maybe, encourage a reexamination of the degree to which our attention is a precious resource that should be spent wisely.

1.2. Resources and Bottlenecks

The idea of an attention economy implies that attention is a limited resource. Describing attention in the metaphor of resources is an old practice (Humphreys & Revelle, 1984; Kahneman, 1973; Navon & Gopher, 1979; Norman & Bobrow, 1975; Wickens, 1984). In this description, there is one or many "pools" of resources that get "depleted" with time, increased effort or decreased motivation, or increasing task demands. This metaphor has been used to explain a range of effects including performance changes with time, skill and motivation, task difficulty and complexity, and dual-task performance.

Given the success of the metaphor, it is tempting to apply it to understanding how cognition will change in an attention economy. It makes intuitive sense that the range of distracting devices that can grab attention at any moment may place small, but constant and pervasive, demands on a pool of mental resources. But the metaphor is not without problems. Navon (1984) compellingly argued in his paper "Resources—A Theoretical Soup Stone?" that the concept of attention as a resource is circular enough to be effectively untestable. Navon's warning suggests the usefulness of resources as a metaphor is not in question, nor whether resources exist, but rather what is questionable is the precise nature of a resource and how it helps us understand how a constantly divided attention can change human experience. This is an important caution when considering how to best understand the effects of an attention economy on cognition.

The "theoretical soup stone" argument was sufficiently compelling that researchers avoided using the concept of resources for a number of years. A reemergence of resource descriptions has been partially supported by a range of techniques examining cerebral processing from a metabolic perspective. Blood oxygenation and flow levels measured by techniques such as functional imaging, near infrared spectroscopy, or Doppler sonography are able to show that cognitive processes demand metabolic resources and how those demands change with variables classically associated with resource theory such as task demands or time. For example, the proposal that talking on a phone while driving reduces the attentional resources needed for driving is indirectly supported by studies showing migration of metabolic resources away from visual areas when language is being processed (Just, Keller, & Cynkar, 2008; Shomstein & Yantis, 2006). Changes in sustained attention have similarly been examined to show how declining alertness changes the ways metabolic resources are allocated (Cohen et al., 1988; Kinomura, Larsson, Gulyás, & Roland, 1996; Lewin et al., 1996; Pardo, Fox, & Raichle, 1991).

Metabolic analyses also point out that different brain regions become involved when tasks must be coordinated. This suggests that task coordination "bottlenecks" are an important consideration as well. Describing attention as a "bottleneck" in processing is another well-worn metaphor of attention (consider Telford, 1931; Welford, 1952 for origins of this approach and Pashler, 1994 for an overview). The general idea is that execution of any task must engage some central mechanism that is only capable of executing one process at a time, or that there are limits to various aspects of cognitive processing, such as bottlenecks at response selection or execution stages. Bottlenecks may also be specific to certain brain regions or types of information. For example, areas of the brain such as the right parietal region have been implicated in a number of processes from the orienting of spatial attention to the processing of spatial language. In one example, work by Atchley and colleagues (Atchley, Dressel, Jones, Burson, & Marshall, 2011) showed that the negative effect of monitoring and verbally responding to speech on the orienting of spatial attention was larger when the verbal task involved direction rather than color decisions. Further, they showed that the effect was selective for the right hemisphere, suggesting a specific neurophysiological bottleneck for a specific type of informational code.

The bottleneck view is sometimes put in opposition to a resource theory that presumes we can do multiple things, but each with fewer resources dedicated to their functioning, producing worse performance (the two approaches are not necessarily exclusive; see Navon & Miller, 2002). An attention economy might reduce the efficacy of cognition simply by placing more processes in the queue. Given a limited amount of time, only so many tasks can get processed and thus some are left undone. Or, dividing attention across tasks might result in each task having fewer resources and consequently each task is done less well. But we would like to work toward a model that describes the effects of an attention economy on specific processes, rather than suggesting a generalized effect of distraction on attention. Indeed, to preview, there may be cases where having multiple tasks vying for attention may produce what appears to be improved performance on tasks such as driving or self-regulation. What is necessary is an understanding of how a variety of cognitive processes are impacted in an attention economy.

1.3. Automatic and Controlled Processing

Although we have argued that the concept of attentional capacity is useful (whether one hypothesizes one or multiple resource pools), researchers have theorized that the amount of resources used in the performance of a task can vary depending on the amount of previous task practice, and that learning can change the nature of the processes that underlie performance (e.g., Posner & Snyder, 1975; Schneider & Shiffrin, 1977). For example, try to remember the last time you learned a complex skill. For many adults, learning how to drive is a particularly memorable example. At the beginning, driving feels effortful: it is difficult to focus on anything other than keeping the car on the road, decision-making is slow, and people often feel clumsy while steering and braking. With sufficient practice, it feels as if the nature of driving has changed. Suddenly, driving seems easier: it is possible to do other tasks (e.g., eat, listen to the radio, yell at other drivers) at the same time, responses to situations on the road are faster and more fluent, and people report that these decisions appear to be made without "thinking." Researchers have described this transition as moving from a situation where people are primarily reliant upon *controlled* cognitive processes to one that where they rely more on *automatic* processes (e.g., Schneider & Shiffrin, 1977).

It has been argued that automatic and controlled processes can be distinguished by a number of characteristic features (e.g., Posner & Snyder, 1975; Schneider & Shiffrin, 1977). Automatic processes are thought to require little intentional effort to elicit (instead, they are cue-driven), consume few attentional resources, occur rapidly, and are not open to conscious introspection. In contrast, controlled processes are thought to be intentionally triggered, consume many attentional resources, are slower, and are open to introspection. In addition, research suggests that automaticity is only likely to come about when the learning environment is relatively stable (i.e., there is a consistent stimulus–response mapping, Schneider & Shiffrin, 1977).

Although influential, this modal view of automaticity has been disputed for a number of reasons (e.g., Hirst, Spelke, Reaves, Caharack, & Neisser, 1980; Logan, 1988; Pashler, 1998). Most prominently, it appears that no one characteristic is necessary and sufficient for distinguishing between processes. For example, attention can influence performance on tasks (e.g., Stroop) that are thought to be reliant on automatic processing (e.g., Kahneman & Henik, 1981). However, we believe the distinction still has utility for understanding the changes that accompany extensive practice if several key points are kept in mind. First, automatic and controlled processes are best viewed as lying on a continuum (e.g., Logan, 1988), with only rare instances found at either pole. Second, automatic and controlled processes interact such that performance on most tasks requires a mixture of both. Third, some improvements that result from practice may be due to improvements in learning to share capacity between two tasks (Pashler, 1998), or from the restructuring of tasks (e.g., Hirst et al., 1980), rather than a direct reduction in the amount of capacity used in performance.

As we have discussed, when an activity becomes automatic it is often triggered by contextual cues rather than intention, actions are performed faster and more fluently, and people are more likely to be able to perform other tasks concurrently. Despite these advantages, automaticity can also lead to errors when we are distracted or interrupted—a common issue in the attention economy. These types of errors have been termed "action slips" (Norman, 1981; Reason, 1990). One type of slip, called a *capture error*, is familiar to most people. Imagine that you get into your car after work and remember that you need to stop on the way home to pick up your spouse's prescription. You drive along your usual route home, listening to your favorite radio station, and then, at the end of your trip, turn off the radio only to realize you forgot to stop. Being the good person you are, you mutter under your breath and head back to the pharmacy. The common explanation of this type of error is that people fail to pay attention at the point where they need to deviate from their usual activity and the environment cues them to continue their habitual behavior (e.g., drive home). Distraction can also lead us to skip (omission error) or repeat (perseveration error) steps in a routine activity. If you have ever heard the unmistakable sound of someone turning the key in the ignition after the car has already started, that is an example of the latter. In such situations, it appears that people do not encode that they have completed the prior step. Altogether, these types of errors suggest that even routines that are relatively automatic can be disrupted by distraction. More broadly, it suggests that controlled processes frequently interact with automatic processes, such that attention may be needed at different points in a relatively automatic activity for it to be successfully carried out (e.g., Reason, 1990).

The distinction between automatic and controlled processes has played a role in theories that attempt to explain a broad range of behavior including learning (Lane, Mathews, Sallas, Prattini, & Sun, 2008; Reber, 1969), memory (e.g., Jacoby, 1991; Schacter, 1997), reasoning (e.g., Stanovich & West, 2000), decision-making (e.g., Bechara, Damasio, Tranel, & Damasio, 1997; Kahneman & Frederick, 2002), and social behavior (e.g., Chen & Chaiken, 1999; Petty & Wegener, 1999). Kahneman (2011) has recently described a general theory of thinking that involves two systems—System 1 and System 2. We briefly describe this view as a potentially useful way to examine the issues we discuss in later sections. In this view, System 1 thinking is automatic, fast, with low demands on attention and low levels of perceived effort and voluntary control. A person's ability to read the emotional state of their partner from a brief glance at their face would be an example of System 1 thinking. System 2 thinking is algorithmic (controlled), slower, with higher demands on attention and greater levels of effort and voluntary control. One key characteristic of System 2 thinking is that it is disrupted when attention is removed from the task. Providing directions to your home over the phone to someone who had never visited would be an example of System 2 thinking. The two systems interact and System 2 is often called upon to monitor and make decisions about courses of action suggested by System 1. This type of monitoring plays a big role in self-control, particularly when there is a conflict between the recommendations of System 1 (Eat chocolate cake!) and the goals of System 2 (Lose weight). However, this type of monitoring requires effort and, if sustained, System 2 can become "depleted" (e.g., Baumeister, Bratslavsky, Muraven, & Tice, 1998), leading to self-control failure. We discuss the implications of this in a later section.

1.4. Information Processing and a Model of the Effect of the Attention Economy on Cognition

IP models describe how information is represented and transformed in physical systems, such as the human brain (e.g., Massaro & Cowan, 1993; for early examples, see Atkinson & Shiffrin, 1968; Sternberg, 1969). In such models, the representation of information and associated processing is typically described in the form of stages (although several stages can operate simultaneously). Thus, key features of this approach include the assumption that information will be modified over time and that each stage of processing takes time to complete (Palmer & Kimchi, 1986). Furthermore, stages can be divided further into substages or component processes. Altogether, these assumptions allow IP models to explain how the disruption of particular elements of IP can positively or negatively impact subsequent actions.

To provide a framework for describing how cognition might be influenced in an attention economy, we use a general model of human information loosely adapted from a model proposed by Wickens (Wickens &

Hollands, 2000). Although there is no one "starting point" in the model (because there is a feedback loop), we will describe its stages in terms of a situation where someone gets information from the environment, say sound and visual input from a conversation with a friend. Note that each stage is characterized broadly and consists of multiple subprocesses. The first stage involves transforming this input via the sensory (S) organs and holding it briefly in a modality-specific sensory store. Subsequently, perceptual (P) processes are used to attempt to interpret the sensory data. This interpretation is carried out by building up from basic features of the input (bottom-up) and also influenced by expectations about the situation (top-down). These expectations are retrieved from long-term memory (LTM) to the extent that the context cues prior experience. In our conversation example, information from perceptual processing would likely be passed on to working memory (WM). WM is generally characterized as a limited-capacity system for manipulating and maintaining information over short time periods (less than 30 s). Because of these features, working memory efficiency can be easily disrupted by distractions or interruptions. Working memory also functions to encode information into LTM for more permanent storage.

The information that is output from perceptual processing and LTM, or from more extensive cognitive processing in working memory, can be thought of as evidence used to influence the *selection* of a possible behavioral response (R). In essence, this is a decision-making stage, and it can occur rapidly. Following the decision, the chosen action is carried out (executed). Attention influences nearly all aspects of IP through the selection of some inputs and not others and by allocating resources to processes to a greater or lesser degree (with overall limitations due to capacity or bottlenecks). Finally, the effects of a person's chosen response on the environment are typically observable, and this provides feedback about whether the response achieved the desired goal. The delay between action and feedback is a key factor in whether people learn and adapt from experience.

To consider how distraction might impact perceptual and cognitive processes in the context of such a model, imagine a woman named Beth who is driving down a residential street at 25 mph, her attention focused solely on the roadway, when a bouncing ball lands in the street about a 100 ft in front of her car. Figure 4.1 illustrates the processes involved using our IP model. First, sensory and perceptual processes such as motion detection and low-level object recognition would be triggered by the ball coming into view. Presumably, prior to the event, Beth would have activated a schema for

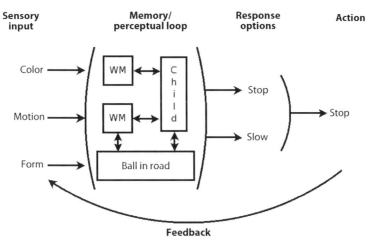

Figure 4.1 A generalized information processing model as applied to a driving task. In this model, sensory inputs (the color, motion, and form associated with a ball rolling into a street) are processed by a memory and perceptual loop that considers context (residential neighborhood) to extract possible associations (children playing). This association results in context-specific response outcomes ("slow down" or "stop quickly") and a chosen action.

"residential streets" while driving in the area, and this would exert a top-down influence on associations triggered in LTM. For example, the representation of "bouncing ball" in the context of a residential street would cue certain associations (e.g., children playing) more than others. In turn, these representations would cue responses associated with such situations in the past (e.g., step on the brakes), making these responses stronger and influencing the selection of an action. Finally, Beth would execute the action by applying the brake and stopping the car before reaching the ball and a pursuing child. In relatively rapid order, she anticipated a potential threat to another person and avoided it.

But what would happen if Beth had been driving distracted instead, say by texting on her phone? Figure 4.2 provides an answer by integrating the prior concepts in this section into one framework. In Fig. 4.2, we have imagined that there are multiple, competing processes operating in parallel. Some processes are effortful or controlled and others are relatively automatic. The general IP approach has been relabeled as a controlled process to reflect that aspects classically associated with the IP approach have characteristics such as intentional memory access, updating, and conscious control. A second, automatic, set of processes has been added to reflect Kahneman's System 1 approach. In this model, the automatic process goes from sensory input

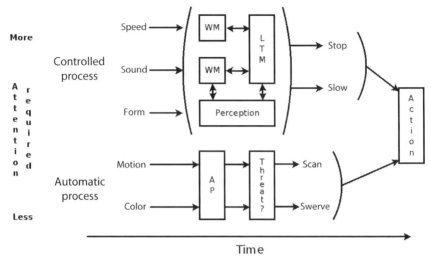

Figure 4.2 A model of task sharing in the attention economy. In this model, the slower, controlled process described in Fig. 4.1 is competing with a faster, automatic process. The former requires more attention, but adds additional sensory inputs (such as driver speed) and a memory/perceptual link to provide response options that are more contextually correct. The latter is active when attention is impoverished. The automatic pathway uses "associative processes" (AP) (Kahneman, 2011) that yield the most basic information to the driver (Is this object a threat?), possibly resulting in inappropriate responses ("Scan the road further" or "Swerve to avoid the ball").

to associative processes (AP) in LTM, which are fast and often based on emotion valence, and then to perception, response selection, and action. Figure 4.2 reflects that the former, controlled process is more complex, allowing for interactions with what we might consider "higher order" cognitive processes of memory, reasoning, and problem solving. However, this processing requires greater attentional resources and it is slower. As we incur an attention debt, we will tend to move toward more exclusively automatic processes.

Even though our extensive experience has made our ability to communicate appear to be an automatic process, it is perhaps one of the most cognitively complex things we do, requiring rapid processing for comprehension, response planning, and response execution. In the example of the driver we have been using, we must assume Beth is putting some effort into her conversation. By incurring this attention debt, she now has less attention for the driving task, leading her to rely more heavily on automatic processes. Automatic mode can lead to potential disruptions at different points in cognitive processing. In line with research on change blindness (see Simons & Rensink, 2005 for a review), it is possible that initial perceptual processing would be disrupted such that the woman would not detect the change in the environment (i.e., the ball coming into the field of view) or that such detection would be delayed. In other words, the framework suggests that she might start with fewer sensory inputs. However, even if these processes were triggered normally, automatic mode driving might prevent the woman from noticing that she was driving on a residential street (i.e., a schema would not be activated), thus disrupting the top-down influence that would typically occur. In this situation, bottom-up processing of the scene would still proceed but the activation of relevant associations would be slowed or disrupted. Put another way, in both these circumstances, distraction would slow the accumulation of evidence necessary for a decision (e.g., Logan & Gordon, 2001; Ploran et al., 2007).

The downstream consequences of disrupted sensory and perceptual processing, failed contextualization, and slowed information accumulation are that response selection and execution is delayed. Furthermore, the problem of a response execution bottleneck means that even effective processing of the relevant information through automatic processes may not lead to the timely initiation of an appropriate response if there is a competing response simultaneously being executed. In the context of our example, such a delay could be deadly. However, as we will discuss in later sections, the consequences of distraction on IP are still significant even when not immediately life-threatening.

2. WHAT ARE THE CONSEQUENCES OF AN ATTENTION DEBT?

2.1. Safety

The possible consequences of depleted attention are most extreme when we consider the costs in terms of human lives lost when drivers choose to drive while distracted. Distractions, defined as things that occupy our attention that are unrelated to the primary task of driving, were an issue well before the era of the attention economy. Drivers have always been faced with other tasks vying for their attention, such as children in the back seat or billboard advertisements trying to capture their interest. And cellular phones are not the first technology that has worried traffic safety professionals. A 1939 *Journal of Applied Psychology* paper titled "Radio Listening and Automobiles" (Suchman, 1939) noted that many drivers, automobile safety clubs, and legislatures worried that radios would result in "interference with proper operation of the vehicle" (p. 148), to the point that, in some states, radios were prohibited in vehicles or from being used in some circumstances such as driving on congested roads. Even at that very early point in the field of psychological science, researchers recognized the power of technology to deplete attention. Suchman noted that one reason the radio might pose a traffic hazard is because it "Diverts the attention of the driver while driving" (p. 154).

Later work by Broadbent (1958) and many others showed that passive and noninteractive information sources such as radios could be filtered out by the attention system. But new technologies are far from passive. The cellular-enabled devices currently carried on or built into vehicles allow for personalized, social contact that is very attractive to our brains and very difficult to filter (see Section 3 for a more detailed analysis). The result in terms of safety is alarming. Automobile crashes represent the most common causes of preventable, nonhealth related, death in the United States (Mokdad, Marks, Stroup, & Gerberding, 2004). The National Safety Council (2010) estimates that about one-quarter of crashes are due to the use of cellular devices while driving. (A problem of similar magnitude also occurs among pedestrians. See Nasar & Troyer, 2013 for a recent analysis.)

While the risks associated with the manual and visual distractions of activities like texting while driving are clear, what is more difficult to characterize are the cognitive effects associated with divided attention for activities as seemingly simple as talking on a hands-free phone while driving. In the framework we outlined in Section 1, there are a number of possibilities for why incurring an attention debt via a conversation on a cellular phone while driving might impair driving performance. At the most basic level of sensory input, we must recognize that resource limits on the processing of information may lead to prioritization of verbal over visual information which lead to inattention blindness and missed sensory input. For example, it has been repeatedly found that conversations while driving result in eye-movement patterns that are restricted to more central locations, limiting the availability of sensory input (e.g., Nunes & Recarte, 2002; Recarte & Nunes, 2003). But to reinforce the view that distractions limit cognitive resources to process available information, there are impairments even when the eyes are in the right place. Attending to a conversation reduces processing of visual information as shown by fMRI studies demonstrating reduced primary (Shomstein & Yantis, 2006) or secondary (Just et al., 2008) visual cortical activity with concurrent auditory processing, or by ERP studies that find reduced P300 amplitudes (Strayer & Drews, 2007).

Even ruminating on a conversation that has been completed may be detrimental to visual scanning and place cognitive load on the driver (Savage, Potter, & Tatler, 2013).

Impoverished attention is not simply a resource issue. Even effects that look sensory in nature, such as restricted eye movements, may have a basis in more central cognitive processes. As Recarte and Nunes (2003) note, eye-movement effects might be due to strategic reallocation of resources to critical central-visual areas. In other words, reduced sensory input may be an attempt by a central mechanism to optimize what resources are available to the visual system. This intriguing notion is supported by recent work integrating driving simulation and fMRI. Schweizer et al. (2013) found that the addition of a secondary auditory task to a driving task resulted in additional activity in prefrontal cortical areas and decreased activity in posterior visual processing areas. Prefrontal areas, otherwise known as areas of "executive control," are engaged in task coordination, so this pattern may simply reflect re-distribution of available metabolic resources. But, it is also possible that the pattern is, as Recarte and Nunes suggest, a reflection of strategic choices by the central executive system to optimize processing in the multiple IP areas (visual and auditory) that are active.

With the addition of more technology to vehicles, it is tempting to want to believe that the cognitive system will become more strategic and that incurring an attention debt might encourage our brains to engage in a set of protective behaviors to compensate. In the context of our model, the suggestion would be that distraction encourages the brain to engage in more controlled processes. One misinterpretation of the Schweizer et al. (2013) study would be just that: distraction encourages a shift from automatic brain regions to regions involved in response selection, attention for action and working memory (Schweizer et al., 2013, p. 7). Such an interpretation would be consistent with naturalistic studies of driving behavior (Dingus et al., 2006) that have claimed to show that cellular phones produce no increase in crash risk or even a slight protective effect for drivers, or studies that suggest drivers engage in compensatory processes such as driving more slowly (Haigney, Taylor, & Westerman, 2000) or straighter (He, McCarley, & Kramer, 2014) when they know they are distracted.

But those interpretations are misleading. For example, consider the effect of improved lane keeping. The notion that drivers make a choice to drive even straighter when distracted is unsupported. The real source of the effect is illustrated by recent work of Medeiros-Ward, Cooper, and

Strayer (2013), who examined lane keeping and distraction as a function of driving difficulty (no wind, predictable gusts and less predictable wind gusts) and concurrent task load (single task, 0 and 2 N-Back tasks). When driving was easiest (no wind), increasing concurrent task load improved lane keeping. The opposite effect was observed when driving was most difficult. This illustrates that the interaction between attentional capacity and performance depends upon the complexity of task to be performed, and it fits well within the framework we have suggested.

When tasks are relatively automatic and simple, or highly trained such as the performance of a sports skill for trained athletes (e.g., Beilock, Carr, MacMahon, & Starkes, 2002), increased attention can introduce controlled processes that are unnecessary and actually detrimental to performance. In the model of Fig. 4.2, the controlled processes that come with more attention include a memory/perceptual loop and metacognitive awareness about performance that leads to individuals "over-controlling" their performance. Using a sports example, a trained golfer asked to think about the mechanics of their shot rather than the outcome of the shot performs worse (Perkins-Ceccato, Passmore, & Lee, 2003) because the addition of the controlled process loop disrupts automatized behaviors. For novices, the controlled loop is necessary to perform a behavior that is not automatic.

As we will see in other sections, incurring an attention debt might actually eliminate controlled processes that interfere with some behaviors, making it tempting to conclude that inattention may be beneficial. But deeper consideration of safety and attention demonstrates why this is a fallacy. It may be true that a driver drives straighter when they have a secondary task in simple driving conditions (see also Atchley & Chan, 2011; Atchley, Chan, & Gregersen, 2013), because inattention reduces controlled processing, but those controlled processes serve other critical functions. Removing the memory loop with inattention reduces navigation success (Drews, Pasupathi, & Strayer, 2008). Furthermore, while most driving is routine, the ability to avoid crashes requires anticipation of nonroutine events. Returning to the example of the woman driving in a residential neighborhood, lack of access to memory schemas might prevent scanning of potential areas of threat and lead her to fixate more centrally on the roadway, resulting in missed critical information. Distraction might also prevent her from developing and holding in memory information that might change automatized behaviors, such as driving more cautiously around the time school ends session, when children might be more likely to appear near the road. In other words, possessing the attentional resources to engage in controlled processes is necessary for highly successful, and safe, behavior in a complex and changing environment.

2.2. Aesthetics and Creativity
2.2.1 Aesthetics
While safety is necessary for survival of the species, creativity and the ability to appreciate beauty are necessary to be fully human. Here too, an attention debt may impoverish us. This problem became clear to the first author during a 2010 visit to the New York Metropolitan Museum of Art. While attempting to appreciate a work of art with my wife, I turned to glare at a man talking loudly on his cellular phone, ruining the experience for everyone inside of the small gallery. During his conversation, the man leaned up against a wall. Unfortunately, the wall was actually a painting by Jackson Pollock. Even the security guard who was about to ask the man to be quiet was so stunned that he was unable to prevent the event from happening.

Quick reflection reveals that there are many less extreme cases, but where the experience of appreciating an artistic endeavor is mediated by technologies that vie for attention. Go to a concert and you will see many of the faces of attendees lit by the screens of their smart phones as they post their experience to social media or watch the performance on their smart phone as they record it, rather than with their own eyes. Walk into an art museum, and even if you do not hear people talking on their phones or touching the art, you will see people texting and glancing up to view the art quickly, or pausing only long enough to take a picture for later posting. Even in the outdoors, the ability to appreciate nature is impacted by mediation from smart phones that encourage treating the experience as one to be captured, remarked upon, posted, and forgotten.

Understanding the effect of an attention economy on aesthetic appreciation requires defining its characteristics. A summary of millennia of debate and discussion is beyond the current scope of this chapter, but a recent review by Reber, Schwarz, and Winkielman (2004) suggests the useful concept that aesthetic appreciation involves the ability of the observer to process the experience. They propose that the "more fluently the perceiver can process an object, the more positive is his or her aesthetic response" (p. 365). For example, priming an artwork with related titles produces higher ratings of liking for the art than priming using unrelated titles or no titles (Belke, Leder, Strobach, & Carbon, 2010). Semantic context improves processing fluency and thus appreciation. Rather than placing beauty solely in the properties of the stimulus itself, beauty is a function of the ability of the observer to mentally process properties of the object in a meaningful way, making the attention of the observer a critical part of aesthetic experience. For example, seeing a painting and saying it "looks nice" is a much more shallow aesthetic experience than seeing the same painting and noting that it "looks nice" *and* that it has additional value by virtue of its place in history, the influence of the artist and the techniques used in creating it, as well as how that piece of work inspired and informed later art. Thus, these latter aspects of aesthetic experience are greatly influenced by the cognitive capacities and experiences of the observer.

To be fair, aesthetic experience may be improved by technology by allowing the experience to be more information rich. Museums have been using this approach for many years using technologies such as audio or visual guides on smart phones to give viewers additional information about works to improve appreciation of them. But if appreciation and a complete aesthetic experience are supported by the ability of observers to process information and make deep connections, then technology also has the power to disrupt those processes.

In the current model, as we incur an attention debt, such as checking social media while perceiving a work of art, two things happen which might reduce the aesthetic experience. First, a division of attention leads to a decline in the depth to which we process stimuli. In such situations, less would be noticed about the object of the experience, such as colors, brushstrokes, or objects in art, harmonies, chords, or textures in music, or sounds, patterns of light or smells in natural experiences. Second, cognition moves from controlled processes that permit access to representations in memory that improve the fluency of experience, to judgments based more on System 1 thinking, that is dominated by the emotional appeal of the object of the aesthetic experience. While enjoyment is a positive outcome, art educators might argue that true appreciation requires fluency. We would also predict less about the experience will be encoded and thus less acquired knowledge for future aesthetic experiences.

These predictions were, in fact, supported by work that appeared in press while this chapter was under review. Work by Linda Henkel (2014), examined the effect of taking pictures of artwork at a museum on subsequent memory for those artworks and their locations in the museum itself. Participants visited a museum and both viewed some objects and photographed others. Subsequent recognition performance (identifying works as previously viewed) was best for viewed objects. This is consistent with the idea that dividing attention between the task of taking a picture and viewing an artwork leads to reduced depth of processing for the work of art and suggests that true appreciation for the art may be impaired. However, Henkel also showed that the photographs themselves served as good retrieval cue. When participants had experimenter-supplied photos as a cue they recalled more old works than when they had to use rote memory. Memory for non-photographed objects was still superior, but the photo helped with overall recognition. We will return to the theme that technology may also serve some positive functions, even in an attention economy, in Section 4.1.

2.2.2 Creativity

Just as the fluency for aesthetic experiences is improved by access to more information and deeper connections between the experience and cognitive processes in the viewer, the ability to think creatively is supported by access to a rich and wide network of knowledge, which can also be disrupted by an attention debt. For example, one aspect of processing that distinguishes low and high verbally creative individuals is that high creatives maintain multiple subordinate word associations for longer periods of time (R. A. Atchley, Keeney, & Burgess, 1999). This would suggest that distraction could harm creative output by disrupting the ability to maintain multiple representations in mind. Consistent with this idea is recent work showing that disconnecting from distracting devices and being immersed in natural settings for an extended period of time can boost the production of creative verbal associations by 50% (R. A. Atchley, Strayer, & Atchley, 2012).

However, it has also been suggested that distraction may actually improve creativity by making individuals more open to remote associations between concepts. In verbal creativity, not fixating on the dominant meaning of a word allows subordinate meanings to remain active, which can foster atypical connections between concepts, and thus "creative" associations. In the model we have developed, one might imagine this as distraction preventing the operation of controlled processes that might cause someone to focus on the most likely interpretation of a word. The finding that attention deficit/hyperactivity disorder, which can be interpreted as a failure of the controlled process loop of our model, may be linked to higher creativity (White & Shah, 2006, 2011) is somewhat consistent with this view.

Another piece of evidence consistent with this general framework is the role of the default network (DFN; see Buckner, Andrews-Hanna, & Schacter, 2008; Greicius, Krasnow, Reiss, & Menon, 2003) in creativity. The DFN is thought to be active during sleep and periods of daydreaming or mind-wandering (Mason et al., 2007). It is often viewed as the opposite of the controlled process loop that engages frontal/parietal, effortful executive processes (Fox et al., 2005). It has been suggested that DFN activity may assist with creative output by supporting the type of remote associations that herald creative responses. Recent fMRI work shows that highly creative individuals who are performing working memory tasks showed less reduction in DFN activity than lower creative individuals (Takeuchi et al., 2011), possibly leaving them open to creative associations despite working memory demands.

As with the tempting link of inattention and lane keeping (Section 2.1), the link between ADHD and creativity does not provide evidence that running an attention debt helps improve creative output. The ADHD link is more readily explained by an increased propensity of these individuals to engage in multiple projects, rather than deep, creative output for a single project. Another intriguing possibility is that ADHD is associated with a less inhibited DFN (Fassbender et al., 2009), and thus individuals possibly have greater exposure to atypical and creative associations. If so, can we "distract" ourselves into creative output by inhibiting the controlled process loop? Two pieces of evidence suggest otherwise. First, the Fassbender et al. work shows that increasing attention load reduces DFN activity, except for individuals with ADHD, so such a strategy may not work for most individuals and may come with a cost for others. Second, as the work on exposure to nature (e.g., R. A. Atchley, Strayer, & Atchley, 2012) suggests, a *decrease* in distractions is more likely to beneficial. Removing distractions and making time for reflection moves creative output to its peak. As Immordino-Yang, Christodoulou, and Singh (2012) suggest, distraction is counterproductive for engaging the DFN in the service of development of complex cognitive abilities like divergent thinking.

In the framework we have been using, these observations suggest a subtle distinction between reduced attention resources due to distraction and the choice to expend fewer resources by not engaging in tasks that require controlled processes. Table 4.2 outlines the features of the distinction between what we call "exogenous and endogenous inattention." In the case of exogenous inattention, the person's choice to engage in multiple tasks involves coordination of multiple tasks that requires the utilization of executive processes, which in turn suppresses DFN activity. In the case of endogenous inattention, the person's choice to not focus on any particular task, such as might occur during a walk or during a waking restful state leads to a disengagement of controlled processes, allowing DFN activity to increase,

Table 4.2 Exogenous Versus Endogenous Inattention

	Exogenous Inattention	Endogenous Inattention
Source	"Bottom-up" requirement to attend to multiple processes	"Top-down" choice to not focus on any task
Controlled processes	Activation of task coordination executive functions	Little controlled process activity
Default network	Suppressed due to executive network activity	Increased as executive network activity declines

possibly improving creative output. If this framework is valid, then running an attention debt is exactly the wrong tack to take to improve creativity.

2.3. The Experience and Regulation of Emotion

So far, with the exception of our discussion of aesthetics, a reader might begin to think that technological distraction primarily influences our intellectual functioning. As we will see, attention affects both our experience of emotions and our ability to regulate them. We first note that contemporary psychology and neuroscience sees cognition and emotion as being tightly intertwined (e.g., Pessoa, 2010; Storbeck & Clore, 2007). For instance, decision-making is impaired when people lack the affective response associated with previous positive or negative experience with a stimulus (e.g., Bechara et al., 1997). In addition, patients with Capgras syndrome can come to believe that family members are imposters because the patient does not experience the expected affective response while recognizing the physical resemblance to their memory of the person (e.g., Hirstein & Ramachandran, 1997). Finally, there is much overlap between the brain systems involved in emotion and cognition (e.g., Davidson, 2003; Storbeck & Clore, 2007). Thus, we can expect that, for some of the same reasons we have seen that distraction disrupts cognitive processing, there will be similar disruptions to affective processing.

Although a precise definition of emotion has evaded the field, we adopt a "modal model" of emotion described by Gross and Thompson (2007). In this model, there are three core features of an emotion. A person must attend to a situation and perceive it as pertinent to his or her goals (the meaning of which elicits the emotion), there is a coupled response in terms of *subjective experience, behavior, and physiology* (Mauss, Levenson, McCarter, Wilhelm, & Gross, 2005), and this response can be up- or downregulated according the physical or social constraints of the situation (i.e., emotion regulation).

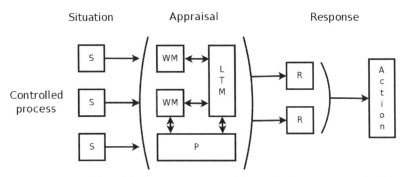

Figure 4.3 The modal model of emotion appraisal (Gross & Thompson, 2007), adapted for the current framework. In this model, situation is mapped onto sensory inputs (S), appraisal is the perceptual/memory loop with working memory (WM), long-term memory (LTM), and perception (P), and response includes response options (R) and action choice.

Consider this model as adapted to the current controlled process framework as described in Section 1.4 (Fig. 4.3). When a person encounters an external (physical) or internal (mentally represented) situation, he or she normally attends to some aspects more than others. This selective processing provides information that serves as the basis for an appraisal of the situation (e.g., its valence), and this appraisal leads to changes in the person's subjective or physical state, or behavior. For example, imagine a man has just left a bar late at night and sees a person wearing a hooded sweatshirt following behind him. The person is walking fast and has their head down, leading the man to assess that the person is a potential threat, which increases his heart rate and blood pressure in preparation for a potential altercation. If, a few seconds later, a streetlight reveals the person is actually a woman with a slight build who appears scared, this is likely to change the man's appraisal, leading to a downregulation of the psychological, physical, and behavioral responses that had been triggered.

Technological distraction can influence emotion processing at several points within this model. First, distraction during the period when a person first encounters a situation can potentially prevent its identification as goal-relevant (when it actually is). As we have suggested previously, the attention economy limits the amount of relevant sensory input by making available attractive, but irrelevant, sensory input. This would decrease the likelihood of an appropriate affective reaction by depriving the appraisal system of the information necessary for a correct assessment, potentially meaning that a potential threat or opportunity would be overlooked. Second, diminished attention may lead to shallow and incomplete processing of the situation by limiting the activation of appropriate schemas, or eliminating the appraisal process altogether and instead leading the person to rely on more immediate System 1 cues to emotional valence. Finally, distraction might impair the response process by restricting consideration to a small subset of possible responses due to insufficient appraisal or elimination of controlled processing.

Consistent with this general framework, more recent work examining the role of DFN in dehumanization of others suggests, much like in creativity, that overspending in the attention economy may produce subtle, but problematic effects for emotion processing. Using fMRI, Jack, Dawson, and Norr (2013) examined responses in the DFN to stimuli such as faces, machines, or animals. Across a variety of conditions, the pattern of results showed that dehumanization was associated with deactivation of the DFN. Much like our previous suggestion about how distraction and diminished attention might reduce activity in DFN and thus reduce creative output, a similar mechanism might produce a reduction in the ability to empathize and see others as human.

However, it is also possible to consider the role of distraction or attentional load on emotional experience more broadly. It has been argued by some researchers that emotions are elicited relatively automatically (e.g., LeDoux, 1996). If this is the case, this would suggest that divided attention engendered by technological distractions would have little effect on emotional experience. By and large though, the evidence is that although emotional stimuli can elicit neural and behavioral responses rapidly, they nevertheless require that a person attend to the stimulus (see Storbeck & Clore, 2007 for a discussion). For example, Pessoa, McKenna, Gutierrez, and Ungerleider (2002) conducted an fMRI study on the processing of emotional (fearful and happy) faces, and found that key brain areas, including the amygdala, were only activated when attentional load was low, but not when it was high. Thus, this suggests that attentional load resulting from technology use has the potential to reduce the extent to which people have emotional responses to stimuli.

The studies described in the previous paragraph typically focus on emotional responses to stimuli that evoke relatively straightforward emotional responses (e.g., disgust elicited by International Affective Picture System photographs; Lang, Bradley, & Cuthbert, 2008). But what about more complex emotions that require extended cognitive processing and elaboration? For instance, the experience of guilt (vs., say anger) requires the person compare his or her behavior to a moral standard. Given that these types of emotions involve a more effortful use of cognitive processes, we would predict their experience would be even more disrupted in the face of attentional load. Thus, it may be difficult to construct and feel complex emotions when distracted, just as it is difficult to have a rich aesthetic experience under the same conditions.

Our experience of emotions is dynamic, and one reason for this is that we are constantly regulating them. Although a description of the substantial research on the topic is beyond the scope of this chapter (see Gross & Thompson, 2007 for a review), we note that distraction is a type of emotion regulation strategy. People using this strategy either focus their attention on aspects of the situation that are consistent with their goals (focusing on positive features or away from negative features) or away from the situation altogether. The primary way this type of strategy differs from typical technological distraction concerns their goal. In the former, the goal is to reduce or enhance the emotional experience of a situation, while in the latter the goal is engage with the technology and effects on emotional experience are simply a byproduct.

Just as technological distraction can imperil safety or reduce the quality of aesthetic experience, the evidence just reviewed suggests that it has the potential to disrupt the richness of our emotional experience of events in our lives. In many ways, these issues are a byproduct of the opportunity costs that occur when we try to maintain attention in both cyber and real-world contexts simultaneously. In Section 3, we describe the reasons we seem to be compelled to pursue this goal in spite of its potential hazards.

3. WHY DO WE OVERSPEND OUR ATTENTION BUDGET?
3.1. Our Social Brain

New information technology can be attractive to people for a number of reasons. Some people enjoy the aesthetics of new devices or applications, and others like to be the first of their friends to obtain a scarce commodity. But the spread of popular applications like Twitter™ and Facebook™, as well as the dramatic worldwide growth in the use of mobile devices, capitalizes upon the important fact that humans seem to have an intense need to be social. Furthermore, this need is deep-rooted. Although many animals have sophisticated social behaviors (e.g., bees; Visscher, 2007), it has been argued that the complexity of primate brains is a byproduct of the complexity of interactions that take place within their social networks (*the social brain hypothesis*, e.g., Dunbar, 1998). In other words, our big brains may be big because we need them to navigate our social world.

Even without the mediation of technology, it is clear that people enjoy thinking and talking about other people, as well as interacting with them. For instance, one study that examined real-world conversations found that approximately 65% of the content concerned social relationships or planned social activities (Dunbar, Marriott, & Duncan, 1997). More directly, there is neural evidence that the process of sharing activates reward centers in the brain in ways that are similar to instrumental rewards such as food (Tamir & Mitchell, 2012). In a series of fMRI studies, participants were given the opportunity to answer questions about their own opinions or the opinions of others. Furthermore, on a given trial, participants chose between answering one of two types of questions that differed with respect to an associated monetary reward. In particular, the researchers were interested in whether people would be willing to pass on the option that maximized their wealth in favor of choosing to talk about themselves (a measure of intrinsic value). Tamir and Mitchell found that describing ones' opinions increased activation in structures in the dopamine reward system (nucleus accumbens and ventral tegmental area), as well as the medial prefrontal cortex (an area associated with self-referential thinking in previous research). Furthermore, participants were willing to give up an average of 17% of their potential winnings in order to talk about themselves. Finally, results also suggested that the rewarding nature of self-disclosure comes about because people find it rewarding both to think about themselves and to share information with other people.

The findings of Tamir and Mitchell (2012) suggest that the anticipation and reward that emanate from the process of social connection are processed by our brains in ways that are similar to primary or secondary reinforcers (note too that there is evidence that physical and social pain are experienced similarly, e.g., Eisenberger, Lieberman, & Williams, 2003). Thus, one reason people have difficulty resisting the urge to pick up a ringing phone or answer a text while driving is that they are anticipating the reward of doing so (see also the issue of the limited life span of social information, Section 3.2). Interestingly, this anticipation may play a role in what has come to be known as "phantom vibration syndrome" (Haupt, 2007). In this situation, people perceive a vibration from their phone or pager when there is not one. Survey research on the topic has found that substantial percentages of people (89% in one sample of undergraduates) report having experienced this sensation (Drouin, Kaiser, & Miller, 2012; Rothberg et al., 2010).

Although much of social media is ostensibly designed to increase the degree to which we share information with each other, it is reasonable to ask whether using the technology while in the company of others has the potential to disrupt our social connections. This type of issue was recently dramatized in a YouTube video entitled "I Forgot My Phone" by Charlene DeGuzman and Miles Crawford (www.youtube.com/watch?v=OINa46HeWg8), which has been viewed approximately 27 million times as of this writing. In the video, DeGuzman goes through her day while in the company of people who are using their phones (e.g., at lunch or a concert) to talk or text with others and take photographs to post online. Her disaffection from her companions is obvious. The broader message is also clear: people are focused on their virtual interactions to the detriment of live ones. Although there is very little research on this particular topic, the response to this video (e.g., Bilton, 2013) suggests that it is very real concern.

With some exceptions (e.g., people with autism; Frith, 2001), humans seek out social connections and find this process rewarding (if sometimes frustrating). We find technologies that capitalize on this motivation to be very difficult to ignore. However, this is not the only reason we are willing to overspend our attention budgets. In Section 3.2, we explore whether our pursuit of social connection in the context of technology is like an addiction and the role of time.

3.2. The Value of Immediate Information

Introductory journalism students at the University of Kansas who were asked to deprive themselves of media for 24 h recorded a number of strong reactions (http://kansan.com/archives/2012/01/25/disconnected-a-day-without-media/). One student noted they had what felt like the beginning of an anxiety attack after 2 h without media. Another noted that the "end of the world" came after 5 min without checking to see if they had any new text messages. With reactions like these and a brain wired for social information that delivers chemical rewards for disclosing personal information to others (Tamir & Mitchell, 2012), it is no wonder that some might think we overspend our attention budget because we are "addicted" to social information.

But what has been made less clear in the discussion of an attention economy is that information is a "substance" with a different temporal value profile than other substances. In other words, information changes value to the user in a fundamentally different way from other items that people value or may be truly addicted to, such as money or chemical substances. Atchley and Warden (2012) sought to illustrate this in a study designed to quantify the "addicting" nature of texting using an intertemporal choice methodology (Rachlin, Raineri, & Cross, 1991). In the study, participants were given choices between small rewards that could be obtained immediately or larger rewards that could be gained by waiting. By varying delay and reward size, the rate of change for which participants valued smaller, sooner rewards, over larger, later rewards can serve as an index of what is known as "delay discounting," or the emphasis someone places on getting the reward "now." For example, the value of a cigarette now compared to many cigarettes at some later time is much greater for someone addicted to smoking than for someone who is a casual smoker (Heyman & Gibb, 2006; Ohmura, Takahashi, & Kitamura, 2005).

In Atchley and Warden (2012), participants made two types of choices. One choice was a standard intertemporal choice for monetary rewards. A second choice paired the monetary reward with the opportunity to respond to information (calling or texting) now or at some future time. For example, a participant might get a choice between "$10.00 now to reply immediately" or "$100 if you wait an hour to reply." In other words, how long is someone willing to wait to send a text and how much money will they "give up" for the opportunity to text right away? Two types of analyses can be applied to these data. First, plotting the point where "smaller sooner" and "larger later" rewards are equal (called the indifference point) over the time delays, produce curves for the discounting rate. The area under the curve serves as an index of discounting. An "addicted" smoker, for example, will devalue later rewards, resulting in a steeply declining slope and little area under the curve. In this analysis, monetary rewards and monetary plus informational rewards produced the same curves. This suggested that there was no evidence of "addiction" to informational rewards since the pattern of decision-making was the same when participants were choosing a little money now or more later, versus a little money and texting now versus more money and texting later.

But another way to look at the data is to ask how *long* it takes for value to decline. In typical intertemporal choice studies that use monetary rewards to establish a baseline choice profile, the delays for the larger, later, rewards are very long, typically ranging as long as weeks and months. Pretesting showed that asking someone to wait weeks or months to reply to a text made little sense so the extreme range of time for informational rewards was changed to

Table 4.3 Time to Lose 25% and 50% of the Value of the Monetary Reward for Monetary and Monetary Plus Informational Rewards as a Function of Social Distance

Choice	Loss of 25% Value	Loss of 50% Value
Less $ now or $100 later	2 weeks	>5 months
Less $ now or $100 later AND...		
Text significant other now or later	<30 min	6 h
Text friend now or later	3 h	15 h
Text acquaintance now or later	≈10 h	≈2 days

Atchley and Warden (2012), Exp. 2.

hours and days. Though the choice curves were the same when normalized for these differences in delay periods, the time for the monetary reward to lose value was strikingly different when the reward was paired with the ability to text. As shown in Table 4.3, money lost 25% of its value in about two weeks. $75 now and $100 in 2 weeks is similar in value. When paired with the ability to respond to a text from their significant other, $75 now and $100 later were judged as equivalent within 30 min. In other words, participants were willing to give up $25 to text their significant other back within one half-hour.

Further, as Table 4.3 illustrates, the delays change as a function of social distance. People were willing to delay responding to texts from friends or acquaintances much longer. This finding shows the choice is not an irrational one, since participants were clearly considering the value of the information when choosing how long to wait. That finding and the equivalent decision-making curves for monetary and monetary plus informational rewards suggest that the "compulsion" to check phones and text at inappropriate times may be less an addiction and more of a rational response to the fact that information loses value rapidly. While monetary or chemical rewards are fungible over any span of time (i.e., a cigarette is just as useful to a smoker now or in a month), information may only have value for a short span of time. If your significant other sends you a text, and you ignore it, you may miss a temporally limited opportunity (e.g., "Come meet me at Joe's for dinner.") that has no value later (as well as other potential consequences).

In an attention economy, some information may have greater subjective value than others. Social contact has always been important and our brains place value on it (see Section 3.1). Social information may drive a greater shift toward overspending our attentional resources. When paired with devices (smart phones) and applications (Facebook) that can deliver that information rapidly and on a massive scale, a normally rational expense of attention to monitor social information of limited temporal value from a small set of physically nearby people, becomes an irrational attempt to monitor and respond to networks much larger than those for which our brains were adapted. Making things worse, as we attempt to respond to such demands, we tax the resources that would help us to regulate what has become an irrational choice.

3.3. Self-Control and Willpower

As we have discussed, technologically based interaction is compelling for a variety of reasons, including the fact that our brains find the process of communicating with others deeply rewarding (e.g., Tamir & Mitchell, 2012) and because this information often has a very short "shelf-life" (Atchley & Warden, 2012). The alerts people receive from texts or other applications thus act as strong cues to importance, diverting attention from ongoing activity. But, what are the broader effects of this type of distraction on people's ability to direct their own behavior?

Self-control is a term that is typically used to describe people's deliberate attempts to pursue their goals in the face of temptations or other obstacles. For example, control theory (Carver & Scheier, 1981) argues that successful self-control involves having an internal standard or goal (e.g., I need to study for a test), monitoring one's current behavior and comparing it to the standard (e.g., I am on Facebook™), and finally acting to reduce any discrepancy (e.g., I turned off my phone and opened my textbook). Interestingly, control theory explicitly highlighted the role of focus of attention in self-regulation. For instance, it was recognized that people must attend to their self-standards during the unfolding of an event in order to respond appropriately (e.g., in order to activate the comparison process; Carver & Scheier, 1981). Thus, attending to a series of texts from a friend might prevent a person from recognizing the need to exercise self-control (e.g., not eating sweets when one is on a diet).

Self-control has also been viewed as a competition between relatively automatic processes and relatively controlled cognitive processes (e.g., Kahneman & Frederick, 2002; Shiv & Fedorikhin, 2002). For example, Kahneman and Frederick argue that tempting stimuli (e.g., a cigarette to a heavy smoker) would activate the faster and less effortful System 1, and that the decision to override this temptation would fall to the slower, capacity-limited and more effortful System 2. In this situation, an increase in mental load has the potential to impair self-control, and this has been borne out in a number of experiments. Shiv and Fedorikhin's (2002, Exp. 1) study provides an excellent example. In their research, participants arrived at the laboratory and were randomly assigned to a high memory load or a low memory load condition. High load participants had to rehearse seven random digits and low memory load participants had to rehearse two random digits while they walked to another experimental room. On the way to this room, participants in a critical condition stopped and were given a brief time to choose between a bowl of fruit and a piece of chocolate cake as a thank you for their participation. High load participants were more likely to choose the tempting chocolate cake while those under lower mental load were more likely to choose the healthy bowl of fruit. By implication, to the extent that technological distractions put us greater mental load, this may have the effect of making it more difficult to use effortful cognitive processes to avoid giving in to the temptations we face (see also Baumeister et al., 1998).

Another way that self-control can be derailed comes about when people need to exert self-control with respect to their technology use. This work bears resemblance to our earlier discussion of the concept of attention as a limited resource. A substantial body of research suggests that self-control (i.e., *willpower*) itself is limited and can be depleted through its extended use (for a general review, see Baumeister, Vohs, & Tice, 2007). This "ego depletion" leads to a short-term decrease in people's ability to exercise self-control on unrelated tasks. In these studies, participants in the critical condition have to complete a task that requires resisting an impulse (e.g., eating radishes while seeing and smelling freshly baked chocolate chip cookies; Baumeister et al., 1998, Exp. 1) while control participants complete a task that does not require self-control. Both groups subsequently complete a new self-control task (e.g., attempting to solve unsolvable problems). The consistent finding is that participants who had to engage self-control in the first task are less likely to effectively use self-control in the second task (e.g., by giving up sooner). Additional research in this area suggests that the psychological effects of depletion may have their basis in the reduction of glucose levels (e.g., Gailliot et al., 2007; but see Job, Walton, Bernecker, & Dweck, 2013), and others have argued that self-regulatory failure is likely to happen when prefrontal function is impaired (whether from ego depletion or otherwise; Heatherton & Wagner, 2011). Altogether, this work suggests that, to the extent that people are attempting to control their technology use (e.g., see the first paragraph of Section 3.2), they may find that the ability to regulate their behavior is impaired in other aspects of their lives.

The foregoing research suggests that technological distraction will nearly always lead to impaired self-control. However, other research suggests a more nuanced situation. For instance, when attentional load reduces people's ability to encode or elaborate upon the hedonic properties of tempting stimuli, this is likely to *improve* self-control (e.g., Van Dillen, Papies, & Hoffman, 2013). In other words, a dieter is unlikely to be tempted by a cookie if distraction prevents him or her from completing the mental and affective processes necessary to build up a craving for it. Researchers have also argued that attentional load primarily restricts the scope of attention to the most salient cues in the environment ("attentional myopia," see Mann & Ward, 2007 for a brief review; see also Shiv & Fedorikhin, 2002). If these cues prime the tempting behavioral option (e.g., delicious foods for a dieter), then increased self-regulation failure is found under load, but if the cues prime the self-control goal (e.g., a scale and diet books), then increased success is found under load (e.g., Mann & Ward, 2004). Thus, both types of research suggest that the effect of greater degrees of technological distraction (and thus load) on self-control is going to vary depending on where attention is focused.

Research has documented the important role that self-control plays in our ability to achieve important educational, career, and life goals (e.g., Ayduk et al., 2000; Shoda, Mischel, & Peake, 1990). Given the foregoing discussion, there are reasons to ask whether the distractions that are engendered in our technological society impair our ability to achieve important self-control goals (even when our technology habits are not the focus of our control efforts). Indeed they might, although not always. In Section 4, we discuss potential ways that technology might enhance self-control efforts and other important activities.

4. CAN WE EXPAND THE ATTENTION ECONOMY?
4.1. Mental and Behavioral Prosthetics

We have spent the majority of this chapter describing ways that the attention economy can disrupt our lives, including reducing our safety, limiting our aesthetic experiences, and making it difficult to exert self-control. But neither of us is a Luddite. Information technology is a tool that has transformed modern life. The side effects we have described often come about because applications and devices are typically designed so that they will be appealing to consumers (and purchased in great numbers), and so often take advantage of the characteristics of our cognitive, emotional, and motivational systems to achieve that goal. Yet, this is not always the case. Technology can be harnessed to support and extend our abilities, and we next discuss three selected examples.

Although older adults may benefit from their extensive knowledge accumulated over their lifetime, research finds that aging leads to declines in attention, memory, and other cognitive processes. For example, the processing speed of cognitive operations is thought to slow in older adults (e.g., Salthouse, 1996). Older adults are also less able to inhibit distracting information than younger adults (e.g., Hasher, Stoltzfus, Zacks, & Rypma, 1991). Episodic memory also appears to decline, as older adults less efficiently encode and remember their life experiences than younger adults (e.g., Craik & Byrd, 1982). Technologies are already being developed to provide cognitive support to the elderly. For instance, *The Memory Mirror* (for a description, see Rogers & Fisk, 2006) is specifically designed to help older adults to remember whether they performed an action (a type of prospective memory), such as taking medication. Whenever medication is removed from a tray, radio frequency identification allows the time to be tracked, which then appears on a timeline in a visual display. Simply by looking at the display, a person can confirm whether they took his or her medication and avoid missing or repeating a dose.

Other technologies are not directly aimed at older adults, but have the potential to help overcome cognitive limitations. Google Glass™ has received much attention for being one of the first wave of consumer-oriented wearable computing devices. Although not all the attention has been favorable (privacy and safety issues have been raised), there are several characteristics that might make it or similar devices useful to older adults. For instance, many current applications for Glass focus on "augmented reality"—providing computer-generated information that supplements what is being seen or heard by the wearer. This type of application could provide helpful assistance for older adults' documented decline in the ability to create associations between elements of an event, such as remembering people's names (e.g., Naveh-Benjamin, Guez, Kilb, & Reedy, 2004). For example, when older adults encounter someone they have met in the past, it is possible that Glass could quickly prime that person's name by briefly flashing it to the screen. Glass is also one of a class of devices (see also, the Vicon Revue™, formerly Microsoft SenseCam) that have been used for "lifelogging"—the documenting and playback of life activities using video or photographs. Despite possible negative implications of lifelogging, there is recent evidence that it can be useful for people with memory difficulties (e.g., Brown et al., 2011) when they regularly use the digital information as a cue to help them remember.

In an earlier section, we discussed how the attention economy might undermine our efforts at self-control. In fact, information technology sometimes engenders habits that compete with other important goals (e.g., safety, such as when we feel compelled to reach for the phone while driving when a text arrives). Yet, technology can also be used to change habits.

One of the first keys to changing a habit involves understanding the cues that trigger it. Although it has been possible for some time to record one's behavior and its context (e.g., writing in a food diary), information technology has made this process considerably easier and more accurate. For example, instead of writing down what has been eaten during a given meal, dieters can take a photograph of their plate before and after a meal using a cell phone camera, and an app will process the information to determine approximate calorie count (e.g., Zhu et al., 2010). Such applications surmount problems with initial estimation of portion sizes, reliance on memory, and the additional cognitive effort of mapping portion sizes to calorie counts. Aids to recording behavior also have the advantage of providing feedback to the user. This type of technology is used quite extensively in the area of fitness. Devices that provide information about location (GPS), heart rate, number of steps (e.g., FitBit™), and other measures are now commonplace, providing clear information about progress and alerting to potential problems (e.g., overtraining). Once someone has initiated behavior change, it can be difficult to maintain that change. One important strategy for dealing with this issue involves making your behavior public. Although groups such as Weightwatchers™ have used such a strategy for many years, a wide range of Websites and applications offer the ability to track and display your efforts (e.g., Strava.com for running and cycling). Others go further. Gympact.com, for instance, allows users to get financial incentives for exercising, as they can earn money from working out and forfeit money if they do not. All of these examples are part of a broader effort to use technology to change behavior. The QuantitativeSelf.com is a Website that is devoted to people who use (often self-developed) technology to track behaviors with the intent of self-improvement. Many users attend local meetings and share the results of their experiments. Finally, there are collaborations that bridge academic and business worlds, such as B.J. Fogg's Stanford Persuasive

Technology Lab. The lab's mission is to support efforts by researchers and designers to create applications that enhance attitude and behavior change.

Our final topic concerns how technology can be harnessed to improve higher education. Because this topic could fill an entire chapter, our discussion is necessarily brief. To begin, we note that much press coverage has recently been devoted to how higher education might be delivered more efficiently via online sources, including for-profit companies like Coursera and Udacity. In particular, it has been claimed that Massive Open Online Courses or MOOCs, are a solution to concerns about the cost of education and its availability to a broader spectrum of people (e.g., Koller, 2011). Initial course offerings have generated excitement, but have also revealed very low completion and pass rates, and this has led to a more circumspect evaluation of their merits (e.g., Kolowich, 2013). There may ultimately be ways of improving such courses, but we believe these findings also illustrate something important about how we think about online education. Students, whether online or "in person," need a set of skills that allow them to direct their own learning. Researchers have referred to such skills as academic self-regulation or self-regulated learning (e.g., Hadwin & Winne, 2012; Zimmerman, 1998). For example, Zimmerman suggests that academic self-regulatory processes include goal setting, strategies for performing tasks, time management skills, metacognitive monitoring, strategies for modifying the environment to improve success, and knowledge about when to seek help from others. There is evidence that undergraduate students often lack these skills when arriving at college, and as a result study in ways that are less than optimal (for a discussion, see Hadwin & Winne, 2012). There are good reasons to believe that this lack of self-regulatory skills could be at the heart of the low completion rates observed in MOOCs and other types of online education. However, there is also evidence that technology can be harnessed to help build these skills (for a review, see Winne & Nesbitt, 2009). For example, Winne and colleagues have developed software (gStudy) that supports students' ability to monitor their learning and to understand when a particular study strategy may or may not be usefully applied. Other attempts at enhancing these skills have used online coursework to help students develop knowledge and skills that will allow them to identify appropriate career goals and make academic decisions that maximize the likelihood of achieving those goals (Atchley, Hooker, Kroska, & Gilmour, 2012). Finally, there are efforts to make educational technology more responsive to human emotions (e.g., frustration) that arise during the learning process (e.g., Graesser, Jackson, & McDaniel, 2007). Such software may help reduce the extent to which students' self-regulatory skills are taxed during the learning process.

In our brief discussion, we have only scratched the surface in discussing ways that technology can better support the processes involved in learning (e.g., by directing attention to relevant features of a concept). Although we are optimistic about its potential, we nevertheless suggest that hard work is necessary to ensure that technology enhances rather than detracts from the learning process.

4.2. Cautionary Tales on the Costs and Benefits of Automation

There is perhaps no more complex place than the cockpit of a passenger jet. It is from commercial aviation that we draw an example of how technology may be a solution for the expanding attention economy by helping us perform well in an increasingly complicated world. It is from the same domain that we point to how ceding control to automation can also pose risk. Both examples involve airline crashes but each had very different outcomes.

The first example is from US Airways flight 1549, which was struck by geese resulting in engine failure shortly after takeoff from New York's La Guardia Airport in January of 2009. The captain of the flight, Chelsey Sullenberger, became a hero for successfully landing the disabled aircraft in the Hudson River, resulting in no losses among his 155-person charge. In his book describing the incident, William Langewiesche (2009) writes that the skill of the pilot and crew were certainly part of the reason disaster was successfully averted, but he also notes that a significant factor was the automation of systems inside the Airbus A320. The fly-by-wire design of A320 is such that the plane will undertake corrective action to prevent crashes in the absence of pilot intervention. With much of the cognitive load for airplane control during the bird strike event offloaded to the aircraft, Captain Sullenberger and crew had the cognitive capacity to plan and execute their ambitious and successful landing in the Hudson.

In the book, the airplane's designer, Bernard Ziegler, poses the curious statement "Sometimes I wonder if we made an airplane that is too easy to fly" (p. 109). He notes that as piloting has become simpler, pilots have become less alert. This is precisely the cautionary message about automation. As suggested in Table 4.2, endogenous inattention or the choice not to engage executive cognitive systems may be beneficial to processes such as creativity. But inattention due to lack of engagement that results in a loss of vigilance or awareness, can have disastrous consequences. Inattention due to fatigue or other causes accounts for over 80,000 crashes per year in the United States, on average (NHTSA, 2011), and is a significant threat to safety on long-distance transportation by ground, sea, or air. One result of making systems more automated is they become less engaging, resulting in drivers, captains, and pilots taking their minds off of their primary task or failing to monitor system states.

A cautionary tale about automation comes from the crash of an Asiana Airlines Boeing 777 in San Francisco in July of 2013. In that crash, which resulted in the loss of two lives on the ground after the crash, the airplane came in too low due to insufficient airspeed on approach and the landing gear struck the seawall protecting the runway. The airplane was in control of a pilot receiving training on the aircraft who was under the direction of a pilot with over 3000 operational hours with a 777. Initial investigation of the crash indicated that one possible reason for the crash was a failure of the pilots to understand the state of automation in the aircraft (NTSB, 2013). Though the airplane was set for a manual landing, the pilots were relying upon the airplane's autothrottle to maintain airspeed. The autothrottle was "armed" or ready to be engaged to maintain airspeed, but whether the pilots failed to complete the process to engage the autothrottle or whether the autothrottle failed, the result was that the crew's erroneous assumptions about the control of airplane airspeed left them without enough time to understand and react to the problem.

These two airline crashes illustrate the fine line between automation as benefit and automation as a cost. On the one hand, we do live in an environment where many of the processes we must control require us to respond to information beyond our capacity, and so we must rely on effective automation to succeed. On the other hand, over-reliance on automation can lead to complacency, mode errors (Sarter & Woods, 1995), and reduced vigilance and increased inattention. In the context of Section 2.1, automation of the driving task by "smart" cars has been suggested as a possible solution to the desire of drivers to engage with social-media technology while driving. While smart vehicles may help prevent some of the crashes associated with distracted driving, what is unclear is if there are hidden costs associated with automation on a massive scale, particularly in the hands of drivers with a much wider range of training and skill levels as compared to airline pilots.

Recent work examining driver error and automated transport systems (Stanton & Salmon, 2009), and driver error and driver distraction (Young & Salmon, 2012), suggests a mixed picture for the role of automation in reducing errors (and crashes) using automated systems. Stanton and

Salmon put classic error taxonomies (Norman, 1981; Rasmussen, 1987; Reason, 1990) in the context of driver error as a basis for suggesting a number of technological solutions to driver error. Automation has the potential to eliminate some types of errors, such as a collision warning system that alerts a driver to an adjacent car prior to a lane change. But, as with the Asiana Airlines crash, failure to understand system state may lead to a host of other problems. As Norman (1981) points out, forming the proper schema for a given situation is critical for successful action. As automation increases, activation of the correct schema may decline as attention moves from the roadway to devices inside the vehicle. (See Young & Salmon, 2012 for a more thorough review.) As Stanton and Young conclude, "As with pilot error, the challenge for the designers will be to introduce technologies that actually reduce driver error, without creating the possibility for new types of error." (p. 236).

5. CONCLUSION

George Miller (2003), in his review of the "cognitive revolution," dates the birth of the cognitive psychology to the early 1950s with the beginnings of rejection of behaviorism as the dominant mode of thought in psychology. In some ways, the battlefield for that revolution was laid out a decade earlier in problems of human factors exposed during the World War II. Failures of human performance such as radio and radar operators missing signals or highly trained pilots crashing airplanes led to recognition that a new understanding of processes inside the "black box" was needed for the growing discipline of cybernetics. From these problems rose work on attention, memory, perception, and problem solving with ties to information theory that helped form a framework for cognitive psychology and later, cognitive science.

In a sense, considering cognition in an attention economy is not a change from the historical roots that helped found the discipline of cognitive science. We are suggesting that new applied problems may lead to new insights into theoretical issues, and that better theoretical understanding may help the design of applications that better support our cognitive processes (e.g., Lane & Meissner, 2008). In this chapter, we propose that an environment that consistently and constantly encourages us to divide our attention between the task at hand and other tasks that our brain finds attractive, serves as a testing ground for assumptions about how our cognitive system works, or does not work, and points toward gaps in knowledge that we must fill. As we have shown (Section 1), classic concepts in cognitive science such as resource theory, automatic and controlled process, and IP models of cognition, when integrated, help us to understand why an attention economy may prove costly to cognitive function, as well as suggest something about "optimal cognition" or the circumstances under which our brain works best. The additional tools now available to us from cognitive neuroscience also reveal data that show we must consider the role of other concepts such as executive and default brain networks to more fully understand how the mind works.

The gaps in our knowledge are also of practical importance. It is clear from Section 2.1 that our devices outstrip our capacity to use them effectively. While this may be in small part an engineering/human factors problem (see Section 4.2), considering the impact of a divided attention on things that make us human, such as our ability to create and appreciate beauty (Section 2.2) and our ability to experience and regulate emotions (Section 2.3), suggests that we cannot reengineer ourselves into optimal capacity in an environment filled with technological distractions. What we need now is to understand how our mind works *best*, not just how it works.

5.1. Toward the Study of Optimal Cognition

One area of research that is open for development involves trying to define and understand the nature of "optimal cognition." What does cognitive function look like when it occurs in environments for which our brain was adapted, rather than those that we have manufactured, and what does this tell us about our mind and our mind's place in the current world? This work will require that cognitive science moves into more ecologically valid field environments that we have been reticent to explore because of concerns about issues of control, detection of subtle effects in behavioral data, or limitations of neuroscience techniques in field environments. But, such work may be critical for the long-term impact of psychology as a discipline. As economist David Laibson noted at the 2011 convention of the Association for Psychological Science, behavioral economists have long had great impact on public policy by borrowing liberally from psychology. One reason: economists do field research that makes their results appear more generalizable to the wider population. Understanding how our brain works best in natural environments is one way that psychology might more effectively demonstrate its impact and relevance to society.

REFERENCES

Atchley, P., Atwood, S., & Boulton, A. (2011). The choice to text and drive in younger drivers: Behavior may shape attitude. *Accident Analysis and Prevention, 43*, 134–142.

Atchley, P., & Chan, M. (2011). Potential benefits and costs of concurrent task engagement to maintain vigilance. *Human Factors, 53*(1), 3–12.

Atchley, P., Chan, M., & Gregersen, S. (2013). A strategically timed verbal task improves performance and neurophysiological alertness during fatiguing drives. *Human Factors*. in press. http://dx.doi.org/10.1177/0018720813500305.

Atchley, P., Dressel, J., Jones, T. C., Burson, R. A., & Marshall, D. (2011). Talking and driving: Applications of crossmodal action reveal a special role for spatial language. *Psychological Research, 75*(6), 525–534.

Atchley, P., Hadlock, C., & Lane, S. (2012). Stuck in the 70s: The role of social norms in distracted driving. *Accident Analysis & Prevention, 48*, 279–284.

Atchley, P., Hooker, E., Kroska, E., & Gilmour, A. (2012). Validation of an online orientation seminar to improve career and major preparedness. *Teaching of Psychology, 39*, 146–151.

Atchley, R. A., Keeney, M., & Burgess, C. (1999). Cerebral hemispheric mechanisms linking ambiguous word meaning retrieval and creativity. *Brain and Cognition, 40*(3), 479–499.

Atchley, R. A., Strayer, D. L., & Atchley, P. (2012). Creativity in the wild: Improving creative reasoning through immersion in natural settings. *PloS One, 7*(12), e51474.

Atchley, P., & Warden, A. C. (2012). The need of young adults to text *now*: Using delay discounting to assess informational choice. *Journal of Applied Research in Memory and Cognition, 1*, 229–234.

Atkinson, R. C., & Shiffrin, R. M. (1968). Human memory: A proposed system and its control processes. *The Psychology of Learning and Motivation, 2*, 89–195.

Ayduk, O., Mendoza-Denton, R., Mischel, W., Downey, G., Peake, P. K., & Rodriguez, M. (2000). Regulating the interpersonal self: Strategic self-regulation for coping with rejection sensitivity. *Journal of Personality and Social Psychology, 79*(5), 776–792.

Baumeister, R. F., Bratslavsky, E., Muraven, M., & Tice, D. M. (1998). Ego depletion: Is the active self a limited resource? *Journal of Personality and Social Psychology, 74*(5), 1252–1265.

Baumeister, R. F., Vohs, K. D., & Tice, D. M. (2007). The strength model of self-control. *Current Directions in Psychological Science, 16*(6), 351–355.

Bechara, A., Damasio, H., Tranel, D., & Damasio, A. R. (1997). Deciding advantageously before knowing the advantageous strategy. *Science, 275*(5304), 1293–1295.

Beilock, S. L., Carr, T. H., MacMahon, C., & Starkes, J. L. (2002). When paying attention becomes counterproductive: Impact of divided versus skill-focused attention on novice and experienced performance of sensorimotor skills. *Journal of Experimental Psychology. Applied, 8*(1), 6–16.

Belke, B., Leder, H., Strobach, T., & Carbon, C. C. (2010). Cognitive fluency: High-level processing dynamics in art appreciation. *Psychology of Aesthetics, Creativity and the Arts, 4*(4), 214–222.

Bilton, N. (September 1, 2013). Disruptions: More connected, yet more alone. *The New York Times*. Retrieved http://www.nytimes.com.

Brehm, J. W., & Cohen, A. R. (1962). *Explorations in cognitive dissonance*. New York: Wiley.

Broadbent, D. E. (1958). *The general nature of vigilance*. London: Pergammon Press.

Brown, G., Berry, E., Kapur, N., Hodges, S., Smyth, G., Watson, P., et al. (2011). SenseCam improves memory for recent events and quality of life in a patient with memory retrieval difficulties. *Memory, 19*(7), 713–722.

Buckner, R. L., Andrews-Hanna, J. R., & Schacter, D. L. (2008). The Brain's default network. *Annals of the New York Academy of Sciences, 1124*(1), 1–38.

Carver, C. S., & Scheier, M. F. (1981). The self-attention-induced feedback loop and social facilitation. *Journal of Experimental Social Psychology, 17*(6), 545–568.

Chen, S., & Chaiken, S. (1999). The heuristic-systematic model in its broader context. In S. Chaiken, & Y. Trope (Eds.), *Dual-process theories in social psychology* (pp. 73–96). New York: Guilford.

Cohen, R. M., Semple, W. E., Gross, M., Holcomb, H. H., Dowling, M. S., & Nordahl, T. E. (1988). Functional localization of sustained attention: Comparison to sensory stimulation in the absence of instruction. *Cognitive and Behavioral Neurology, 1*(1), 3–20.

Craik, F. I. M., & Byrd, M. (1982). Aging and cognitive deficits. In F. I. M. Craik, & S. Trehub (Eds.), *Aging and cognitive processes* (pp. 191–211). USA: Springer.

Davenport, T. H., & Beck, J. C. (2001). *The attention economy: Understanding the new currency of business*. Boston, MA: Harvard Business Press.

Davidson, R. J. (2003). Affective neuroscience and psychophysiology: Toward a synthesis. *Psychophysiology, 40*(5), 655–665.

Dingus, T. A., Klauer, S. G., Neale, V. L., Petersen, A., Lee, S. E., Sudweeks, J., et al. (2006). *The 100-car naturalistic driving study, phase II—Results of the 100-car field experiment DOT HS 810 593*. National Highway Traffic Safety Administration, USDOT.

Drews, F. A., Pasupathi, M., & Strayer, D. L. (2008). Passenger and cell phone conversations in simulated driving. *Journal of Experimental Psychology. Applied, 14*(4), 392–400.

Drouin, M., Kaiser, D. H., & Miller, D. A. (2012). Phantom vibrations among undergraduates: Prevalence and associated psychological characteristics. *Computers in Human Behavior, 28*(4), 1490–1496.

Dunbar, R. I. M. (1998). The social brain hypothesis. *Evolutionary Anthropology, 6*, 178–190.

Dunbar, R. I. M., Marriott, A., & Duncan, N. D. C. (1997). Human conversational behavior. *Human Nature, 8*(3), 231–246.

Eisenberger, N. I., Lieberman, M. D., & Williams, K. D. (2003). Does rejection hurt? An fMRI study of social exclusion. *Science, 302*(5643), 290–292.

Fassbender, C., Zhang, H., Buzy, W. M., Cortes, C. R., Mizuiri, D., Beckett, L., et al. (2009). A lack of default network suppression is linked to increased distractibility in ADHD. *Brain Research, 1273*, 114–128.

Festinger, L. (1962). *A theory of cognitive dissonance: Vol. 2.* Palo Alto, CA: Stanford University Press.

Fox, M. D., Snyder, A. Z., Vincent, J. L., Corbetta, M., Van Essen, D. C., & Raichle, M. E. (2005). The human brain is intrinsically organized into dynamic, anti-correlated functional networks. *Proceedings of the National Academy of Sciences, 102*(27), 9673–9678.

Frith, U. (2001). Mind blindness and the brain in autism. *Neuron, 32*(6), 969–979.

Gailliot, M. T., Baumeister, R. F., DeWall, C. N., Maner, J. K., Plant, E. A., Tice, D. M., et al. (2007). Self-control relies on glucose as a limited energy source: Willpower is more than a metaphor. *Journal of Personality and Social Psychology, 92*(2), 325–336.

Graesser, A. C., Jackson, G. T., & McDaniel, B. (2007). AutoTutor holds conversations with learners that are responsive to their cognitive and emotional states. *Educational Technology, 47*, 19–22.

Greicius, M. D., Krasnow, B., Reiss, A. L., & Menon, V. (2003). Functional connectivity in the resting brain: A network analysis of the default mode hypothesis. *Proceedings of the National Academy of Sciences, 100*(1), 253–258.

Gross, J. J., & Thompson, R. A. (2007). Emotion regulation: Conceptual foundations. In J. Gross (Ed.), *Handbook of emotion regulation* (pp. 3–24). New York: Guilford.

Hadwin, A. F., & Winne, P. H. (2012). Promoting learning skills in undergraduate students. In J. R. Kirby & M. J. Lawson (Eds.), *Enhancing the quality of learning: Dispositions, instruction and learning processes* (pp. 201–227). New York: Cambridge University Press.

Haigney, D., Taylor, R., & Westerman, S. (2000). Concurrent mobile (cellular) phone use and driving performance: Task demand characteristics and compensatory processes. *Transportation Research Part F: Traffic Psychology and Behaviour, 3*(3), 113–121.
Hasher, L., Stoltzfus, E. R., Zacks, R. T., & Rypma, B. (1991). Age and inhibition. *Journal of Experimental Psychology Learning Memory and Cognition, 17,* 163–169.
Haupt, A. (June 12, 2007). Good vibrations? Bad? None at all. *USA Today.* Retrieved from www.usatoday.com.
He, J., McCarley, J. S., & Kramer, A. F. (2014). Lane keeping under cognitive load performance changes and mechanisms. *Human Factors, 56,* 414–426.
Heatherton, T. F., & Wagner, D. D. (2011). Cognitive neuroscience of self-regulation failure. *Trends in Cognitive Sciences, 15,* 132–139.
Henkel, L. A. (2014). Point-and-shoot memories the influence of taking photos on memory. *Psychological Science, 25,* 396–402.
Heyman, G. M., & Gibb, S. P. (2006). Delay discounting in college cigarette chippers. *Behavioural Pharmacology, 17,* 669–679.
Hirst, W., Spelke, E. S., Reaves, C. C., Caharack, G., & Neisser, U. (1980). Dividing attention without alternation or automaticity. *Journal of Experimental Psychology. General, 109,* 98–117.
Hirstein, W., & Ramachandran, V. S. (1997). Capgras syndrome: A novel probe for understanding the neural representation of the identity and familiarity of persons. *Proceedings of the Royal Society of London. Series B: Biological Sciences, 264*(1380), 437–444.
Humphreys, M. S., & Revelle, W. (1984). Personality, motivation, and performance: A theory of the relationship between individual differences and information processing. *Psychological Review, 91*(2), 153–183.
Immordino-Yang, M. H., Christodoulou, J. A., & Singh, V. (2012). Rest is not idleness implications of the brain's default mode for human development and education. *Perspectives on Psychological Science, 7*(4), 352–364.
Jack, A. I., Dawson, A. J., & Norr, M. (2013). Seeing human: Distinct and overlapping neural signatures associated with two forms of dehumanization. *NeuroImage, 79,* 313–328.
Jacoby, L. L. (1991). A process dissociation framework: Separating automatic from intentional uses of memory. *Journal of Memory and Language, 30,* 513–541.
Job, V., Walton, G. M., Bernecker, K., & Dweck, C. S. (2013). Beliefs about willpower determine the impact of glucose on self-control. *Proceedings of the National Academy of Sciences of the United States of America, 110,* 14837–14842.
Just, M. A., Keller, T. A., & Cynkar, J. (2008). A decrease in brain activation associated with driving when listening to someone speak. *Brain Research, 1205,* 70–80.
Kahneman, D. (1973). *Attention and effort.* Englewood Cliffs, NJ: Prentice-Hall.
Kahneman, D. (2011). *Thinking, fast and slow.* New York: Macmillan.
Kahneman, D., & Frederick, S. (2002). Representativeness revisited: Attribute substitution in intuitive judgment. In T. Gilovich, D. Griffin, & D. Kahneman (Eds.), *Heuristics and biases: The psychology of intuitive judgment* (pp. 49–81). New York: Cambridge University Press.
Kahneman, D., & Henik, A. (1981). Perceptual organization and attention. In M. Kubovy, & J. Pomerantz (Eds.), *Perceptual organization* (pp. 181–211). Hillsdale, NJ: Lawrence Erlbaum Associates.
Kinomura, S., Larsson, J., Gulyás, B., & Roland, P. E. (1996). Activation by attention of the human reticular formation and thalamic intralaminar nuclei. *Science, 271,* 512–515.
Koller, D. (December 5, 2011). Death knell for the lecture: Technology as a passport for personalized education. *The New York Times.* Retrieved from http://www.nytimes.com.
Kolowich, S. (August 8, 2013). The MOOC revolution may not be as disruptive as imagined. *The Chronicle of Higher Education.* Retrieved from http://chronicle.com.

Lane, S. M., Mathews, R. C., Sallas, B., Prattini, B., & Sun, R. (2008). Facilitating interactions of model and experience-based processes: Implications for type and flexibility of representation. *Memory & Cognition, 36*, 157–169.

Lane, S. M., & Meissner, C. A. (2008). A 'middle road' approach to bridging the basic-applied divide in eyewitness identification research. *Applied Cognitive Psychology, 22*, 779–787.

Lang, P. J., Bradley, M. M., & Cuthbert, B. N. (2008). *International affective picture system (IAPS): Affective ratings of pictures and instruction manual: Technical Report A-8.* Gainesville, FL: University of Florida.

Langewiesche, W. (2009). *Fly by wire: The geese, the glide, the miracle on the Hudson.* New York: Macmillan.

LeDoux, J. E. (1996). *The emotional brain.* New York: Simon and Schuster.

Lenhart, A., Ling, R., Campbell, A., & Purcell, K. (2010). *Teens and mobile phones.* Pew Internet & American Life Project.http://www.pewinternet.org/Reports/2010/Teens-and-Mobile-Phones.aspx.

Lewin, J. S., Friedman, L., Wu, D., Miller, D. A., Thompson, L. A., Klein, S. K., et al. (1996). Cortical localization of human sustained attention: detection with functional MR using a visual vigilance paradigm. *Journal of Computer Assisted Tomography, 20*, 695–701.

Logan, G. D. (1988). Toward an instance theory of automatization. *Psychological Review, 95*(4), 492–527.

Logan, G. D., & Gordon, R. D. (2001). Executive control of visual attention in dual-task situations. *Psychological Review, 108*, 393–434.

Mann, T., & Ward, A. (2004). To eat or not to eat: Implications of the attentional myopia model for restrained eaters. *Journal of Abnormal Psychology, 113*, 90–98.

Mann, T., & Ward, A. (2007). Attention, self-control, and health behaviors. *Current Directions in Psychological Science, 16*(5), 280–283.

Mason, M. F., Norton, M. I., Van Horn, J. D., Wegner, D. M., Grafton, S. T., & Macrae, C. N. (2007). Wandering minds: The default network and stimulus-independent thought. *Science, 315*(5810), 393–395.

Massaro, D. W., & Cowan, N. (1993). Information processing models: Microscopes of the mind. *Annual Review of Psychology, 44*, 383–425.

Mauss, I. B., Levenson, R. W., McCarter, L., Wilhelm, F. H., & Gross, J. J. (2005). The tie that binds? Coherence among emotion experience, behavior, and physiology. *Emotion, 5*, 175–190.

McMaster, C., & Lee, C. (1991). Cognitive dissonance in tobacco smokers. *Addictive Behaviors, 16*(5), 349–353.

Medeiros-Ward, N., Cooper, J., & Strayer, D. (2013). Hierarchical control and driving. *Journal of Experimental Psychology: General*, in press. http://dx.doi.org/10.1037/a0035097.

Miller, G. A. (2003). The cognitive revolution: A historical perspective. *Trends in Cognitive Sciences, 7*(3), 141–144.

Mokdad, A. H., Marks, J. S., Stroup, D. F., & Gerberding, J. L. (2004). Actual causes of death in the United States, 2000. *JAMA, 291*(10), 1238–1245.

Nasar, J. L., & Troyer, D. (2013). Pedestrian injuries due to mobile phone use in public places. *Accident Analysis & Prevention, 57*, 91–95.

National Highway Transportation Safety Administration (2011). *Traffic safety facts 2010: A compilation of motor vehicle crashes data from the fatality analysis reporting system and the general estimates system* (Report No. DOT-HS811-659). Washington DC: USDOT, NHTSA. http://www-nrd.nhtsa.dot.gov/Pubs/811659.pdf (Retrieved 03.03.12).

National Safety Council Estimates that At Least 1.6 Million Crashes Each Year Involve Drivers Using Cell Phones and Texting, (2010). http://www.nsc.org/Pages/NSCestimates16millioncrashescausedbydriversusingcellphonesandtexting.aspx (Retrieved 11.11.13).

Naveh-Benjamin, M., Guez, J., Kilb, A., & Reedy, S. (2004). The associative memory deficit of older adults: Further support using face-name associations. *Psychology and Aging, 19*(3), 541–546.
Navon, D. (1984). Resources—A theoretical soup stone? *Psychological Review, 91*(2), 216–234.
Navon, D., & Gopher, D. (1979). On the economy of the human-processing system. *Psychological Review, 86*(3), 214–255.
Navon, D., & Miller, J. (2002). Queuing or sharing? A critical evaluation of the single bottleneck notion. *Cognitive Psychology, 44*(3), 193–251.
Norman, D. A. (1981). Categorization of action slips. *Psychological Review, 88*(1), 1–15.
Norman, D. A., & Bobrow, D. G. (1975). On data-limited and resource-limited processes. *Cognitive Psychology, 7*(1), 44–64.
NTSB focuses on pilots' communication, autopilot, in Asiana briefing. (July 10, 2013). *Puget Sound Business Journal*, (Retrieved 27.10.13).
Nunes, L., & Recarte, M. A. (2002). Cognitive demands of hands-free-phone conversation while driving. *Transportation Research Part F: Traffic Psychology and Behaviour, 5*(2), 133–144.
Ohmura, Y., Takahashi, T., & Kitamura, N. (2005). Discounting delayed and probabilistic monetary gains and losses by smokers of cigarettes. *Psychopharmacology, 182*(4), 508–515.
Palmer, S. E., & Kimchi, R. (1986). The information processing approach to cognition. In T. J. Knapp, & L. C. Robertson (Eds.), *Approaches to cognition: Contrasts and controversies* (pp. 37–77). Hillsdale, NJ: Erlbaum.
Pardo, J. V., Fox, P. T., & Raichle, M. E. (1991). Localization of a human system for sustained attention by positron emission tomography. *Nature, 349*(6304), 61–64.
Pashler, H. (1994). Dual-task interference in simple tasks: data and theory. *Psychological Bulletin, 116*(2), 220–244.
Pashler, H. (1998). *The psychology of attention*. Cambridge, MA: MIT Press.
Perkins-Ceccato, N., Passmore, S. R., & Lee, T. D. (2003). Effects of focus of attention depend on golfers' skill. *Journal of Sports Sciences, 21*(8), 593–600.
Pessoa, L. (2010). Emotion and cognition and the amygdala: From "what is it?" to "what's to be done?". *Neuropsychologia, 48*(12), 3416–3429.
Pessoa, L., McKenna, M., Gutierrez, E., & Ungerleider, L. G. (2002). Neural processing of emotional faces requires attention. *Proceedings of the National Academy of Sciences, 99*(17), 11458–11463.
Petty, R. E., & Wegener, D. T. (1999). The elaboration likelihood model: Current status and controversies. In S. Chaiken, & Y. Trope (Eds.), *Dual process theories in social psychology* (pp. 41–72). New York, NY: Guilford Press.
Ploran, E. J., Nelson, S. M., Velanova, K., Donaldson, D. I., Petersen, S. E., & Wheeler, M. E. (2007). Evidence accumulation and the moment of recognition: Dissociating perceptual recognition processes using fMRI. *The Journal of Neuroscience, 27*(44), 11912–11924.
Posner, M. I., & Snyder, C. R. R. (1975). Facilitation and inhibition in the processing of signals. *Attention and Performance, V*, 669–682.
Rachlin, H., Raineri, A., & Cross, D. (1991). Subjective probability and delay. *Journal of the Experimental Analysis of Behavior, 55*(2), 233–244.
Rasmussen, J. (1987). *Information processing and human-machine interaction. An approach to cognitive engineering*. North-Holland: Amsterdam.
Reason, J. (1990). *Human error*. New York, NY: Cambridge University Press.
Reber, A. S. (1969). Transfer of syntactic structure in synthetic languages. *Journal of Experimental Psychology, 81*(1), 115–119.
Reber, R., Schwarz, N., & Winkielman, P. (2004). Processing fluency and aesthetic pleasure: Is beauty in the perceiver's processing experience? *Personality and Social Psychology Review, 8*(4), 364–382.

Recarte, M. A., & Nunes, L. M. (2003). Mental workload while driving: Effects on visual search, discrimination, and decision making. *Journal of Experimental Psychology. Applied*, *9*(2), 119–137.

Rogers, W. A., & Fisk, A. D. (2006). Cognitive support for elders through technology. *Generations*, *30*(2), 38–43.

Rothberg, M. B., Arora, A., Hermann, J., Kleppel, R., Marie, P. S., & Visintainer, P. (2010). Phantom vibration syndrome among medical staff: A cross sectional survey. *British Medical Journal*, *341*, 1292–1293.

Salthouse, T. A. (1996). The processing-speed theory of adult age differences in cognition. *Psychological Review*, *103*(3), 403–428.

Sarter, N. B., & Woods, D. D. (1995). How in the world did we ever get into that mode? Mode error and awareness in supervisory control. *Human Factors*, *37*(1), 5–19.

Savage, S. W., Potter, D. D., & Tatler, B. W. (2013). Does preoccupation impair hazard perception? A simultaneous EEG and eye-tracking study. *Transportation Research Part F: Traffic Psychology and Behaviour*, *17*, 52–62.

Schacter, D. L. (1997). Memory distortion: History and current status. In D. L. Schacter, J. T. Coyle, G. D. Fishbach, M. M. Mesulam, & L. E. Sullivan (Eds.), *Memory distortion: How minds, brains, and societies reconstruct the past* (pp. 1–43). Cambridge, MA: Harvard University Press.

Schneider, W., & Shiffrin, R. M. (1977). Controlled and automatic human information processing: I. Detection, search, and attention. *Psychological Review*, *84*(1), 1–66.

Schweizer, T. A., Kan, K., Hung, Y., Tam, F., Naglie, G., & Graham, S. J. (2013). Brain activity during driving with distraction: An immersive fMRI study. *Frontiers in Human Neuroscience*, *7*, 1–11.

Shiv, B., & Fedorikhin, A. (2002). Spontaneous versus controlled influences of stimulus-based affect on choice behavior. *Organizational Behavior and Human Decision Processes*, *87*(2), 342–370.

Shoda, Y., Mischel, W., & Peake, P. K. (1990). Predicting adolescent cognitive and self-regulatory competencies from preschool delay of gratification: Identifying diagnostic conditions. *Developmental Psychology*, *26*(6), 978–986.

Shomstein, S., & Yantis, S. (2006). Parietal cortex mediates voluntary control of spatial and nonspatial auditory attention. *The Journal of Neuroscience*, *26*(2), 435–439.

Simon, H. A. (1971). Designing organizations for an information-rich world. In M. Greenberger (Ed.), *Computers, communications, and the public interest* (pp. 37–72). Baltimore, MD: John's Hopkins University Press.

Simons, D. J., & Rensink, R. A. (2005). Change blindness: Past, present, and future. *Trends in Cognitive Sciences*, *9*(1), 16–20.

Stanovich, K. E., & West, R. F. (2000). Individual differences in reasoning: Implications for the rationality debate? *Behavioral and Brain Sciences*, *23*(5), 645–665.

Stanton, N. A., & Salmon, P. M. (2009). Human error taxonomies applied to driving: A generic driver error taxonomy and its implications for intelligent transport systems. *Safety Science*, *47*(2), 227–237.

Sternberg, S. (1969). The discovery of processing stages: Extensions of Donders' method. *Acta Psychologica*, *30*, 276–315.

Storbeck, J., & Clore, G. L. (2007). On the interdependence of cognition and emotion. *Cognition and Emotion*, *21*(6), 1212–1237.

Strayer, D. L., & Drews, F. A. (2007). Cell-phone-induced driver distraction. *Current Directions in Psychological Science*, *16*(3), 128–131.

Suchman, E. A. (1939). Radio listening and automobiles. *Journal of Applied Psychology*, *23*(1), 148–157.

Takeuchi, H., Taki, Y., Hashizume, H., Sassa, Y., Nagase, T., Nouchi, R., et al. (2011). Failing to deactivate: The association between brain activity during a working memory task and creativity. *NeuroImage, 55*(2), 681–687.

Tamir, D. I., & Mitchell, J. P. (2012). Disclosing information about the self is intrinsically rewarding. *Proceedings of the National Academy of Sciences, 109*(21), 8038–8043.

Telford, C. W. (1931). The refractory phase of voluntary and associative responses. *Journal of Experimental Psychology, 14*(1), 1–36.

Van Dillen, L. F., Papies, E., & Hoffman, W. (2013). Turning a blind eye to temptation: How task load can facilitate self-regulation. *Journal of Personality and Social Psychology, 104*, 427–443.

Visscher, P. K. (2007). Group decision making in nest-site selection among social insects. *Annual Review of Entomology, 52*, 255–275.

Welford, A. T. (1952). The psychological refractory period and the timing of high speed performance—A review and a theory. *British Journal of Psychology: General Section, 43*(1), 2–19.

White, H. A., & Shah, P. (2006). Uninhibited imaginations: Creativity in adults with attention-deficit/hyperactivity disorder. *Personality and Individual Differences, 40*(6), 1121–1131.

White, H. A., & Shah, P. (2011). Creative style and achievement in adults with attention-deficit/hyperactivity disorder. *Personality and Individual Differences, 50*(5), 673–677.

Wickens, C. D. (1984). Processing resources in attention. In R. Parasuraman, & D. R. Davies (Eds.), *Varieties of attention* (pp. 63–102). Orlando, FL: Academic Press.

Wickens, C. D., & Hollands, J. G. (2000). Complex systems, process control, and automation. In C. D. Wickens, & J. G. Hollands (Eds.), *Engineering psychology and human performance* (3rd ed., pp. 538–550). Upper Saddle River, NJ: Prentice Hall.

Winne, P. H., & Nesbitt, J. C. (2009). Supporting self-regulated learning with cognitive tools. In D. J. Hacker, J. Dunlosky, & A. C. Graesser (Eds.), *Handbook of metacognition in education* (pp. 259–277). New York: Taylor & Francis.

Young, K. L., & Salmon, P. M. (2012). Examining the relationship between driver distraction and driving errors: A discussion of theory, studies and methods. *Safety Science, 50*(2), 165–174.

Zhu, F., Bosch, M., Woo, I., Kim, S., Boushey, C. J., Ebert, D. S., et al. (2010). The use of mobile devices in aiding dietary assessment and evaluation. *IEEE Journal of Selected Topics in Signal Processing, 4*, 756–766.

Zimmerman, B. J. (1998). Academic studying and development of personal skill: A self-regulatory perspective. *Educational Psychologist, 33*, 73–86.

CHAPTER FIVE

Memory Recruitment: A Backward Idea About Masked Priming

Glen E. Bodner[*,1], **Michael E.J. Masson**[†]

[*]Department of Psychology, University of Calgary, Calgary, Alberta, Canada
[†]Department of Psychology, University of Victoria, Victoria, British Columbia, Canada
[1]Corresponding author: e-mail address: bodner@ucalgary.ca

Contents

1. Masked Priming — 180
   1.1 One Paradigm — 181
   1.2 Two Ironies — 181
2. Three Accounts of Masked Priming — 182
   2.1 Prospective Accounts — 182
   2.2 Memory-Recruitment Account — 183
   2.3 Bayesian Reader Account — 184
3. Four Masked Priming Phenomena — 185
   3.1 Masked Nonword Priming (with an Aside on Frequency Attenuation) — 185
   3.2 Prime-Proportion Effects on Masked Priming — 197
   3.3 Duration of Masked Priming — 203
4. The Status of the Memory-Recruitment Account — 205
   4.1 Memory Recruitment Redux/Denouement — 205
   4.2 Other Challenges to Memory Recruitment — 206
5. Moving Accounts of Masked Priming Forward — 208
References — 209

Abstract

Accounts of priming typically assume that primes activate existing representations, thus *prospectively* altering target processing. In contrast, Bodner and Masson (1997) described a memory-recruitment account of priming in which the processing operations applied to primes—even masked primes—are encoded into a new memory instance that can be *retrospectively* recruited to contribute to target processing if the context and task conditions support recruitment. Our chapter updates three lines of research we have pursued since our last update (Masson & Bodner, 2003) in attempting to contrast various priming accounts. The first line examines when and why nonwords, which do not have existing representations, show masked priming. The second line examines when and why masked priming is sensitive to prime-proportion manipulations. The third line examines whether masked priming effects can be lasting. After summarizing some of the successes and failures of our backward account, we acknowledge that we failed to provide unequivocal evidence for it. We end with some suggestions for moving accounts of masked priming forward.

1. MASKED PRIMING

Pioneers in the study of unconscious cognition had their work cut out for them (e.g., Forster & Davis, 1984; Greenwald, 1992; Kunst-Wilson & Zajonc, 1980; Marcel, 1983). Given Freud's famously controversial take on the unconscious, it was necessary to set the bar high for empirical evidence of its existence (e.g., Holender, 1986). The realm of subliminal/unconscious/masked priming effects, the topic of our chapter, also has controversial roots. In 1957, market researcher James Vicary infamously claimed that tachistoscopic presentations of "eat popcorn" and "drink Coca Cola" during screenings of the movie *Picnic* increased sales of both products, but his claims were bogus (Pratkanis, 1992). Despite that initial stumble, evidence of unconscious priming is now firmly established (e.g., Dehaene et al., 1998), though specific effects are still occasionally attributed to conscious perception or awareness (e.g., Desender, Van Lierde, & Van den Bussche, 2013). Coming full circle, Vicary's claim has recently been substantiated: Subliminal primes can affect drink brand choice if participants are thirsty enough (Karremans, Stroebe, & Claus, 2006). Current debates now center on the basis and limits of unconscious processes, and on how they interface with conscious processes.

In 1997, we made our own controversial claims about unconscious processes, specifically about the basis and limits of masked priming effects (see Section 2.2). We then attempted to push masked priming past several of its purported limits in the hope of substantiating our somewhat salacious claim about its basis. A decade ago, we reviewed the state of the evidence for our account in an edited book on the state of the art of masked priming (Kinoshita & Lupker, 2003). Masson and Bodner's (2003) chapter showcased our optimism about the viability of a retrospective memory-recruitment based account of masked priming. This chapter provides a less sanguine bookend to that auspicious (audacious) chapter. We review and update the lines of evidence that formed the basis of our previous chapter and conclude that we may have pushed the limits of our account beyond a breaking point. At best, we failed to provide unequivocal evidence for it, and in the meantime, others have built up a considerable pile of evidence that challenges it. At worst, we were just plain wrong. Fortunately, Freud made available to us a whole taxonomy of putative unconscious defense mechanisms, some of which allow us to suggest or at least hope that the data generated by ourselves and by others in the course of evaluating our account have provided some insights about masked priming that will usefully inform other accounts of unconscious processes.

1.1. One Paradigm

Forster and Davis (1984) developed the masked priming paradigm for the sole purpose of studying the processes involved in visual word recognition. We, like many other researchers, have relied on this one now-classic paradigm in our studies. In our implementation, three stimulus events are presented in succession in the same location on a computer screen: a pattern mask is shown for 495 ms (e.g., &&&&&), it is immediately replaced by a lowercase letter-string prime for 45 or 60 ms (e.g., chair), which in turn is immediately replaced by an uppercase letter-string target to which the participant responds (e.g., CHAIR). Because of the masking and/or brief presentation, most participants are unaware of the primes, and we have verified the effectiveness of our masking procedures using both subjective awareness reports and objective prime-judgment tasks (e.g., Bodner & Dypvik, 2005).

Priming effects are myriad and varied. They occur whenever responses to targets are systematically and differentially affected by two or more types of prime in measures of reaction time and/or error rate. Varying the types of masked primes that are compared (e.g., repetition or semantic vs. unrelated; response congruent vs. response incongruent), the prime-target stimulus onset asynchrony (SOA), and the target task (e.g., binary judgments, most often word/nonword "lexical" decisions; stimulus identification tasks, most often naming) provides researchers with a potentially powerful tool for mapping mental processes and structures (e.g., Forster, Mohan, & Hector, 2003).

1.2. Two Ironies

As will become clear, there are two overarching ironies to our work using this paradigm. The first irony is that the masked priming paradigm was developed specifically to eliminate the potential contributions of memory processes to priming effects, yet we have used it specifically to study the potential contributions of memory processes to priming effects. The second irony is that we have used the masked priming paradigm to argue that masked priming effects might be a misnomer: they might not reflect a prospective "priming" process at all. We warned you that our claims would be controversial. Of course, making such claims is easy. Substantiating them is the tough row to hoe.

2. THREE ACCOUNTS OF MASKED PRIMING

Accounts of masked priming are available in three main flavors. Prospective accounts attribute masked priming to the prime event "priming" existing abstract representations. In contrast, our memory-recruitment account attributes masked priming to a retrospective memory-recruitment process that is initiated once the target is presented. And the newest kid on the block, the Bayesian Reader account, attributes masked priming to the perceptual system being "tricked into treating the prime and the target as a single object" (Norris & Kinoshita, 2008, p. 434; see Masson & Isaak, 1999, for a similar suggestion). Section 2 provides a brief sketch of each account, but we doodle much more for our account because it is the only account "on trial" in this chapter. Indeed, Section 3 exclusively reviews the four bodies of masked priming evidence we have used to evaluate our account. Because of this selective emphasis, we have tried to avoid championing or maligning the other two accounts except to mention where they fit or do not fit with these sets of data.

2.1. Prospective Accounts

The theory-laden term "priming" implies that the prime creates some forward-acting processing momentum that works to facilitate target processing. In the lexical-entry opening account (Forster & Davis, 1984), a masked word prime provides an automatic head start, equivalent to the prime-target SOA, in opening the word's entry in the mental lexicon (e.g., Forster, 1999). Priming will occur if the target appears during the brief window of time that its entry is open, because its contents can be accessed faster than on unrelated prime trials where there was no head start.

Prospective accounts are by no means limited to lexical or even localist representations. Primes might activate abstract orthographic, phonological, or semantic representations (e.g., Bowers, 2003), sublexical or letter level representations (e.g., Davis, Kim, & Forster, 2008), and/or word-level representations other than the prime via a spreading activation process (e.g., Neely, 1977) or in a competitive network model (e.g., Davis, 2003). Priming effects can also be conceptualized as resulting from the activation of distributed representations in a connectionist network (e.g., Masson, 1995).

Finally, in paradigms measuring response priming (i.e., facilitation when prime and target bias the same binary response rather than opposite responses), priming may reflect preactivation of motor-response areas (e.g., Dehaene et al., 1998). In common, these prospective accounts attribute priming to the activation of existing representations.

2.2. Memory-Recruitment Account

The chief purpose of masking primes was to eliminate the influence of memory-based processes, thus allowing domain-specific word-recognition (particularly, *lexical*) processes to be isolated. The memory-recruitment account essentially argues that this goal failed, and posits that a memory-based unified account of both masked and long-term priming effects may be viable (Bodner & Masson, 1997; Masson & Bodner, 2003). As reviewed in Masson and Bodner (2003), the ingredients for our account were sourced primarily from four inspirations. First, Forster and Davis (1984) raised (and then attempted to rule out) the possibility that memory contributes to masked priming. Second, we were inspired by instance-based accounts of cognition, particularly Kolers' claims that processing operations are chronically encoded (cf. temporary activation of existing representations), and that priming effects reflect skill transfer that occurs when prime and target require overlapping processing operations (e.g., Kolers & Roediger, 1984). The facts that we can remember things and that our responses can be influenced by prior experiences are pretty good evidence that our past experiences were encoded in some manner. And the fact that we can read a sentence faster a full year later if it is presented in the same format is good evidence that we can recruit specific instances of prior processing (Kolers, 1976; Logan, 1988). Third, demonstrations of a subliminal mere-exposure effect with novel stimuli suggest that priming does not always reflect the activation of existing representations (e.g., Kunst-Wilson & Zajonc, 1980; Whittlesea & Price, 2001).

Fourth, we essentially just borrowed the retrieval account of priming put forward by Whittlesea and Jacoby (1990) and applied it to masked priming. Beginning with their startling punchline, Whittlesea and Jacoby found faster naming responses to a target (e.g., GREEN) when it was preceded by the briefly presented prime pair GREEN-pLaNt rather than the pair GREEN-PLANT (and in comparison to a host of other control conditions). Mixed-case degradation of the second prime was argued to increase recruitment of the processing performed on the first prime, which in turn made that processing more available to facilitate repetition priming of the target. In contrast, by prospective accounts, the influence of the first prime cannot be conditional on the second prime being degraded, so there is no basis to predict larger priming in the degraded condition. We maintain that this is a nifty and neglected effect.

Putting these ingredients together, the memory-recruitment account proposes that when a masked prime is presented, the cognitive system begins to process it, likely by applying the same task-specific processing operations to the masked prime that will be applied to the visible target. But, unlike in activation accounts, the processing operations applied to the prime are encoded in a new instance, albeit one that is too impoverished to be consciously accessed. We originally referred to this encoding as evincing a "nonlexical" basis for priming (Bodner & Masson, 1997), but we highlighted the memory connection by calling it an "episodic resource" (Bodner & Masson, 2001). We quickly dropped the "episodic" term, given that participants cannot consciously recollect the primes. A point we did not make in our past descriptions of the account is that the prime will also cue prior processing records from similar stimuli or situations (i.e., prior instances), which will be applied toward the processing of the prime.

When the target is presented, the cognitive system will shift from processing the prime to processing the target (we consider potential variants to this shift in Section 4). The target's presentation will again cue prior processing records from similar stimuli or situations, and the most salient of these is the processing that was applied to the prime mere milliseconds ago. Thus, the cognitive system will recruit the prime processing and will apply it in aid of processing the target. When this processing overlaps, facilitation of target responses should result. When this processing does not overlap, interference can occur. Importantly, if masked priming is a memory effect, then it follows that it should be modulated by the sort of task and context effects that modulate other memory effects. These claims set the stage for the various tricks we tried to get masked primes to perform in Section 3. In sum, we have advocated a simple sort of "reverse psychology" of the traditional prospective view for explaining masked priming.

2.3. Bayesian Reader Account

Norris and Kinoshita (2008) have given us a third way to think about masked priming, based on Bayesian principles of decision making. In brief, the Bayesian Reader account claims that the cognitive system does not treat the prime as a separate event from the target (see also the ROUSE model of Huber, Shiffrin, Lyle, & Quach, 2002). Instead, the available perceptual evidence based on a conflation of prime and target processing is combined with information about the target's likelihood based on prior experiences or "priors" to reach an optimal decision about the target's class or identity in the task at hand. The algorithm for this process can be implemented in a formal Bayesian Reader model (Norris, 2006) that can be used to run simulations of priming studies. This is a well-specified account, except the model is agnostic regarding whether the "priors" are local or distributed abstract representations, or memory-based instances. For this reason, and because the bulk of our studies were designed to pit the memory-recruitment account against prospective accounts, we do not dwell on this important, emerging account (see Kinoshita & Norris, 2012, for a recent overview).

3. FOUR MASKED PRIMING PHENOMENA

Masson and Bodner (2003) evaluated the memory-recruitment account by attempting to "deconstruct" three then-prevalent dissociations between masked and "unmasked" priming, and by highlighting a novel fourth parallel between these two types of priming. The key dissociations were that masked priming effects, in contrast to unmasked priming effects, were (1) confined to words, (2) equal for low- and high-frequency words, and (3) highly ephemeral. The novel parallel was our finding that both masked and unmasked priming effects can be sensitive to prime-proportion manipulations. This section updates the status of these four masked priming phenomena, drawing heavily on our own work and some of the challenges it has faced.

3.1. Masked Nonword Priming (with an Aside on Frequency Attenuation)

On the surface, the question of whether nonwords show masked repetition priming would seem to have a strong potential for cleaving apart lexical, memory recruitment, and Bayesian accounts of masked priming. Novel nonwords have not been experienced before, thus they have no existing lexical entry to be primed, unlike for words. Thus, on the lexical account, nonwords should not show masked priming (e.g., Forster & Davis, 1984). By the memory-recruitment account, on the other hand, the processing applied to a nonword prime is encoded, and when this processing overlaps with the processing required of the target, target processing should be facilitated—so nonwords *should* show masked priming. And, by the Bayesian Reader account, nonwords should not show priming in the standard paradigm (cf. the Norris & Kinoshita, 2008, referent-based same-different judgment paradigm) because again, a masked prime has no nonword "prior" to update.

Before Bodner and Masson (1997), there were only a few reports of reliable masked nonword priming (Forster, 1985; Sereno, 1991), a situation that supported the validity of the masked priming paradigm as a tool for isolating lexical processes (see Forster, 1998; Forster et al., 2003). Indeed, when Bodner set out to complete the series of lexical-decision task experiments that would comprise Bodner and Masson (1997) as part of a first graduate research course with Masson, we did not anticipate that we would find nonword priming.

3.1.1 An Aside on Frequency Attenuation

To digress, our original goal was to provide new tests of whether the *frequency-attenuation effect* (i.e., greater priming for low- than for high-frequency words) could be found with masked primes, comparable to what had been found with unmasked primes. Forster and Davis (1984) did not find this frequency by priming interaction using their new paradigm, which they took as key support for their lexical-entry opening account. Based on the memory-recruitment idea, we reasoned that the processing of the prime event might be more distinct in memory for low- than for high-frequency words—but participants might need to be encouraged to rely heavily on the prime processing (as opposed to processing records from other prior experiences with the items) to reveal this interaction (after Whittlesea & Jacoby, 1990).

To this end, we made the lexical-decision task more difficult, either by using mIxEd-cAsE targets (e.g., pErD), or by using uppercase pseudohomophone nonwords (e.g., BRANE, which sounds like BRAIN but must be judged a nonword in the lexical-decision task). Both manipulations failed to produce the expected frequency by priming interaction. However, subsequent studies have obtained it either by using a stronger frequency manipulation (Bodner & Masson, 2001) or by ensuring the low-frequency words are known to participants (Kinoshita, 2006; Norris & Kinoshita, 2008). The latter results are thus consistent with the memory-recruitment account (by aligning masked and long-term priming results) and, to our knowledge, have yet to be reconciled with the lexical account or discussed in the context of the Bayesian Reader account.

3.1.2 Bodner and Masson (1997)

Turning back to our reminiscence, we expected a frequency by priming interaction but did not find it, and we did not expect nonword priming but we found it (see Fig. 5.1). Specifically, we replicated the absence of nonword priming with regular, pronounceable uppercase (hereafter, *standard*) nonwords (−7 ms; Experiment 1), but mixed-case nonwords showed repetition priming (93 ms; Experiment 2A), as did pseudohomophone nonwords (38 ms; Experiment 3). We then engaged in some of our patented *post hoc* head scratching. Why did we find nonword priming, but only in the latter two cases?

Our explanation for this pattern appealed to a trade-off between two potential influences of repetition primes on target processing in the lexical-decision task, which we refer to here as *target facilitation* versus a *fluency bias*. On the target facilitation side, we assume that the overlap in the processing of the prime and the target on repetition trials should work to facilitate lexical decisions. We further assume the extent to which participants rely on this overlap and achieve this facilitation will depend on task difficulty, the prime's utility, etc. On the fluency bias side, we assume that more fluency is experienced when processing word targets than nonword targets, and that differences in fluency are used to help make lexical

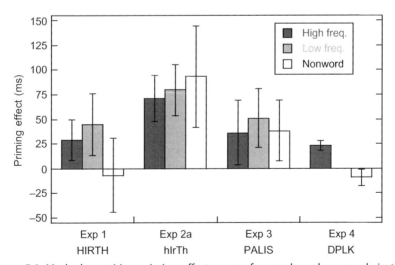

Figure 5.1 Masked repetition priming effect means for words and nonwords in the lexical-decision task (with sample nonword targets) in Bodner and Masson (1997). Bars show the 95% confidence interval for each priming effect. *Adapted from figure 1 of Bodner and Masson (1997).*

decisions. We further assume that repetition priming increases target processing fluency. Therefore, repetition priming of a nonword target will normally make it seem more like a word, which should work against making a nonword response (Feustel, Shiffrin, & Salasoo, 1983).

With standard nonwords, repetition primes facilitate target processing while also creating a "word" response bias that works against making a correct nonword response in the lexical-decision task. We conjecture that these two influences roughly cancel each other out under usual circumstances: the more one relies on the prime, the greater the fluency bias against making a correct response. In contrast, making targets harder to process by using mixed-case targets should not only *increase* recruitment of the processing applied to the prime event (Whittlesea & Jacoby, 1990), thus increasing target facilitation, but also *decrease* the overall experience of fluency when processing these unfamiliar targets and should reduce participants' reliance on fluency as an indicator of lexical status. And with pseudohomophone nonwords, the lexical-decision task is made more difficult because phonology cannot be used to distinguish word and nonword targets. Prime recruitment and thus target facilitation is again increased, tipping the balance between facilitation and fluency bias in favor of the former.

Having produced null and positive nonword priming and a *post hoc* account of each, we created an *a priori* test of our account by trying to engineer a negative nonword priming effect. To this end, Bodner and Masson (1997) tested only high-frequency words (e.g., DOOR) and illegal consonant string nonwords (e.g., TWLT). Lexical decisions could now be based on superficial analysis of orthographic regularity, which should *increase* reliance on the fluency bias, and in turn this should interfere with correct responding on repetition-primed nonword trials. Consistent with our trade-off account, we obtained a negative nonword priming effect (−9 ms; Experiment 4).

Masson and Isaak (1999) further tested the memory-recruitment account by using the naming task where a fluency bias should be less likely to operate. Here, participants must say each target aloud, so there is no binary judgment that can be influenced one way or the other by an experience of processing fluency. As a result, priming should be driven by target facilitation alone. Not only did Masson and Isaak find robust nonword priming in this task, but also it was similar in magnitude to the priming obtained for word targets. However, Forster (1998) suggested that masked priming effects in the naming task occur at an articulatory level (i.e., participants try to pronounce the primes), hence nonwords prime and prime just as well as words. Because of this concern, we do not discuss at length masked priming effects from the naming task in our chapter.

As a graduate student, Bodner naïvely assumed that this set of nonword priming effects effectively resolved the debate about whether masked priming reflects a prospective or retrospective process. But it turned out that no one else was quite as taken with them. For years, these findings were more often than not treated as anomalous exceptions to the general rule that nonwords do not show masked priming. Indeed, there were so many "but see" and "cf." references to our nonword findings that the first author refers to his name in this research area as "Buttsy Bodner". Detailed criticisms of these effects and/or of our interpretations have also been offered (Forster, 1998; Forster et al., 2003, Kinoshita & Norris, 2011; Norris & Kinoshita, 2008, 2010) and debated (Bowers, 2010; Masson & Bodner, 2003). Rather than rehashing these debates here, Section 3.1.3 examines the one nonword priming result that generated the most surprise and subsequent study, namely the mixed-case effect. The remaining bits of Section 3 then provide updates on recent investigations of nonword priming.

3.1.3 Explaining (Away) Mixed-Case Nonword Priming

One reason Forster (1998) called Bodner and Masson's (1997) mixed-case nonword priming effect "perplexing" was its magnitude. The effect was numerically greater for nonwords than for words. The mixed-case nonword priming effect has since been replicated by Bodner and Masson (2001, Experiment 2B, 15 ms) and Kinoshita and Norris (2011, Experiment 1, 27 ms, but not in Experiment 2, 11 ms), but in each case, its magnitude has been much more modest. Kinoshita and Norris (2011) noted that Bodner and Masson's (1997) participants' lexical decisions were very slow, and suggested that this may have contributed to our large mixed-case nonword priming effect. We concur.

In addition, Kinoshita and Norris (2011) offered two alternative explanations for mixed-case nonword priming. The first is that the effect might be driven by the physical continuity between lowercase letters in a repetition prime and its mixed-case target (e.g., word-wOrD). In a control experiment, Bodner and Masson (1997, Experiment 2B) found that replacing the nonoverlapping letters in each repetition prime with new letters to make a functionally unrelated prime (e.g., wirk-wOrD) eliminated priming for both words and nonwords. Thus, we concluded that physical continuity across the lowercase letters in repetition primes and targets was not the locus of the effect. However, Kinoshita and Norris (2011) took issue with this control experiment, suggesting that physical continuity might operate only when all the letters in repetition primes and targets are the same (as in Bodner & Masson, 1997, Experiment 2A). To address this issue, Kinoshita and Norris (2011, Experiments 1 and 2) manipulated whether primes were presented in the same font and size (allowing physical continuity for lowercase letters) or a different font and size (eliminating physical continuity for all letters) relative to their mixed-case targets. They found no evidence of reduced priming in the different font/size condition in either experiment, leading them to reject their own physical-continuity explanation.

The second alternative explanation for mixed-case nonword priming offered by Kinoshita and Norris (2011) is that it was an artifact of the perceptual similarity and hence confusability between lowercase "l" and both lowercase and uppercase "I/i" in Courier font. In a *post hoc* analysis of a replication of Bodner and Masson (1997, Experiment 2A), Kinoshita and Norris (2011, Experiment 1) found mixed-case nonword priming in the lexical-decision task for "ambiguous" nonwords such as "lOvInK" but not for "unambiguous" nonwords such as "jAsAnT". For this chapter, we conducted a reanalysis of Bodner and Masson (1997, Experiment 2A) and we did not find a difference in mixed-case nonword priming across our 13 ambiguous and 35 unambiguous critical nonword targets. Our ambiguous nonwords showed 88 ms of priming and our unambiguous nonwords showed 90 ms of priming, contrary to the letter-ambiguity hypothesis.

In their second experiment, Kinoshita and Norris (2011) created a new set of mixed-case nonword targets that did not include lowercase "l," and the 11-ms of priming they obtained for these targets failed to reach significance. Their nonsignificant effect ($p=0.06$ by subjects) is difficult to interpret, however, given that 37 of their 80 nonword targets contained "i" or "I" and thus were ambiguous by their own operational definition. To support the letter-ambiguity hypothesis, Kinoshita and Norris would need to have found significant priming for their ambiguous nonwords and a nonsignificant priming effect for their unambiguous nonwords. The balance of evidence leads us to suggest that mixed-case nonword priming is not typically or exclusively due to the letter ambiguity identified by Kinoshita and Norris.

3.1.4 Using a Backward Task to Test a Backward Idea

Davis et al. (2008) proposed yet another alternative to memory recruitment to explain mixed-case nonword priming. They argued that mixed-case targets direct processing toward individual letters instead of lexical units, and "this extra process of checking letter identity may result in a priming effect for nonword targets based on letter representations" (p. 675). They further argued that difficult target formats other than mixed case should not induce a letter-level process and thus should not yield nonword priming. To test this *sublexical claim*, they introduced a *backward lexical-decision task* in which targets must be processed from right-to-left before a lexical decision is made (e.g., DAOR for word target ROAD, FRAL for nonword target LARF). On the memory-recruitment account, this task should increase prime recruitment and target facilitation relative to the fluency bias associated with the lexical-decision task, hence backward nonword priming should occur. With forward primes and backward targets, Davis et al. (2008) found repetition priming for words but not for nonwords, thus providing an important new challenge to the memory-recruitment account.

Working with Bodner, former graduate student Aaron Brown confirmed that nonword priming is absent in the backward lexical-decision task (using uppercase targets) under the same parameters that generate mixed-case nonword priming in the usual lexical-decision task (see Fig. 5.2). Brown tested 48 participants per group, the stimuli were from Bodner

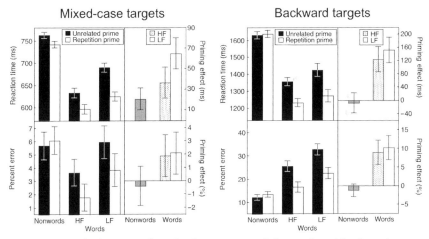

Figure 5.2 Masked priming for mixed-case targets (left panel) and backward targets (right panel) in the lexical-decision task (see text). Mean reaction times, error rates, and priming effects are plotted as a function of prime type for nonword targets and high-frequency (HF) and low-frequency (LF) word targets. Error bars for reaction times and errors are 95% within-subjects confidence intervals for comparing pairs of means across prime type. Error bars for word priming effects are 95% within-subjects confidence intervals for comparing priming across target frequency. Error bars for nonword priming effects are 95% confidence intervals for comparing these effects against zero.

and Masson (2001, Experiment 2), and the prime-target SOA was 45 ms. Critically, nonword priming was not significant in the backward task (−7 ms) but was significant with mixed-case targets (21 ms) and the latter effect was not modulated by the aforementioned letter ambiguity issue. Unlike Davis et al. (2008), the frequency of the word targets was also manipulated, and we obtained a frequency by priming interaction but only in the mixed-case group. This interaction suggests that priming with mixed-case targets reflects more than a sublexical process, at least for the word targets.

One interpretation of this dissociation between mixed-case and backward priming is that the former reflects a sublexical process rather than memory recruitment, and the latter reflects a lexical process. Alternatively, mixed-case targets might negate the fluency bias against nonword priming, but backward targets might not. With backward targets, participants may continue to experience their target processing as more fluent on repetition (vs. unrelated) trials, and this fluency bias may work against making rapid nonword responses. Our experience doing the backward task is that once one adjusts to reading targets from right to left, the task, though laborious, is regular and predictable. In contrast, with mixed-case targets, different combinations of uppercase and lowercase letters are continually encountered, making responding to targets less regular and predictable. A fluency bias may be more likely to survive in a more stable environment such as processing backward (vs. mixed-case) targets.

This *ad hoc* "out" aside, we concede that mixed-case nonword priming does not provide unequivocal evidence of a fluency bias. As a result, mixed-case nonword priming cannot be taken as unequivocal support for the memory-recruitment account (cf. Bodner & Masson, 1997). Unfortunately, at a practical level, even if the backward lexical-decision task isolates lexical processes, researchers interested in the lexicon are unlikely to use it given the long response times and the high error rates it produces. Therefore, we return to looking at priming for good old standard nonwords, but with some new tricks, in Sections 3.1.5 and 3.1.6.

3.1.5 Nonword Priming: Should we Stay or Should We No-Go?

Having surrendered our much-contested mixed-case nonword priming effect, it behooves us to show that masked nonword priming can occur with standard targets when it is not undermined by a fluency bias. As mentioned earlier, there have been occasional reports of standard masked nonword priming (Bodner & Masson, 2001, 2003; Forster, 1985; Sereno, 1991), but Forster (1998) reported that across 40 of his own standard lexical-decision experiments only 3 produced significant nonword priming, and that the mean nonword priming effect was only 9 ms.

Perea, Gomez, and Fraga (2010) speculated that the absence (or small magnitude) of standard nonword priming in the lexical-decision task might be due to priming occurring only for the positive/default response option and not for the negative/alternative response option in any given binary task. Consistent with this idea are the results from Norris and Kinoshita's (2008) same-different judgment paradigm. In this paradigm, a referent item is shown in plain view before a masked priming trial, and the participant's task is to decide whether the target matches the referent or not. Using this paradigm, Norris and Kinoshita (2008) reported priming for both words and nonwords on positive "same" trials but neither showed priming on negative "different" trials (see also Kinoshita & Norris, 2011).

Using the standard masked priming paradigm, Perea et al. (2010) tested whether more nonword priming would be obtained in a nonword-based go/no-go task—in which participants make "yes" responses to nonwords and withhold responding to words (Siakaluk, Buchanan, & Westbury, 2003)—than in the usual lexical-decision task. Instead, they found significant, equivalent priming in these respective tasks (14 vs. 11 ms), leading them to conclude that making "no" (vs. "yes") responses to nonwords does not work against nonword priming. On the one hand, their significant nonword priming effects give the memory-recruitment account another gasp of air, but on the other hand, the null interaction suggests either that a fluency bias does not operate against nonword priming in the lexical-decision task or the go/no-go task did not reduce it.

Recently, and in collaboration with graduate students Aaron Brown and Andreas Breuer, we attempted to show that a fluency bias works against nonword priming even in the nonword go/no-go task. Our experiment was inspired by Unkelbach (2006), who showed that task factors can be manipulated in ways that can produce striking fluency bias reversals (e.g., making fluency favor "new" rather than "old" responses on a recognition test). Our crucial condition, Condition A, involved two key changes to the method used by Perea et al. (2010). First, the prime context was adjusted to make fluency predictive of a nonword target. To this end, the proportion of repetition (vs. unrelated) prime trials was 0.8 for nonword targets but 0 for word targets (rather than 0.5 for both target types as in Perea et al.). Thus, prime-induced fluency strongly signaled a nonword response. Second, to guide participants to rely on this *reversed fluency bias*, the target context was adjusted to induce a task-wide bias toward the nonword response. This was accomplished by using a 60/40 nonword/word ratio (rather than 50/50 as in Perea et al.). Taken together, prime-induced fluency should create a bias toward making a nonword response, and the target-type ratio should work to make the nonword response prepotent. Condition B removed this prepotency by using a 50/50 nonword/word ratio. Condition C used an 80/20 nonword/word ratio to make the nonword response strongly prepotent, but the proportion of repetition (vs. unrelated) prime trials was 0.5 for nonword and word targets, so fluency did not exclusively signal a nonword response. There were 24 participants per group, the stimuli were from Bodner and Masson (2001, Experiment 1), and the prime-target SOA was 45 ms. As shown in Fig. 5.3, robust nonword priming occurred in Condition A (27 ms) but not in Condition B (3 ms) or C (6 ms). This experiment suggests that overcoming the fluency bias can be very challenging, even when some of the context and task elements are set up to promote nonword priming.

Perea et al. (2010) obtained a larger priming effect for words than for nonwords in their lexical-decision task, and they argued that this result "strongly suggests that there is a lexical component to masked priming" (p. 373). We do not think this conclusion logically follows, however, for two reasons. First, when some nonword priming occurs, it does not follow that the fluency bias has been eliminated. It merely demonstrates that enough of the fluency bias has been overcome to reveal positive nonword

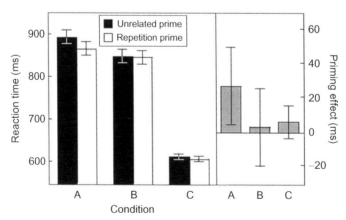

Figure 5.3 Masked priming effects in three nonword go/no-go task conditions (see text). Mean reaction times are plotted as a function of prime type for nonword targets. Error bars for reaction are 95% within-subjects confidence intervals for comparing pairs of means across prime type. Error bars for priming effects are 95% confidence intervals for comparing priming effects against zero.

priming (Bodner & Masson, 1997). Second, rather than reflecting a lexical process, larger priming effects for words compared with nonwords could reflect the prime-initiated recruitment of prior experiences with the prime other than the prime episode (see Whittlesea & Jacoby, 1990). As mentioned in Section 2.2, the processing of the prime should also sponsor memory recruitment. This form of memory recruitment, which does not exist for nonwords, would selectively facilitate repetition priming for word targets. It might also explain the frequency-attenuation effect, if prior experiences with low- versus high-frequency words are more distinct in memory. We have not written of these possibilities before.

3.1.6 Nonword Priming in an All-Nonword Task: New Evidence of a Fluency Bias

Perea et al.'s (2010) finding that nonword priming was not greater when participants made a "yes" rather than a "no" response to nonwords was not fully convincing, unfortunately, because different tasks were used to make this comparison (i.e., nonword go/no-go vs. lexical decision, respectively). Bodner, Johnson, and Masson (2014) designed a novel test of whether fluency from repetition primes might bias a "yes" response rather than a "no" response to nonwords *within the same task*. This test can be accomplished only by creating a binary all-nonword task. Our participants decided whether each five-letter nonword target contained more vowels than consonants. If a fluency bias promotes "yes" responses, then priming should be greater for "yes" nonwords (e.g., SEERA) than for "no" nonwords (e.g., BULGA) in this novel task.

In one experiment, we tested 110 participants (70 in one replication, 40 in another; the results were the same and are combined here), there were 200 trials, the proportion of repetition (vs. unrelated) prime trials and of yes (vs. no) nonwords was 0.5, assignment of hand to yes/no response was counterbalanced (and had no effect), and the prime-target SOA was 45 ms. As shown in Fig. 5.4, the critical interaction between nonword type and priming was significant. Nonword priming was significant for "yes" nonwords (22 ms) but not for "no" nonwords (6 ms). Participants made slightly more errors on repetition (vs. unrelated) trials, but this was true of both nonword types.

This dissociation suggests that nonword priming might be underestimated if fluency biases "yes" over "no" responses in the lexical-decision task, and perhaps biases "same" over "different" responses in the Norris and Kinoshita (2008) referent task (Bowers, 2010; but see Norris & Kinoshita,

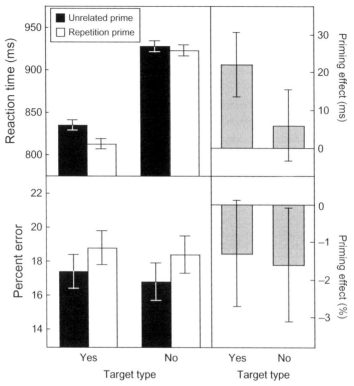

Figure 5.4 Masked priming effects for "yes" and "no" nonword targets in an all-nonword vowel-judgment task (Bodner et al., 2014). Mean reaction times and error rates are plotted as a function of prime type for each type of nonword target. Error bars for reaction times are 95% within-subjects confidence intervals for comparing pairs of means across prime type. Error bars for priming effects are 95% confidence intervals for comparing priming effects against zero.

2010). It further suggests that another reason nonword priming may often fail to be observed: The mere presence of words! When word and nonword targets occur within a task (especially in the lexical-decision task), participants likely give high priority to word targets, for which they have more processing experience. Even in the nonword-based go/no-go task, participants likely first attempt to rule out that the target is a word before committing a nonword response. As a result, fluency from repetition primes may typically be counted toward the dominant or more fluent response option (typically the "word" response), thus making it difficult to observe nonword priming. It is tantalizing for memory-recruitment enthusiasts (of which there are at least two convalescing cases) to speculate that greater priming for "yes" than "no" responses could explain why masked priming is usually greater for words than for nonwords in the lexical-decision task. Unfortunately, one cannot simply create a "nonlexical-decision task" where participants are asked to decide whether targets are nonwords or not. We have tried this, and our participants reported that they simply flipped the task instructions.

The nonword priming effects reviewed in Sections 3.1.5 and 3.1.6 provide a semblance of optimism for our claim that masked primes are encoded and can influence nonword target processing when not countered by a fluency bias. Of course, it is always possible to attribute these effects to a purely prospective sublexical locus rather than to memory recruitment. At a minimum, though, masked nonword priming results are problematic for a *purely* lexical account. They are also problematic for the Bayesian Reader account (Norris & Kinoshita, 2008) when there is no nonword prior to be updated by the prime (cf. the same-different referent paradigm). In Section 3.2, we switch gears to consider another masked priming phenomenon that we anticipated would provide better evidence for a memory-recruitment account.

3.2. Prime-Proportion Effects on Masked Priming

Beginning with the first author's dissertation work (Bodner & Masson, 2001, 2003), we have largely pursued a second line of evidence for the memory-recruitment account, namely the surprising sensitivity of masked priming to prime-proportion manipulations. As Masson and Bodner (2003) put it, "we reasoned that if masked priming and long-term priming share a common mechanism, then masked priming might ... be enhanced by a high degree of contextual overlap between study and test episodes" (p. 78). Overlap can be defined as the list-wide proportion of trials with (vs. without) overlap in one or more of the operations required for processing both the prime and target (e.g., orthographic, phonological, semantic, motor). Typically, we have manipulated this proportion between groups (0.8 vs. 0.2). Because participants are largely unaware of the primes, it is unlikely that they engage in conscious, strategic modulation of processing based on awareness of the prime proportion. Instead, increased priming in high-proportion-overlap conditions reflects an adaptive modulation of the use of information arising from an unconscious source.

In print, we motivated our tests of prime-proportion effects on masked priming by appealing to: (1) participants' sensitivity to the list-wide structure of stimuli, without awareness, in implicit learning studies (e.g., Reber & Allen, 1978; Vokey & Brooks, 1992); (2) a proportion-old effect on recognition tests (Allen & Jacoby, 1990; Jacoby, 1983); and (3) a proportion congruent Stroop effect (Cheesman & Merikle, 1986). However, the true origin of the idea was the failure of the first author's Master's thesis work to show an influence of a spatially based prime-proportion manipulation on short-SOA unmasked semantic priming (Bodner, 1997). At that time, we had just completed the experiments comprising Bodner and Masson (1997), so we essentially took a blind leap and tested whether a repetition-prime-proportion manipulation would modulate masked priming in the lexical-decision task. This was a long shot given that the dominant account of masked priming appealed to an automatic, prime-context-insensitive lexical-entry opening mechanism (Forster & Davis, 1984).

3.2.1 Effects with Word Stimuli

Bodner and Masson (2001) reported 12 lexical-decision experiments, 8 of which showed greater repetition priming for words when 0.8 rather than 0.2 of the trials contained repetition (vs. unrelated) primes (see Fig. 5.5, panel A). Across those eight experiments, the average priming effect was 32 ms in the 0.2 group and 57 ms in the 0.8 group—a substantial difference in a realm of tiny differences! An underlying trope of this chapter is that we can learn from failures. When we examined our failures, we noticed that they all involved substantial trial-to-trial variation in target processing difficulty. For example, Experiment 2 used a mixture of very high-frequency (i.e., easy) word targets and very low-frequency (i.e., hard) word targets. We also noticed (and showed statistically) that across these four experiments substantial priming occurred in the 0.2 conditions. From the memory-recruitment account (as we elaborate below), this pattern suggested that when variation in target processing difficulty is high, participants increase their use of the primes, regardless of their list-wide validity for the task at hand. Consistent with this claim, we found that adding a set of medium-frequency word targets "smoothed out" this variation and allowed a prime-proportion effect to emerge (Experiment 6).

In the word-recognition domain, we also reported an influence of relatedness proportion on masked semantic priming in the lexical-decision task (Bodner & Masson, 2003). This effect was especially surprising given that such effects had typically been obtained only with unmasked primes, using SOAs that were long enough to allow application of conscious strategies such as generating expectancies about the target based on the prime

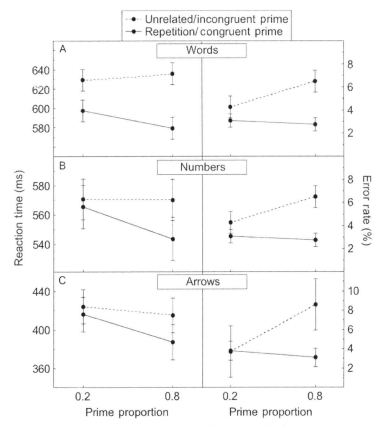

Figure 5.5 Bias pattern of prime-proportion effects on masked priming. Mean reaction times and error rates are plotted as a function of prime-proportion condition for (A) word stimuli in the lexical-decision task from Bodner and Masson (2001; word data, pooled across eight sets of data), (B) number stimuli in the parity-judgment task from Bodner and Dypvik (2005; data pooled across target type and Experiments 1–3), and (C) arrow stimuli in the left/right task from Bodner and Mulji (2010). Bars are 95% between subject confidence intervals, computed separately for repetition/congruent prime trials and unrelated/incongruent prime trials, and are appropriate for comparing a given trial type across prime-proportion groups. *Adapted from figure 5 of Bodner and Dypvik (2005).*

(see Neely, 1991). However, in the last decade, there has been one published failure to replicate this effect (Grossi, 2006), and no successful replications of it. In conjunction with the absence of proportion-dependent semantic priming effects with unmasked primes at short SOAs (e.g., Bodner, 1997; Perea & Rosa, 2002), Bodner and Masson's (2003) findings could be Type I errors and therefore warrant an attempt at replication.

In contrast, there are many replications of repetition-proportion modulated masked priming. Bodner and Masson (2004) reported this effect in the naming task (see also Kinoshita, Forster, & Mozer, 2008). In the lexical-decision task, Bodner, Masson, and Richard (2006) used "no prime" trials to establish that the larger priming effect in the high (vs. low) proportion group reflects both increased facilitation from repetition primes, and increased interference from unrelated primes. They also found that priming is influenced by the proportion of repetition trials, rather than by the proportion of unrelated trials (cf. Kinoshita et al., 2008). Bodner and Stalinski (2008) further showed that the effect can also occur within subjects, across blocks (see also Kinoshita et al., 2008) and under cognitive load (though surprisingly it was absent in the no-load condition). And, linking to Section 3.1, masked nonword priming often emerges when a high repetition-proportion is used (Bodner & Masson, 2001, Experiments 1, 2A, and 4A; Bodner & Masson, 2003, Experiment 2), though not always (Bodner & Stalinski, 2008).

3.2.2 Effects in Other Stimulus Domains

Proportion-dependent masked priming has also been reported in several other stimulus domains, thus implicating a domain-general mechanism if not memory recruitment *per se*. In these paradigms, response priming is the basic effect: facilitation (typically) occurs when the prime and target bias the same binary response (congruent trials) rather than opposite responses (incongruent trials). Bodner and Dypvik (2005; see Fig. 5.5, panel B) and Kinoshita, Mozer, and Forster (2011) both obtained proportion-dependent masked response priming in an odd/even parity-judgment task using number stimuli. Indeed, Bodner and Dypvik obtained a striking reversal in the direction of priming and in the proportion effect using exactly the same items—only the task was varied. Parity judgments were facilitated on parity-congruent trials (e.g., 1–7) relative to parity-incongruent trials (e.g., 6–7) when the parity-congruency proportion was 0.8 (vs. 0.2), but magnitude judgments relative to 5 were facilitated on magnitude-congruent trials (e.g., 6–7) relative to magnitude-incongruent trials (e.g., 1–7) when the magnitude-congruency was 0.8 (vs. 0.2).

Proportion-dependent masked response priming has also been found for left/right judgments to nonalphanumeric stimuli (Jaskowski, Skalska, & Verleger, 2003), and most recently to arrow stimuli (Bodner & Lee, 2014; Bodner & Mulji, 2010; see Fig. 5.5, panel C; Klapp, 2007; Perry & Lupker, 2010). Interestingly, an influence of prime-proportion extends even to free-choice trials (within a set of fixed-choice trials with unambiguous arrow targets) where a masked prime (e.g., >) precedes an ambiguous target (e.g., < >). Bodner and Mulji (2010) showed that the proportion of congruent fixed-choice trials modulated how quickly and how frequently participants choose the response associated with the prime (e.g., >) as their free-choice response, though the form taken by this modulation is debated (Bodner & Lee, 2014; Perry & Lupker, 2010). An important and surprising twist in this paradigm is that the direction of response priming, and of the influence of prime proportion, completely reverses at prime-target SOAs above 100 ms. That is, responses are slower on response-congruent (vs. incongruent) trials, particularly when the proportion of response-congruent trials is greater (Klapp, 2007; Perry & Lupker, 2010). We discuss the importance of this finding in Section 4.2.

3.2.3 Accounting for These Effects

The occurrence of prime-proportion effects on masked priming across these stimulus domains is consistent with the operation of a domain-general memory-recruitment process (e.g., see Bodner & Dypvik, 2005). The cognitive system may "tune in" to the list-wide utility of the masked primes for performing the target task, and may modulate its reliance on recruiting the prime accordingly. The best evidence we have mustered for this possibility comes from an examination of the form taken by these effects. As illustrated in Fig. 5.5, increased recruitment of the prime in the 0.8 (vs. 0.2) group produces a consistent bias effect across binary judgment tasks: it results in faster responses on the 0.8 repetition/congruent prime trials, but it also results in more errors on the 0.2 unrelated/incongruent prime trials. Thus, increased prime recruitment results in both a benefit and a cost. From an activation-based account, increased activation of the prime in the 0.8 group should produce these benefits, but how or why increased activation produces costs across these domains is less clear.

Unfortunately, the domain-general occurrence of prime-proportion effects, and their underappreciated bias pattern, does not exclusively "rule in" a memory-recruitment explanation. Rather than computing and adapting to the prime proportion directly, participants may be adapting to these manipulations indirectly, for example, through their influence on error rate (e.g., Jaskowski et al., 2003) or response times (e.g., Desender & Van den Bussche, 2012; Van Opstal, Buc Calderon, Gevers, & Verguts, 2011). In some cases, researchers have argued that high-proportion groups increase prime activation (Klapp, 2007) or that low-proportion groups suppress prime activation (Perry & Lupker, 2010). Klapp's adaptive associative-strength account fits particularly well with demonstrations of prime-proportion effects in a response priming paradigm (Bodner & Lee, 2014). Finally, despite evidence to the contrary (e.g., Bodner & Dypvik, 2005; Bodner et al., 2006; Bodner & Mulji, 2010), it has even been suggested that these effects might reflect conscious influences due to insufficient masking (e.g., Desender & Van den Bussche, 2012).

A detailed alternative account of prime-proportion effects is the *Adaptation to the Statistics of the Environment* (ASE) account (Kinoshita et al., 2008, 2011), which posits that the cognitive system adapts its response deadline as a function of current and recent trial difficulty to minimize response time and error rate. Formal ASE models predict and produce prime-proportion effects when it is assumed that repetition/congruent (easy) trials are more sensitive than unrelated/incongruent (hard) trials to list-wide trial difficulty. To date, the ASE account has been successfully applied to prime-proportion effects in the naming and parity-judgment tasks. Moreover, in each case, the ASE account also fit new results that either contradict the memory-recruitment account or for which the account makes no clear prediction.

We are fans of the ASE account, but that approach is not without its challenges. To begin, it does not explain prime-proportion effects for words in the lexical-decision task (see Kinoshita et al., 2008, p. 645). It is also unclear whether ASE can account for the error portion of the bias pattern, given that it has been used to model only response times thus far. Moreover, the ASE model predicts that prime-proportion effects should occur only in speeded tasks. Recently, we have obtained repetition-proportion effects on both response times and accuracy in masked priming in a nonspeeded fragment-completion task (Bodner & Johnson, 2009; see also Weidemann, Huber, & Shiffrin, 2008), which challenges the ASE account. In addition, the ASE account cannot explain modulation in masked priming when there is no observable response time difference across prime-context conditions (Van Opstal et al., 2011). Finally, it is unclear whether the ASE account can accommodate reversals in the direction of response priming across SOAs (e.g., Klapp, 2007), a pattern that is also problematic for the memory-recruitment account (see Section 4.2).

If issues such as these can be addressed, we concede that the ASE account provides a much better-specified and mechanistic account of prime-proportion effects than does the admittedly vague memory-recruitment account. Fortunately, even if our account is incorrect, it is proved to be useful in helping motivate the investigation of an important new phenomenon, namely the adaptive modulation of masked priming by variations in prime context. We are pleased to note that whether such adaptive modulations reflect "smart" or "dumb" mechanisms are currently an active area of research (e.g., Desender et al., 2013).

3.3. Duration of Masked Priming

If the processing applied to a masked prime event is encoded into memory in a lasting form, then by the memory-recruitment account it follows that it might be possible to show lasting masked priming effects. In contrast, on prospective accounts, the activation or opening of existing representations is typically posited to be very short-lived (e.g., Forster & Davis, 1984; Greenwald, Draine, & Abrams, 1996; cf. Becker, Moscovitch, Behrmann, & Joordens, 1997). And, by the Bayesian Reader account, masked priming should be limited to adjacent prime-target pairings that become conflated in the act of perception. Consistent with the latter accounts, initial tests suggested that masked priming was limited to a single trial and could be detected after no more than a second or two between prime and target presentations (e.g., Ferrand, 1996; Forster, Booker, Schacter, & Davis, 1990; Forster & Davis, 1984; Greenwald et al., 1996; Humphreys, Besner, & Quinlan, 1988; Versace & Nevers, 2003). In contrast, priming effects with unmasked stimuli can be very long lasting (e.g., Kolers, 1976). This sharp dissociation between masked and unmasked priming could be taken as a failure of the memory-recruitment account, though it might not be too surprising if such an impoverished trace does not have a lasting influence (see Masson & Bodner, 2003).

However, the subliminal mere-exposure effect suggests that this dissociation may not be so sharp. Famously, Kunst-Wilson and Zajonc (1980) found that brief repeated exposures to polygons increased their selection over novel foils in a subsequent forced-choice preference task. Importantly, if less famously, Whittlesea and Price (2001) replicated this result using a variety of pictorial stimuli in both two-alternative forced-choice preference and recognition tasks; they also reported that a single exposure was insufficient to produce these priming effects. Given that participants in these studies had not experienced these particular stimuli before, it seems reasonable to assume that they somehow encoded aspects of them into memory.

Inspired by these findings, Masson and Bodner (2003) reported some work-in-progress in which a single 45-ms masked word prime presented on trial N (e.g., bell-TOAD) generated priming of target lexical decisions

(39 ms; BELL) and masked perceptual identification (11%; *bell* followed by a postmask) a few seconds later on trial $N+1$. We never published this pair of experiments because we felt that the results did not sufficiently challenge the lexical account. One could simply posit that lexical entries remain open for a few seconds, after all. In retrospect, however, the persistence of masked priming from one trial to another does appear to provide an important challenge for the Bayesian Reader account. In our design, the prime would be conflated with an unrelated target on trial N, and there was no prime and hence no prior to be updated prior to the target's presentation on trial $N+1$.

As hinted at in Masson and Bodner (2003), we instead pursued longer duration effects that we thought would be more impressive. Our ambition exceeded our grasp. We failed like Icarus. In a series of unpublished lexical-detection experiments, we often found effects but we had enough difficulty replicating them that we ultimately banished all of them to our file drawers. Our failure to demonstrate consistent long-lasting masked priming should thus be taken as a challenge to the memory-recruitment account. We briefly describe four of our most recent attempts here, both to show our cards and to inspire others either to improve upon or avoid these tacks.

In one attempt, a masked word prime on trial N was repeated on trial $N+6$, and the five intervening trials required either lexical decisions (no primes) or symmetry judgments to polygons (to reduce retroactive interference). In a second attempt, during an exposure phase, masked word primes were presented on three consecutive trials involving a straight/curved judgment to the letter-string targets (e.g., EEEE/GGGG). During the test phase about a minute later, lexical decisions to primed versus unprimed targets were compared. In a third attempt, lexical decisions were required throughout but unbeknownst to participants, masked word primes were presented on four trials prior to their appearance as targets. Different exposure-test blocking variants resulted in average lags of 50, 80, or 130 trials (about 3 min on average). In our most recent attempt, with graduate student Andreas Breuer, we investigated whether masked word primes, across eight lexical-decision training trials, can become associated with either a word or nonword response that was required for the target on each training trial. On test trials, we measured whether lexical decisions were faster to word-response trained words than to nonword-response trained words. This last attempt was inspired by Marcos (2007), who found that repeated pairings of masked "+" versus "o" primes with "<" versus ">" targets, respectively, in an association phase generated robust response priming in a testing phase.

Although Bornstein's (1989) review and meta-analysis of the mere-exposure effect suggests that the effect is robust with word stimuli (see his table 1), we have not been able to achieve reliable evidence that repeated exposure to masked word primes influences future responses. And yet, one recent finding makes us hesitate to close the door too firmly on this possibility. In a study using patients with epilepsy, Gaillard et al. (2007) presented brief (29 ms) masked words three times, at intervals ranging from 5 s to 47 min. The patients' task was to decide whether each masked word was threatening or not; these judgments were at chance for the initial two word presentations (i.e., there was no behavioral priming effect). Nonetheless, using implanted intracranial electrodes, the researchers found evidence that the local field potential generated by presentation of the masked words often differed across the two initial presentations. They concluded that a "single presentation of a masked word can durably affect neural architecture" (p. 1527). So, although our labs' efforts over the past decade to update Masson and Bodner (2003) regarding the dissociation between masked and unmasked priming have not been successful "there may still be gold in them thar hills."

4. THE STATUS OF THE MEMORY-RECRUITMENT ACCOUNT

The findings reviewed in Section 3 do not provide a complete evaluation of the memory-recruitment account. They merely update Masson and Bodner (2003) regarding the balance of progress/regress we have made in each of the domains we have investigated. Our goal in Section 4 is to now summarize, as frankly as possible, where those updates leave the account, and to acknowledge a few other serious challenges and limitations. Section 5 then highlights a few key issues for accounts of masked priming to address.

4.1. Memory Recruitment Redux/Denouement

We can think of only one masked nonword priming result that would seriously reanimate the memory-recruitment account: A long-lasting influence of a single masked nonword presentation, either on a behavioral measure or on a brain measure such as the local field potential effects, Gaillard et al. (2007) demonstrated with word stimuli. Short-lived influences of a single masked nonword prime can always be chalked up to a sublexical (e.g., letter level) activation process rather than to memory recruitment. Long-lived influences of multiple masked nonword prime exposures could be chalked up to the formation, activation, or modification of a newly formed abstract representation. So, although the evidence reviewed in Section 3.1 reinforces the claim that a fluency bias can work against nonword priming, we have not succeeded in establishing that the nonword priming revealed when this fluency bias is reduced or eliminated necessarily reflects memory recruitment.

As for the finding that masked priming effects are larger for low- than for high-frequency words (Section 3.1.2), the memory-recruitment account of this result has not been well motivated. The prime resource might be more distinctive in memory for low-frequency words, as suggested by Bodner and Masson (1997), but the effect could also simply reflect there being more room to show priming for low-frequency items, given their longer reaction times. On the other hand, the possibility that this interaction reflects prime-initiated recruitment of other processing experiences in memory, which would be more distinct for low (vs. high) frequency words, could render that this interaction is more important than we have realized (see Section 3.1.5).

Finally, although the memory-recruitment account provided a handy motivation for studying prime-proportion effects on masked priming, we concede that these effects do not compel a retrospective priming process. Some of these effects (e.g., Bodner & Mulji, 2010) can be attributed to an adaptive associative-activation process (e.g., Klapp, 2007), and others (e.g., Bodner & Dypvik, 2005; Bodner & Masson, 2004) can be attributed to an adaptive adjustment of the response deadline (e.g., Kinoshita et al., 2008, 2011). On the other hand, Klapp's (2007) account is silent regarding prime-proportion effects that occur without repetitions of primes and targets (e.g., Bodner & Masson, 2001), and the ASE account does not predict the effect in nonspeeded tasks (Bodner & Johnson, 2009) or even in the lexical-decision task (Bodner & Masson, 2001; Bodner et al., 2006). One small victory for the memory-recruitment account is that it tried to offer a unified explanation of prime-proportion effects across various tasks, stimulus domains, and prime types (Bodner & Dypvik, 2005).

4.2. Other Challenges to Memory Recruitment

Over the years, we have doubtlessly missed many other masked priming results that challenge the memory-recruitment account. Here, we highlight one specific challenge and one general challenge. The specific challenge is that the memory-recruitment account cannot easily explain negative ("inhibitory") masked priming effects when there is overlap in prime-target processing. For example, in the word domain, Nakayama, Sears, and Lupker (2008) reported that orthographic neighbor primes (e.g., heap-HELP) resulted in slower reaction times than unrelated control primes (e.g., area-HELP). Bowers (2010) picked on the Bayesian Reader account's inability to accommodate such effects, but on the memory-recruitment account overlap should also facilitate target responses (as noted by Nakayama et al.)—unless that overlap works against making the correct target response (as we considered at length for nonword priming in Section 3.1). Relatedly, although we have used the memory-recruitment account to explain some response-priming effects (e.g., Bodner & Dypvik, 2005; Bodner & Mulji, 2010), the account is incompatible with the negative-compatibility effect (NCE), and with the prime-proportion effect on the NCE (Klapp, 2007), as noted by Perry and Lupker (2010). The NCE occurs when responses are faster after response-incompatible primes than after response-compatible primes. For example, in a left/right task, a left-facing arrow (relative to a right-facing arrow) sometimes facilitates responses to a right-facing arrow. Curiously, the NCE typically emerges at prime-target SOAs above 100 ms, whereas the usual positive-compatibility effect typically occurs at shorter SOAs (e.g., Schlaghecken & Eimer, 2000). In fairness to the memory-recruitment account, this reversal of response priming is hard to explain. The dominant "activation then inhibition" account seems to redescribe the data pattern rather than to explain it in a satisfactory way (e.g., Schlaghecken & Eimer, 2000).

At a more general level, the memory-recruitment account and its trusty sidekick fluency bias have been criticized for being poorly specified and *post hoc*, most vociferously by Forster (e.g., Forster, 1998; Forster et al., 2003) and Kinoshita (Kinoshita et al., 2008; Kinoshita & Norris, 2011, 2012). Are the contents of a "processing resource" vaguer than the contents of a "lexical entry" or "prior"? Perhaps not. Could they be better specified? Absolutely. But in the absence of a strong set of findings that provide unambiguous support for our account, and in the absence of a ringing endorsement from researchers regarding its utility, there is not much incentive to do so. Instead, we have been impressed with the development of better-specified accounts of masked priming, such as the Bayesian Reader account (e.g., Norris & Kinoshita, 2008), and of masked prime-proportion effects, such as the ASE account (e.g., Kinoshita et al., 2008, 2011). As long as the possibility that a memory process can "remain on" when primes are masked is not turned off in the consciousness of researchers, we hope that our account will continue to have some influence, and not solely in a "Buttsy" sense.

5. MOVING ACCOUNTS OF MASKED PRIMING FORWARD

Having masked our share of primes, Section 5 fashions some parting thoughts that will hopefully make a reasonable substitute for genuine wisdom. To begin, let us pitchfork away the straw men, and concede that masked priming paradigms are unlikely to provide pure measures of lexical, sublexical, or memory processes. Participants likely bring multiple processes to bear on the processing of masked primes. Therefore, we will need better-specified accounts of each active process, and careful tests of whether each process is influenced by context and task factors. Relatedly, accounts of masked priming have not typically attempted to address effects in both speeded (response-time based) and nonspeeded (accuracy based) tasks, across both classification (e.g., binary response) and identification (e.g., naming, masked perceptual identification, word fragment completion) tasks, with repeated and nonrepeated stimuli across trials, and when response priming is measured versus controlled. A merit of the memory-recruitment account was that it attempted to provide a simple, unified explanation of priming and prime-proportion effects that cut across these categories.

Layered on top of these considerations is the issue of whether masked priming effects are modulated by conscious awareness—not direct awareness of the primes—but awareness of the variations in one's target processing that arise from priming (for a recent review, see Desender & Van den Bussche, 2012). Only recently has clear evidence of unconscious modulation of masked priming effects been reported (Desender et al., 2013). For example, Van Opstal et al. (2011) found that a masked prime can bias either of two opposing responses depending on the *unconscious* context, even when the masked context manipulation did not affect overall reaction times and thus could not sponsor a response deadline shift, contrary to the ASE account. Researchers should keep in mind that masked priming effects are not necessarily driven solely by unconscious processes so long as targets are plainly visible and participants are aware of their responses to them. On the other hand, having established that masked priming effects are not much influenced by prime awareness, researchers might wish to "open up" their research by trying different prime durations and/or prime-target SOAs, which could reveal very different types of priming (e.g., Schlaghecken & Eimer, 2000). For example, using the same set of manipulations we consistently obtained nonword priming effects at a 60-ms SOA (Bodner & Masson, 1997) but not at a 45-ms SOA (Bodner & Masson, 2001).

Although we did not succeed in providing unequivocal evidence for prime recruitment, the idea that priming reflects an overlap in processing operations can be salvaged (see Bodner & Masson, 2001). One possibility is that rather than being recruited, the processing that is begun when a prime is presented continues when the prime is replaced with the target, and becomes integrated with the processing applied to the target (see Masson & Isaak, 1999). This idea is still very distinct from the idea that the prime activates an existing abstract representation. A related possibility is that the processing applied to the prime becomes mistaken for the processing applied to the target (rather than being integrated)—a source confusion error. This variant is consistent with the perceptual conflation between prime and target processing that forms the basis of the Bayesian Reader account of masked priming, except the conflation does not necessarily arise at the perceptual level; conflation could also arise at other levels of processing (e.g., phonological, semantic, motor). We have not pursued these possibilities because we were attempting to explore parallels between long-term priming and masked priming. Given that long-term priming reflects a retrospective process, and given that our initial attempts to show long-lasting masked priming effects panned out (Masson & Bodner, 2003), we emphasized the "recruitment" possibility. The absence of consistent long-lasting masked priming makes these other alternatives more attractive.

Although our own rhetoric nearly tempts us, neither of us plans to run more masked priming experiments. To help inure us, both of us have finally retired the OS 9 Macs and software we used to run most of our masked priming experiments. Therefore, the fate of the memory-recruitment account will naturally fall out of the directions taken and not taken by other researchers. We take pride in what we have contributed to this literature by stirring the pot. If nothing else, the contents of a stirred pot are less likely to get burned. Although we did not accomplish everything we had hoped, we are optimistic that a backward idea about masked priming can still help move research on unconscious processes forward.

REFERENCES

Allen, S. W., & Jacoby, L. L. (1990). Reinstating study context produces unconscious influences of memory. *Memory & Cognition, 18*, 270–278.

Becker, S., Moscovitch, M., Behrmann, M., & Joordens, S. (1997). Long-term semantic priming: A computational account and empirical evidence. *Journal of Experimental Psychology Learning, Memory, and Cognition, 23*, 1059–1082.

Bodner, G. E. (1997). Isolating retrospective priming processes using relatedness proportion manipulations. University of Victoria, Unpublished Master's thesis.

Bodner, G. E., & Dypvik, A. T. (2005). Masked priming of number judgments depends on prime validity and task. *Memory & Cognition, 33*, 29–47.

Bodner, G. E., & Johnson, J. C. S. (2009). Repetition proportion affects masked priming in nonspeeded tasks. *Psychonomic Bulletin & Review, 16*, 497–502.

Bodner, G. E., Johnson, J. C. S., & Masson, M. E. J. (2014). Reasserting an influence of fluency on masked nonword priming: Evidence from an all-nonword task. Manuscript submitted for publication.

Bodner, G. E., & Lee, L. (2014). Masked response priming across three prime proportions: A comparison of three accounts. Manuscript submitted for publication.

Bodner, G. E., & Masson, M. E. J. (1997). Masked repetition priming of words and nonwords: Evidence for a nonlexical basis for priming. *Journal of Memory and Language, 37*, 268–293.

Bodner, G. E., & Masson, M. E. J. (2001). Prime validity affects masked repetition priming: Evidence for an episodic resource account of priming. *Journal of Memory and Language, 45*, 616–647.

Bodner, G. E., & Masson, M. E. J. (2003). Beyond spreading activation: An influence of relatedness proportion on masked semantic priming. *Psychonomic Bulletin & Review, 10*, 645–652.

Bodner, G. E., & Masson, M. E. J. (2004). Beyond binary judgments: Prime validity modulates masked repetition priming in the naming task. *Memory & Cognition, 32*, 1–11.

Bodner, G. E., Masson, M. E. J., & Richard, N. T. (2006). Repetition proportion biases masked priming of lexical decisions. *Memory & Cognition, 34*, 1298–1311.

Bodner, G. E., & Mulji, R. (2010). Prime proportion affects masked priming of fixed and free-choice responses. *Experimental Psychology, 57*, 360–366.

Bodner, G. E., & Stalinski, S. M. (2008). Masked repetition priming and proportion effects under cognitive load. *Canadian Journal of Experimental Psychology, 62*, 127–131.

Bornstein, R. F. (1989). Exposure and affect: Overview and meta-analysis of research, 1968-1987. *Psychological Bulletin, 106*, 265–289.

Bowers, J. S. (2003). An abstractionist account of masked and long-term priming. In S. Kinoshita, & S. J. Lupker (Eds.), *Macquarie Monographs in Cognitive Science. Masked priming: The state of the art* (pp. 39–55). New York, NY: Psychology Press.

Bowers, J. S. (2010). Does masked and unmasked priming reflect Bayesian inference as implemented in the Bayesian Reader? *European Journal of Cognitive Psychology, 22*, 779–797.

Cheesman, J., & Merikle, P. M. (1986). Distinguishing conscious from unconscious perceptual processes. *Canadian Journal of Experimental Psychology, 40*, 343–367.

Davis, C. J. (2003). Factors underlying masked priming effects in competitive network models of visual word recognition. In S. Kinoshita, & S. J. Lupker (Eds.), *Macquarie Monographs in Cognitive Science. Masked priming: The state of the art* (pp. 121–170). New York, NY: Psychology Press.

Davis, C., Kim, J., & Forster, K. I. (2008). Being forward not backward: Lexical limits to masked priming. *Cognition, 107*, 673–684.

Dehaene, S., Naccache, L., Le Clec'H, G., Koechlin, E., Mueller, M., Dehaene-Lambertz,- G., et al. (1998). Imaging unconscious semantic priming. *Nature, 395*, 597–600.

Desender, K., & Van den Bussche, E. (2012). Is consciousness necessary for conflict adaptation? *Frontiers in Human Neuroscience, 6*, 1–13.

Desender, K., Van Lierde, E., & Van den Bussche, E. (2013). Comparing conscious and unconscious conflict adaptation. *PLoS One, 8*, e55976.

Ferrand, L. (1996). The masked repetition priming effect dissipates when increasing the interstimulus interval: Evidence from word naming. *Acta Psychologica, 91*, 15–25.

Feustel, T. C., Shiffrin, R. M., & Salasoo, A. (1983). Episodic and lexical contributions to the repetition effect in word identification. *Journal of Experimental Psychology. General, 112*, 309–346.

Forster, K. I. (1985). Lexical acquisition and the modular lexicon. *Language and Cognitive Processes, 1*, 87–108.

Forster, K. I. (1998). The pros and cons of masked priming. *Journal of Psycholinguistic Research, 27*, 203–233.

Forster, K. I. (1999). The microgenesis of priming effects in lexical access. *Brain and Language, 68*, 5–15.

Forster, K. I., Booker, J., Schacter, D. L., & Davis, C. (1990). Masked repetition priming: Lexical activation or novel memory trace? *Bulletin of the Psychonomic Society, 28*, 341–345.

Forster, K. I., & Davis, C. (1984). Repetition priming and frequency attenuation in lexical access. *Journal of Experimental Psychology Learning, Memory, and Cognition, 10*, 680–698.

Forster, K. I., Mohan, K., & Hector, J. (2003). The mechanics of masked priming. In S. Kinoshita, & S. J. Lupker (Eds.), *Macquarie Monographs in Cognitive Science. Masked priming: The state of the art* (pp. 3–37). New York, NY: Psychology Press.

Gaillard, R., Cohen, L., Adam, C., Clemencequ, S., Hasboun, D., Baulac, M., et al. (2007). Subliminal words durably affect neuronal activity. *Neuroreport, 18*, 1527–1531.

Greenwald, A. G. (1992). New look 3: Unconscious cognition reclaimed. *American Psychologist, 47*, 766–779.

Greenwald, A. G., Draine, S. C., & Abrams, R. L. (1996). Three cognitive markers of unconscious semantic activation. *Science, 273*, 1699–1702.

Grossi, G. (2006). Relatedness proportion effects on masked associative priming: An ERP study. *Psychophysiology, 43*, 21–30.

Holender, D. (1986). Semantic activation without conscious identification in dichotic listening, parafoveal vision, and visual masking: A survey and appraisal. *Behavioral and Brain Sciences, 9*, 1–23.

Huber, D. E., Shiffrin, R. M., Lyle, K. B., & Quach, R. (2002). Mechanisms of source confusion and discounting in short-term priming 2: Effects of prime similarity and target duration. *Journal of Experimental Psychology. Learning, Memory, and Cognition, 28*, 1120–1136.

Humphreys, G. W., Besner, D., & Quinlan, P. T. (1988). Event perception and the word repetition effect. *Journal of Experimental Psychology General, 117*, 51–67.

Jacoby, L. L. (1983). Perceptual enhancement: Persistent effects of an experience. *Journal of Experimental Psychology Learning, Memory, and Cognition, 9*, 21–38.

Jaskowski, P., Skalska, B., & Verleger, R. (2003). How the self controls its "automatic pilot" when processing subliminal information. *Journal of Cognitive Neuroscience, 15*, 1–10.

Karremans, J. C., Stroebe, W., & Claus, J. (2006). Beyond Vicary's fantasies: The impact of subliminal priming and brand choice. *Journal of Experimental Social Psychology, 42*, 792–798.

Kinoshita, S. (2006). Additive and interactive effects of word frequency and masked repetition in the lexical decision task. *Psychonomic Bulletin & Review, 13*, 668–673.

Kinoshita, S., Forster, K. I., & Mozer, M. C. (2008). Unconscious cognition isn't that smart: Modulation of masked repetition priming effect in the naming task. *Cognition, 107*, 623–649.

Kinoshita, S., & Lupker, S. J. (2003). *Masked priming: The state of the art*. New York, NY: Psychology Press.

Kinoshita, S., Mozer, M. C., & Forster, K. I. (2011). Dynamic adaptation to history of trial difficulty explains the effect of congruency proportion on masked priming. *Journal of Experimental Psychology. General, 140*, 622–636.

Kinoshita, S., & Norris, D. (2011). Does the familiarity bias hypothesis explain why there is no masked priming for "NO" decisions? *Memory & Cognition, 9*, 319–334.

Kinoshita, S., & Norris, D. (2012). Task-dependent masked priming effects in visual word recognition. *Frontiers in Psychology, 3*, 1–12.

Klapp, S. T. (2007). Nonconscious control mimics a purposeful strategy: Strength of Stroop-like interference is automatically modulated by proportion of compatible trials. *Journal of Experimental Psychology. Human Perception and Performance, 33*, 1366–1376.

Kolers, P. A. (1976). Reading a year later. *Journal of Experimental Psychology: Human Learning and Memory, 2*, 554–565.

Kolers, P. A., & Roediger, H. L., III (1984). Procedures of mind. *Journal of Verbal Learning and Verbal Behavior, 23*, 425–449.

Kunst-Wilson, W. R., & Zajonc, R. B. (1980). Affective discrimination of stimuli that cannot be recognized. *Science, 207*, 557–558.

Logan, G. D. (1988). Toward an instance theory of automatization. *Psychological Review, 95*, 492–527.

Marcel, A. (1983). Conscious and unconscious perception: An approach to the relations between phenomenal experience and perceptual processes. *Cognitive Psychology, 15*, 197–237.

Marcos, J. (2007). Associative learning of discrimination with masked stimuli. *Learning and Motivation, 38*, 75–88.

Masson, M. E. J. (1995). A distributed memory model of semantic priming. *Journal of Experimental Psychology Learning, Memory, and Cognition, 21*, 3–23.

Masson, M. E. J., & Bodner, G. E. (2003). A retrospective view of masked priming: Toward a unified account of masked and long-term repetition priming. In S. Kinoshita, & S. J. Lupker (Eds.), *Macquarie Monographs in Cognitive Science. Masked priming: The state of the art* (pp. 57–94). New York, NY: Psychology Press.

Masson, M. E. J., & Isaak, M. I. (1999). Masked priming for words and nonwords in the naming task: Further evidence for a nonlexical basis for priming. *Memory & Cognition, 27*, 399–412.

Nakayama, M., Sears, C. R., & Lupker, S. J. (2008). Masked priming with orthographic neighbors: A test of the lexical competition assumption. *Journal of Experimental Psychology. Human Perception and Performance, 34*, 1236–1260.

Neely, J. H. (1977). Semantic priming and retrieval from lexical memory: Roles of inhibitionless spreading activation and limited-capacity attention. *Journal of Experimental Psychology General, 106*, 226–254.

Neely, J. H. (1991). Semantic priming effects in visual word recognition: A selective review of current findings and theories. In D. Besner & G. W. Humphreys (Eds.), *Basic processes in reading: Visual word recognition* (pp. 264–336). Hillsdale, NJ: Erlbaum.

Norris, D. (2006). The Bayesian reader: Explaining word recognition as an optimal Bayesian decision process. *Psychological Review, 113*, 327–357.

Norris, D., & Kinoshita, S. (2008). Perception as evidence accumulation and Bayesian inference: Insights from masked priming. *Journal of Experimental Psychology. General, 137*, 433–455.

Norris, D., & Kinoshita, S. (2010). Explanation versus accommodation: Reply to Bowers (2010). *European Journal of Cognitive Psychology, 22*, 1261–1269.

Perea, M., Gomez, P., & Fraga, I. (2010). Masked nonword repetition effects in yes/no and go/no-go lexical decision: A test of the evidence accumulation and deadline accounts. *Psychonomic Bulletin & Review, 17*, 369–374.

Perea, M., & Rosa, E. (2002). Does the proportion of associatively related pairs modulate the associative priming effect at very brief stimulus-onset asynchronies? *Acta Psychologica, 110*, 103–124.

Perry, J. R., & Lupker, S. J. (2010). A prospective view of the impact of prime validity on response speed and selection in the arrow classification task with free choice trials. *Attention, Perception, & Psychophysics, 72*, 528–537.

Pratkanis, A. R. (1992). The cargo-cult science of subliminal persuasion. *Skeptical Inquirer, 16*, 260–272.
Reber, A. S., & Allen, R. (1978). Analogic and abstraction strategies in synthetic grammar learning: A functionalist interpretation. *Cognition, 6*, 193–221.
Schlaghecken, F., & Eimer, M. (2000). A central-peripheral asymmetry in masked priming. *Perception & Psychophysics, 62*, 1367–1382.
Sereno, J. A. (1991). Graphemic, associative, and syntactic priming effects at a brief stimulus onset asynchrony in lexical decision and naming. *Journal of Experimental Psychology. Learning, Memory, and Cognition, 17*, 459–477.
Siakaluk, P. D., Buchanan, L., & Westbury, C. (2003). The effect of semantic distance in yes/no and go/no-go semantic categorization tasks. *Memory & Cognition, 31*, 100–113.
Unkelbach, C. (2006). The learned interpretation of cognitive fluency. *Psychological Science, 17*, 339–345.
Van Opstal, F., Buc Calderon, C., Gevers, W., & Verguts, T. (2011). Setting the stage subliminally: Unconscious context effects. *Consciousness and Cognition, 20*, 1860–1864.
Versace, R., & Nevers, B. (2003). Word frequency effect on repetition priming as a function of prime duration and delay between the prime and target. *British Journal of Psychology, 94*, 389–408.
Vokey, J. R., & Brooks, L. R. (1992). Salience of item knowledge in learning artificial grammars. *Journal of Experimental Psychology. Learning, Memory, and Cognition, 18*, 328–344.
Weidemann, C. T., Huber, D. E., & Shiffrin, R. M. (2008). Prime diagnosticity in short-term repetition priming: Is primed evidence discounted, even when it reliably indicates the correct answer? *Journal of Experimental Psychology. Learning, Memory, and Cognition, 34*, 257–281.
Whittlesea, B. W. A., & Jacoby, L. L. (1990). Interaction of prime repetition with visual degradation: Is priming a retrieval phenomenon? *Journal of Memory and Language, 29*, 546–565.
Whittlesea, B. W. A., & Price, J. R. (2001). Implicit/explicit memory versus analytic/nonanalytic processing: Rethinking the mere exposure effect. *Memory & Cognition, 29*, 234–246.

CHAPTER SIX

Role of Knowledge in Motion Extrapolation: The Relevance of an Approach Contrasting Experts and Novices

André Didierjean*,[1], Vincent Ferrari[†], Colin Blättler[†]
*University of Franche-Comté & Institut Universitaire de France, Besançon, France
[†]Research Center of the French Air Force (CReA), Salon-de-Provence, France
[1]Corresponding author: e-mail address: andre.didierjean@univ-fcomte.fr

Contents

1. Introduction	216
2. Representational Momentum	217
2.1 Experimental Demonstration of the Phenomenon	217
2.2 RM Shares Characteristics with Physical Movement	218
3. Understanding the Impact of observers' Knowledge of Objects	221
3.1 RM Is Influenced by Knowledge on the Context in Which the Motion Occurred	221
3.2 The Knowledge Involved in RM Is Sometimes Naïve Conceptions of Physical Principles	223
3.3 The Role of Knowledge With Regard To the Specific Characteristics of Each Object	224
4. RM Is Modulated by Expert Knowledge	225
4.1 Integrating Dynamic and Natural Scenes in RM Experimental Paradigms	225
4.2 RM Among Experienced and Inexperienced Drivers	226
4.3 "True Novices." A Study with Expert and Novice Pilots	229
5. Conclusion	232
References	233

Abstract

One of the most powerful adaptive mechanisms available to the visuocognitive system for avoiding localization errors is to anticipate the probable evolution of the dynamic event as the environmental scenes are being perceived. For about 30 years now, this phenomenon has been studied in psychology in a field named "representational momentum" (RM). RM refers to the tendency of participants to "remember" the stopping point of an event as being farther along in the direction of movement than it was in reality. In this chapter, we will focus on one aspect of this phenomenon: the role of knowledge present in memory. First, we will show that different forms of knowledge are likely to influence RM effect. Second, we will focus on one specific form of knowledge: expert knowledge. We will present studies using an expert–novice paradigm providing insight with regard to the mechanisms involved in RM effect. These studies notably show that RM effect is partly a "domain-specific" phenomenon, involving knowledge specific to each category of scenes and objects.

1. INTRODUCTION

The world we live in is a world that is constantly in motion. Objects move and even environments are constantly changing. Moreover, while we observe targets in motion, we too are often moving. For instance, when driving, we come across or overtake other cars in motion. The ability to anticipate the possible evolution of the moving targets we encounter is undoubtedly a critical element in man's adaptation to his environment. In the absence of this adaptation, and taking into account the delay in information processing, our decisions would be based on an obsolete representation of the world. A large body of psychological research has analyzed how the cognitive system processes this environmental constraint in real time: as soon as a scene has been cognitively processed, it has already changed.

In this chapter, we will focus on one specific aspect of this issue: how the cognitive system handles a brief interruption in the perceptual flow. When we are driving for instance, our perception is often interrupted. We blink, check our speed on the dashboard, or turn on windshield-wipers. Yet, after this brief interruption, although the scene has changed, we experience strong feelings of continuity with the scene preceding the interruption. For about 30 years now, this phenomenon has been studied in psychology within the field referred to as *representational momentum* (RM).

RM refers to the tendency of observers to "remember" the final position of a moving target as displaced forward in the direction of target motion (Freyd & Finke, 1984). The first part of this chapter seeks to describe this perceptual bias (for a more general description of this field, see Hubbard, 2005). Specifically, we will illustrate how the RM effect develops on the basis of physical characteristics of the object's movement (its speed, its direction) and its context. Second, we will show that within the framework of an RM task, processing the movement activates generic knowledge among observers, modulating the RM effect. We will also show that specific knowledge influences the RM effect. We will then present studies which, by contrasting experts and novices, argue in favor of a domain-specific effect, meaning, involving knowledge specific to each category of scenes and objects.

2. REPRESENTATIONAL MOMENTUM
2.1. Experimental Demonstration of the Phenomenon

In the seminal study by Freyd and Finke (1984), a rotation movement was implied by presenting a rectangle in three different orientations in succession. Each rectangle was presented for 250 ms and the interval between each presentation was 250 ms. Then a fourth rectangle was shown that either was in exactly the same position as the third rectangle or tilted in the same or opposite direction to that of the implied motion. Participants were asked to determine whether the fourth orientation was similar to the third (see Fig. 6.1).

Freyd and Finke (1984) results showed that participants had more trouble rejecting the rectangles whose orientation extended the implied motion than those indicating a backward movement. Similar results were not found when no movement was induced (for instance, when the order of the third and second orientations was reversed). According to the authors, participants appeared to encode the spatial position of the third orientation slightly ahead in the same direction as the implicit path of motion. They suggested that this pattern resulted from memory for the orientation of the final inducing

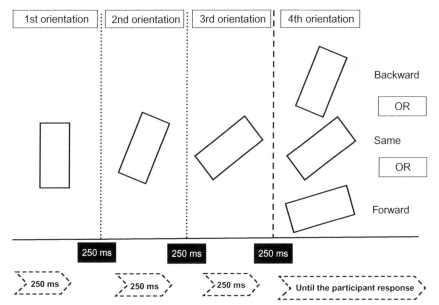

Figure 6.1 Procedure from Freyd and Finke (1984). The successive presentation of three orientations of a rectangle induces a movement of rotation of this rectangle.

stimulus being displaced forward, and given that they hypothesized this displacement reflected the effects of implied momentum, they referred to the forward displacement as RM. This phenomenon, RM, is a fundamental adaptation process that can even be observed using a static image implying motion. Freyd (1983) showed two photographs depicting an on-going action (for instance, a child jumping). These two photographs were presented in succession either in chronological order (n then $n+1$) or in reverse order ($n+1$ then n). Moreover, in some of the trials, the two photographs were identical (n then n). Participants were asked to state whether the pairs were identical or not. Results showed that the photographs presented in chronological order were harder to reject than those presented in reverse order (see also Freyd, Pantzer, & Cheng, 1988; Futterweit & Beilin, 1994).

While RM was initially revealed using very simple stimuli, it has also been observed using complex stimuli. Several studies have demonstrated, for example, that the movement of a target increasing in size (i.e., one whose size increases as it approaches) or shrinking (i.e., diminishes in size as the target moves away) provokes encoding the size of the target as larger when it is increasing and as smaller when it is decreasing (Hayes, Sacher, Thornton, Sereno, & Freyd, 1996; Hubbard, 1996; Nagaï & Yagi, 2001). Similarly, Munger, Solberg, and Horrocks (1999) presented three complex dimensional figures inducing rotation movements. Their results show that complex objects rotating in depth in the visual system also lead to an extrapolation of movement.

2.2. RM Shares Characteristics with Physical Movement

In one of their first studies, Freyd and Finke (1985) hypothesized the existence of an analogy between the anticipated and the real movement of an object. To test this hypothesis, they analyzed the object's velocity effect on RM. Using a protocol that was largely identical to the one used in their previous study (Freyd & Finke, 1984), two experimental conditions were compared: the induced movement was either quick or slow. Their results showed stronger RM effect when figures were presented with higher velocity of motion. Extending these studies, Finke, Freyd, and Shyi (1986) analyzed the impact of acceleration or deceleration of induced movement. They observed that when a figure appeared to accelerate, the spatial position represented by the observer was largely distorted as further along in the path of motion. By contrast, deceleration in the display of the figure reduced RM effect (for similar results, see also Finke & Shyi, 1988).

Following these preliminary studies on RM, Hubbard and Bharucha (1988) used a slightly different experimental paradigm. They showed participants a target (a point) moving in a continuous and rectilinear motion, either vertically (top to bottom or bottom to top, depending on the trials) or horizontally (right to left or left to right, depending on the trials). See Fig. 6.2 for an illustration. This movement is therefore an apparent motion and not an induced motion as was the case in the experiences described previously. After a few seconds, the target vanished without warning, and after the target had vanished, the observers used a computer mouse to position the cursor at the display coordinates at which they judged the target to have vanished.

Results showed that participants' memory for the location of the target was displaced along the direction of motion. This RM effect occurred with both vertical and horizontal motion.

An interesting aspect of this study is that Hubbard and Bharucha (1988) observed an unexpected result (see Fig. 6.2). Their findings showed that RM effect was smaller for bottom-to-top than for top-to-bottom displacement. Moreover, these authors also reported that horizontally moving targets were

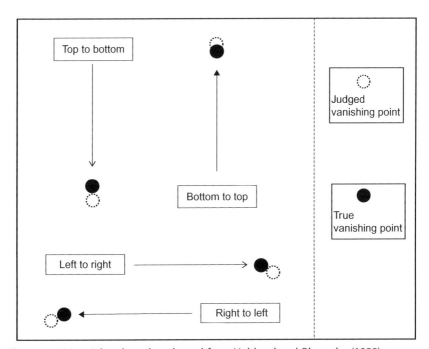

Figure 6.2 Material and results adapted from Hubbard and Bharucha (1988).

displaced downward below the path of motion (in addition to being displaced forward along the axis of motion). More recently, Hubbard (2001) reported that vertically moving targets that vanished high in the picture plane (i.e., descending targets that had fallen a shorter distance and ascending targets that had risen a longer distance) exhibited smaller forward displacement than did vertically moving targets that vanished low in the picture plane (i.e., descending targets that had fallen a longer distance and ascending targets that had risen a shorter distance). Hubbard (2001, 2005) argued that all these results were probably produced by the observer's knowledges about physical gravity laws. Gravity acts to decrease the forward velocity of a rising object and increase the forward velocity of a falling object.

Extending these results on the effect of gravity, Hubbard (1995) also studied the effects of friction on RM. He presented participants with a moving target (a square) which, depending on the experimental condition, was either in contact or not, with another static surface (a rectangle). He hypothesized that if knowledge of principles of physics has an impact on RM effect, when a moving target is in contact with another surface (existence of friction), a reduction in RM would be observed. Results effectively show that RM is smaller when targets are in contact with another surface (see also Hubbard, 1998; Kerzel, 2002).

These results provide convincing evidence that RM processes are influenced by observers' knowledge of physical principles, such as gravity or friction.

The studies presented highlight certain similarities between RM and real displacement from a spatial perspective. A few studies have analyzed whether these similarities exist as well from a temporal perspective. Freyd and Johnson (1987) addressed this question using Freyd and Finke's paradigm (1984, see Fig. 6.1). In their study, they varied the latency between the third and fourth orientation presented (from 10 to 900 ms). Their results showed that the RM effect increased with increased retention intervals. This highlights a new similarity between RM and real displacement: a moving object whose motion is suddenly hidden covers a longer distance when the retention interval is longer.

In sum, RM is a fundamental and adaptive phenomenon that has been highlighted across numerous situations. Confronted with a moving object, when the perception is interrupted for a short while, an observer always judges the last position of the object as further along in the direction of motion and further off in time than it was in reality. Moreover, this phenomenon is modulated by observers' knowledge of physical characteristics.

3. UNDERSTANDING THE IMPACT OF OBSERVERS' KNOWLEDGE OF OBJECTS

3.1. RM Is Influenced by Knowledge on the Context in Which the Motion Occurred

Following first RM studies that have been presented in the section 2.1, some studies explored how RM effect is influenced by knowledge. These studies showed that RM was influenced not only by major principles of physics such as gravity but also by knowledge on the context in which the motion took place.

In one such study, Bertamini (1993) presented observers with an image on which a circle was drawn on an inclined plane. Using a paradigm that was largely similar to that used by Freyd and Finke (1984), this first image disappeared from the screen and was replaced by a second image. In this second image, the circle was positioned either slightly above the initial position or slightly below it. Participants were asked to indicate whether the circle's position was identical for the two images. Results showed that images positioned below the initial circle were harder to reject than those positioned above the circle. This can be intepretated by the fact that context influences observers. In the real world, a ball on an inclined plane rolls downward. This knowledge appears to influence RM. To further extend his research, the author used different conditions, varying the angle of inclination of the plane. Results showed that the steeper the inclination, the stronger the RM effect. The context of the target object—the inclined plane in this case—is therefore taken into account by the mechanisms responsible for RM.

In a series of studies that also addressed the effect of context (Hubbard & Bharucha, 1988), participants were shown a target enclosed within a frame, moving either horizontally or vertically at a constant speed. From time to time, the target bounced off the inner walls of the frame. Depending on the trials, it disappeared prior to collision with a wall of the frame, at the moment of collision with the closest wall or after collision. Participants were asked to position the cursor over where they considered the target to have vanished. Results showed that in positions prior to collision or at the moment of collision, the direction of displacement was opposite to the direction of motion. This suggests that participants anticipated that the target would rebound on the walls of the frame, thereby changing its direction. In line with this, studies carried out by Verfaillie and d'Ydewalle (1991) show that complex motion "patterns" can influence extrapolation. The paradigm used was similar to that used by Freyd and Finke (1984); however, Verfaillie and d'Ydewalle introduced conditions in which successive rotations of a rectangle changed direction from time to time (see Fig. 6.3). The moving target could thus be described from a local perspective (clockwise motion) as well as from a global perspective with regard to the periodic motion of the moving target (clockwise then counterclockwise motion, etc.).

The key point in this analysis concerns the cases where the target disappears just before the breaking point. The results clearly show that the extrapolation of motion is no longer observed at these points of disruption. This demonstrates that the memorization of the final orientation of the rectangle presented is influenced by the anticipation of the target's global motion and not merely by an extrapolation of its local motion. These findings suggest that observers could have extracted the regularities that govern this global motion. Observers thus anticipate motion using acquired knowledge (the extracted regularities) and not simply on the basis of perceived motion. Understanding the nature of the different forms of knowledge involved in this effect is thus a fundamental issue.

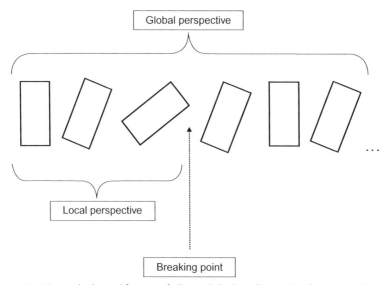

Figure 6.3 Material adapted from Verfaillie and d'Ydewalle (1991). The rectangle is presented successively in different orientations that induce a rotational movement. At various times the rotation moves in the opposite direction (breaking point).

3.2. The Knowledge Involved in RM Is Sometimes Naïve Conceptions of Physical Principles

A number of studies have shown that physical knowledge used in RM effect is often implicit and naïve rather than explicit expert knowledge. This distinction is particularly well illustrated in a study carried out by Freyd and Jones (1994). These authors analyzed RM in a situation where a ball was shot through a spiral tube (see Fig. 6.4). Participants were asked to state where the ball was positioned a few moments after exiting the tube.

Results showed that participants selected the spiral path as the ball's anticipated trajectory (i.e., a trajectory influenced by a spiral form, see section B of Fig. 6.4). However, results from a posttest questionnaire showed that over 60% of the participants chose "straight path" as the ball's expected trajectory after exiting a spiral tube (see section A of Fig. 6.4). The RM effect observed therefore reflects naïve physics rather than explicit knowledge of physical laws among participants (Zago & Lacquaniti, 2005). Similar results have been found by Kozhevnikov and Hegarty (2001) who focussed on explicit and implicit knowledge of physical principles. In this study that was carried out among physics experts and novices, the authors elaborated an RM paradigm that required specific physical laws (notably gravity). Results showed that both novices and experts (despite the fact that the latter were able to correctly state physical laws) continued to exhibit implicit impetus beliefs. In this experiment, when impetus beliefs and Newtonian theory made different predictions, experts exhibited the same implicit impetus beliefs as novices when asked to respond in an RM paradigm.

The findings we presented above are consistent with the view that RM is under the influence of "naïve" knowledge rather than expert knowledge.

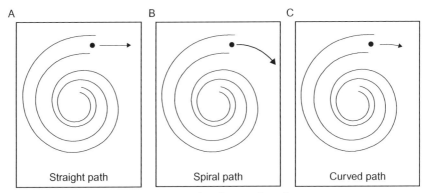

Figure 6.4 Material adapted from Freyd and Jones (1994).

Nevertheless, we think that these studies have given themselves little chance to observe an influence of expert knowledge. In particular, this could be a consequence of the highly artificial aspect of the situations presented in most of these studies. Studies on expert memory have shown that expert knowledge is essentially highly specific knowledge, which cannot be transferred to situations that are not closely linked to the domain of expertise (see, for instance, Chase & Simon, 1973; Unterrainer, Kaller, Halsband, & Rahm, 2006; for a review, see Gobet, 1998; Didierjean & Gobet, 2008). In the following sections, we will show that object-specific knowledge can also influence RM and that the impact of RM can also be highlighted using valid ecological material. We will then show that based on this kind of paradigm, it is possible to demonstrate that expert knowledge influences RM, and thereby advance our understanding on the nature of knowledge involved.

3.3. The Role of Knowledge With Regard To the Specific Characteristics of Each Object

One of the most elegant studies showing object-specific effects on RM was conducted by Vinson and Reed (2002) (see also Reed & Vinson, 1996). These authors carried out an RM experiment using drawings representing objects. Each drawing was successively presented four times during 250 ms and was shifted each time 15 mm higher or lower than the previous one. A fifth drawing was then shown and subjects were to determine whether this last one was at the same position as the fourth drawing shown. The authors demonstrated that the size of RM was related to the nature of objects. A greater memory shift was induced by a weight stimulus when implied motion was downward and by a rocket stimulus when implied motion was upward. A building did not elicit different memory shifts for upward and downward movement. Vinson and Reed also showed that despite having *identical visual features*, the "rocket" and "building" stimuli produced different results (see Fig. 6.5). While the rocket showed greater memory shift for upward implied motion, the same drawing labeled "building" did not elicit similar results. These findings show that RM is affected by participants' knowledge of perceived objects. Why is it then that the few studies that have attempted to vary the expertise level of participants have failed to show an impact of expert knowledge (for instance, Kozhevnikov & Hegarty, 2001; Zago & Lacquaniti, 2005)? Probably because the paradigms used are far removed from the "natural" conditions

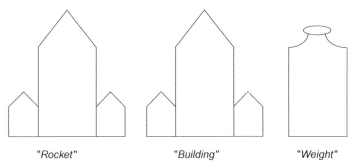

Figure 6.5 Material adapted from Vinson and Reed (2002).

where expertise occurs. In the next section, we will present a study that shows that the effects of RM can also be illustrated using more ecological material.

4. RM IS MODULATED BY EXPERT KNOWLEDGE

This section seeks to show that expert knowledge, which most of the time is very specific within a given domain, modulates RM. Its objective is twofold: first, we will show why integrating natural and realistic scenes is an indispensable condition in highlighting the effects of expert knowledge on RM. Second, we will present the experimental results from a series of studies conducted among experts and novices in different domains; these results show that the RM effect is modulated by expertise, enabling us to extend our understanding of the knowledge at stake.

4.1. Integrating Dynamic and Natural Scenes in RM Experimental Paradigms

We think that classic RM tasks, such as those we have presented above, do not enable an observer to bring into play his/her expert knowledge, as the situations presented are rather artificial. Which observer is expert in the perceptual processing of a rectangle turning around, a shifting point or a pointing building? Analyzing how the RM effect is modulated by expertise undoubtedly requires the development of an experimental paradigm presenting a dynamic scene within a realistic frame and specific to a domain of expertise.

Thornton and Hayes (2004) presented several experiments demonstrating RM effects with tasks using relatively natural scenes. One of their experiments presented synthesized images of movie sequences showing a driver's view along a scenic roadway. This virtual environment contained a straight, single-lane gray road receding in depth over a green, textured ground plane. The overall impression was that of a viewer in a car approaching a small village, driving through the village, and then continuing along the open road. Videos depicted a synthesized image of a road as seen from inside the car driving at 58, 65, or 72 km/h. The observer's task was to detect an "unexpected" interruption in the sequence. Participants watched road scene videos that were temporarily interrupted by a black screen lasting 250 ms. After the interruption, the film continued and the participants had to judge whether the scene resumed at exactly the same point as it had stopped (normal-resumption condition) or at some other point. When the scene resumed at a different point, it could be either with a shift forward or with a shift backward. The results obtained showed that forward shifts were more difficult to reject than backward shifts. This study thus showed that RM can also be found in the case of natural scenes, further confirming the adaptive dimension of anticipation mechanisms. In the next section, we will show how this paradigm can be used to analyze whether RM is influenced by explicit knowledge that is specific by nature.

4.2. RM Among Experienced and Inexperienced Drivers

In several studies (Blättler, Ferrari, Didierjean, & Marmèche, 2012; Blättler, Ferrari, Didierjean, Van Elslande, & Marmèche, 2010), we tried to test the impact of domain-specific expertise, automobile driving, on RM, using films of road scenes, and to find out whether the improved anticipation ability that comes with greater expertise is transferred to scenes from domains that are far removed from the individual's domain of expertise.

In a first study, experienced automobile drivers and inexperienced automobile drivers performed a movement-anticipation task on realistic road scenes (i.e., automobile driving filmed by an onboard camera). Our idea was to use an RM task in order to find out whether an expertise effect occurs as early as the perceptual encoding phase.

In this experiment, the participants were divided into two groups on the basis of their driving experience: "inexperienced drivers," who did not have their driver's license, and "experienced drivers," who had been driving regularly (for at least 2 h a day) for an average of 18 years. They viewed road scenes filmed by an onboard camera. The car was constantly moving at a speed of 60 km/h. The scenes were interrupted by the display of a black screen lasting 250 ms and then resumed in one of three conditions: a shift forward (with respect to the car's direction of movement), a shift backward (in the direction opposite to the car's movement), or no shift (at exactly the same point as before the interruption, normal-resumption condition). In the shift conditions, the size of the forward and backward shifts was manipulated (3, 6, 9, and 12 m). Figure 6.6 gives an illustration of a standard frame, a 12-m shift forward, and a 12-m shift backward.

The task was a same/different comparison task. Participants had to compare the last scene viewed before the cut, to the first scene viewed after the cut, and decide whether or not the two scenes were the same (i.e., whether the vehicle was in the same location in both scenes). Our hypotheses were that if more RM effect is observed in experienced drivers than inexperienced ones, then in the normal-resumption condition, experienced drivers should make significantly more errors than inexperienced ones. In the forward-shift and backward-shift conditions, if participants anticipate, they should have more trouble deciding on forward shifts (than on backward shifts) whether or not the first image seen after the cut is different from the last image seen before the cut. Accordingly, if experienced drivers anticipate more than inexperienced ones, then we can expect the asymmetry between forward and backward shifts (on "same" responses) to be greater for experienced drivers than for inexperienced ones.

First, the results of this experiment indicated that all participants of both driving-expertise levels exhibited an RM effect; the error rate was significantly higher for forward shifts than for backward ones. This finding obtained with real videos corroborates those obtained with synthesized images by Thornton and Hayes (2004). Concerning the main goal of this study, that is, to explore the effect of domain-specific knowledge on motion anticipation, the results showed that the experienced drivers did indeed anticipate more than the inexperienced. For example, the experienced

12 m backward   Standard frame   12 m forward

Figure 6.6 Example of material used in Blättler et al. (2010, Experiment 1). The standard frame (in the middle) was the last image seen before the cut. The video resumed after a backward shift of 12 m or a forward shift of 12 m.

drivers made more errors when the video resumed at exactly the same point as before the cut. Knowledge acquired from years of driving modulates the effect of RM on driving-scene judgements. These results extend earlier findings from the few studies demonstrating RM modulation by the observer's domain-specific conceptual knowledge of the moving object (Vinson & Reed, 2002). They also show, as noted in certain models of expert memory (for a review, see Didierjean & Gobet, 2008), that expert perception of scenes differs from that of novices right from the perceptual encoding phase.

In a second part of this experiment, we aimed at determining whether this expertise effect is due to the existence of a general anticipation ability acquired with driving expertise, or whether the knowledge developed by experienced drivers is domain specific. In this second part, the same experienced drivers and inexperienced drivers as in the first part performed two RM tasks with stimuli not involved in driving. One task showed a black square moving from left to right across the screen; the other showed a film of a person running (see Fig. 6.7). In each trial, 2 s after the beginning of the video, a black screen was displayed for 250 ms. After the interruption, the video resumed in one of the same conditions as in the first experiment (normal-resumption condition, forward-shift conditions, and backward-shift conditions). Our goal was to find out if the knowledge mobilized in RM tasks is partly task specific. Most studies on cognitive expertise have shown that expert knowledge is not transferred to material that is not from the expert's domain (e.g., Chase & Simon, 1973; Ericsson, 1985; Hatano & Osawa, 1983; Unterrainer et al., 2006; see however Gauthier, Williams, Tarr, & Tanaka, 1998; Tanaka, Curran, & Sheinberg, 2005). With this

 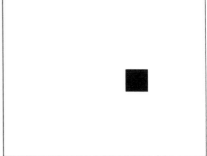

Figure 6.7 Examples of material used in the second part of the Blättler et al. (2010)'s article. Left: The image is a screen print of a video showing a person running from right to left. Right: The image is a screen print of an animated square moving from left to right.

hypothesis, we can expect no differences between experienced and inexperienced drivers in terms of movement anticipation.

The results showed that for both natural scenes and artificial scenes, all participants exhibited an RM effect. As a whole, the participants made judgement errors in the normal-resumption condition, and their forward-shift and backward-shift responses were asymmetrical (i.e., there were more mistakes on forward shifts than on backward ones). These results thus provide further evidence of an RM effect in dynamic situations. Unlike the first part of the experiment, however, there was no anticipation difference between the two groups of participants (experienced or inexperienced drivers). The main finding of this second part of the experiment is that knowledge acquired in a specific domain (here, automobile driving), which led to RM modulation with experience, was not transferred to dissimilar domains.

Correlations were calculated in order to relate the participants' performance in both parts of the experiments. No correlations were found between the different types of scenes, for either group of participants. This second result argues in favor of the presence of RM components specific to the scenes presented. In a second study, we tried to extend these results to a new expertise domain. We used novices and expert pilots and simulated aircraft landing scenes (Blättler, Ferrari, Didierjean, & Marmèche, 2011).

4.3. "True Novices." A Study with Expert and Novice Pilots

Our main goal was to find out whether RM would be observed for "true" novices, or whether this effect requires some minimal amount of knowledge of the scenes observed. One of the limitations of the study we have presented above was that the inexperienced drivers were not "true" novices. As car passengers, the novices must have seen the same types of visual scenes as the experienced drivers. Indeed, Jordan and Hunsinger (2008) argued that even riding in an automobile can modify the person's perception of the driving situation he/she observes. This question is important at a more general level because, although RM is a particularly robust phenomenon (Courtney & Hubbard, 2008; Ruppel, Fleming, & Hubbard, 2009) that has been observed in many different situations, in the vast majority of studies, the observers were not actually real novices relative to the scenes presented.

In our experiment, visual simulations based on synthesized images of aircraft landing scenes, seen from the viewpoint of the pilot, were used in an RM task. We tested 15 expert pilots from the French Air Force and

21 novice participants, who had never been in the cockpit of an airplane or on board an aircraft simulator. The speed chosen for the landing was a standard speed for a military jet fighter (i.e., the distance the aircraft travels during 125 ms is about 7 m at a speed of 200 km/h). As in our precedent studies, the scenes were interrupted by the display of a black screen lasting 125 ms and then resumed in one of three conditions: a shift forward (with respect to the aircraft's direction of motion), a shift backward (in the direction opposite to the plane's motion), or no shift (i.e., at exactly the same point as before the interruption). In the shift conditions, the size of the forward and backward shifts was manipulated (125, 250, 375, and 500 ms). Participants had to compare the last image seen before the cut to the first image seen after the cut and decide whether the scene had shifted backward or forward.

First, as in our experiments with expert drivers, we observed that expert pilots anticipate more than novices do in their knowledge domain. When the scene resumed at exactly the same point as before the cut, the piloting experts answered "backward shift" significantly more often than the novices did. When the video resumed with a forward shift, the experts again responded "backward shift" significantly more often than the novices did, especially on the smallest forward shifts.

Second, the main goal of the present study was to find out whether RM would be observed for "true" novices, or whether this effect requires some minimal amount of knowledge of the scenes observed. Here, the RM effect was not detected for the novices. A few rare experiments have shown that RM can be eliminated when the direction of motion cannot be anticipated (e.g., Kerzel, 2002) or when distractors are presented during the retention interval (e.g., Kerzel, 2003). Distractors during the retention interval seem to stop the mental extrapolation of the target. The presence of such distractors may disrupt the flow of attention allocated to the moving target and thereby cause RM to decrease. With this finding in mind, we tested in a control experiment the hypothesis that with a longer inter stimuli interval (ISI), more time could be allotted to the mental extrapolation of the dynamic scene, and that this additional time might allow RM to show up, even among novices. Therefore, in a control experiment, ISI duration was doubled (from 125 to 250 ms) and the same shift sizes were used. The results were very similar to those obtained in our first experiment. For novices in these experimental conditions, we were not able to demonstrate RM. To rule out the possibility that the novices were perhaps an outlier group with unusually small RM in general, a control task was proposed to these same novices. We chose the classical (Hubbard, 2001) task of a moving square on a plain background, the same as the one we used in our previous research (Blättler et al., 2010). Results showed that our novices, as all participants of previous research, exhibited an RM effect.

Our main question in this research was whether or not the mechanisms responsible for RM might be generic (i.e., general or not domain specific). In this study, experts showed a strong RM effect, whereas anticipation was not detected for the novices in several experimental conditions. Taken together, these results clearly support the hypothesis that RM relies at least partially on specific knowledge stored in long-term memory.

The RM observed here with the expert pilots can be considered to reflect very good adaptation by the visual system of experts. In this line, Hayhoe (2009) showed that memory may play a part in controlling visually guided behavior. Observers are thought to learn the dynamic properties of the world in order to direct their gaze where it is needed. In dynamic environments such as driving, they would learn the complex properties of the moving environment. For Hayhoe, evidence of such learning is the fact that saccades are often directed toward a location in a scene in advance of an expected event. For example, in Land and McLeod's (2000) study of cricket, batsmen anticipated the ball's bouncing point so that the eye arrived at that point 100–200 ms before the ball did. The ability to predict where the ball will bounce would rely on previous experience of the ball's trajectory. The saccades were always preceded by a fixation on the ball as it left the bowler's hand, suggesting that the bouncing-point predictions were based on both current sensory data and prior experience of the ball's motion. The authors concluded that observers store internal models of the dynamic properties of the world that can be used to position the gaze in anticipation of a predicted event. The participants' anticipatory saccades and pursuit movements revealed that acquisition of visual information is planned for a predicted state of the world. Such predictions have to be based on a stored memory representation. And the accuracy of the predictions reveals the quality of the information in the stored memory or internal model. Spatial and temporal accuracy of eye saccades and fine-tuning of these movements following a change in the moving object's dynamic properties would indicate that subjects have an accurate internal model of the object's spatiotemporal path, and that they rapidly update this model when errors occur. As Hayhoe (2009) stressed, the development of internal models occurs over long periods as a result of extensive practice. The data we collected seem to point in this direction. It takes years of experience before an expert pilot becomes capable of anticipating the spatiotemporal evolution of landing scenes in order to fill in the visual gap in what is perceived. Such anticipation processes are likely to help pilots manage the control strategies they use. Following the pioneering work by De Groot (1965) and Chase and Simon (1973), a large number of studies have shown that expertise in a domain considerably modifies the perceptual encoding of domain-specific elements present in the scene (e.g., Reingold, Charness, Pomplun, & Stampe, 2001). Thus, it is possible that expert pilots extract different information that promotes RM.

5. CONCLUSION

The objective of this chapter was to present some of the studies which show that RM is influenced by knowledge. One of the recurrent questions in cognitive psychology concerns knowing whether generic mechanisms, in which similar processes are applied to all situations, underlie a given behavior, or whether specific mechanisms that are different for each situation are used. Analyzing this issue is complex as in most of the domains studied in psychology, participants are all experts in the task proposed (for instance in most of the studies on face recognition), or on the contrary, all novices (for example in the tasks used to analyze working memory). In both cases, it is difficult to determine what falls within specific knowledge and what falls within generic knowledge. As the studies we have presented show, comparing experts and novices in the RM domain offers an interesting tool with which we can address this issue. Our results show that at least partly, RM is undoubtedly influenced by specific knowledge with regard to each category of scenes.

Putting into perspective the studies in the domain of cognitive expertise and RM undoubtedly offer an additional advantage. Over the years, the cognitive expertise domain has developed theories that provide precise description of the architecture of expert knowledge in memory (see, for instance, Gobet & Simon, 1996, 2000). These models have pointed out that in expert memory, knowledge develops in a highly specific form, named "chunk" (e.g., Chase & Simon, 1973; Gobet et al., 2001). In chess for instance, chunks are familiar patterns of pieces commonly found in chess games. Expertise is acquired through the learning of a very large number of chunks indexed by a discrimination network. Such networks enable the rapid categorization of domain-specific patterns and account for the speed with which expert players "see" the key elements of a problem. In these theories, chunks have an anticipatory character: they possess information on the most probable follow-up of actions which activate them. To date, this characteristic of expert memory has been essentially demonstrated with strategic knowledge, for instance tactical schemas in basketball (e.g., Didierjean & Marmèche, 2005) or chess openings (e.g., Ferrari, Didierjean, & Marmèche, 2006). Putting into perspective the studies in the domain of cognitive expertise and RM is undoubtedly interesting in these two domains. Studies on expertise propose specific models of knowledge involved in anticipation. For their part, studies on RM present a well-grounded experimental and theoretical framework to extend these models to the first phases of perceptual encoding.

REFERENCES

Bertamini, M. (1993). Memory for position and dynamic representations. *Memory & Cognition, 21,* 449–457.

Blättler, C., Ferrari, V., Didierjean, A., & Marmèche, E. (2011). Representational momentum in aviation. *Journal of Experimental Psychology. Human Perception and Performance, 37,* 1569–1577.

Blättler, C., Ferrari, V., Didierjean, A., & Marmèche, E. (2012). Role of expertise and action in motion extrapolation in real road scenes. *Visual Cognition, 20,* 998–1001.

Blättler, C., Ferrari, V., Didierjean, A., Van Elslande, P., & Marmèche, E. (2010). Can expertise modulate representational momentum? *Visual Cognition, 18,* 1253–1273.

Chase, W. G., & Simon, H. A. (1973). Perception in chess. *Cognitive Psychology, 4,* 55–81.

Courtney, J. R., & Hubbard, T. L. (2008). Spatial memory and explicit knowledge: An effect of instruction on representational momentum. *Quarterly Journal of Experimental Psychology, 61,* 1778–1784.

De Groot, A. D. (1965). *Thought and choice in chess.* The Hague: Mouton Publishers.

Didierjean, A., & Gobet, F. (2008). Sherlock Holmes—An expert's view of expertise. *British Journal of Psychology, 99,* 109–125.

Didierjean, A., & Marmèche, E. (2005). Anticipatory representation of visual basketball scenes by novice and expert players. *Visual Cognition, 12,* 265–283.

Ericsson, K. A. (1985). Memory skill. *Canadian Journal of Psychology, 39,* 188–231.

Ferrari, V., Didierjean, A., & Marmèche, E. (2006). Dynamic perception in chess. *The Quarterly Journal of Experimental Psychology, 59,* 397–410.

Finke, R. A., Freyd, J. J., & Shyi, G. C. (1986). Implied velocity and acceleration induce transformations of visual memory. *Journal of Experimental Psychology: General, 115,* 175–188.

Finke, R. A., & Shyi, G. C. (1988). Mental extrapolation and representational momentum for complex implied motions. *Journal of Experimental Psychology: Learning, Memory, and Cognition, 14,* 112–120.

Freyd, J. J. (1983). The mental representation of movement when static stimuli are viewed. *Perception & Psychophysics, 33,* 575–581.

Freyd, J. J., & Finke, R. A. (1984). Representational momentum. *Journal of Experimental Psychology: Learning, Memory, and Cognition, 10,* 126–132.

Freyd, J. J., & Finke, R. A. (1985). A velocity effect of representational momentum. *Bulletin of the Psychonomic Society, 23,* 443–446.

Freyd, J. J., & Johnson, J. Q. (1987). Probing the time course of representational momentum. *Journal of Experimental Psychology: Learning, Memory, and Cognition, 13,* 259–268.

Freyd, J. J., & Jones, K. T. (1994). Representational momentum for a spiral path. *Journal of Experimental Psychology: Learning, Memory, and Cognition, 20,* 968–976.

Freyd, J. J., Pantzer, T. M., & Cheng, J. L. (1988). Representing statics as forces in equilibrium. *Journal of Experimental Psychology: General, 117,* 395–407.

Futterweit, L. R., & Beilin, H. (1994). Recognition memory for movement in photographs: A developmental study. *Journal of Experimental Child Psychology, 57,* 163–179.

Gauthier, I., Williams, P., Tarr, M. J., & Tanaka, J. (1998). Training 'greeble' experts: A framework for studying expert object recognition processes. *Vision Research, 38,* 2401–2428.

Gobet, F. (1998). Expert memory: A comparison of four theories. *Cognition, 66,* 115–152.

Gobet, F., Lane, P. C. R., Croker, S., Cheng, P. C. H., Jones, G., Oliver, I., et al. (2001). Chunking mechanisms in human learning. *Trends in Cognitive Sciences, 5,* 236–243.

Gobet, F., & Simon, H. A. (1996). Templates in chess memory: A mechanism for recalling several boards. *Cognitive Psychology, 31,* 1–40.

Gobet, F., & Simon, H. A. (2000). Five seconds or sixty? Presentation time in expert memory. *Cognitive Science, 24,* 651–682.

Hatano, G., & Osawa, K. (1983). Digit memory of grand experts in abacus-derived mental calculation. *Cognition, 15,* 95–110.

Hayes, A. E., Sacher, G., Thornton, I. M., Sereno, M. E., & Freyd, J. J. (1996). Representational momentum in depth using stereopsis. *Investigative Ophthalmology & Visual Science, 37,* S467.

Hayhoe, M. M. (2009). Visual memory in motor planning and action. In J. R. Brockmole (Ed.), *The visual world in memory.* Hove: Psychology Press.

Hubbard, T. L. (1995). Environmental invariants in the representation of motion: Implied dynamics and representational momentum, gravity, friction, and centripetal forces. *Psychonomic Bulletin & Review, 2,* 322–338.

Hubbard, T. L. (1996). Displacement in depth: Representational momentum and boundary extension. *Psychological Research, 59,* 33–47.

Hubbard, T. L. (1998). Some effects of representational friction, target size, and memory averaging on memory for vertically moving targets. *Canadian Journal of Experimental Psychology, 52,* 44–49.

Hubbard, T. L. (2001). The effect of height in the picture plane on the forward displacement of ascending and descending targets. *Canadian Journal of Experimental Psychology, 55,* 325–329.

Hubbard, T. L. (2005). Representational momentum and related displacements in spatial memory: A review of the findings. *Psychonomic Bulletin & Review, 12,* 822–851.

Hubbard, T. L., & Bharucha, J. J. (1988). Judged displacement in apparent vertical and horizontal motion. *Perception & Psychophysics, 44,* 211–221.

Jordan, J. S., & Hunsinger, M. (2008). Learned patterns of action-effect anticipation contribute to the spatial displacement of continuously moving stimuli. *Journal of Experimental Psychology: Human Perception and Performance, 34,* 113–124.

Kerzel, D. (2002). A matter of design: No representational momentum without predictability. *Visual Cognition, 9,* 66–80.

Kerzel, D. (2003). Attention maintains mental extrapolation of target position: Irrelevant distractors eliminate forward displacement after implied motion. *Cognition, 88,* 109–131.

Kozhevnikov, M., & Hegarty, M. (2001). Impetus beliefs as default heuristics: Dissociation between explicit and implicit knowledge about motion. *Psychonomic Bulletin & Review, 8,* 439–453.

Land, M. F., & McLeod, P. (2000). From eye movements to actions: How batsmen hit the ball. *Nature Neuroscience, 3,* 1340–1345.

Munger, M. P., Solberg, J. L., & Horrocks, K. K. (1999). The relationship between mental rotation and representational momentum. *Journal of Experimental Psychology: Learning, Memory, and Cognition, 25,* 1557–1568.

Nagaï, M., & Yagi, A. (2001). The pointedness effect on representational momentum. *Memory & Cognition, 29,* 91–99.

Reed, C. L., & Vinson, N. G. (1996). Conceptual effects on representational momentum. *Journal of Experimental Psychology: Human Perception and Performance, 22,* 839–850.
Reingold, E. M., Charness, N., Pomplun, M., & Stampe, D. M. (2001). Visual span in expert chess players: Evidence from eye movements. *Psychological Science, 12,* 48–55.
Ruppel, S. E., Fleming, C. N., & Hubbard, T. L. (2009). Representational momentum is not (totally) impervious to error feedback. *Canadian Journal of Experimental Psychology, 63,* 49–58.
Tanaka, J. W., Curran, T., & Sheinberg, D. L. (2005). The training and transfer of real-world perceptual expertise. *Psychological Science, 16,* 145–151.
Thornton, I. M., & Hayes, A. E. (2004). Anticipating action in complex scenes. *Visual Cognition, 11,* 341–370.
Unterrainer, J. M., Kaller, C. P., Halsband, U., & Rahm, B. (2006). Planning abilities and chess: A comparison of chess and non-chess players on the Tower of London task. *British Journal of Psychology, 97,* 299–311.
Verfaillie, K., & d'Ydewalle, G. (1991). Representational momentum and event course anticipation in the perception of implied periodical motions. *Journal of Experimental Psychology: Learning, Memory, and Cognition, 17,* 302–313.
Vinson, N. G., & Reed, C. L. (2002). Sources of object-specific effects in representational momentum. *Visual Cognition, 9,* 41–65.
Zago, M., & Lacquaniti, F. (2005). The internal model of gravity for hand interception: Parametric adaptation to zero-gravity visual targets on Earth. *Journal of Neurophysiology, 94,* 1346–1357.

CHAPTER SEVEN

Retrieval-Based Learning: An Episodic Context Account

Jeffrey D. Karpicke*,[1], Melissa Lehman*, William R. Aue*,[†]

*Department of Psychological Sciences, Purdue University, West Lafayette, Indiana, USA
[†]Department of Psychology, Syracuse University, Syracuse, New York, USA
[1]Corresponding author: e-mail address: karpicke@purdue.edu

Contents

1. Introduction	238
2. Current Status of Retrieval Practice Research	239
2.1 The Effects of Retrieval Practice on Learning	240
2.2 Delimiting the Key Effects in the Retrieval Practice Literature	245
3. Analysis of Existing Explanations of Retrieval Practice	247
3.1 Strength and Retrieval Effort	248
3.2 Storage and Retrieval Strength	249
3.3 Bifurcation	250
3.4 Transfer Appropriate Processing	250
3.5 Encoding Variability	251
3.6 Elaborative Retrieval	252
4. An Episodic Context Account of Retrieval-Based Learning	258
4.1 Overview of the Episodic Context Account	258
4.2 Context Representation and Encoding	259
4.3 Context Reinstatement During Retrieval	260
4.4 Context Updating During Successful Retrieval	261
4.5 Retrieval Practice Restricts the Search Set	262
5. Evidence Supporting an Episodic Context Account	263
5.1 Effects of Retrieval Practice and Initial Retrieval Difficulty	263
5.2 Recollection of Context on a Criterial Test	266
5.3 Manipulations of Initial Context Retrieval	271
6. General Discussion and Final Comments	275
6.1 Context Variability and Study-Phase Retrieval	275
6.2 Conclusion	278
Acknowledgments	278
References	278

Abstract

Practicing retrieval is a powerful way to promote learning and long-term retention. This chapter addresses the theoretical underpinnings of retrieval-based learning. We review methodological issues in retrieval practice research, identify key findings to be accounted for, and evaluate current candidate theories. We propose an episodic context account of retrieval-based learning, which explains retrieval practice in terms of context reinstatement, context updating, and restriction of the search set. Retrieval practice involves attempting to reinstate a prior learning context, and when retrieval is successful, the representation of context is updated to include features of retrieved contexts and the current context. Future retrieval is enhanced because updated context representations can be used to restrict the search set and hone in on a desired target. The context account accommodates a wide variety of phenomena in the retrieval practice literature and provides a comprehensive and cohesive account of retrieval-based learning.

1. INTRODUCTION

We often think of our minds as places that hold copies or records of our past experiences, and perhaps as a consequence, we tend to identify the process of "learning" with the acquisition of new knowledge and experiences—the creation of new information in memory. When learning is viewed as the process of getting information into one's mind, an emphasis naturally falls on the processes involved in encoding knowledge and experiences. Learners may not worry much about how they will retrieve and reconstruct knowledge when they need to use it in the future, but even if they do, they likely view retrieval as the mere expression of knowledge obtained from prior experiences—the evidence that prior learning occurred—but no more. It is in this sense that retrieval is considered "neutral" for learning because the process of accessing knowledge is not thought to change knowledge.

The approach described in this chapter, referred to as *retrieval-based learning*, is based on the finding that accessing knowledge does indeed change one's knowledge. When people practice retrieval, the act of retrieving knowledge in the present enhances one's ability to retrieve and use that knowledge again in the future. Retrieval is not neutral; it does not merely involve accessing static pieces of information held in a storage system. Instead, every time a person retrieves knowledge, that knowledge is changed. Retrieval-based learning is an advantageous feature of our memory systems, one that we might build in if we were designing memory from scratch (Nairne, 2010). Retrieval is typically purposeful and goal directed; when knowledge is successfully reconstructed in the present, it likely happened for a reason, so improving the future retrievability of that knowledge would seem advantageous so that similar problems could be solved again when they occur in the future. Indeed, with every act of retrieval, there is some change that occurs that improves one's ability to retrieve and reconstruct that knowledge in the future.

This chapter is concerned with the nature of the changes that occur as a consequence of retrieval. There has been a surge of research on retrieval practice in the past decade, but this research also has a long history. The fact that active recall improves learning was noted by Francis Bacon in *Novum Organum* (1620) and by William James in the *Principles of Psychology* (1890). Experimental studies of the effects of retrieval on learning date back at least to Abbott (1909), and over 70 years ago, McGeoch (1942, pp. 196–200) summarized the state of research on "Recall During Practice" in his book, *The Psychology of Human Learning*, the gold-standard textbook at the time. Indeed, retrieval practice is not new to *The Psychology of Learning and Motivation* series. Only a few years ago, Delaney, Verkoeijen, and Spirgel (2010) devoted a section of their review of the spacing effect to retrieval practice and Roediger, Putnam, and Smith (2011) surveyed "ten benefits of testing." Nevertheless, as noted by Delaney et al. and Roediger et al., theoretical progress in understanding the nature of retrieval-based learning has been limited.

Section 2 describes methodological issues in retrieval practice research and identifies the key effects that need to be explained by any theory of retrieval practice. Section 3 turns to an overview and analysis of existing accounts of retrieval practice. Several ideas commonly invoked when discussing retrieval practice provide little insight into underlying mechanisms—the deep structure of retrieval practice effects. One exception is the theory that retrieval practice effects stem from semantic elaboration during retrieval. We evaluate the rationale and evidence for this elaboration account. Section 4 sketches an account of retrieval-based learning that we call an *episodic context account*. In Section 5 we review the current evidence in light of the context account, discuss the account in relation to other theoretical ideas, and conclude by offering suggestions for future work based on the predictions of the context account.

2. CURRENT STATUS OF RETRIEVAL PRACTICE RESEARCH

As noted above, there has been a recent surge in research on retrieval practice. In addition to the two reviews mentioned above, recent overviews have been provided by Roediger and Karpicke (2006a),

McDaniel, Roediger, and McDermott (2007), Roediger and Butler (2011), Carpenter (2012), Karpicke (2012), and Karpicke and Grimaldi (2012), among others. This review is focused on theoretical explanations of retrieval-based learning, and our aims in this section are, first, to clarify some methodological and conceptual issues surrounding retrieval practice research and, second, to delimit the key effects that must be accounted for by any theory of retrieval practice.

2.1. The Effects of Retrieval Practice on Learning

If a person experiences an event or studies new material and his or her memory is assessed at a later time, the ability to recall the material will decrease as the time between the study and test event increases. The systematic study of forgetting began with Ebbinghaus (1885/1964), and it has long been known that the appropriate way to evaluate forgetting is to test different people or different sets of materials at different points in time. If one were to test the same person or the same material repeatedly, the act of assessing memory at one point in time would influence the measurement of forgetting at a subsequent point in time. The "best practices" for measuring forgetting were emphasized in textbooks by McGeoch (1942) and Deese (1958), for example, during what was perhaps the peak of interest in the study of forgetting curves. The recommended methods for studying forgetting are noteworthy because they acknowledge, tacitly or explicitly, that each act of retrieval influences subsequent retrieval. These effects were traditionally viewed as contaminants that must be removed from experiments to obtain pure measures of forgetting.

The effects of prior retrieval on subsequent retrieval (and the "contaminating" effects on the measurement of forgetting) were demonstrated clearly in an experiment by Hanawalt (1937). He had subjects study simple geometric line drawings and reproduce them at different points in time: immediately, 1 day, 1 week, 1 month, or 2 months after the original study period. Some groups of subjects reproduced the drawings only once at one of the retention intervals (single recall), while another group reproduced the drawings repeatedly at each retention interval (repeated recall). Figure 7.1 shows the proportion of figures correctly reproduced in the single recall and repeated recall conditions. Whereas the typical forgetting curve appears in the single recall condition, there is little or no forgetting over time in the repeated recall condition. Today, we view the effects depicted in Fig. 7.1 as benefits of repeated retrieval rather than as contaminating effects

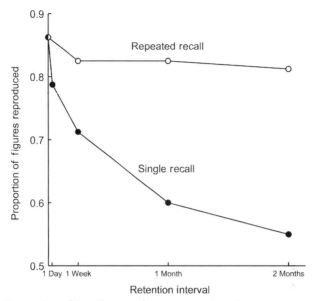

Figure 7.1 Proportion of line-drawing figures correctly redrawn at varying retention intervals under repeated recall or single recall conditions. A typical forgetting trend is observed in the single recall condition, whereas little or no forgetting is seen in the repeated recall condition. *Data are from Hanawalt (1937).*

of retrieval on the measurement of forgetting. The benefit of retrieval practice can be seen at each retention interval. For instance, at the 1-week interval, subjects benefitted from prior recall immediately after learning; at 1 month, subjects benefitted from prior retrieval at the immediate and 1-week intervals; and large benefits of repeated recall were seen 2 months after the original learning episode. Each time subjects practiced retrieving the line drawings, the act of retrieval enhanced the ability to reconstruct the drawings again in the future.

Fast forward to present times and there have been perhaps hundreds of recent demonstrations of retrieval practice effects. One example from Smith, Roediger, and Karpicke (2013) illustrates some important points about the nature of retrieval practice effects. Subjects first studied word pairs that included a category name and an item from the category as a to-be-recalled target (e.g., *vegetable—cucumber*). In the second phase of the experiment, subjects either restudied the word pairs or saw the cue and first two letters of the target (*vegetable—cu____*). For these items, subjects were told to think back the study episode and recall the word that completed the word stem (as we will discuss later, these intentional retrieval instructions are important; Karpicke & Zaromb, 2010). Then in the third and final phase of the experiment, the subjects freely recalled the target words. We refer to this as the *criterial test*, and Fig. 7.2 shows the proportion of words recalled on this test. The results show that practicing retrieval of the target words enhanced recall on the criterial test relative to having restudied the word pairs in phase 2 in the experiment. Smith et al. also varied whether subjects were required to produce a response (overt retrieval) or merely think about the target word in their minds (covert retrieval) in phase 2, and they found little or no effect of overt versus covert retrieval across a series of four experiments. The main point for present purposes is that practicing retrieval of the target words enhanced recall on the criterial test relative to studying the target words.

The Smith et al. experiment highlights some important points about retrieval practice effects. First, subjects did not restudy the target items in the retrieval practice condition. The effect shown in Fig. 7.2 is purely due to the act of retrieval, rather than a combination of retrieval and restudy (or feedback) effects. Second, given that the key effect has to do with

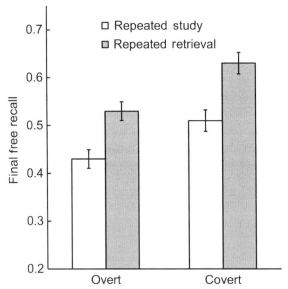

Figure 7.2 Proportion of words recalled on a criterial free recall test as a function of prior repeated study or repeated retrieval practice (where targets were recalled overtly or covertly). Practicing retrieval of the target words enhanced recall on the criterial test relative to restudying the target words. *The figure is redrawn using data from Smith et al. (2013), Experiment 4.*

retrieval in the absence of restudying, successful retrieval is essential. Subjects in the Smith et al. experiment correctly recalled the targets 72% of the time during initial retrieval practice, and the effects in that condition are being compared to the effects of restudying 100% of the items in the repeated study condition. Thus, the comparison is biased in favor of the restudy condition, because all items were reexperienced in that condition, yet there is still a benefit of retrieval practice on the criterial test. Third, the criterial free recall test (phase 3 in the experiment) occurred about 15 min after the initial recall test (phase 2). It is sometimes claimed that the effects of retrieval practice do not appear in the short term and only occur when there is a delay between the learning experience and the final test. Clearly, that is not true; retrieval practice effects are alive and well even in the short term.

The findings of Smith et al. (2013) highlight three key attributes of retrieval practice that are worth emphasizing. First, the best way to examine the effect of retrieval itself is to examine retrieval without restudy or feedback, thereby isolating the effect of retrieval rather than the combined effects of retrieval and subsequent encoding during restudy. Second, the benefits of retrieval practice depend on successful retrieval. When subjects recall relatively little in a retrieval practice condition, one is unlikely to see an effect relative to restudying (for instance, in retrieval practice experiments by Hogan & Kintsch, 1971, subjects recalled about 30% of the items during initial recall, and benefits of retrieval practice over restudying were not seen on immediate criterial tests). When studying the generation effect (Slamecka & Graf, 1978), researchers have been careful to use conditions that ensure successful generation of most if not all target items, yet curiously, when studying testing/retrieval practice effects researchers tend to neglect the importance of initial retrieval success. Third, under the right conditions, benefits of retrieval practice relative to restudying are observable in the short term, a few minutes after the experimental procedure.

An additional noteworthy aspect of retrieval practice is that repeated retrieval and repeated study conditions likely do not represent "pure" manipulations of retrieval practice. Some retrieval of a prior episodic context probably occurs in repeated study conditions. Indeed, "study-phase retrieval" and "reminding" have long been explanations for spaced practice effects (see Greene, 2008). Those ideas essentially attribute spacing effects to retrieval practice and hinge upon the assumption that retrieval practice occurs in repeated study conditions, even when subjects are not instructed to think back to prior events. Interestingly, McGeoch (1942) noted these points in his discussion of "Recall During Practice":

> There are wide variations in the extent to which a subject depends on the direct stimulus pattern of the material being practiced. Assume that he is memorizing a list of words. At the extreme of complete dependence on the stimulus pattern he repeats each word as he perceives it, but does not attempt to anticipate any word or to recall a word before it is actually presented. At the opposite extreme, beginning with the second presentation he attempts to recall as much as possible of the material without having it presented to his receptors. Between the extremes lie innumerable combinations of presentation and independent recall. (p. 196)

McGeoch continues:

> It is probable that the experiments have seldom compared 'pure' reading or presentation with recitation. Instead, the readings may have involved some recitation, so that the comparisons have been between small amounts of recitation and larger ones. The reports of the subjects and the observation of their behavior permit a statement of some of the basic variables underlying the effectiveness of the relatively larger amounts of recall during practice. (p. 199)

There are a variety of ways to deal with the retrieval success problem and make a fair comparison across restudy and retrieval practice conditions. Two approaches are unsatisfactory. First, one could provide feedback or restudy opportunities after every retrieval attempt. This ensures that subjects reexperience the items even if they cannot recall them, but it clouds inferences about the mnemonic effect of retrieval because the effect is now a combination of direct and mediated effects that cannot be teased apart (Roediger & Karpicke, 2006a). A second possibility is to conditionalize final recall on initial recall. A conditional analysis may provide interesting information, but it raises a host of additional item-selection problems. The items recalled initially are by definition "easier" items, and they are likely to be recalled again on a criterial test by virtue of their easiness alone, rather than because of a retrieval practice manipulation. Conditional analyses are correlational, and inherent item characteristics are tangled with any mnemonic effect of retrieval. Neither the provision of feedback nor a conditional analysis is a satisfactory approach to addressing the retrieval success problem in retrieval practice experiments.

We propose two general solutions to address retrieval success issues. First, experiments can be designed so that levels of initial retrieval success are relatively high, and under such circumstances, one is likely to observe retrieval practice effects even in the short term (i.e., at the end of an experimental session). Karpicke and Zaromb (2010) and Smith et al. (2013) provide examples of how one might accomplish this. Second, methods have been developed to bring subjects to criterion, ensuring that they have successfully recalled each item once prior to introducing the manipulation of repeated study or repeated retrieval practice. There are a variety of ways to implement a criterion procedure (e.g., see Grimaldi & Karpicke, 2014; Karpicke, 2009; Karpicke & Roediger, 2007b, 2008; Pyc & Rawson, 2009). Karpicke and Smith (2012) present and discuss a few possible criterion methods.

We suspect that some researchers may ignore retrieval success problems in retrieval practice experiments because the work is viewed as a "testing effect" rather than as a retrieval practice effect. The locus of the positive effects on learning, however, is in repeated, successful retrieval. Retrieval can occur in a variety of activities that are not "tests." In educational settings, many classroom activities could be modified to incorporate active retrieval (see Blunt & Karpicke, in press). Likewise, tests do not always require people to practice retrieval, as is the case when students take tests with the relevant material available during the test (open-book tests; Agarwal, Karpicke, Kang, Roediger, & McDermott, 2008). The emphasis on "testing" producing learning has sometimes obscured the locus of the effect. It is not testing, *per se*, that produces learning; it is the act of practicing retrieval that produces learning. Retrieval practice will occur with varying degrees of success during a test, it may occur during a condition where students are nominally told to "study," it may not occur on tests where retrieval is not necessary, and it may occur in other activities that do not seem test-like at all.

2.2. Delimiting the Key Effects in the Retrieval Practice Literature

We can now delimit the key effects that would need to be explained by an account of retrieval-based learning and eliminate some effects that are not germane to theorizing about retrieval practice. First, our focus is on the direct effects of retrieval practice, rather than on the mediated effects of retrieval on subsequent encoding or studying (e.g., Grimaldi & Karpicke, 2012; Kornell, Hays, & Bjork, 2009). Second, it is sometimes claimed that the effects of retrieval practice only occur after a delay, and in a similar vein, it has been noted that repeated study and retrieval practice conditions sometimes interact with the timing of the final test, such that repeated study is better in the short term and retrieval practice is better in the long term. Retrieval practice effects do indeed occur at short retention intervals, as described earlier (Karpicke & Zaromb, 2010; Smith et al., 2013). The retention interval interaction is essentially a result of item-selection artifacts favoring the restudy condition, and as such, it is not an important phenomenon in need of a mechanistic explanation. As described earlier, when a repeated study condition reexperiences many more items than a retrieval practice condition, it is no surprise that repeated study would produce better performance than retrieval practice. The "benefit" of repeated study in the short term is illusory; if retrieval success were near perfect (by using one of the methods outlined above), and item reexposure were close to identical across repeated study and retrieval practice conditions, there would be no advantage of repeated study in the short term. Indeed, the benefits of retrieval practice would likely be observed (e.g., Smith et al., 2013).

There are four key effects that, at a minimum, would need to be explained by any theory of retrieval-based learning (see Table 7.1). The first is the main effect of retrieval practice—that practicing retrieval enhances performance on a criterial test relative to an appropriate control condition (either a no-test baseline control condition or a repeated study condition). The next three essentially constitute a set of effects that collectively can be considered effects of "difficult" initial retrievals. This includes the following effects: (1) tests that involve recall tend to produce greater effects than tests that involve recognition (e.g., Glover, 1989; see too Butler & Roediger, 2007); (2) spacing an initial retrieval practice event produces greater effects than massed retrieval (e.g., Jacoby, 1978; Whitten & Bjork, 1977; see too Karpicke & Bauernschmidt, 2011); and (3) recalling with weakly related semantic cues produces greater effects relative to recalling with strong semantic cues (Carpenter, 2009; see too Carpenter & DeLosh, 2006). In these three scenarios, the conditions that produce larger gains in retention (initial recall, spacing an initial retrieval trial, and recalling with weak semantic cues) are thought to afford more difficult retrieval relative to the conditions that produce smaller gains (initial recognition, massed retrieval, and recalling with strong semantic cues).

Table 7.1 Key Effects of Retrieval Practice to Be Explained by Theoretical Accounts of Retrieval-Based Learning

1. Retrieval practice enhances retention on a criterial test relative to control conditions (no-test or repeated study conditions)
2. Initial retrieval practice under recall conditions produces greater effects relative to initial retrieval practice under recognition conditions
3. Spaced initial retrieval practice produces greater effects than massed initial retrieval
4. Retrieval practice with weak cues produces greater effects than retrieval practice with strong cues

Certainly, there are additional effects that a robust theory would need to handle—for instance, practicing retrieval alleviates the buildup of proactive interference; practicing retrieval enhances recollection on tests that require context retrieval; orienting retrieval toward greater context retrieval produces larger effects; and other phenomena, which we will return to later in this report. Nevertheless, the four central effects described above provide a starting point for any explanation of retrieval practice. In the next section, we examine several existing explanations and evaluate whether the ideas elucidate the underlying mechanisms that may be responsible for retrieval practice effects.

3. ANALYSIS OF EXISTING EXPLANATIONS OF RETRIEVAL PRACTICE

McGeoch (1942) offered four possible explanations for the effect of retrieval practice on learning, some of which align remarkably well with contemporary ideas. He wrote:

(1) Recitation furnishes the subject with progressive knowledge of results. This information (a) acts as an incentive condition, (b) brings the law of effect directly to bear, (c) favors early elimination of wrong responses, and (d) by informing the subject which items have been learned, promotes a more effective distribution of effort over the material. (2) Recitation favors articulation of the items and leads to the utilization of accent and rhythm. (3) It likewise promotes grouping of the items, localization in the series, and the search for meaningful connections. (4) In recitation the subject is practicing the material more nearly in the way in which it is to be tested and used – that is, without direct stimulation from the copy. It constitutes, therefore, a more immediately relevant form of practice. (pp. 199–200)

McGeoch's first explanation falls in the realm of indirect or mediated effects, rather than the direct mnemonic effects of retrieval on learning. His second explanation, which places an emphasis on articulation, is consistent with current ideas about the "production effect" (e.g., MacLeod, Gopie, Hourihan, Neary, & Ozubko, 2010), but has not been shown to be crucially important for retrieval practice effects (Putnam & Roediger, 2013; Smith et al., 2013). McGeoch's third and fourth explanations bear close relations to two theories described below. The idea that retrieval practice leads students to practice in the way that material will be used in the future is essentially the same as the transfer-appropriate processing idea of retrieval-based learning (see Roediger & Karpicke, 2006a, 2006b). The idea of "searching for meaningful connections" appears similar to the semantic elaboration account, which is given close attention at the end of this section.

This section discusses the most prominent accounts that have been proposed to explain retrieval-based learning, beginning with explanations that attribute retrieval-based learning to modifications of memory trace strength, followed by accounts that propose that retrieval-based learning is due either to practice with retrieval tasks or to encoding variability produced by retrieval tasks. We then turn to an account that attributes retrieval-based learning to semantic elaboration processes.

3.1. Strength and Retrieval Effort

One of the earliest explanations for the mnemonic benefits of retrieval assumed that retrieval processes affect the *strength* of memory traces. This idea assumes that representations of information are stored in memory and those representations can be strengthened in such a way that makes them more retrievable. In a foundational paper, Bjork (1975) proposed that when an item is retrieved from memory, the representation of that item memory is strengthened in some manner. He also proposed that the level of strengthening that takes place is a function of the *effort* required to retrieve the item, an idea termed the retrieval effort hypothesis. Specifically, Bjork suggested that retrieval operated in a way similar to levels of processing during encoding, with retrieval as a deeper level of processing relative to shallow restudying and with more effortful retrieval operations producing even deeper processing and thus greater strengthening (see too Bjork, 1994).

The retrieval effort theory provides an intuitive account of a variety of retrieval phenomena. Initially developed to account for negative recency effects (Craik, 1970), retrieval effort also helped to explain findings that the longer it takes subjects to retrieve words, given their definitions, the more likely those items are to be recalled on a later test (Gardiner, Craik, & Bleasdale, 1973; but see Karpicke & Bauernschmidt, 2011). Retrieval effort has been operationalized and manipulated in a variety of ways such as changing learning criterion (Pyc & Rawson, 2009), providing less informative cues (Carpenter & DeLosh, 2006), or delaying the initial test (Karpicke & Roediger, 2007a, 2007b).

Ultimately, retrieval effort is a redescription of some retrieval practice phenomena and does not delineate mechanisms that would produce the mnemonic effects of retrieval on subsequent retention. The concept of retrieval effort can be problematic, too, because it is not always clear what constitutes effortful retrieval, and the relation between time and effort is ambiguous. Response times are often considered measures of effort, with slower times representing greater effort. It is equally plausible that faster response times reflect greater effort. For instance, it is reasonable to think that running 1 mile requires more effort than walking it, yet running will take less time than walking. These issues aside, retrieval effort is still only a measure that may or may not be correlated with underlying mechanisms that produce the mnemonic effects of retrieval, but it does not specify what those mechanisms might be.

3.2. Storage and Retrieval Strength

An idea related to Bjork's (1975) retrieval effort proposal is the theory of disuse proposed by Bjork and Bjork (1992). A key element of the theory is the differentiation of retrieval strength from storage strength. They suggest that retrieval is a function of both the quality of the item in memory (which they termed storage strength) and the ability of a test cue to elicit the item (retrieval strength; see too Raaijmakers & Shiffrin, 1981; Tulving & Thomson, 1973). To explain the benefit of retrieval, Bjork and Bjork (1992) assumed that both storage and retrieval strength are increased when an item is restudied, and the strengths are increased to a greater degree when an item is recalled. Additionally, they assumed that the increment in strengths is, in part, a function of retrieval difficulty. When an item with low-current retrieval strength is successfully retrieved (i.e., a difficult retrieval), it will receive a greater increment in strengths than an item with high-retrieval strength (i.e., an easily retrieved item).

Bjork and Bjork's (1992) theory of disuse represents, in part, a more concrete version of Bjork's (1975) retrieval effort hypothesis, and the concepts of retrieval strengths and their interplay with storage strengths are consistent with a variety of contemporary models of memory. Moreover, the verbal theory provided by Bjork and Bjork (1992) would seem to account for the key attributes of retrieval-based learning described above. However, the storage/retrieval strength idea simply assumes that strengths increase when an item is recalled; that is, it assumes that retrieval-based learning occurs without proposing a mechanistic explanation for how it occurs. In addition, the primary mechanism for incrementing storage and retrieval strengths is retrieval effort during a test, which is influenced by the retrieval strength of a to-be-recalled item relative to a set of competitors. While Bjork and Bjork describe what a difficult item is in their model (i.e., an item with low-retrieval strength relative to a set of competitors), it is not always clear how to define a "difficult" item in a variety of retrieval situations.

3.3. Bifurcation

Another variant of a strength hypothesis is Kornell, Bjork, and Garcia's (2011) *bifurcation* account, which offers a description of the forgetting rates for retrieved versus restudied items. It is sometimes the case that restudied items are recalled better than tested items on an immediate criterial test, whereas the tested/retrieved items are recalled better than restudied items on a delayed test (e.g., Hogan & Kintsch, 1971; Roediger & Karpicke, 2006b). According to the bifurcation model, initial tests produce a bifurcated item distribution, in which items that are successfully retrieved are strengthened, while items that are not successfully retrieved are not. Items that are restudied are strengthened, but to a lesser degree than retrieved items. The model also assumes that items are recalled on a test if they exceed a threshold that varies as a function of test "difficulty" (Halamish & Bjork, 2011). The differential strengthening of retrieved versus restudied items results in advantages for restudied items on an immediate test because more of the items have been strengthened beyond the retrieval threshold. However, after a delay, all items are weakened (i.e., forgotten) at the same rate, and now many restudied items fall below the retrieval threshold, whereas the retrieval practice items, which gained more strength initially, remain above threshold.

In support of the idea, Kornell et al. (2011) showed that when all items are retrieved during initial testing, preventing bifurcation, the aforementioned interaction with delay does not occur; similarly, when repeated study occurs under conditions that presumably produce bifurcation, the interaction is once again present. The bifurcation idea provides a descriptive account of a particular pattern of results, but it is somewhat limited in scope. Kornell et al. (2011, p. 86) acknowledge that their distribution-based framework is merely a descriptive account of this particular pattern of data and is not intended to indicate the underlying mechanisms of retrieval-based learning. Like other strength accounts, the bifurcation model simply relies on the idea that retrieved items are strengthened more than studied items without specifying how or why such strengthening would occur. In addition, as we outlined earlier, the retention interval interaction that the bifurcation model explains is essentially an item-selection artifact that occurs under a particular set of conditions. It is not crucial for understanding the deep structure of retrieval-based learning.

3.4. Transfer Appropriate Processing

Another descriptive account of retrieval practice proposes that intervening retrieval serves as practice that is similar to the conditions of a final criterial test.

Transfer-appropriate processing refers to the idea that test performance will be greatest when the cognitive processes required on a criterial test are similar to the cognitive processes that occurred during original learning (Kolers & Roediger, 1984; Morris, Bransford, & Franks, 1977). Some researchers have argued that retrieval practice may be beneficial because the processes necessary for successful initial retrieval are similar to those employed during later retrieval (e.g., Landauer & Bjork, 1978; Roediger & Karpicke, 2006a, 2006b). This idea has been substantiated to some degree by the finding that performance on a criterial test is best when the final test questions are identical to initial test questions (e.g., Butler, 2010; Johnson & Mayer, 2009; McDaniel & Fisher, 1991; see also Brewer, Marsh, Meeks, Clark-Foos, & Hicks, 2010). However, a strict interpretation of transfer-appropriate processing would predict that performance should be best when the intervening and criterial test formats are identical and thus require exactly the same overlapping mental processes. Some authors have reported such a matching pattern (e.g., Duchastel & Nungester, 1982), but many others have not. Instead, free recall (Carpenter & DeLosh, 2006; Glover, 1989) or short answer test formats (Butler & Roediger, 2007; Kang, McDermott, & Roediger, 2007; McDaniel, Anderson, Derbish, & Morrisette, 2007) have generally been found to produce the best performance regardless of the criterial test format.

It may be the case that, very generally speaking, similarity of processing during original learning and criterial performance is important. However, transfer-appropriate processing still only offers a redescription of the basic retrieval practice effect. The relevant data do not support the idea that retrieval practice effects are greatest when initial and final test formats are matched. The idea of transfer-appropriate processing also does not appear to make clear predictions about the benefit of spaced versus massed retrieval or retrieving with weak versus strong cues, two of the key effects we identified earlier. In sum, transfer-appropriate processing is essentially a statement about the similarity of original learning and later test situations, and it does not specify underlying mechanisms that would produce retrieval practice effects.

3.5. Encoding Variability

Encoding variability has occasionally been proposed as an explanation for retrieval-based learning, although the idea has been discussed less frequently than other ideas reviewed in this section. Encoding variability refers to the idea that when items or materials are experienced multiple times, the materials are encoded in different (variable) ways during each encounter, and this is assumed to increase the number of retrieval routes a person has to access material in the future (Martin, 1968; Melton, 1970). Encoding variability has been explored most extensively as an explanation for the spacing effect, the finding that material is learned better when multiple presentations of an item are spaced over time relative to when presentations are presented back to back with no intervening items (massed practice; see Bower, 1972; Greene, 2008).

Empirical tests of encoding variability as an explanation for retrieval practice have been scarce, and the extant data are mixed. For example, McDaniel and Masson (1985) observed a benefit on a criterial extra-list cued recall test when the intervening test used a different extra-list cue, which may support an encoding variability interpretation. Conversely, Butler (2010) found that varying the conditions of retrieval practice by presenting different questions across repeated tests did not increase retention relative to a condition in which the same questions were presented on repeated tests. However, perhaps the greatest problem for any account based on encoding variability is that attempts to induce variable encoding directly have shown no effect or even decreases in memory performance (e.g., Benjamin & Tullis, 2010; Greene & Stillwell, 1995; Postman & Knecht, 1983; Verkoeijen, Rikers, & Schmidt, 2004).

Our main purpose in mentioning encoding variability is to distinguish that concept from the idea of *contextual* variability, which refers to the specific idea that different temporal/contextual features can be encoded as part of the representation of repeated events. Indeed, contextual variability theories of the spacing effect have received both empirical and theoretical support (Delaney et al., 2010; Greene, 1989; Lohnas & Kahana, in press; Raaijmakers, 2003). In later sections of this chapter, we describe how contextual variability may play an important role in retrieval-based learning.

3.6. Elaborative Retrieval

An explanation that has received considerable attention in recent years attributes the effects of retrieval practice to semantic elaboration that is assumed to occur during the process of retrieval. This theory is known as the "elaborative retrieval hypothesis" (Carpenter, 2009, 2011), though here we refer to it specifically as the *semantic elaboration account* in an attempt to clarify what is meant by "elaboration."

Elaboration generally refers to the process of encoding additional features or attributes in the representation of an event, and this typically refers to semantic or meaning-based aspects of items. When one condition enhances memory performance relative to another, the enhancement can often be attributed to elaboration or "deep processing," perhaps only based on the fact that one condition produced better memory performance than another (Karpicke & Smith, 2012). There is still no universally agreed upon index of elaboration, decades after Craik and Tulving (1975) initiated the search for one. As such, in many circumstances, elaboration essentially remains a "just-so story" when it is invoked to explain memory phenomena.

The semantic elaboration account is clearer than past accounts in describing the type of elaboration assumed to occur during retrieval. The idea is that when subjects use retrieval cues to search for a target response, several items that are semantically related to the cue become activated during the search process (Carpenter, 2009, 2011). For example, when attempting to recall the target word *bread* when given a weakly associated cue such as *basket*, several words that are associated with the cue (like *eggs, wicker, fruit,* and so on) are thought to become activated, and these semantic associates are assumed to serve as retrieval routes from *basket* to *bread* on a future criterial test. The elaboration account further assumes that there is little if any generation of semantic associates when word pairs like *basket-bread* are repeatedly studied because subjects do not need to search for the target. Similarly, difficult retrieval conditions are assumed to produce more extensive semantic searches relative to less difficult conditions. For example, when a cue is strongly associated to a target (e.g., *toast* as the cue for *bread*), recall of the target is easier, producing a less extensive search of memory and thus less semantic elaboration. "Weak" cues would produce more extensive searches and more elaboration. In experiments related to the semantic elaboration account, weak cues have been defined as ones with weak semantic associations to targets or ones that provide less information about targets (e.g., if the target word were *cabin,* the cue *c _ _ _ _* would be "weaker" than the cue *c a b _ _*).

The strength of the semantic elaboration account is that it proposes a mechanism for retrieval-based learning: the generation of several semantically/associatively related words during retrieval is assumed to occur and is assumed to produce retrieval practice effects. In addition, the elaboration account attempts to explain key effects in the retrieval practice literature. However, the semantic elaboration account has been challenged on both logical and empirical grounds, as described next.

First, much of the evidence in support of the semantic elaboration account is correlational. For example, Carpenter (2011) showed that practicing retrieval enhanced performance on a criterial cued recall test where the cues were mediators, nonstudied words that were semantically related to the studied pairs. For example, for the word pair *mother–child*, the nonstudied word *father* might be given as a cue to retrieve the target *child*. The idea is that the word *father* came to mind during initial retrieval and mediates the association between *mother* and *child*. Carpenter's (2011) findings were taken as evidence that the activation of semantic mediators occurred during retrieval. However, the generation of semantic mediators, and thus the amount of elaboration, was never directly manipulated. It is perfectly possible that some mechanism other than the generation of semantic associates produced the retrieval practice effect, and the benefits of retrieval practice were seen with extra-list mediators as cues, even though those words never came to mind during initial retrieval. In other words, rather than viewing the activation of mediators as a cause of retrieval-based learning, it may be that some other mechanism produced retrieval-based learning and also produced an effect on final mediator-cued recall.

Second, the idea behind elaborative retrieval seems inconsistent with the principle of cue overload: As more items become associated with a single retrieval cue, the likelihood of recovering a particular target decreases (see Nairne, 2002, 2006; Raaijmakers & Shiffrin, 1981; Surprenant & Neath, 2009; Watkins & Watkins, 1975; Wixted & Rohrer, 1993). The semantic elaboration idea is that subjects generate several semantically related words related to a retrieval cue. This ought to produce massive cue overload, making memory performance worse, yet the generation of semantically related words is proposed to explain the improvement in memory due to retrieval practice. The phenomenon of cue overload is well established, and indeed, the number of words that are implicitly associated with a retrieval cue is negatively associated with recall of target words (Nelson & McEvoy, 1979), which is the opposite of the semantic elaboration idea. Even if we assumed that, rather than becoming part of the search set, the semantically associated information serves as additional retrieval cues, this is still difficult to reconcile with the cue overload principle, as these items are not provided at test and thus would have to be retrieved prior to being used as cues. For example, if a subject were given a cue and generated three associated mediators before reaching the target, the three mediators would still need to be retrieved to access the target on a later test. Thus, four items, rather than one, would be associated with the retrieval cue.

Third, the semantic elaboration account appears at odds with the phenomenon of retrieval-induced forgetting. In retrieval-induced forgetting experiments, subjects study cue–target word pairs where multiple targets share the same cue (e.g., *fruit-orange* and *fruit-banana*) and then practice retrieval of some of targets that were paired with each cue (e.g., subjects might practice *fruit-or_ _ _ _*, but *banana* would not be practiced). The retrieval-induced forgetting effect is that retrieval practice of the targets (*orange* in this example) interferes with subsequent recall of nonpracticed items (*banana*; see Anderson, Bjork, & Bjork, 1994). The semantic elaboration account proposes that several semantically related words are activated during retrieval; presumably, this would mean that nonpracticed items benefit from activation during retrieval practice. If this were generally true, it is difficult to see why retrieval-induced forgetting would occur. Regardless of the particular mechanism proposed to explain retrieval-induced forgetting (see Raaijmakers & Jakab, 2013; Storm, 2011), it is hard to reconcile that effect with the proposal that many semantic associates become activated during retrieval.

The aforementioned concerns are logical and conceptual in nature. As noted above, an advantage of the semantic elaboration account is that it proposes a candidate mechanism for retrieval practice effects that can be induced and experimentally tested. If semantic elaboration is the mechanism responsible for retrieval practice effects, then inducing semantic elaboration directly should produce the same or similar effects as practicing retrieval. Unfortunately, the data from experiments comparing elaboration to retrieval practice have not supported this straightforward prediction.

Some experiments have shown that elaboration tasks do not produce the same results as retrieval practice tasks, which is troubling if retrieval practice effects are presumed to arise from elaboration. For example, Karpicke and Zaromb (2010) had subjects either generate target words from fragments (like *eat—di__*) or practice retrieval by recalling the target words from a prior study episode. Active generation is often considered an elaborative task, and both tasks required subjects to produce the target words. Nevertheless, Karpicke and Zaromb consistently found that retrieving the prior occurrence of the target word produced greater effects on a later criterial test than did generating the words. (The Karpicke and Zaromb experiments are described in greater detail in Section 5.3.)

Karpicke and Blunt (2011) also compared the effects of practicing retrieval to the effects of completing an elaborative study task. They had subjects read educational texts and either practice retrieval, by writing down as much as they could remember in the absence of the texts, or create concept maps while viewing the text. Concept mapping is an elaborative study activity where subjects make a node-and-link diagram of the concepts in a set of materials. The task requires subjects to focus on the organizational structure of the material and draw connections among concepts (Novak & Gowin, 1984). Karpicke and Blunt showed that practicing retrieval produced more learning than elaborative concept mapping, a finding that is hard to reconcile with the idea that retrieval practice effects stem from semantic elaboration.

Additional experiments have provided more direct tests of the elaborative retrieval account by inducing exactly the type of semantic elaboration purported to occur during retrieval. In a series of experiments, Karpicke and Smith (2012) had subjects learn lists of word pairs and practice repeated retrieval of the items or engage in various elaborative study tasks. Two experiments examined the effects of forming interactive images of the word pairs. In a critical experiment (Experiment 3), in the repeated elaboration condition, subjects repeatedly generated semantic mediators that connected the cue and target words. The experimental procedure directly induced the type of elaboration proposed to occur during retrieval, and the prediction was that repeated elaboration would produce effects similar or identical to those produced by repeated retrieval practice. Figure 7.3 shows performance on a criterial test 1 week after the original learning phase. Repeated retrieval produced large gains in learning relative to repeatedly studying the items and relative to not reexperiencing the items (in the "drop" condition). Most importantly, repeated elaboration did not produce effects like those seen from practicing retrieval. Again, these data provide a direct challenge to the idea that semantic elaboration is the mechanism responsible for retrieval practice effects. Directly inducing semantic elaboration, in the way proposed by the elaborative retrieval hypothesis, did not produce effects like those produced by practicing repeated retrieval.

The semantic elaboration account faces a number of additional challenges as a general explanation for retrieval-based learning. Retrieval practice effects occur under conditions in which semantic elaboration seems unlikely—for example, when the tasks employ nonverbal materials, such as pictures, symbols, or faces (Carpenter & DeLosh, 2005; Carpenter & Kelly, 2012; Coppens, Verkoeijen, & Rikers, 2011; Kang, 2010), and when cue–target word pairs consist of identical words (e.g., *table–table*; Karpicke & Smith, 2012), which presumably obviate semantic elaboration or the generation of mediators. Even under these circumstances, where it is difficult to imagine how semantic elaboration would occur, the positive effects of repeated retrieval practice are still observed. Additionally, if semantic

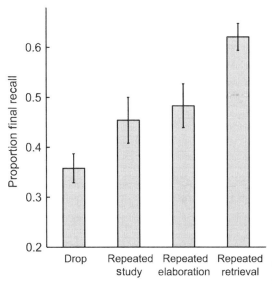

Figure 7.3 Proportion of words recalled on a criterial test in drop, repeated study, repeated elaboration, and repeated retrieval conditions. Repeated retrieval produced large gains in learning relative to repeated studying, whereas repeated elaboration did not. *Figure is reprinted from Karpicke and Smith (2012).*

elaboration occurs during initial cued recall and creates alternate retrieval routes from cues to targets, then the benefits of retrieval practice should be most evident when those cues are provided again on a criterial test. However, initial cued recall produces benefits on subsequent free recall (e.g., Karpicke & Zaromb, 2010; Smith et al., 2013), and in some cases initial cued recall does not improve final cued recall (Carpenter & DeLosh, 2006; Glover, 1989). It is also difficult to see how semantic elaboration from cues to targets would enhance subsequent recall and recognition of the cue words (Carpenter, 2011; Carpenter, Pashler, & Vul, 2006).

In describing encoding variability as an explanatory account of repetition and spacing effects, Greene (2008) wrote, "The notion that some variant of encoding variability underlies the spacing effect has been popular among theorists even in the absence of direct evidence that encoding variability benefits memory at all" (p. 74). A similar statement can be made for semantic elaboration: The idea that semantic elaboration underlies retrieval practice effects remains popular even though attempts to induce elaboration directly have not shown that it benefits memory in the same way as retrieval practice.

Although it may be true that some semantic information becomes activated during retrieval, a broad array of findings suggest that semantic elaboration does not offer a robust explanation of retrieval-based learning. It is important to note that these challenges pertain specifically to the assumption that the retrieval process produces *semantic* elaboration by activating several semantically related words. Perhaps retrieval produces some other form of "elaboration," but if so, such elaboration would need to be explicitly defined. In the next section, we propose an alternative account of retrieval-based learning, the episodic context account, that is based on established ideas in memory theory and that explains a wealth of evidence in the retrieval practice literature.

4. AN EPISODIC CONTEXT ACCOUNT OF RETRIEVAL-BASED LEARNING

4.1. Overview of the Episodic Context Account

Four basic assumptions drawn from memory models underlie the episodic context account. Most of these assumptions are shared by many general theoretical accounts of encoding and retrieval processes, and the context account applies these ideas to retrieval-based learning. We outline the four basic assumptions here and then describe the details of the account in more detail below. First, we assume that events occur within a slowly changing representation of temporal context, and that people encode information about items/events and about the temporal context in which events occur (Howard & Kahana, 2002; Lehman & Malmberg, 2013; Raaijmakers & Shiffrin, 1981). Information about events is stored as an incomplete copy of lexical/semantic item features and temporal context features (Shiffrin & Steyvers, 1997). Second, during retrieval, subjects use cues available in the present to attempt to reconstruct what occurred in the past. When the context during retrieval has changed significantly from the context during study, subjects attempt to *reinstate* the temporal context associated with the study period and use the reinstated temporal context features to guide a search process (Lehman & Malmberg, 2013). Third, when an item that was studied in a past context (context A) is retrieved in the present (context B), the context representation associated with that item is *updated*, such that it includes a composite of A and B context features (e.g., Lohnas & Kahana, in press). Finally, on a later test, subjects again attempt to reinstate context in the service of retrieval, and the updated context representation allows subjects to *restrict their search set*, the set of items considered as candidates for retrieval (Raaijmakers & Shiffrin, 1981). Because items that were studied in context A and retrieved in context B are associated with features of both contexts, the reinstatement of features from context A, context B, or both will serve as effective retrieval cues. When items are repeatedly retrieved in multiple temporal contexts, they become associated with a variety of contextual features that serve as effective retrieval cues on later tests. Ultimately, repeated retrieval may produce a decontextualization process wherein items become more retrievable but are no longer only associated with a specific context (e.g., the original study context).

We propose that these four basic assumptions allow the episodic context account to explain a variety of findings in the retrieval-based learning literature, including those that have been used to support other accounts. As described in more detail below, some of these processes may be differentially affected by the nature of a retrieval practice task, such that more or less contextual reinstatement may occur depending on the demands of the retrieval situation. The context account offers an explanation for the differential effects of retrieval-based learning on different types of tests and retention intervals. The following sections expand on the assumptions of the context account.

4.2. Context Representation and Encoding

The first assumptions of the context account are based in models of memory that assume a role of episodic context. The context account assumes that when material is studied, information is encoded about the items that were encountered in an incomplete and error-prone manner (Shiffrin & Steyvers, 1997). This is assumed to include, but is not necessarily limited to, semantic and phonetic features of the words. Importantly, information about the context in which the event occurred is also stored (Atkinson & Shiffrin, 1968; Howard & Kahana, 2002; Klein, Shiffrin, & Criss, 2007; Lehman & Malmberg, 2009, 2013; Mensink & Raaijmakers, 1989; Raaijmakers & Shiffrin, 1981; Shiffrin & Steyvers, 1997). Thus, memory representations include both item information and context information.

The term "context" can refer to a variety of aspects of an event, including the external environment (e.g., Smith, 1979) and a person's internal mental state (Klein et al., 2007). The episodic context account focuses on the importance of temporal context, a representation of context that changes with the passage of time (Howard & Kahana, 2002). In general, temporal context features are assumed to change at a slow pace (Bower, 1972; Estes, 1955; Howard & Kahana, 2002; Lehman & Malmberg, 2013; Mensink & Raaijmakers, 1989); however, rapid changes in context can occur when there are significant changes in tasks, goals, or setting

(Lehman & Malmberg, 2013; see too Jang & Huber, 2008). The way context features change from one moment to the next differs across models. Some models assume that context features drift in a random manner (Lehman & Malmberg, 2009, 2013; Mensink & Raaijmakers, 1989), whereas retrieved-context models assume that context change is driven by the retrieval of preexperimental contexts that are associated with items (Howard & Kahana, 2002; Polyn, Norman, & Kahana, 2009; Sederberg, Howard, & Kahana, 2008). The episodic context account offered here is neutral about the exact nature of temporal context change. Regardless of the type of contextual drift one assumes, the key point is that context on trial n is more similar to the context on trial $n + 1$ than it is to the context on trial $n + 10$. The contexts associated with events that occur in close proximity are likely to be very similar, whereas the contexts associated with events repeated at longer lags will be less similar (Howard & Kahana, 2002; Klein et al., 2007; Mensink & Raaijmakers, 1989).

4.3. Context Reinstatement During Retrieval

During retrieval, a person's goal is to remember what occurred at a particular place and time in the past, using cues available in the present. Consistent with most memory theories, the context account assumes that retrieval is accomplished by comparing available cues to the contents of memory. Memory representations with features that match those of the retrieval cues are assembled into a set of potentially recallable items called a *search set* (Raaijmakers & Shiffrin, 1981). Retrieval is determined by the diagnostic value of retrieval cues, the ability of a cue to uniquely specify a target to the exclusion of competing candidates (Nairne, 2002, 2006; Raaijmakers & Shiffrin, 1981). In other words, the effectiveness of a cue in eliciting a target is positively related to the match between the target and the cue and negatively related to the match between the cue and other candidates stored in memory. Because a search set will likely include both target and nontarget candidates, successful retrieval of a desired target will be most likely when the search set has been restricted (Raaijmakers & Shiffrin, 1981; Wixted & Rohrer, 1993, 1994; Watkins & Watkins, 1975).

While some tasks, such as cued recall, provide subjects with cues with which to probe memory, others, such as free recall, require subjects to generate their own cues. It is worth reiterating that the most robust retrieval practice effects tend to be observed under free recall conditions. When few cues are provided in the retrieval environment, the reinstatement of temporal context plays an especially critical role in retrieval. When temporal context is used as a cue, traces that are most likely to be retrieved are those associated with context features similar to the current retrieval context. Due to contextual drift, the retrieval context will likely be different from the study context. However, because context drifts slowly, the context cue during immediate retrieval will likely still match features of the context associated with traces in memory. As the length of the delay between study and retrieval increases, more contextual drift occurs and the retrieval context is less similar to the context associated with list items. Thus, in order to accomplish a recall task, some of the temporal context information that was present during study must be reinstated to serve as a retrieval cue (Lehman & Malmberg, 2013). The more context has shifted between study and retrieval, and the fewer other cues available, the more contextual reinstatement must be relied on as a retrieval strategy.

4.4. Context Updating During Successful Retrieval

The primary assumption that drives the episodic context account is that retrieval of an item updates the context representation stored with that item, making the retrieved item more recallable in the future. During subsequent retrieval attempts, when temporal context has drifted from the study context, items with updated context representations will be more retrievable via temporal context cues relative to items that have not been updated. Context updating creates a set of items that are more distinctly associated with future temporal contextual cues.

During retrieval in context B, the study context (context A) must be reinstated in order to recall the studied items (Lehman & Malmberg, 2013). When items are successfully retrieved on an initial test (in context B), features from the reinstated context A and the current context B are added to a composite context representation. Thus, the context representations of successfully retrieved items contain features that are associated with both contexts A and B, such that the reinstatement of either context A or context B in the future will serve to evoke the item from memory.

When context has changed very little between study and test (e.g., during massed retrieval), reinstatement of the study context will be less helpful (or unnecessary) to accomplish retrieval, given that the reinstated features will be similar to the current test features. Thus, the retrieved items will enjoy limited benefits from additional encoding of contextual features given that many of these features may be redundant. However, when the study and test contexts are different (e.g., during spaced retrieval), unique context features are added during successful retrieval. During future retrieval, context cues that are similar to A or B will match the context associated with the item. The longer the lag between study and initial retrieval, the more context change occurs, and the more distinct the additional context features will be for successfully retrieved items. As discussed in more detail below, this account of retrieval-based learning is similar to contextual accounts proposed to explain the spacing effect (e.g., Delaney et al., 2010; Lohnas & Kahana, in press; Lohnas, Polyn, & Kahana, 2011; Raaijmakers, 2003). According to contextual variability accounts of spacing effects, spaced repetitions occur in more varied contexts than massed repetitions, producing a larger set of retrieval cues that will be potentially effective for cueing the target information. According to the context account of retrieval-based learning, repeated retrieval leads to the updating of context features each time items are retrieved. The end result is that repeatedly retrieved items are associated with multiple contexts, producing a context representation that will match a variety of context cues.

4.5. Retrieval Practice Restricts the Search Set

The context account proposes that context reinstatement is used to guide a search process and that context is used to restrict the search set, the subset of items treated as candidates during retrieval (Raaijmakers & Shiffrin, 1981). Memory performance will be best when retrieval cues uniquely specify a target to the exclusion of competing candidates; performance can be improved when the cue–target match is increased, when the match between cues and competitors is decreased, and when the size of the search set is restricted to fewer candidates. The episodic context account assumes that the context features associated with successfully retrieved items are effective in uniquely specifying those items because updated context representations help subjects restrict the search set. When the context representation is a composite of A and B features, and subjects attempt to retrieve the items again on a future criterial test, they can restrict their search only to items associated with both A and B contexts. Because only previously retrieved items have representations associated with both context A and context B, the search set can be restricted to those items only. The distinct set of context features associated with retrieved items may aid in list discrimination (e.g., Chan & McDermott, 2007; Szpunar, McDermott, & Roediger, 2008; Verkoeijen, Tabbers, & Verhage, 2011) because items that are strongly associated with contexts A and B (i.e., those that were studied in context A and retrieved in context B) will be likely to be retrieved in response to a cue that includes features of contexts A or B, but unlikely to be retrieved in response to a retrieval cue that includes features of context C (a context in which they did not occur).

The context reinstatement process that occurs during retrieval practice may produce additional effects on the representation of context. First, as predicted by retrieved-context models, the reactivation of context A that occurs during retrieval may cause the current context to become updated with features from the retrieved context A (Howard & Kahana, 2002). In addition, the reinstatement of context A may facilitate future reinstatement of context A. In either case, items that are retrieved in context B via the reinstatement of context A may benefit not only because an updated composite context is created but also because the context features that are reinstated on an initial test are likely to be reinstated and used as cues on future tests. Indeed, recent evidence suggests that practice reinstating a specific environmental context may facilitate later contextual reinstatement necessary to accomplish a recall task, which Masicampo and Sahakyan (in press) have referred to as facilitated reinstatement (see also Brinegar, Lehman, & Malmberg, 2013). If context reinstatement is facilitated on a future test, then the context used as a cue will be more likely to contain features that match those stored with items that were previously retrieved, and the search set will be restricted to those items.

5. EVIDENCE SUPPORTING AN EPISODIC CONTEXT ACCOUNT

5.1. Effects of Retrieval Practice and Initial Retrieval Difficulty

The episodic context account explains the basic retrieval practice effect in terms of context reinstatement, context updating, and restriction of the search set. When people practice retrieval, they attempt to reinstate a prior learning context as they search for and try to recover items, and when retrieval is successful, the representation of context is updated to include features of the retrieved context and the current context. When people attempt retrieval again in the future, they are now better able to restrict the search set and hone in on the desired target by virtue of the updated context representation. In principle, these processes can and sometimes do occur during study events (i.e., study-phase retrieval). If subjects study material and are reminded of a prior occurrence, we assume that processes of context updating and search set restriction may occur while studying. Without intentional retrieval instructions, study-phase retrieval is not obligatory in a repeated study condition. Similarly, we assume that there is a difference in the degree of context updating that occurs with incidental retrieval, which is a person's "mode" during study-phase retrieval, relative to intentional retrieval, which occurs during retrieval practice as people deliberately search memory for information about the prior occurrence of a learning episode. Thus, the context account specifies underlying mechanisms that produce the mnemonic benefits of retrieval practice.

The context account also offers explanations for the effects of "difficult" retrievals outlined earlier (see Table 7.1). First, although retrieval practice effects occur with a variety of initial retrieval formats, the effects are most robust and observed most consistently when initial retrieval involves free recall. This general finding is consistent with the context account: Free recall requires subjects to reinstate a prior context with minimal cues, whereas other retrieval situations (such as recognition tests) may not require as much context reinstatement. Similarly, in cued recall tasks, the nature of the available cues will determine the degree to which subjects must attempt to reinstate context. For instance, practicing retrieval with only the first letter of a target produces a greater gain relative to practicing retrieval with three letters of the target provided (Carpenter & DeLosh, 2006). The context account proposes that subjects must reinstate more episodic context when fewer cues are provided, and greater recollection of the episodic context drives the gains in learning. The context account offers a ready explanation for the general advantage of recall-like retrieval practice conditions.

Second, the context account explains why a spaced initial retrieval produces more learning than massed retrieval. Consider what happens during massed retrieval practice: When an item is studied and successfully retrieved immediately after the occurrence, the temporal context has changed very little between study and retrieval. Context reinstatement may not be necessary, but even if it occurs, context updating under massed retrieval conditions will produce a context representation essentially like one that would exist without retrieval practice. On the contrary, when successful retrieval is spaced relative to a prior study episode, and retrieval occurs in a context that is substantially different from the study context, the context representation is updated to include features of the retrieved and current context. Subjects can then use the distinctive updated context to guide the search process when they attempt retrieval again in the future.

Third, and importantly, the context account readily explains why retrieval with weak semantic cues would produce a greater mnemonic effect relative to retrieval with strong cues, a finding that has been taken as key evidence favoring a semantic elaboration account (Carpenter, 2009). When cues are strongly associated to targets based on preexperimental features such as semantic relatedness, retrieval can be accomplished without much reliance on reinstating episodic context. For instance, if the strong associate *table* is given as a cue to recall *chair*, the target may come to mind easily due to its strong semantic association rather than because of the recollection of episodic context. In contrast, when cues and targets have little or no preexperimental association, reinstatement of prior context is obligatory. To recall *chair* when given a weak associate like *glue* as the retrieval cue, subjects must reinstate episodic occurrence information about when they studied the pair *glue–chair*. The episodic context account explains the advantage of practicing retrieval with weak cues in terms of context reinstatement rather than semantic elaboration purported to occur during retrieval (Carpenter, 2009).

Thus, the context account offers explanations for the general advantage of retrieval practice over repeated studying, the advantage of initial recall versus recognition, the advantage of spaced versus massed initial retrieval, and the advantage of retrieving with weak associates relative to retrieving with strong associates. A strength of the context account is that it specifies mechanisms (degree of context reinstatement and context updating) for the effects of "difficult" initial retrievals. Difficult retrieval conditions are ones that require greater context reinstatement. We hasten to note that similar ideas have been expressed by previous authors. Glover (1989) suggested that benefits of retrieval were dependent on the "completeness" of the retrieval event and Dempster (1996) proposed that "the effectiveness of an intervening test was an inverse function of the availability of retrieval cues" (p. 33). Each statement is essentially about the degree of context reinstatement required during a retrieval opportunity. Importantly, not all "difficult" retrieval situations benefit subsequent retention. For example, dividing attention during retrieval makes retrieval practice more difficult but does not increase the mnemonic benefit of retrieval (Dudukovic, DuBrow, & Wagner, 2009; Gaspelin, Ruthruff, & Pashler, 2013). It is not "difficulty" *per se* that enhances learning; it is the degree to which retrieval practice requires context reinstatement.

The episodic context account offers explanations for several additional effects in the retrieval practice literature, listed in Table 7.2. Specifically,

Table 7.2 Additional Effects of Retrieval Practice that Support the Episodic Context Account of Retrieval-Based Learning

Retrieval practice enhances subsequent context recollection
 1. Retrieval practice enhances "Remembering" on a criterial test
 2. Retrieval practice enhances recollection on a criterial test, as measured by process dissociation
 3. Retrieval practice enhances temporal source memory and list discrimination on a criterial test
 4. Retrieval practice reduces the effects of proactive interference
 5. Retrieval practice produces a restricted search set and faster response times on a criterial test

Initial context retrieval during retrieval practice enhances subsequent retention
 6. Intentional retrieval (being in an episodic retrieval mode) produces greater retrieval practice effects relative to incidental retrieval
 7. Reinstating the initial study context during retrieval practice enhances retention
 8. Recalling temporal context during initial retrieval practice enhances retention

the context account makes predictions about recollection of context on the criterial test and about the role of retrieving context during initial retrieval practice. We discuss these topics in turn in the next sections.

5.2. Recollection of Context on a Criterial Test

The episodic context account makes specific predictions about what types of final criterial tests will be sensitive to the effects of retrieval-based learning. Because retrieval-based learning occurs when contextual information is reinstated and updated, criterial tests that rely on the use of contextual information should be more sensitive to retrieval practice effects relative to criterial tests that can be accomplished without reliance on temporal context. Indeed, final free recall tests, which involve probing memory with context cues, are more sensitive to the effects of prior retrieval practice relative to final recognition tests, where performance can be accomplished by familiarity or automatic retrieval rather than recollection of context (see Darley & Murdock, 1971; Hogan & Kintsch, 1971; Glover, 1989). However, recognition tests that require subjects to use temporal contextual information ought to be sensitive to prior retrieval practice. This prediction has been confirmed in a variety of studies that we review here.

In an important paper, Chan and McDermott (2007) examined the effects of initial retrieval practice on final recognition memory tests that assessed context recollection, either by estimating subjects' recollection or by directly requiring subjects to recollect prior context. Subjects studied lists of words and then either freely recalled the lists or completed a distracter task. Across a series of experiments, Chan and McDermott examined performance on final recognition tests that assessed recollection with process dissociation (Jacoby, 1991), with source memory judgments (Johnson, Hashtroudi, & Lindsay, 1993), or with remember/know judgments (Tulving, 1985). Chan and McDermott showed that, according to all of these measures, practicing retrieval enhanced context recollection on the criterial test (see too McDermott, 2006; Verkoeijen et al., 2011). These findings are consistent with the episodic context account: Because people reinstate and update context as they practice retrieval, the ability to recollect context is improved on future tests.

In a similar line of research, Karpicke, McCabe, and Roediger (2006) examined the effects of repeated retrieval practice with a variant of process dissociation developed to estimate recollection and automatic retrieval in free recall (McCabe, Roediger, & Karpicke, 2011). Subjects studied four lists, each containing 20 items from a single category (e.g., 20 four-legged animals). One group repeatedly studied the lists four times, while a second group studied once and repeatedly recalled the lists in three consecutive free recall tests (see Roediger & Karpicke, 2006b). The subjects then took final tests either immediately (at the end of the session) or 1 week after the learning phase. In the criterial test phase, the subjects took inclusion tests for two lists (two categories): They were told to recall as many studied words as they could, guessing when necessary in order to produce 20 responses. Subjects took exclusion tests for the other two lists/categories: They were instructed to produce 20 new category members that they had not studied in the original learning phase. The key data from the exclusion tests are the proportions of exclusion errors—words from the studied lists that are mistakenly produced on the test. The results of the inclusion and exclusion tests can be combined to obtain estimates of recollection and automatic retrieval (Jacoby, 1991; see McCabe et al., 2011 for details).

Figure 7.4 shows the key results of the experiment on the 1-week delayed final tests. On the immediate final tests, repeated studying produced better performance than repeated free recall on the inclusion tests (77% vs. 68%; see Roediger & Karpicke, 2006b). Performance under exclusion instructions was near floor, so the process dissociation procedure could

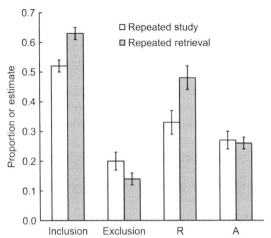

Figure 7.4 The left portion shows the proportion of words correctly produced on an inclusion test and the proportion of words incorrectly produced on an exclusion test. The inclusion and exclusion test data were used to calculate estimates of recollection (R) and automaticity (A) using Jacoby's (1991) process dissociation procedure. Repeated retrieval practice selectively enhanced the recollection estimate and did not affect the automaticity estimate. *Data are from Karpicke et al. (2006).*

not be applied. Thus, the analysis is focused on the 1-week data, which show that subjects in the repeated retrieval condition recalled more than subjects in the repeated study condition on the final inclusion test. In addition, subjects in the repeated retrieval group made fewer exclusion errors than subjects in the repeated study group. Inclusion and exclusion performance can be combined to obtain estimates of recollection and automatic retrieval, and Fig. 7.4 shows repeated retrieval practice selectively enhanced the recollection estimate and did not affect the automaticity estimate. The results suggest that repeated retrieval improved subjects' abilities to recollect which items occurred in the original learning phase so that they could include them on the inclusion test and also correctly exclude them on the exclusion test.

The episodic context account emphasizes that while the recollection of temporal context is essential for retrieval, other surface features of contexts are not as important for remembering occurrence information, and therefore, these features are not likely to be reinstated or updated during retrieval practice. Brewer et al. (2010) provided important evidence about the types of contextual information that are enhanced with retrieval practice. Subjects studied two lists that contained words spoken by male or female speakers. They then either freely recalled each list or completed a distracter task (similar to Chan & McDermott, 2007). On the criterial test, the subjects were shown each word and asked to identify either the list that the word came from (a list discrimination task, which requires temporal judgments) or the gender of the voice that read the word. Initial retrieval practice improved final list discrimination performance but did not enhance the ability to remember the gender of the person who spoke the word. It is noteworthy that similar research on the generation effect has shown that generating words disrupts memory for certain contextual details such as the color or font of a word (see Mulligan, Lozito, & Rosner, 2006). Brewer et al.'s results are consistent with the episodic context account, which proposes that subjects rely on temporal context cues to accomplish free recall, that elements of temporal context were updated during retrieval practice, and that enhanced memory for temporal context is evident on criterial tests.

The research described so far suggests that practicing retrieval enhances the ability to recollect what occurred at a particular place and time. Another way to examine this ability is to have people study several lists of words and instruct them to recall only the last list. The ability to constrain retrieval only to the most recent items, excluding items that occurred on earlier lists, is an index of the degree to which people are able to reinstate and restrict their search to specific prior context. Szpunar et al. (2008) devised a procedure to examine the role of retrieval practice in this way, and we have recently carried out experiments using this method to test predictions of the episodic context account (Lehman, Smith, & Karpicke, in press). Lehman et al. (in press) had subjects study five lists and then freely recall the last (fifth) list. In a control condition, subjects studied and performed a brief distracter task between lists. In the retrieval practice condition, subjects studied and then freely recalled each list after studying it. Finally, in an elaboration condition, after studying each list, the subjects were shown with the words and instructed to generate semantic associates for each word. This task was aimed at inducing the type of elaboration proposed by the semantic elaboration account (Carpenter, 2009; Karpicke & Smith, 2012). Following the fifth list, subjects in all conditions took a criterial recall test on which they were told to recall only words from the most recent (fifth) list. The subjects also completed a final free recall test over all lists at the end of the experiment, but here we focus on the data from the fifth list free recall test.

Figure 7.5 shows the proportion of words recalled from the fifth list (correct recall) and from prior lists (prior-list intrusions). Retrieval practice enhanced correct recall, relative to the control condition, and almost eliminated recall of prior-list intrusions. Importantly, semantic elaboration did

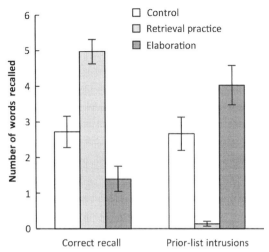

Figure 7.5 The left portion shows the proportion of words correctly recalled, and the right portion shows the proportion of intrusions from prior lists under control, retrieval practice, and elaboration conditions. Retrieval practice enhanced correct recall, relative to the control condition, and all but eliminated recall of prior-list intrusions. Semantic elaboration, on the contrary, reduced correct recall and increased the recall of intrusions. *Data are from Lehman et al. (in press).*

not produce results like those produced by retrieval practice. In fact, elaboration reduced correct recall and increased the production of prior-list intrusions relative to the control condition. Lehman et al. (in press) also examined cumulative recall during the recall period as an indicator of the size of subjects' search sets (Wixted & Rohrer, 1994). When subjects recall from smaller, more restricted search sets, there is an early and rapid approach to asymptote during recall, whereas when subjects recall from larger search sets, there is a slower and more gradual approach to asymptote. Figure 7.6 shows cumulative recall, which includes recall of correct items and intrusions. An analysis of the retrieval dynamics depicted in Fig. 7.6 confirmed that retrieval practice produced a restricted search set, whereas semantic elaboration led to an expanded search set (see too Bäuml & Kliegl, 2013). Overall, Lehman et al.'s results support the predictions of the episodic context account: Practicing retrieval required subjects to reinstate and update context representations, and this improved subjects' abilities to restrict their search to a particular context. Lehman et al.'s results are also important because they cast additional doubt on the idea that semantic elaboration operates in the same way as retrieval practice (Karpicke & Smith, 2012).

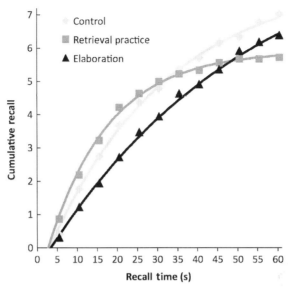

Figure 7.6 Cumulative recall curves showing the cumulative number of words recalled (correct recalls plus intrusions) under control, retrieval practice, and elaboration conditions. Retrieval practice produced a restricted search set, as evidenced by the early and rapid approach to asymptote. Semantic elaboration created an expanded search set, as evidenced by the slower and more gradual approach to asymptote. *Data are from Lehman et al. (in press).*

In sum, several lines of evidence show that practicing retrieval enhances the ability to recollect details of prior episodic contexts, which supports the episodic context account of retrieval-based learning. The next section reviews evidence that manipulating the recollection of episodic context during learning is critically important for retrieval-based learning.

5.3. Manipulations of Initial Context Retrieval

One criticism levied against the elaborative retrieval account is that there have been few attempts to test the theory by directly inducing the kind of semantic elaboration proposed to produce retrieval practice effects (and such attempts have not shown that semantic elaboration produces effects similar to retrieval practice effects; Karpicke & Smith, 2012). The episodic context account must be held to the same standard of evidence. Specifically, the context account leads to the prediction that manipulating the degree to which subjects recollect prior episodic context should be critical for producing retrieval practice effects. Indeed, there have been direct tests of this idea, and the results support the theory that remembering the episodic context matters for retrieval practice.

Karpicke and Zaromb (2010) carried out a series of experiments in which they manipulated whether subjects read (studied) target items, generated the target items, or retrieved the targets from a prior study episode. In their experiments, subjects first studied a list of target words (e.g., *love*). In a second phase, subjects either read the words paired with a related cue word (e.g., *heart—love*) or were given fragments of the target words (e.g., *heart— l_v_*). In a *generate* condition, the subjects were instructed to complete the word fragments with the first word that came to mind, whereas in a *recall* condition, the subjects were told to think back the study episode and recall a word that completed the fragment. This instruction directed subjects to reinstate the prior study context and placed them in what Tulving (1983) referred to as an "episodic retrieval mode." Importantly, there were no differences in the proportion of targets produced under the two conditions (subjects produced 70–75% of the targets in both conditions across a series of four experiments). In the third and final phase of the experiment, subjects freely recalled the target words, and Fig. 7.7 shows the proportion of words recalled on the criterial test. Whereas generating the targets produced no benefit relative to reading the words, retrieving the targets did produce

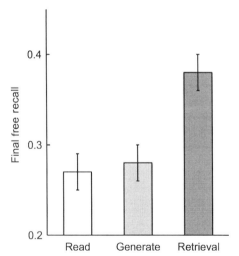

Figure 7.7 Proportion of words recalled on a criterial free recall test under read, generate, and retrieval practice conditions. Whereas generating the targets produced no benefit relative to reading the targets, retrieving the targets did produce an advantage on the final free recall test. *Data are from Karpicke and Zaromb (2010).*

a benefit on the final free recall test. (Karpicke and Zaromb also found similar benefits in other experiments where the criterial test involved item recognition.) The results are consistent with the episodic context account: Intentional retrieval, which involves thinking back to the study context, produced a larger effect on the criterial test than did incidental retrieval (generating the targets without thinking back to the study context).

Karpicke, Lehman, and Gallo (2014) examined the effects of initial retrieval orientation on subsequent recall. The general design was similar to the one used by Karpicke and Zaromb (2010). In the first phase of the experiment, subjects studied a list that contained a mixture of pictures and words presented in red ink (see Gallo, Weiss, & Schacter, 2004). In a second phase, subjects were shown a series of words (this time in black ink), some of which were old studied words and some of which were new, and the subjects were instructed to do one of three things. One group was instructed to form a mental image of each word, a task traditionally considered an elaborative study task. A second group took a standard yes/no recognition test. A third group took a "source constrained" recognition test: They were instructed to say "yes" only if they had studied the word previously as a picture (Gallo et al., 2004; Jacoby, Shimizu, Daniels, & Rhodes, 2005). Thus, both the standard and constrained recognition groups made recognition judgments, but subjects in the constrained condition were required to recollect details about the previous study context. Finally, at the end of the experiment the subjects freely recalled the words. Figure 7.8 shows the proportion of words recalled on the final test (collapsed across whether the items were originally presented as pictures or words). Making a recognition judgment produced greater final recall than did forming a mental image, which represents another demonstration of retrieval practice producing more learning than an elaborative study task (Karpicke & Blunt, 2011; Karpicke & Smith, 2012; Lehman et al., in press). Most importantly, the constrained recognition condition produced better performance than the standard recognition condition. Requiring subjects to recollect details from the study context produced the greatest effects on subsequent retention, a result that supports the episodic context account.

Finally, Whiffen and Karpicke (2013) tested a strong prediction of the episodic context account: If one were to hold all aspects of item presentation constant and manipulate only whether subjects were instructed to think about when an item had previously occurred in time, the act of making that temporal judgment should produce a retrieval practice effect on a later criterial test. Whiffen and Karpicke used a list discrimination task to require

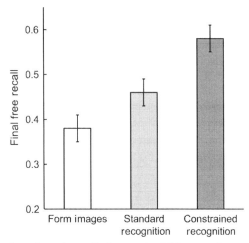

Figure 7.8 Proportion of words recalled on a criterial free recall test after forming mental images of the words, taking a standard yes/no recognition test over the words, or taking a constrained recognition test, in which subjects were asked to remember the original context of the study event. Recognition judgments produced better recall than forming mental images, and constrained recognition condition produced better performance than the standard recognition condition. *Data are from Karpicke et al. (2014).*

subjects to recollect prior temporal occurrence. Subjects studied two short lists of words, separated by a brief distracter task, and were then shown the words again with the two lists mixed together. In the restudy condition, the subjects were simply told to restudy the words in preparation for a final recall test, whereas in the list discrimination condition, the subjects were also told to indicate whether each word came from the first or second list (a list discrimination judgment). The subjects then freely recalled the words, and Fig. 7.9 shows the key results. The left portion of Fig. 7.9 shows the proportion of words recalled on the final test and shows that simply making a list discrimination judgment enhanced final recall. Whiffen and Karpicke also examined temporal clustering on the final test in terms of how often subjects grouped their output based on which list the word came from (this is done by calculating an adjusted ratio of clustering score with "list" as the grouping factor). The temporal clustering scores, shown in the right portion of Fig. 7.9, indicate that subjects relied on temporal order as an output strategy in the retrieval practice condition, clustering their output around list much more than subjects did in the list discrimination condition. The results confirm an important prediction of the context account: Simply thinking about the prior episodic context of an event enhances subsequent memory.

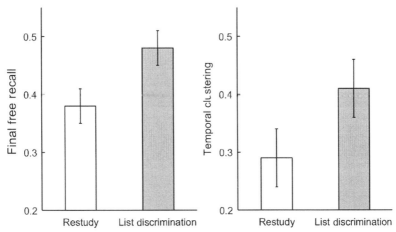

Figure 7.9 The left panel shows the proportion of words recalled on a criterial free recall test after studying the words or making temporal (list discrimination) judgments about the words. Simply making a list discrimination judgment enhanced final recall relative to the restudy condition. The right panel shows clustering scores, which represent the degree to which subjects organized their recall output temporally. Temporal clustering was more prevalent for the list discrimination condition indicating that subjects relied on temporal order as an output strategy relative to the restudy condition. *Data are from Whiffen and Karpicke (2013).*

The research reviewed in the previous sections supports the episodic context account of retrieval-based learning. Practicing retrieval enhances performance on criterial tests that assess recollection of episodic context, and retrieval practice conditions that emphasize the reinstatement of prior context produce especially large effects on criterial tests. In the remainder of this chapter, we describe how the episodic context account relates to other general theories that emphasize context reinstatement and retrieval.

6. GENERAL DISCUSSION AND FINAL COMMENTS
6.1. Context Variability and Study-Phase Retrieval

The episodic context account presented here is closely related to some accounts that have been proposed to explain the spacing effect (for reviews, see Benjamin & Tullis, 2010; Delaney et al., 2010). The theoretical explanation for the spacing effect that has received the most empirical support attributes spacing effects to a combination of *contextual variability* and *study-phase retrieval*. In this section, we discuss the relation of these ideas to the episodic context account of retrieval-based learning.

According to contextual variability accounts of the spacing effect, the occurrence of a studied item in two different contexts produces a varied set of retrieval cues that are effective for eliciting the item on a later test (Glenberg, 1979; Melton, 1970; see also Lohnas et al., 2011). Because context drifts throughout the study of a list, items that occur in two or more positions on the list experience greater contextual variability than items that are studied in a massed fashion, and the greater the distance between two presentations, the more contextual variability occurs (e.g., Glenberg, 1979; Greene, 1989). Study-phase retrieval accounts propose that spacing effects occur when, upon the second presentation of an item, people retrieve the prior presentation and additional information is added to the memory trace when the prior presentation is retrieved (Greene, 1989; Hintzman & Block, 1973). According to accounts that combine contextual variability and study-phase retrieval, the magnitude of the spacing effect will be greatest when study-phase retrieval is difficult but not impossible, because such conditions produce the greatest contextual variability in encoded traces. For many decades, theoretical explanations of the spacing effect have assumed a role for temporal context (Glenberg, 1979; Greene, 1989; Hintzman & Block, 1973; Kahana & Greene, 1993). These accounts have also assumed that spacing effects will occur only when retrieval tasks require reliance on contextual cues (Greene, 1989; Kahana & Greene, 1993).

Recently, Raaijmakers (2003) proposed an account of spacing effects that implements contextual variability and study-phase retrieval assumptions in a formal model of memory (Raaijmakers & Shiffrin, 1981). In Raaijmakers's model, the likelihood of retrieving an item is a function of the item's context strength, which represents the degree of association between the item and the context cue used to probe memory. The model incorporates the assumption that context drifts over time and that as time passes the current context becomes less similar to the context associated with the studied item, thereby decreasing the trace's context strength (Mensink & Raaijmakers, 1989). Additionally, when a studied item is repeated, subjects may or may not retrieve the trace stored during the prior presentation. If the prior presentation is retrieved, then additional contextual elements are stored with the trace. Importantly, the larger the contextual change between repetitions, the stronger the link to context that is formed (i.e., the greater the increase in context strength).

Delaney et al. (2010) extended Raaijmakers (2003) account, proposing that the amount of additional contextual information that is encoded on spaced presentations during study-phase retrieval is a function of the lag between presentations of the items. When repetitions occur close together on a list, the strength of the item is high during the second presentation, and the increase in context strength will be small. However, when the repetitions are far apart on the list, the strength will be low during the second presentation, and the increase in context strength will be larger. Similarly, various other recent accounts of spacing effects have attributed the benefit of spaced study to some combination of contextual variability and study-phase retrieval (Benjamin & Tullis, 2010; Lohnas & Kahana, in press; Verkoeijen et al., 2004).

Study-phase retrieval/contextual variability accounts of spacing effects share several features with the episodic context account of retrieval-based learning proposed here. The accounts assume that context fluctuates over time, that retrieval produces extra contextual encoding that reflects variation in context, that the amount of variation in encoded context plays a role in the magnitude of the benefit of additional encoding, and that only retrieval tasks that rely on the use of contextual cues will be sensitive to the benefits produced by additional contextual encoding. It is surprising that the most prominent accounts of the spacing effect attribute the advantage of spaced study to contextual encoding driven by retrieval processes, yet none of the prominent accounts of retrieval-based learning (e.g., strengthening, retrieval effort, transfer-appropriate processing, and elaborative retrieval) attributes retrieval practice to contextual factors.

The episodic context account of retrieval-based learning extends the ideas of contextual variability and study-phase retrieval in a few notable ways. The context account emphasizes the importance of intentional rather than incidental retrieval. Whereas study-phase retrieval refers to incidental retrieval that occurs when a person notices or is reminded of a prior occurrence during restudy, retrieval practice refers to conditions where people must intentionally reinstate a study context and remember what occurred during a prior learning episode. The amount of contextual updating is likely greater for intentionally retrieved items than it is for incidentally retrieved items. The context account also assumes that retrieval creates an updated context representation that contains a composite of features from prior contexts and from the current context in which retrieval occurs. The context account further proposes that because context reinstatement is used to guide a search process, people can use distinctive contexts produced by repeated retrieval practice to restrict their search and thereby improve memory performance. In sum, the episodic context account is the natural extension of contextual variability and study-phase retrieval accounts of spacing effects, combined with assumptions from several foundational memory models (e.g., Howard & Kahana, 2002; Raaijmakers & Shiffrin, 1981; Shiffrin & Steyvers, 1997), to provide a comprehensive and cohesive account of retrieval-based learning.

6.2. Conclusion

The episodic context account is a broad and general account of retrieval-based learning. It provides an account of the key effects in the retrieval practice literature, it accommodates a wide variety of additional retrieval practice effects, and it helps explain some findings that are challenging for other accounts to explain. It is congruent with contextual variability and study-phase retrieval accounts of the spacing effect, and it is founded on assumptions from a variety of fundamental models of memory. Future theoretical work should aim to elucidate specific predictions of the account that can be empirically tested, and the assumptions of the context account remain to be implemented in a formal model. Finally, and perhaps most importantly, the episodic context account identifies the defining feature of retrieval-based learning as the successful remembering of prior learning experiences. The notion that people learn when they practice remembering prior learning experiences can inform future research on retrieval-based learning as well as the design of educational activities to promote student learning.

ACKNOWLEDGMENTS

The writing of this report and some of the research described was supported in part by grants from the National Science Foundation (DRL-1149363 and DUE-1245476) and the Institute of Education Sciences in the U.S. Department of Education (R305A110903). The opinions expressed in this article are those of the authors and do not represent the views of the National Science Foundation, the Institute of Education Sciences, or of the U.S. Department of Education.

REFERENCES

Abbott, E. E. (1909). On the analysis of the factors of recall in the learning process. *Psychological Monographs, 11*, 159–177.
Agarwal, P., Karpicke, J., Kang, S., Roediger, H., III, & McDermott, K. (2008). Examining the testing effect with open-and closed-book tests. *Applied Cognitive Psychology, 22*(7), 861–876.
Anderson, M. C., Bjork, E. L., & Bjork, R. A. (1994). Remembering can cause forgetting: Retrieval dynamics in long-term memory. *Journal of Experimental Psychology: Learning, Memory, and Cognition, 20*, 1063–1087.
Atkinson, R. C., & Shiffrin, R. M. (1968). Human memory: A proposed system and its control processes. In K. W. Spence, & J. T. Spence (Eds.), *The psychology of learning and motivation* (pp. 89–195). New York, NY: Academic Press.

Bacon, F. (2000). *Novum organum*. L. Jardine & M. Silverthorne, Trans, Cambridge, England: Cambridge University Press (Original work published 1620).
Bäuml, K.-H. T., & Kliegl, O. (2013). The critical role of retrieval processes in release from proactive interference. *Journal of Memory and Language, 68*, 39–53.
Benjamin, A. S., & Tullis, J. (2010). What makes distributed practice effective? *Cognitive Psychology, 61*(3), 228–247.
Bjork, R. A. (1975). Retrieval as a memory modifier. In R. Solso (Ed.), *Information processing and cognition: The Loyola Symposium* (pp. 123–144). Hillsdale, NJ: Erlbaum.
Bjork, R. (1994). Memory and metamemory considerations in the training of human beings. In J. Metcalfe, & A. P. Shimamura (Eds.), *Metacognition* (pp. 185–205). Cambridge: The MIT Press.
Bjork, R. A., & Bjork, E. L. (1992). A new theory of disuse and an old theory of stimulus fluctuation. In A. Healy, S. Kosslyn,, & R. Shiffrin (Eds.), *From learning processes to cognitive processes: Essays in honor of William K Estes*: Vol. 2. (pp. 35–67). Hillsdale, NJ: Erlbaum.
Blunt, J. R., & Karpicke, J. D. (in press). Learning with retrieval-based concept mapping. *Journal of Educational Psychology*.
Bower, G. H. (1972). Stimulus-sampling theory of encoding variability. In A. W. Meltion, & E. Martin (Eds.), *Coding processes in human memory* (pp. 85–123). Washington, DC: Winston.
Brewer, G. A., Marsh, R. L., Meeks, J. T., Clark-Foos, A., & Hicks, J. L. (2010). The effects of free recall testing on subsequent source memory. *Memory, 18*, 385–393.
Brinegar, K., Lehman, M., & Malmberg, K. J. (2013). Improving memory after environmental context change: A strategy of "preinstatement" *Psychonomic Bulletin & Review, 20*, 528–533.
Butler, A. C., & Roediger, H. L., III (2007). Testing improves long-term retention in a simulated classroom setting. *European Journal of Cognitive Psychology, 19*, 514–527.
Butler, A. C. (2010). Repeated testing produces superior transfer of learning relative to repeated studying. *Journal of Experimental Psychology Learning, Memory, and Cognition, 36*, 1118–1133.
Carpenter, S. K. (2009). Cue strength as a moderator of the testing effect: The benefits of elaborative retrieval. *Journal of Experimental Psychology Learning, Memory, and Cognition, 35*, 1563–1569.
Carpenter, S. K. (2011). Semantic information activated during retrieval contributes to later retention: Support for the mediator effectiveness hypothesis of the testing effect. *Journal of Experimental Psychology. Learning, Memory, and Cognition, 37*, 1547–1552.
Carpenter, S. K. (2012). Testing enhances the transfer of learning. *Current Directions in Psychological Science, 21*, 279–283.
Carpenter, S. K., & DeLosh, E. L. (2005). Application of the testing and spacing effects to name-learning. *Applied Cognitive Psychology, 19*, 619–636.
Carpenter, S. K., & DeLosh, E. L. (2006). Impoverished cue support enhances subsequent retention: Support for the elaborative retrieval explanation of the testing effect. *Memory & Cognition, 34*, 268–276.
Carpenter, S. K., & Kelly, J. W. (2012). Tests enhance retention and transfer of spatial learning. *Psychonomic Bulletin & Review, 19*, 443–448.
Carpenter, S. K., Pashler, H., & Vul, E. (2006). What types of learning are enhanced by a cued recall test? *Psychonomic Bulletin & Review, 13*, 826–830.
Chan, J. C. K., & McDermott, K. B. (2007). The testing effect in recognition memory: A dual process account. *Journal of Experimental Psychology Learning, Memory, and Cognition, 33*, 431–437.
Coppens, L. C., Verkoeijen, P. P. J. L., & Rikers, R. M. J. P. (2011). Learning Adinkra symbols: The effect of testing. *Journal of Cognitive Psychology, 23*(3), 351–357.

Craik, F. I. M. (1970). The fate of primary memory items in free recall. *Journal of Verbal Learning and Verbal Behavior, 9*, 143–148.
Craik, F. I. M., & Tulving, E. (1975). Depth of processing and the retention of words in episodic memory. *Journal of Experimental Psychology General, 104*(3), 268–294.
Darley, C. F., & Murdock, B. B. (1971). Effects of prior free recall testing on final recall and recognition. *Journal of Experimental Psychology, 91*, 66–73.
Deese, J. (1958). *The psychology of learning* (2nd ed.). New York, NY: McGraw-Hill.
Delaney, P., Verkoeijen, P., & Spirgel, A. (2010). Spacing and testing effects: A deeply critical, lengthy, and at times discursive review of the literature. In B. H. Ross, & B. H. Ross (Eds.), *The psychology of learning and motivation: Advances in research and theory*: Vol. 53. (pp. 63–147). San Diego, CA: Elsevier Academic Press.
Dempster, F. N. (1996). Distributing and managing the conditions of encoding and practice. In E. L. Bjork, & R. A. Bjork (Eds.), *Human memory* (pp. 197–236). San Diego, CA: Academic Press.
Duchastel, P., & Nungester, R. (1982). Testing effects measured with alternate test forms. *The Journal of Educational Research, 75*(5), 309–313.
Dudukovic, N. M., DuBrow, S., & Wagner, A. D. (2009). Attention during memory retrieval enhances future remembering. *Memory & Cognition, 37*(7), 953–961.
Ebbinghaus, H. (1885). *Memory: A contribution to experimental psychology*. New York: Teachers College, Columbia University.
Estes, W. K. (1955). Statistical theory of spontaneous recovery and regression. *Psychological Review, 62*, 145–154.
Gallo, D. A., Weiss, J. A., & Schacter, D. L. (2004). Reducing false recognition with criterial recollection tests: Distinctiveness heuristic versus criterion shifts. *Journal of Memory and Language, 51*, 473–493.
Gardiner, F., Craik, F., & Bleasdale, F. (1973). Retrieval difficulty and subsequent recall. *Memory & Cognition, 1*(3), 213–216.
Gaspelin, N., Ruthruff, E., & Pashler, H. (2013). Divided attention: An undesirable difficulty in memory retention. *Memory & Cognition, 41*(7), 978–988.
Glenberg, A. (1979). Component-levels theory of the effects of spacing of repetitions on recall and recognition. *Memory & Cognition, 7*(2), 95–112.
Glover, J. A. (1989). The "testing" phenomenon: Not gone but nearly forgotten. *Journal of Educational Psychology, 81*, 392–399.
Greene, R. L. (1989). Spacing effects in memory: Evidence for a two-process account. *Journal of Experimental Psychology. Learning, Memory, and Cognition, 15*, 371–377.
Greene, R. L. (2008). Repetition and spacing effects. In J. Byrne (Ed.), *Learning and memory: A comprehensive reference* (pp. 65–78). Oxford, UK: Elsevier.
Greene, R. L., & Stillwell, A. M. (1995). Effects of encoding variability and spacing on frequency discrimination. *Journal of Memory and Language, 34*, 468–476.
Grimaldi, P. J., & Karpicke, J. D. (2012). When and why do retrieval attempts enhance subsequent encoding? *Memory & Cognition, 40*, 505–513.
Grimaldi, P. J., & Karpicke, J. D. (2014). Guided retrieval practice of educational materials using automated scoring. *Journal of Educational Psychology, 106*, 58–68.
Halamish, V., & Bjork, R. (2011). When does testing enhance retention? A distribution-based interpretation of retrieval as a memory modifier. *Journal of Experimental Psychology. Learning, Memory and Cognition, 37*(4), 801–812.
Hanawalt, N. G. (1937). Memory trace for figures in recall and recognition. *Archives of Psychology (Columbia University), 216*, 89.
Hintzman, D. L., & Block, R. A. (1973). Memory for the spacing of repetitions. *Journal of Experimental Psychology, 99*, 70–74.
Hogan, R., & Kintsch, W. (1971). Differential effects of study and test trials on long-term recognition and recall. *Journal of Verbal Learning and Verbal Behavior, 10*(5), 562–567.

Howard, M. W., & Kahana, M. J. (2002). A distributed representation of temporal context. *Journal of Mathematical Psychology, 46*, 269–299.

Jacoby, L. L. (1978). On interpreting the effects of repetition: Solving a problem versus remembering a solution. *Journal of Verbal Learning and Verbal Behavior, 17*, 649–667.

Jacoby, L. L. (1991). A process dissociation framework: Separating automatic from intentional uses of memory. *Journal of Memory and Language, 30*, 513–541.

Jacoby, L. L., Shimizu, Y., Daniels, K. A., & Rhodes, M. G. (2005). Modes of cognitive control in recognition and source memory: Depth of retrieval. *Psychonomic Bulletin & Review, 12*, 852–857.

James, W. (1890). *The principles of psychology*. New York: Henry Holt and Company.

Jang, Y., & Huber, D. E. (2008). Context retrieval and context change in free recall: Recalling from long-term memory drives list isolation. *Journal of Experimental Psychology. Learning, Memory, and Cognition, 34*, 112–127.

Johnson, M. K., Hashtroudi, S., & Lindsay, D. S. (1993). Source monitoring. *Psychological Bulletin, 114*, 3–28.

Johnson, C. I., & Mayer, R. E. (2009). A testing effect with multimedia learning. *Journal of Educational Psychology, 101*, 621–629.

Kahana, M. J., & Greene, R. L. (1993). The effects of spacing on memory for homogeneous lists. *Journal of Experimental Psychology. Learning, Memory, and Cognition, 19*, 159–162.

Kang, S. H. K. (2010). Enhancing visuospatial learning: The benefit of retrieval practice. *Memory & Cognition, 38*(8), 1009–1017.

Kang, S., McDermott, K., & Roediger, H. (2007). Test format and corrective feedback modify the effect of testing on long-term retention. *European Journal of Cognitive Psychology, 19*(4–5), 528–558.

Karpicke, J. D. (2009). Metacognitive control and strategy selection: Deciding to practice retrieval during learning. *Journal of Experimental Psychology. General, 138*, 469–486.

Karpicke, J. D. (2012). Retrieval-based learning: Active retrieval promotes meaningful learning. *Current Directions in Psychological Science, 21*, 157–163.

Karpicke, J. D., & Bauernschmidt, A. (2011). Spaced retrieval: Absolute spacing enhances learning regardless of relative spacing. *Journal of Experimental Psychology. Learning, Memory, and Cognition, 37*, 1250–1257.

Karpicke, J. D., & Blunt, J. R. (2011). Retrieval practice produces more learning than elaborative studying with concept mapping. *Science, 331*, 772–775.

Karpicke, J. D., & Grimaldi, P. J. (2012). Retrieval-based learning: A perspective for enhancing meaningful learning. *Educational Psychology Review, 24*, 401–418.

Karpicke, J. D., Lehman, M., & Gallo, D. A. (2014). Retrieval-based learning: The role of initial retrieval orientation. Unpublished manuscript.

Karpicke, J. D., McCabe, D. P., & Roediger, H. L. (2006). Testing enhances recollection: Process dissociations and metamemory judgments. In *Poster presented at the 47th annual meeting of the psychonomic society, Houston, TX*.

Karpicke, J. D., & Roediger, H. L. (2007a). Expanding retrieval practice promotes short-term retention, but equally spaced retrieval enhances long-term retention. *Journal of Experimental Psychology. Learning, Memory, and Cognition, 33*, 704–719.

Karpicke, J. D., & Roediger, H. L. (2007b). Repeated retrieval during learning is the key to long-term retention. *Journal of Memory and Language, 57*(2), 151–162.

Karpicke, J., & Roediger, H. (2008). The critical importance of retrieval for learning. *Science, 319*(5865), 966–968.

Karpicke, J. D., & Smith, M. A. (2012). Separate mnemonic effects of retrieval practice and elaborative encoding. *Journal of Memory and Language, 67*, 17–29.

Karpicke, J. D., & Zaromb, F. M. (2010). Retrieval mode distinguishes the testing effect from the generation effect. *Journal of Memory and Language, 62*, 227–239.

Klein, K. A., Shiffrin, R. M., & Criss, A. H. (2007). Putting context in context. In J. S. Nairne (Ed.), *The foundations of remembering: Essays in honor of Henry L. Roediger III*. New York: Psychology Press.

Kolers, P. A., & Roediger, H. L. (1984). Procedures of mind. *Journal of Verbal Learning and Verbal Behavior, 23*, 425–449.

Kornell, N., Bjork, R. A., & Garcia, M. A. (2011). Why tests appear to prevent forgetting: A distribution-based bifurcation model. *Journal of Memory and Language, 65*, 85–97.

Kornell, N., Hays, M. J., & Bjork, R. A. (2009). Unsuccessful retrieval attempts enhance subsequent learning. *Journal of Experimental Psychology. Learning, Memory, and Cognition, 35*, 989–998.

Landauer, T. K., & Bjork, R. (1978). Optimum rehearsal patterns and name learning. In M. M. Gruneberg, P. E. Morris, & R. N. Sykes (Eds.), *Practical aspects of memory: Vol. 1*. (pp. 625–632). London: Academic press.

Lehman, M., & Malmberg, K. J. (2009). A global theory of remembering and forgetting from multiple lists. *Journal of Experimental Psychology. Learning, Memory, and Cognition, 35*(4), 970.

Lehman, M., & Malmberg, K. J. (2013). A buffer model of encoding and temporal correlations in retrieval. *Psychological Review, 120*(1), 155–189.

Lehman, M., Smith, M. A., & Karpicke, J. D. (in press). Toward an episodic context account of retrieval-based learning: Dissociating retrieval practice and elaboration. *Journal of Experimental Psychology: Learning, Memory, and Cognition*.

Lohnas, L. J., & Kahana, M. J. (in press). A retrieved context account of spacing and repetition effects in free recall. *Journal of Experimental Psychology. Learning, Memory and Cognition*.

Lohnas, L. J., Polyn, S. M., & Kahana, M. J. (2011). Contextual variability in free recall. *Journal of Memory and Language, 64*(3), 249–255.

MacLeod, C. M., Gopie, N., Hourihan, K. L., Neary, K. R., & Ozubko, J. D. (2010). The production effect: Delineation of a phenomenon. *Journal of Experimental Psychology. Learning, Memory, and Cognition, 36*, 671–685.

Martin, E. (1968). Stimulus meaningfulness and paired-associate transfer: An encoding variability hypothesis. *Psychological Review, 75*, 421–441.

Masicampo, E. J., & Sahakyan, L. (in press). Imagining another context during encoding offsets context-dependent forgetting. *Journal of Experimental Psychology: Learning, Memory, and Cognition*. [Epub ahead of print].

McCabe, D. P., Roediger, H. L., & Karpicke, J. D. (2011). Automatic processing influences free recall: Converging evidence from the process dissociation procedure and remember-know judgments. *Memory & Cognition, 39*, 389–402.

McDaniel, M., Anderson, J., Derbish, M., & Morrisette, N. (2007). Testing the testing effect in the classroom. *European Journal of Cognitive Psychology, 19*(4–5), 494–513.

McDaniel, M., & Fisher, R. (1991). Tests and test feedback as learning sources. *Contemporary Educational Psychology, 16*(2), 192–201.

McDaniel, M. A., & Masson, M. E. J. (1985). Altering memory representations through retrieval. *Journal of Experimental Psychology. Learning, Memory, and Cognition, 11*, 371–385.

McDaniel, M. A., Roediger, H. L. I., & McDermott, K. B. (2007). Generalizing test-enhanced learning from the laboratory to the classroom. *Psychonomic Bulletin & Review, 14*(2), 200–206.

McDermott, K. B. (2006). Paradoxical effects of testing: Repeated retrieval attempts enhance the likelihood of later accurate and false recall. *Memory & Cognition, 34*, 261–267.

McGeoch, J. A. (1942). *The psychology of human learning*. New York: Longmans.

Melton, A. W. (1970). The situation with respect to the spacing of repetitions and memory. *Journal of Verbal Learning and Verbal Behavior, 9*(5), 596–606.

Mensink, G. J. M., & Raaijmakers, J. G. W. (1989). A model for contextual fluctuation. *Journal of Mathematical Psychology, 33*, 172–186.

Morris, C. D., Bransford, J., & Franks, J. (1977). Levels of processing versus transfer appropriate processing. *Journal of Verbal Learning and Verbal Behavior*, *16*(5), 519–533.
Mulligan, N. W., Lozito, J. P., & Rosner, Z. A. (2006). Generation and context memory. *Journal of Experimental Psychology Learning, Memory, and Cognition*, *32*, 836–846.
Nairne, J. S. (2002). The myth of the encoding-retrieval match. *Memory*, *10*, 389–395.
Nairne, J. S. (2006). Modeling distinctiveness: Implications for general memory theory. In R. R. Hunt, & J. Worthen (Eds.), *Distinctiveness and memory* (pp. 27–46). New York: Oxford University Press.
Nairne, J. S. (2010). Adaptive memory: Evolutionary constraints on remembering. In B. H. Ross (Ed.), *The psychology of learning and motivation*: Vol. 53. (pp. 1–32). Burlington: Academic Press.
Nelson, D. L., & McEvoy, C. L. (1979). Encoding context and set size. *Journal of Experimental Psychology Human Learning and Memory*, *5*(3), 292–314.
Novak, J. D., & Gowin, D. B. (1984). *Learning how to learn*. New York: Cambridge University Press.
Polyn, S. M., Norman, K. A., & Kahana, M. J. (2009). A context maintenance and retrieval model of organizational processes in free recall. *Psychological Review*, *116*(1), 129–156.
Postman, L., & Knecht, K. (1983). Encoding variability and retention. *Journal of Verbal Learning and Verbal Behavior*, *22*, 133–152.
Putnam, A. L., & Roediger, H. L. (2013). Does response mode affect amount recalled or the magnitude of the testing effect? *Memory & Cognition*, *41*(1), 36–48.
Pyc, M. A., & Rawson, K. A. (2009). Testing the retrieval effort hypothesis: Does greater difficulty correctly recalling information lead to higher levels of memory? *Journal of Memory and Language*, *60*, 437–447.
Raaijmakers, J. (2003). Spacing and repetition effects in human memory: Application of the SAM model. *Cognitive Science*, *27*(3), 431–452.
Raaijmakers, J. G. W., & Jakab, E. (2013). Rethinking inhibition theory: On the problematic status of the inhibition theory for forgetting. *Journal of Memory and Language*, *68*, 98–122.
Raaijmakers, J. G. W., & Shiffrin, R. M. (1981). Search of associative memory. *Psychological Review*, *88*, 93–134.
Roediger, H., & Butler, A. (2011). The critical role of retrieval practice in long-term retention. *Trends in Cognitive Sciences*, *15*(1), 20–27.
Roediger, H. L., & Karpicke, J. D. (2006a). Test-enhanced learning: Taking memory tests improves long-term retention. *Psychological Science*, *17*, 249–255.
Roediger, H. L., & Karpicke, J. D. (2006b). The power of testing memory: Basic research and implications for educational practice. *Perspectives on Psychological Science*, *1*, 181–210.
Roediger, H. L., Putnam, A. L., & Smith, M. A. (2011). Ten benefits of testing and their applications to educational practice. In J. P. Mestre, & B. H. Ross (Eds.), *The psychology of learning and motivation: Cognition in education*: Vol. 55. (pp. 1–36). San Diego, CA: Elsevier Academic Press.
Sederberg, P. B., Howard, M. W., & Kahana, M. J. (2008). A context-based theory of recency and contiguity in free recall. *Psychological Review*, *115*(4), 893–912.
Shiffrin, R. M., & Steyvers, M. (1997). A model for recognition memory: REM—Retrieving effectively from memory. *Psychonomic Bulletin & Review*, *4*, 145–166.
Slamecka, N. J., & Graf, P. (1978). The generation effect: Delineation of a phenomenon. *Journal of Experimental Psychology Human Learning and Memory*, *4*(6), 592–604.
Smith, S. M. (1979). Remembering in and out of context. *Journal of Experimental Psychology: Human Learning and Memory*, *5*, 460–471.
Smith, M. A., Roediger, H. L., & Karpicke, J. D. (2013). Covert retrieval practice benefits retention as much as overt retrieval practice. *Journal of Experimental Psychology. Learning, Memory, and Cognition*, *39*, 1712–1725.

Storm, B. C. (2011). The benefit of forgetting in thinking and remembering. *Current Directions in Psychological Science, 20*, 291–295.

Surprenant, A. M., & Neath, I. (2009). *Principles of memory*. New York: Psychology Press.

Szpunar, K. K., McDermott, K. B., & Roediger, H. L., III (2008). Testing during study insulates against the buildup of proactive interference. *Journal of Experimental Psychology. Learning, Memory, and Cognition, 34*, 1392–1399.

Tulving, E. (1983). *Elements of episodic memory*. New York: Oxford University Press.

Tulving, E. (1985). Memory and consciousness. *Canadian Psychology, 26*, 1–12.

Tulving, E., & Thomson, D. M. (1973). Encoding specificity and retrieval processes in episodic memory. *Psychological Review, 80*(5), 352–373.

Verkoeijen, P. P. J. L., Rikers, R. M. J. P., & Schmidt, H. G. (2004). Detrimental influence of contextual change on spacing effects in free recall. *Journal of Experimental Psychology. Learning, Memory, and Cognition, 30*, 796–800.

Verkoeijen, P. P. J. L., Tabbers, H. K., & Verhage, M. L. (2011). Comparing the effects of testing and restudying on recollection in recognition memory. *Experimental Psychology, 58*(6), 490–498.

Watkins, O. C., & Watkins, M. J. (1975). Buildup of proactive inhibition as a cue-overload effect. *Journal of Experimental Psychology Human Learning and Memory, 1*(4), 442–452.

Whiffen, J., & Karpicke, J. D. (2013). The role of temporal context in retrieval practice. In *Poster presented at the 54th annual meeting of the psychonomic society, Toronto, ON*.

Whitten, W. B., & Bjork, R. A. (1977). Learning from tests: Effects of spacing. *Journal of Verbal Learning and Verbal Behavior, 16*, 465–478.

Wixted, J. T., & Rohrer, D. (1993). Proactive interference and the dynamics of free recall. *Journal of Experimental Psychology. Learning, Memory, and Cognition, 19*, 1024–1039.

Wixted, J. T., & Rohrer, D. (1994). Analyzing the dynamics of free recall: An integrative review of the empirical literature. *Psychonomic Bulletin & Review, 1*, 89–106.

CHAPTER EIGHT

Consequences of Testing Memory

Kenneth J. Malmberg[*,1], Melissa Lehman[†], Jeffrey Annis[*], Amy H. Criss[‡], Richard M. Shiffrin[§]

[*]Department of Psychology, University of South Florida, Tampa, Florida, USA
[†]Department of Psychological Sciences, Purdue University, West Lafayette, Indiana, USA
[‡]Department of Psychology, Syracuse University, Syracuse, New York, USA
[§]Department of Brain and Psychological Sciences, Indiana University, Bloomington, Indiana, USA
[1]Corresponding author: e-mail address: malmberg@usf.edu

Contents

1. Introduction 285
2. Benefits of Memory Testing 287
   2.1 Generalization of the Testing Effect 288
   2.2 Why Does Testing Improve or Harm Memory? 290
3. Costs of Testing Memory: Output Interference 298
4. The Influence of One Test on the Next: Sequential Dependencies 302
5. Past Decisions Influence Future Decisions: Shifts in Bias 306
6. Conclusions 308
References 308

Abstract

Studies using a wide variety of conditions and a diverse set of procedures show that testing memory affects future behavior. The studies have used differing terminology and have been ascribed to differing specialty areas of the literature. Partly, for this reason, the various phenomena have been described in ways, suggesting they differ in substance. In this chapter, we relate many of these phenomena and show that they might be due to a set of common memory processes, processes that can act through conscious, strategic or unconscious, implicit means. The critical strand that links the phenomena is that memory is a continuous process that constantly stores and retrieves information.

1. INTRODUCTION

In typical laboratory investigations of human memory, learning occurs when one is asked to study a set of to-be-remembered items. During study, participants are either left to their own devices or assigned a variety of tasks that guide the learning in a particular direction. In these tasks, it is typical for memory to be tested in one or more ways after some delay. The three phases are referred to as study, retention, and test. Ebbinghaus (1885) established that the amount of information forgotten increases with increases in the length of retention interval, and the literature developed since then has focused primarily on how the conditions during study are related to performance when memory is tested. In much of the early literature, it was assumed that only study, not testing, impacts future memory. Evidence to the contrary was often obscured by designs, randomizations, and analyses that made it hard or impossible to see the effects of testing. However, recent years have seen an upsurge of investigations examining and demonstrating remarkably strong effects of testing. This should not be a surprise given that we can obviously remember what was tested, observe what transpires during testing, and learn from the results of testing. The general rule is that the act of remembering affects subsequent learning and retrieval. Many of the effects are beneficial, but some are harmful. In this chapter, we review both and discuss how memory models can explain them.

There is actually a fairly long history of studies of the effects of testing, but most of the older studies confounded testing and studying. A set of older studies and models by Izawa (1970, 1971) examined the "potentiating" effects of testing, but did not at the time engender further research. Roediger and Karpicke (2006) showed that testing a memory can produce better learning than studying a second time, sparking a renewed interest in the consequences of testing memory. The studies have inspired both systematic investigations into applications and a better understanding of basic processes involved in learning, remembering, and forgetting. Because the various findings are not well organized by a common theoretical framework and are found in different areas of psychological science, we aim in this chapter to relate the various findings with the help of memory theory.

As just mentioned, a driving force behind the recent investigations is the finding that eventual retrieval of some initially studied information can be increased more by an intermediate act of retrieval than by an intermediate act of study. This phenomenon is often referred to as *the testing effect* or *the retrieval practice effect*. Such benefits of retrieving information from memory are robust, occurring for a range of materials and test types (see Roediger & Karpicke, 2006 for a review). In fact, the layperson may have benefited from similar procedures, such as flashcards, when studying for exams (albeit typically such use involves both testing and study).

However, there are actually quite a large number of "testing effects." Some are positive as in the many studies of learning, and the testing effects just mentioned. Others are negative. For instance, retrieval from memory has negative consequences for the future retrieval of other information, generally termed *interference* and studied extensively in list learning experiments in the 1950s and 1960s (see Crowder, 1976 for a review). Another set of retrieval tasks producing negative memory effects are referred to as *retrieval-induced forgetting* (Anderson, Bjork, & Bjork, 1994, 2000; Jakab & Raaijmakers, 2009; Raaijmakers & Jakab, 2013a, 2013b; there is an ongoing debate concerning the degree to which such effects are due to *active suppression* or *competition*). Yet other paradigms demonstrate *output interference* during the course of successive testing (Criss, Malmberg, & Shiffrin, 2011; Raaijmakers & Shiffrin, 1980; Wickens, 1970).

Other test effects can be either positive or negative. For example, decisions made on the basis of what is retrieved from memory often affect in the future what we believe we have or have not experienced (Malmberg & Annis, 2012). In addition, *sequential dependencies* occur for both events that were and were not experienced; these consequences of testing memory are robust and tend to produce systematic mnemonic bias rather than changes in overall levels of accuracy.

These brief citations are enough to suggest that a number of processes are at work during testing. It is abundantly clear that testing and retrieving has significant implications for what we will remember in the future. We shall see that major factors are the storage of new information during testing (producing both positive and negative effects), and strategic changes induced by learning from the results of testing. Specifically, we consider three classes of processes by which memory testing can alter performance on subsequent tests: (a) storing new memory traces during testing; (b) enhancing, modifying, or updating existing memory traces; and (c) altering learning and retrieval strategies. Examining how these factors work is an aim of this chapter. We first review some of what is known about the consequences of testing memory.

2. BENEFITS OF MEMORY TESTING

Starting in the late 1800s (e.g., Ebbinghaus, 1885), there has been a long history of studies of learning and forgetting. Such learning produces memory for recent events, such as lists of words or words pairs, and also produces knowledge. Nelson and Shiffrin (2013) describe how a common set of memory processes can produce both types of learning. Many articles and books have dealt with learning and memory, typically dealing with tasks in which testing involves both testing and studying. This chapter instead focuses on more recent tasks in which the effects of testing are separated (at least partially) from the effects of studying.

2.1. Generalization of the Testing Effect

Studies examining the "testing effect" on retention often utilize free recall tests, whereby a list of to-be remembered items is studied and after a retention interval, one is asked to recall as many items from the study list in any order. In the control condition, one is given a second chance to study the items. The key question concerns whether testing memory provides any substantial improvement in memory beyond the benefits of additional study, as measured during a subsequent round of free recall. This final measure of memory retention is referred to as a *criterion test*. When the retention interval between the first and second round of testing is lengthened, forgetting of the original material increases in both conditions, but the rate of forgetting is greater for items given additional study compared to items that were recalled in the first round of testing (Roediger & Karpicke, 2006).

Of course, we often want to remember specific events, in contrast to remembering an entire class of events as in free recall. For instance, in cued recall participants study pairs of items and are tested with one member of the pair provided as a cue (a testing procedure somewhat like a short answer or fill-in-the-blank test found in educational settings). In recognition tests, participants must decide whether a tested item had (a "target") or had not (a "foil") been studied on a prior list (a situation analogous to a true–false test or a multiple-choice test found in educational and legal settings, such as identifying a suspect from a lineup).

Researchers have asked whether the benefits found for testing in free recall extend to cued recall and recognition. They report that initial free recall testing reduces the rate of forgetting more than initial cued recall or yes/no recognition testing (Carpenter & DeLosh, 2006; Glover, 1989). In fact, it appears that initial yes/no recognition has little effect compared to restudying regardless of the task used on the final test of memory (Carpenter & DeLosh, 2006). Likewise, evidence for an effect of initial free recall on final recognition testing is mixed (Carpenter & DeLosh, 2006; Darley & Murdock, 1971; Jones & Roediger, 1995; Roediger & McDermott, 1995). Hence, recognition testing appears to be much less effective than free recall testing in reducing the subsequent rate of forgetting, and recognition testing appears to benefit much less strongly than free recall testing when used as the criterion task.

Some of the variability reported in studies of test effects may be due to differing processes used in different tasks, differences likely caused by differing tasks and materials (see Gillund & Shiffrin, 1984; Malmberg, 2008 for a review of the way theory can take such differences into account). For instance, Chan and McDermott (2007) speculated that retrieval practice increases performance on recognition tests that rely on "recollective" processes (Mandler, 1980). Recollective processes are often associated with or defined by memory for details of an encoding event and may be due to the use of processes during recognition that are also required for cued or free recall. Chan and McDermott found that retrieval practice increased performance on a list discrimination test and increased "remember" responses, although there was little effect of retrieval practice on final yes–no recognition hit rates. They concluded that retrieval practice increased the tendency to make a recognition decision based on the retrieval of episodic details of the events and decreased the tendency to make a recognition decision based on the familiarity of the test item. Whether recollective processes are used to a significant degree during recognition testing is a debatable issue (Dunn, 2004; Malmberg, 2008; Malmberg, Zeelenberg, & Shiffrin, 2004), and likely depends on procedural details including timing, incentives, and instructions, because the use of recollective processes to make recognition judgments surely requires more time and effort than judgments made on the basis of familiarity.

It is also likely that the benefits of testing do not apply equally to all aspects of to-be-remembered events. Brewer, Marsh, Meeks, Clark-Foos, and Hicks (2010) presented participants with two lists consisting of words spoken by both male and female speakers. Half of the participants completed a free recall test after each list, and the others completed an arithmetic task. A final source memory task followed in both conditions, which required participants to identify either the original study list from which the word was read or the gender of the speaker that read the item. Initial free recall testing increased final list discrimination performance, suggesting that the free recall practice improves the encoding and/or access to the temporal aspects of the events, but it did not increase gender discrimination performance, indicating that other aspects of the event, such as the representation of the source, are not enhanced by free recall testing. Taking this result together with the finding that recognition and cued recall do not benefit from testing to the extent that free recall does, it appears likely that more of the benefit imparted by retrieval is the result of the storage of additional features representing the context in which the testing occurred than the storage of additional perceptual features about the items to be remembered.

2.2. Why Does Testing Improve or Harm Memory?

Theories are constrained by the findings that testing provides more benefits for eventual free recall of a given item than benefits for eventual cued recall and recognition, especially when the initial testing also uses free recall. One hypothesis holds that free recall testing makes the memory in question more accessible by altering or adding to its contextual representation (Karpicke, Lehman, & Aue, 2014). Indeed, free recall is heavily dependent on the use of context information (Lehman & Malmberg, 2013; Malmberg & Shiffrin, 2005), and changes in context have been implicated in forgetting going back decades (Lehman & Malmberg, 2009; McGeoch, 1942; Mensink & Raaijmakers, 1989). Another hypothesis holds that testing causes an increase in item information and/or inter-item information than does study alone. For instance, there is a large amount of evidence that people are usually overconfident in their ability to recall specific items in the future, and they underestimate the amount of time it takes to learn pairs of words in anticipation of a cued recall test of memory, but when given the opportunity to test their learning prior to the criterion test, subjects are able to increase the amount of time allocated to studying the most difficult to remember pairs, at least when there is ample time to do so (Koriat & Bjork, 2005, 2006; Nelson & Leonesio, 1988; Son & Metcalfe, 2000). And of course, one should consider encoding models that assume free recall testing results in the storage of various combinations of these forms of information.

Another hypothesis holds that free recall testing may lead the subject to improve their retrieval strategy. Retrieval strategies are especially important in performing free recall, and they may be less important in item recognition or cued recall. However, it is quite difficult to think about changes in retrieval strategies without considering related changes in encoding. For instance, a more (or less) effective retrieval strategy may be implemented during or after the course of a single series of recall or recognition trials. Presumably, if it was adopted at some point during a series of tests, the new retrieval strategy would have some effect during the current round of testing and an effect during a subsequent round of testing, take for instance, associative recognition, which requires subjects to discriminate between pairs of items that were studied together (intact pairs) from pairs of items that were studied but not studied as part of the same pair (rearranged pairs). It is possible that the subject begins an initial round of testing with a strategy that utilizes information representing the familiarity of the test pair, but after a small number of associative recognition trials that a subject realizes that a recollective strategy, such as recall to reject, may improve their accuracy on subsequent trials (cf. Malmberg, Holden, & Shiffrin, 2004; Malmberg & Xu, 2007; Xu & Malmberg, 2007). If this strategy were also used during criterion testing and if similar encoding did not take place in the control condition, then the benefits of testing would be apparent. However, the switch in retrieval strategy may co-occur with a new encoding strategy to support it. Consider again the associative recognition task. Experience with a few trials of the associative recognition task may inspire the subject to focus on encoding of associative information during the course of initial testing, strengthening the inter-item associations originally acquired during study (cf. Palmeri & Flanery, 2002, e.g., from categorization literature). If so, should one attribute the benefits of testing to the change in retrieval or the change in encoding? This question is difficult to answer without careful experimentation.

It seems reasonable to assume that both the retrieval strategy and the information retrieved will affect what is encoded during the test trial and the subsequent effects of testing. For instance, tasks like cued recall and associative recognition may encourage the encoding of inter-item associative information, but tasks or strategies that require retrieval of temporal context may result in more extensive encoding of temporal context during the course of testing. If the criterion task also requires access to temporal context, then test effects should be observed, in a manner akin to transfer-appropriate processing (Morris, Bransford, & Franks, 1977). However, if the criterion task requires access to different information, say associative information for a recall task, then encoding of temporal context features would be less beneficial. Information stored that is particular to a given memory task is what distinguishes in memory the performance of different tasks, and we will return to the effects of switches in task switching when we discuss output interference in a later section of this chapter. For now, we note that the benefits of testing are sometimes diminished when there is a conflict in the memory task performed during initial testing (e.g., free recall) and criterion testing (e.g., recognition).

However, it is also noted that matches in task context (e.g., recognition) do not necessarily predict benefits of memory testing (Carpenter & DeLosh, 2006). To receive benefits from memory testing, it is necessary to encode or store information that is not easily stored during the course of studying. In free recall, the items "tested" are only those generated by subject. According to some models, the cue set used to probe memory is determined in large part by the inter-item associations stored during study (cf. Lehman &

Malmberg, 2013; Raaijmakers & Shiffrin, 1980). It then follows that the order in which items are retrieved during free recall is decidedly nonrandom during free recall, and this provides a potentially rich reflection of the organization of memory traces stored during study and prior testing, but free recall does not provide a perfect image of the list of studied items, and in these cases, there is an opportunity to improve memory. Especially, for longer lists of items, there is likely to be mismatch between the study list—the order in which items were studied and/or the contents of the list itself—and what is retrieved during memory testing. This points to a possible component of the benefits to free recall of testing; use of inter-item associations during memory testing may increase the strength of those associations formed during initial learning. In addition, if the traces are also updated with temporal context features, then the benefits may persist over a period of time. If the same associations are strengthened during study in the control condition, similar encoding benefits could be available. However, the study conditions need to be just right; otherwise, there is a risk of adding new weak traces, especially when the order in which items are initially studied is different from the order in which items are restudied, because having many weak associative cues may be less effective than having single strong cues when performing free recall.

The fact that recognition testing and cued recall testing often involve all of the material on the study list distinguishes these tasks from free recall. Similarly, in the control condition, all items are studied. For paired associate cued recall, one might expect memory testing would provide the subject with knowledge about which pairs have been learned and which have not been learned because subjects are quite poor at predicting how likely they are to remember a cue–target combination in the future, unless some retention interval intervenes (Nelson & Dunlosky, 1991). Testing should therefore impart some benefit through the storage of item and/or associative information over and above study, especially if feedback in the form of the correct answer is provided when mistakes are made. In the Carpenter and DeLosh (2006) experiment, however, paired associate cued recall was not utilized in order to create a common study condition, in which single items were studied. Rather, subjects were cued with the first letter of each target word, and this version of cued recall is more similar to item recognition insofar as associations between items are not important in order to complete the task, and since feedback was not provided, it is unclear what advantage testing memory would have over additional study.

Assessing the benefits of recognition testing is complicated by the fact that unstudied items are tested in addition to the studied items. Although there may be some benefits of encoding additional item or contextual features during testing that distinguish targets from foils, the storage of traces representing the foil test trials will cause some additional interference if these traces are accessed during the criterion test. We will have much more to say concerning the consequences of recognition testing in subsequent sections.

Improvements in learning attributable to testing that are due to contextual storage and to cognitive control may both occur. Two studies by Lehman and Malmberg were aimed to study and perhaps provide separate evidence for these factors. In the published study (Lehman & Malmberg, 2013), participants completed several study–test cycles for free recall, with different words in each cycle. There were improvements in free recall over the course of eight study–test cycles. Thus, whatever harm might have been caused by interference from the storage of words studied and tested on earlier lists was overcome by factors that improved memory as cycles continued, such as improved storage and retrieval processes and strategies. Interestingly, when individual differences were analyzed, the improved performance was due almost entirely to the subjects who had the highest overall rate of free recall. The advantage of the high performers over the low performers extended throughout the free-recall serial position curve, a not surprising result showing that overall encoding and retrieval were better for high performers, but also showing that the advantage was not limited to short-term memory (recency portions of the serial position curve) or long-term memory (the rest of the serial positions). A more detailed analysis showed that the high performers were increasingly likely to begin retrieval with the final item on the list over cycles, whereas the low performers were more likely to begin retrieval with the item in the first serial position and less likely to switch this strategy. This finding indicates that the retrieval cues used to probe memory were different in the two groups, and that the high performers were increasingly using a short-term-memory-first retrieval strategy as cycles continued.

The unpublished results from a similar recognition memory study (Lehman, in press) were that the gains found over cycles of free recall did not appear when recognition was used (there was a slight decrease over cycles). This could suggest that the gain found in free recall was not due to better storage of items, but there are several other possibilities. For example, participants could store co-rehearsed items increasingly well over cycles of free recall, but such storage might not much improve recognition when recognition judgments are based on item familiarity. In this case, interference due to storage and test of prior lists could dominate performance.

2.2.1 On the Efficiency of Test Taking Strategies

Test takers can be quite adaptable, even in the absence of explicit feedback, altering their retrieval strategies to improve overall performance. K. J. Malmberg and J. Annis (unpublished) were interested in the extent to which default test-taking strategies were efficient (see Malmberg, 2008 for a discussion of the efficiency of recognition memory). Efficiency is a critical issue for many testing situations such as standardized one-chance testing with a time deadline.

Figure 8.1 shows the results of an experiment that utilized an associative recognition procedure to test memory. Subjects studied five lists of pairs of words, each list with different words. On a given list, eight word pairs were studied one, two, or six times with random spacing. The associative recognition test involved discriminating pairs of words that were studied together (intact pairs) from pairs of words that were studied but not studied together (rearranged pairs). Subjects were asked to respond "old" to intact pairs and "new" to rearranged pairs. The task is difficult because items comprising intact and rearranged pairs were in fact studied, and therefore "familiar," but only the intact pairs should be endorsed.

We were interested in the efficiency of task performance over all test trials for a given list. Efficiency is a joint function of the speed and accuracy with which the test trials are completed. The efficient test taker maximizes accuracy while minimizing the amount of time allotted to the task (see Malmberg, 2008 for a discussion of the interaction of subjective goals and efficiency). In one condition, subjects performed the testing at their own pace, as in most laboratory experiments. In another condition, subjects were given a 36-s deadline to complete the same 24 test trials. Testing with a time limit is typical of the way that most exams are given in educational or standardized testing settings. The 36-s deadline was deemed to be sufficiently challenging based on the reaction time observations of dozens of subjects in prior experiments (e.g., Malmberg & Xu, 2007; Xu & Malmberg, 2007).

Figure 8.1 shows the results, panels (A), (B), (C), and (D) showing data averaged across the five lists. Panel (A) plots hit rates and false alarm rates, neither of which were significantly different in self-paced versus deadline conditions. Panel (B) shows that self-paced subjects took longer to complete the testing. This suggests that under conditions commonly found in the laboratory subjects tend to perform this task relatively inefficiently. Panel (C)

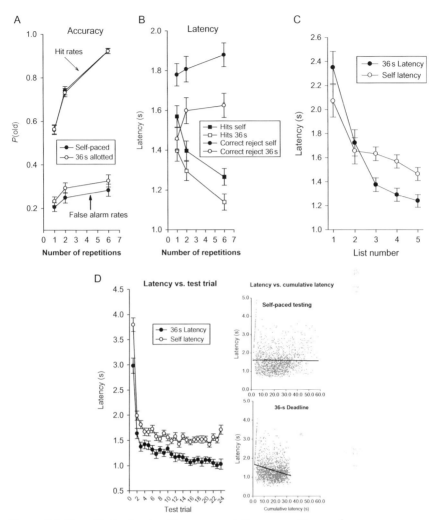

Figure 8.1 The effects of a deadline on associative recognition performance.

shows the average response latency for each list. After two study–test cycles, subjects who were given a deadline began to perform the task more quickly. Panel (D) shows that the gain in efficiency was achieved over all 24 test trials in a given cycle; subjects did not simply begin to respond more quickly as the deadline neared. These results indicate the typical subject with a deadline learns to perform the memory tests more efficiently than the typical subject without a deadline, but practice performing the memory tasks is required in order to do so.

2.2.2 Memory Testing Affects Metacognitive Judgments

One factor by which experience leads participants to change their learning and retrieval strategies involves metacognitive judgments. In one experiment, K. J. Malmberg and T. O. Nelson (unpublished) asked subjects to classify words as being relatively "easy" to remember or relatively difficult to remember (an ease-of-learning judgment or EOL). The words varied in the frequency with which they are used in natural language. On average, common words (high frequency or HF) were judged to be easier to remember than rare words (low frequency or LF) about 64% of the time [$t(57) = 4.24$]. Table 8.1 shows that when given the opportunity to study these words, along with words that were not given EOL judgments, subjects tended to study the words judged as relatively difficult to remember longer, [$F(1,57) = 4.31$, MSE = 1.34], but there was little difference in the amount of time subjects allocated to studying high common and rare words [$F < 1$].

Figure 8.2 shows that when memory was subsequently tested using yes–no recognition procedure, hit rates were greater for rare words than for common words, but the patterns of false alarm rates were dependent on the EOL judgment given. The outcome of EOL judgments (i.e., easy vs. difficult) reliably affected both hit rates and false alarm rates [$F(1,57) = 42.30$, MSE = 0.26]. The interaction of word frequency and EOL judgment was not significant [$F(1,49) = 0.22$]. By contrast, the simple effect of normative word frequency on the false alarm rate was significant only for words judged difficult to learn [$t(57) = 3.31$] and not for words judged easy to learn [$t(57) = 0.29$], and the interaction between word frequency and EOL judgment was significant [$F(1,57) = 4.95$, MSE = 0.13]. Thus, although rare words were better recognized than common words, only those words that were judged to be relatively difficult to learn produced the mirror-patterned word-frequency effect, and amount of time spent studying a word was predicted by the metacognitive judgment assessing it as easy to be learned.

Table 8.1 Amount of Self-Paced Study Time (s) Allocated to Words

EOL	Normative Word Frequency		
	LF	HF	$\bar{X}$
"Easy"	2.80 (0.20)	2.90 (0.23)	2.85 (0.22)
"Difficult"	3.05 (0.20)	2.95 (0.22)	3.00 (0.21)
None	2.93 (0.21)	2.97 (0.20)	2.94 (0.21)
$\bar{X}$	2.91 (0.20)	2.94 (0.22)	

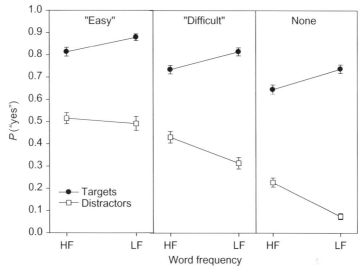

Figure 8.2 The relationship between ease-of-learning judgments given and normative word frequency.

Importantly, Benjamin (2003) reported that LF words were judged easier to learn subsequent to recognition testing, suggesting the possibility that recognition testing could be used to improve the allocation of study time.

In summary, there appear to be three classes of processes by which memory testing can alter performance on subsequent tests: (a) storing new memory traces during testing; (b) enhancing, modifying, or updating existing memory traces; and (c) altering learning and retrieval strategies.

2.2.3 What Is Stored During Memory Testing?

When an item is tested, it is important to know whether a new trace will be stored, or whether a prior trace for the tested item will be updated or modified. This issue has been raised to explain "differentiation" in the articles by Ratcliff, Clark, and Shiffrin (1990) and Shiffrin, Ratcliff, and Clark (1990) and modeled thereafter (e.g., Shiffrin & Steyvers, 1997, 1998). Those articles dealt with repeated study events rather than testing and argued that extra item storage in an existing trace decreased similarity to other items, thereby improving performance for other items, whereas storage of a new trace added noise and decreased performance for other items. Their list-strength results suggested that repeated study events often resulted in adding information to existing traces. The same issues arise when one considers storage of test events, though this has not yet been the subject of empirical research.

Considering the cases when testing an item does add information to its existing episodic trace, the kinds of information added may be information about the item itself (e.g., its spelling or meaning), information linking the item to others, or information linking the item to context. The ways that this added information determines later performance will depend on the relative proportions of storage of each of these types, the ways the information is used in a given task, and obviously on whether the subsequent testing is of the item itself (in which case storage during testing is generally beneficial) or of other items (in which case storage during testing will be generally harmful).

It is also possible that storage during testing will not just add information but modify existing information, especially if the information stored initially was stored inaccurately (e.g., initial storage of a word may have involved a misspelling, but upon testing, the spelling in the existing trace is corrected). Related to modification of existing traces is a recent literature on "reconsolidation," suggesting that reactivation of an existing recent trace places it in a malleable state that then allows it to be stored again in a different form (Lattal & Wood, 2013; Schiller & Phelps, 2011; see Rodriguez-Ortiz & Bermúdez-Rattoni, 2007 for a review): Injection of neuroinhibitors (in nonhumans) after reminders call a trace to mind can cause the initially stored memory to be lost. Here, testing has negative consequences, but due to the chemical treatment following retrieval rather than the retrieval itself. The mechanisms by which the memories are harmed are not entirely clear. It is possible, for example, that the treatments add a great deal of context noise to the existing memory. It is quite reasonable and consistent with prior research that the retrieval of an item's memory trace may add test context to existing context and existing item information. This should have especially significant benefits when the criterion test involves free recall and/or source memory since these are tasks that depend heavily on the use of context as retrieval cues (Lehman & Malmberg, 2013; Malmberg & Shiffrin, 2005). Tasks like recognition and cued recall may be less affected because item information is a more important component of the retrieval probe.

3. COSTS OF TESTING MEMORY: OUTPUT INTERFERENCE

Testing typically provides benefits to the items that are tested, but typically has costs to memory for items that are not tested, and sometimes costs to items tested but not retrieved. Such costs are mostly due to storage of information associated with the test and thus are similar for study events, test events, or the situations in which both occur. The costs of testing memory were very important to researchers during the verbal-learning heyday (Crowder, 1976). To take just one example of many findings and studies, Brown (1958) and Peterson and Peterson (1959) showed that forgetting of a small list of items increases with the duration of a retention interval filled with another task or activity (such as arithmetic). This intervening activity has two important effects: it suppresses rehearsal and adds to memory the intervening material. Keppel and Underwood (1962) proposed that forgetting is directly related to the amount of testing (and studying) that occurs between study and test of a given item. In these paradigms, the deleterious effects of testing are evidenced by loss of what is usually termed short-term memory. The nature, time course, and cause of short-term memory loss are issues being studied by scientists today, but cannot be reviewed in this chapter.

Of course, interference effects are legion in long-term memory, as seen in over a century's worth of list learning studies. These costs associated with memory testing and studying of some items upon memory for other items are typically attributed to the storage of new traces and/or to the strengthening of existing traces and most often explained by competition. The idea is that a probe of memory tends to produce activation of similar traces: New material and/or new traces are stored during testing. At least some of the resultant traces tend to have increased similarity to the item that is the target of a later test. Increased activation of those more similar traces decreases activation of the target trace because retrieval from memory is a competitive process.

The forgetting caused by memory storage and retrieval has been traditionally termed *interference*; when the focus is on testing, the term *output interference* has been used. Researchers in recent years have also termed such interference *retrieval-induced forgetting*. This term is neutral concerning the causes of forgetting, but researchers using this term have tended to favor an explanation involving suppression or inhibition of traces that would otherwise interfere. One form of evidence comes from studies using cued recall (e.g., Anderson, Bjork, & Bjork, 1994, 2000): Lists of pairs of words are studied, each with a common cue, such as a category label (FURNITURE), and the targets of memory testing are exemplars of that category (CHAIR, TABLE, BED, etc.). Following the study list, practice is given for the retrieval of some of the targets by presenting the cue that specifies the target of retrieval (FURNITURE-B_). Such practice is intended to produce inhibition of activation of the traces of the category members whose first letter is not B. When memory for all category members is then tested with the category cue, the practiced items are better recalled and the unpracticed items are worse recalled. A variety of conditions and controls are used in an attempt to demonstrate that such findings are due to active suppression of unwanted memories rather than competition from the practiced items. However, this issue is highly contentious because essentially all the results can be explained by some form of competition (e.g., Raaijmakers & Jakab, 2013a, 2013b). At the time of this writing, it appears that the greatest portion of the costs associated with retrieving other information is due to competition but the degree to which active suppression occurs as well is not yet known. Whatever the causes, it is accepted that the costs of testing are due to storage of the tested traces, whether it acts directly by increasing strength of the tested items or indirectly by causing suppression of the traces that would otherwise interfere.

It is of course the case that costs and benefits associated with storage and retrieval are found in many paradigms (Lehman & Malmberg, 2009). An interesting phenomenon in this regard is that known as "part-list cuing" (e.g., Slamecka, 1968, 1969). After study of a list of items, some of the list items are provided at test, supposedly as cues that might help free recall of the remaining items, but in fact, free recall is harmed rather than helped. Because it is well known that associations between items occur during list study, intuition suggests that the part-list cues will help free recall by fostering use of associative links. Raaijmakers and Shiffrin (1980) showed this intuition to be incorrect: Their SAM model did store associations and did make use of these during free recall, but nonetheless reliably predicted the observed results regardless of the choices of parameters for the model. The reasons are complex, but a major factor is the fact that associated items tend to fall into different groups. If it could be arranged that one item were provided from each group, then recall would indeed be helped, as often observed in categorized recall (e.g., see Raaijmakers & Shiffrin, 1981). However, the random choice of part-list cues too often results in cues that fall within a single group, thereby harming free recall.

Although it is generally the case that storage and retrieval of items other than the target of a later test harm performance, there is at least one important exception, known as the list-strength effect (Ratcliff et al., 1990; Shiffrin et al., 1990). Strengthening some list items during study helps rather than harms recognition of other list items. The theoretical account is based on *differentiation*: Making a trace stronger and more accurate decreases its similarity to a later test probe of a different item. This account requires that additional study causes a strengthened trace (most of the time) rather than storage of an additional trace. It is interesting to note that testing of some list items harms rather than helps subsequent recognition testing of other items (described in more detail below), suggesting that testing after list study causes storage of a separate test trace rather than a combined single trace, though it is perfectly possible and perhaps likely that the separate test trace will contain information about both study and test for the tested item.

The accounts above of differentiation and storage of additional information in the same trace or different traces leave out a critical factor that has been important in all modeling of the empirical phenomena: The difference between context cues and content cues. In short, context cues are common to all list items, so additional storage of context makes all traces more similar, in contrast to storage of content which makes different traces less similar. Thus, the observed effects are a balance of these two opposing factors. A critical link in understanding how this works was found by Malmberg and Shiffrin (2005) who obtained evidence that repeated massed study produces just "one shot of context," but increasing storage of content. This idea has not been explored in testing.

As mentioned briefly above, output interference is observed not only in free and cued recall but also in recognition. In fact, output interference in recognition memory testing is particularly important as a constraint on theory. Increases in the number of items studied on a list generally result in only small impairments, at least when one uses controls to reduce the impact of such factors as serial position effects and lag effects. Dennis and Humphreys (2001) pointed this out and suggested that the primary (perhaps only) cause of forgetting of words in recognition was *context noise*, interference caused not by activation of similar list items, but rather caused by activation of traces of the test item itself that were stored prior to the list study. Context noise surely contributes to recognition difficulty, but the relative amount of interference due to *item noise* (e.g., from similar items on the list) and due to context noise remains in dispute (Criss & Shiffrin, 2004; Criss et al., 2011; Dennis & Humphreys, 2001).

It is possible that small list length effects in recognition are in part the result of context changes from study to test: If the probe cue uses context significantly different from the context stored during list study, then the similarity of a test probe to stored traces of other words would be quite low because the traces would be dissimilar in both content and context. If so, only the trace of the test word, if it exists, would tend to be activated.

However, this hypothesis implies that storage of the test traces themselves would be quite similar to subsequent tests. If so, test traces would tend to be activated (depending also on content similarity) and would cause interference for subsequent tests. Such interference has been found in many studies and can be quite strong. Recognition accuracy has been found to decrease over tests in forced choice testing (Criss et al., 2011; Murdock & Anderson, 1975) and in old–new testing (Criss et al., 2011). The natural interpretation is interference caused by storage of test traces that are similar enough in context and content to be activated when a different item is subsequently tested.

The role of item interference from the storage of item information is further revealed by experiments that demonstrate how output interference may be reduced. Wickens, Born, and Allen (1963; see also Wickens, 1970) reported the results of several experiments demonstrating what Watkins and Watkins (1975) referred to as the release from proactive interference or *release from PI*. In a typical study, trigrams of stimuli from some category are studied and followed by a period of distraction activity that serves to empty short-term memory. The test performance then measures retrieval from long-term memory. Different trials use different stimuli. If successive trials use stimuli from the same category, then performance drops, but a switch to a new category causes performance to revert to the initially higher level. The typical interpretation is that there is increasing competition as traces of items in the same category accumulate, competition that abates when the switch to a new category occurs. In a recent experiment, we found a form of release from PI within successive recognition tests following list study. The study list contained items from several categories, presented in random order. The sequence of forced choice tests was blocked by category. Performance dropped over tests within category but reverted to the initial level when testing of a new category began (Malmberg, Criss, Gangwani, & Shiffrin, 2012).

4. THE INFLUENCE OF ONE TEST ON THE NEXT: SEQUENTIAL DEPENDENCIES

Responses on successive test trials often interact, for many different reasons. In recall, for example, what is recalled on one trial may be used as a probe or source of additional information on the next trial. In recognition, the response (or stimulus) on trial n predicts the nature and speed of the response on trial $n+j$, even when items tested were not in fact studied

(Kachergis, Cox, & Shiffrin, 2013; Malmberg & Annis, 2012; Ratcliff & McKoon, 1978). For instance, when recognition is tested using a yes–no procedure and the order of target and foil test trials is determined randomly, a "yes" response is more to follow a "yes" response than a "no" response, and "yes" responses are made more quickly when they follow a "yes" response than when they follow a "no" response. These correlations are positive and known as *assimilation*. In other instances, the current response is negatively correlated with prior responses (or stimuli) and this is known as *contrast*. For instance, when recognition memory is tested using a judgment of frequency (JOF) procedure, the JOF on trial $n+1$ is often greater if the prior stimulus was an infrequently studied item than it was a frequently studied item (J. Annis & K. J. Malmberg, in press; Malmberg & Annis, 2012). In contrast to the decline in accuracy associated with output interference, overall accuracy of yes–no recognition is unaffected since the magnitude of the assimilation is similar for both target and foil test trials (Malmberg & Annis, 2012). In this sense, the decreases in accuracy with increases in testing and sequential dependencies are distinct phenomena that require separate accounts.

Taken together, assimilation and contrast comprise a set of *sequential dependencies*, and several recent studies have documented them in recognition memory testing. The cogent reader may not be surprised by this finding since sequential dependencies have long been known to exist in sequences of perceptual decision trials (Collier, 1954a, 1954b; Collier & Verplanck, 1958; Verplanck, Collier, & Cotton, 1952). Indeed, the sequential dependencies found in a series of absolute identification trials were a basis for linking memory and perception in Miller (1956). However, the patterns of sequential dependencies observed in memory testing can be quite different than those observed in perceptual testing, like absolute identification, and organizing these observations in a theoretical framework may go a long way in developing a better general understanding of cognition, as well as the individual systems that support it.

A key question, borrowed from the perception literature, concerns whether assimilation is the result of shifts in response bias and/or shifts in the nature of the information on which the recognition decision is made (Lockhead, 2004; Treisman & Williams, 1984). According to the former hypothesis, response biases are based on the prior probabilities of target versus foil test trials. If one is in midst of a long series of mostly target trials and bias reflects recent experience, then one should be more biased to respond "yes" than if one is in the midst of a long series of foil trials. However, sequential dependencies are found in recognition testing in the absence of direct knowledge about the nature of the memory tests, and therefore prior responses must be the basis for determining the bias. According to the later hypothesis, assimilation is the result of a positive correlation between the sources of information on which consecutive decisions are made. We refer to this as carryover, and we have developed a model of carryover that shares some assumptions of compound cue models (Annis & Malmberg, 2013; cf. Ratcliff & McKoon, 1988). Nevertheless, it is quite possible that sequential dependencies arise from both transient fluctuations in response bias and carryover.

To tease apart the contributions of bias and carryover, one must make some assumptions. When interpreting the data from several recent experiments, Malmberg and Annis worked within a signal detection framework by assuming that response bias is influenced only by the prior probabilities of the classes of stimuli and the costs and rewards associated with various outcomes; so long as the evidence on which the decision is made is a continuous random variable, what is represented by the information used to make the decision is not important (Green & Swets, 1966). In other words, sequential dependencies produced by bias should be similar regardless of whether memory or perception is being tested (Malmberg & Annis, 2012).

In one experiment in which recognition memory and absolute identification were directly compared, subjects were presented with words that varied at six levels on two dimensions: the frequency with which they were encountered and the font size in which the words were displayed. During this phase of the experiment, subjects performed absolute identification based on the font size of the words, and assimilation was observed, with contrast observed at lags >1. Following the study list, recognition memory for the words was tested with the JOF procedure. Assimilation was again observed in the JOFs, but contrast was not observed at lags >1. Rather, contrast was observed in adjacent memory tests between the prior stimulus and the current response. In another experiment, feedback was manipulated. Feedback is often provided in perception experiments and is thought to influence the subject's knowledge about the prior probabilities of the stimulus classes, and contrast is only observed at lags >1 and only when feedback is provided (Holland & Lockhead, 1968). For JOFs, on the other hand, contrast occurs in the absence but not in the presence of feedback. As a package, this pattern of sequential dependencies observed in JOFs is different from those commonly reported for absolute identification.

Other research has observed that assimilation diminishes with increases in the ISI during absolute identification tests (Matthews & Stewart, 2009) but not during recognition testing (Malmberg & Annis, 2012). Thus, there are reports of differences in the patterns of sequential dependencies in recognition and perception testing, and therefore, they are most likely not caused by simple changes in response bias within the standard signal detection framework. It is possible that these different patterns of sequential dependencies are related to differences in memory and perception systems and/or subtle differences in the procedures used for examining them.

Modeling the sequential dependencies observed in recognition testing may help us better understand the nature of memory traces and evidence used to make memory decisions. For instance, sequential dependencies are also found in recognition memory testing when the confidence ratings procedure is used (Malmberg & Annis, 2012); a "yes" response is more likely following a highly confident "yes" response than following a low-confidence "yes" response. In addition, a "yes" response was more likely following a low-confidence "yes" than following a miss (i.e., "no" response). Hence, the amount of assimilation was correlated with the amount of evidence used to make the yes–no decision on the prior trial. This suggests that the nature of the evidence is either a continuous random variable or a discrete random variable with at least three categories: not retrieved, weakly retrieved, or strongly retrieved.

Schwartz, Howard, Jing, and Kahana (2005) examined the relationship between the order in which items were studied and the order in which items were tested. When items were studied in adjacent positions, but not distant serial positions, and tested in adjacent positions, they found that hits were more likely following a high-confidence response on the immediately prior test trial, which they stated provided evidence that the high confidence associated with first response is due to a recollection of the co-occurrence of the two items on the study list. However, there was a boost in hit rates even when items were studied in distant serial positions and therefore did not co-occur and were unlikely to be rehearsed together (Kachergis et al., 2013; Malmberg & Annis, 2012). In addition, similar boosts in false alarm rates are observed even when the first item in the test sequence was not studied (Malmberg & Annis, 2012). Since recollection can be ruled out as the cause of the increase in the tendency to recognize an unstudied item, sequential dependencies either do not depend on the recollection of an item on a prior test trial or may also reflect a combined strength of evidence obtained on adjacent test trials.

5. PAST DECISIONS INFLUENCE FUTURE DECISIONS: SHIFTS IN BIAS

On one hand, it is only sensible to acknowledge that the criterion for responding old or new may change during the course of a recognition test (cf. Treisman & Williams, 1984). However, there exists very little evidence to suggest this is so. The classic paradigm for eliciting changes in response bias involves manipulating the contents of the test list. Specifically, changing the proportion of targets on the test list typically elicits a change in the location of the criterion exactly as expected in a signal detection framework, that is, participants become more conservative as the proportion of foils increases if participants are informed of the relative proportion of targets (or foils) on the test list (e.g., Criss, 2009, 2010). When this information is withheld, there is little to no evidence of a change in response bias (Healy & Kubovy, 1978). In a striking example, Cox and Dobbins (2011) presented target-free or distractor-free lists for recognition decisions without informing participants, but the tendency to respond "old" was nearly identical for a target-free and distractor-free list as for standard lists containing half targets and half foils (see also G. Koop, A. H. Criss, & K. J. Malmberg, in preparation).

Although subjects in typical recognition experiments do not seem very sensitive to the proportion targets and foils test trials, feedback appears to be a critical factor that modulates changes in response bias during the course of recognition testing (Estes & Maddox, 1995). In fact, one experiment conducted by K. J. Malmberg and J. Xu (unpublished) found that providing feedback concerning the proportion of correct responses only after all memory testing was complete influenced response bias on subsequent lists using a continuous recognition procedure. Since feedback is almost never provided in memory testing experiments, the upshot is that there is little evidence indicating systematic shifts in response bias occur.

Another common scenario where the criterion is assumed to change during the course of testing is when the expected memorability of the test item varies. For example, early theories of the word-frequency mirror effect assumed that participants adjusted the amount of evidence required to endorse an item as studied depending on the expected accuracy for each class of items (e.g., Glanzer & Adams, 1990). Low-frequency targets are easy to remember, and therefore, a higher level of evidence is required to endorse a LF word, reducing the false alarm rate. The WFE is now attributed to stimulus attributes such as feature frequency (Malmberg, Steyvers, Stephens, & Shiffrin, 2002; Shiffrin & Steyvers, 1997); however, the idea that expected familiarity of the test stimuli is a driving force behind the criterion placement remains (e.g., Hirshman, 1995).

Direct attempts to elicit changes in criterion on this basis in a trial-by-trial manner have not been successful. For example, in one experiment, Stretch and Wixted (1998) had participants study some items one time and other items five times. They emphasized the differences in expected memory by color-coding items such that strongly encoded targets and a subset of foils were presented in red font, and weakly encoded targets and the remaining foils were presented in green font even when fully informed about the experimental design. There are many similar examples, showing that participants do not change their criteria during the test list in response to changes in difficulty. The one apparent exception seems to be when the difficulty of the test is altered, not by changing the nature of the targets but by changing the nature of the foils.

Brown, Steyvers, and Hemmer (2007) changed the nature of target items in a blocked fashion going from either easy (randomly chosen) or difficult (mirror image of studied items) foils. Not surprisingly, the false alarm rate was substantially higher for the difficult foils. The critical finding was that the hit rate also changed with block—increasing when the foils became easier and decreasing when foils become more difficult to reject (see Benjamin & Bawa, 2004 for similar data). Brown et al. interpreted this as strong evidence of a change in criterion during the test. An alternative explanation comes from Turner, Van Zandt, and Brown (2011) who describe a model where stimulus representations develop over the course of the experiment and these changes in stimulus representation result in data that are typically interpreted as a criterion change. In other words, even cases that appear to result from changes in the criteria may in fact result from changes in the distributions of memory evidence. The Turner et al. model provides important insight about the role of feedback in memory, which we will return to. However, the model is a signal detection model and has nothing to say about the encoding and retrieval processes that underlie memory or the processes that resulting updated representations. Within the REM framework, representations are updated during test by updating the best matching memory trace if the test item is judged to be old and storing a new trace if the test item is judged to be new (Criss et al., 2011).

A critical feature of the Turner et al. model is that feedback (externally provided by the experimenter or internally generated from a subject's own response when feedback is not provided) is used to establish accurate representations. Interestingly, providing feedback during recognition is the single manipulation that produces compelling criterion shifts, at least under some conditions. Han and Dobbins (2008, 2009) provided accurate feedback for correct responses and biased feedback for incorrect responses. In one condition, they provided feedback indicating that all false alarms were actually correct, and in another, they provided feedback indicating that all misses were actually correct. Performance showed that participants did change their criterion in response to this biased feedback. These studies used standard recognition lists with half targets and half foils. In contrast, Koop et al. used distractor-free and target-free lists. Recall that when no feedback is provided, performance in these "pure" lists is identical to lists with half targets and half foils. In all cases, presenting feedback causes the criterion setting to be closer to optimal. That is, for pure lists, the presence of feedback causes the probability of calling a test item old to move toward one for the distractor-free list and zero for the target-free list.

6. CONCLUSIONS

Recent interest in the positive consequences of memory testing has spawned a number of systematic empirical investigations of the circumstances in which one would expect to observe them. Here, we presented some of these results in a broad context that reflects the variety of influences of memory testing on subsequent testing. These consequences are sometimes positive, but often they are negative, depending on the manner in which memory is tested. A comprehensive understanding will explain both types of outcomes within a framework that views memories as the outcome of a continuous parallel process of encoding and retrieval. The extant literature suggests to us that such an account will also necessarily require both a description of the nature of the information encoded during memory testing and a description of the control processes invoked to carry out the testing. In addition, a comprehensive account of the consequences of memory testing will describe how prior tests of memory affect future decisions one makes.

REFERENCES

Anderson, M. C., Bjork, R. A., & Bjork, E. L. (1994). Remembering can cause forgetting: Retrieval dynamics in long-term memory. *Journal of Experimental Psychology: Learning, Memory, and Cognition, 20*, 1063–1087.

Anderson, M. C., Bjork, E. L., & Bjork, R. A. (2000). Retrieval-induced forgetting: Evidence for a recall-specific mechanism. *Psychonomic Bulletin & Review, 7*, 522–530.

Annis, J., & Malmberg, K. J. (2013). A model of positive sequential dependencies in judgments of frequency. *Journal of Mathematical Psychology, 57*, 225–236.
Benjamin, A. S. (2003). Predicting and postdicting the effects of word frequency on memory. *Memory & Cognition, 31*, 297–305.
Benjamin, A. S., & Bawa, S. (2004). Distractor plausibility and criterion placement in recognition. *Journal of Memory and Language, 51*, 159–172.
Brewer, G. A., Marsh, R. L., Meeks, J. T., Clark-Foos, A., & Hicks, J. L. (2010). The effects of free recall testing on subsequent source memory. *Memory, 18*, 385–393.
Brown, J. (1958). Some tests of the decay theory of immediate memory. *Quarterly Journal of Experimental Psychology, 10*, 12–21.
Brown, S. D., Steyvers, M., & Hemmer, P. (2007). Modeling experimentally induced strategy shifts. *Psychological Science, 18*, 40–45.
Carpenter, S. K., & DeLosh, E. L. (2006). Impoverished cue support enhances subsequent retention: Support for the elaborative retrieval explanation of the testing effect. *Memory & Cognition, 34*, 268–276.
Chan, J. C. K., & McDermott, K. B. (2007). The testing effect in recognition memory: A dual process account. *Journal of Experimental Psychology. Learning Memory and Cognition, 33*, 431–437.
Collier, G. (1954a). Intertrial association at the visual threshold as a function of intertribal Interval. *Journal of Experimental Psychology, 48*, 330–334.
Collier, G. (1954b). Probability of response and intertrial association as functions of monocular and binocular stimulation. *Journal of Experimental Psychology, 47*, 75–83.
Collier, G., & Verplanck, W. S. (1958). Nonindependence of successive responses at threshold as a function of interpolated stimuli. *Journal of Experimental Psychology, 55*, 429–437.
Cox, J. C., & Dobbins, I. G. (2011). The striking similarities between standard, distractor-free, and target-free recognition. *Memory and Cognition, 39*, 925–940.
Criss, A. H., & Shiffrin, R. M. (2004). Context noise and item noise jointly determine recognition memory: A comment on Dennis & Humphreys (2001). *Psychological Review, 111*(3), 800–807.
Criss, A. H. (2009). The distribution of subjective memory strength: List strength and response bias. *Cognitive Psychology, 59*, 297–319.
Criss, A. H. (2010). Differentiation and response bias in episodic memory: Evidence from reaction time distributions. *Journal of Experimental Psychology. Learning, Memory, and Cognition, 36*, 484–499.
Criss, A. H., Malmberg, K. J., & Shiffrin, R. M. (2011). Output interference in recognition memory. *Journal of Memory and Language, 64*, 316–326.
Crowder, R. G. (1976). *Principles of learning and memory*. Hillsdale, NJ: Erlbaum.
Darley, C. F., & Murdock, B. B. (1971). Effects of prior free recall testing on final recall and recognition. *Journal of Experimental Psychology, 91*, 66–73.
Dennis, S., & Humphreys, M. S. (2001). A context noise model of episodic recognition memory. *Psychological Review, 108*, 452–478.
Dunn, J. A. (2004). RK: A matter of confidence. *Psychological Review, 111*, 524–542.
Ebbinghaus, H. (1885). *Memory: A contribution to experimental psychology*. New York, NY: Teachers College, Columbia University.
Estes, W. K., & Maddox, W. T. (1995). Interactions of stimulus attributes, base rates, and feedback in recognition. *Journal of Experimental Psychology. Learning Memory and Cognition, 21*, 1075–1095.
Gillund, G., & Shiffrin, R. M. (1984). A retrieval model for both recognition and recall. *Psychological Review, 91*, 1–67.
Glanzer, M., & Adams, J. K. (1990). The mirror effect in recognition memory: Data and theory. *Journal of Experimental Psychology. Learning Memory and Cognition, 16*, 5–16.

Glover, J. A. (1989). The "testing" phenomenon: Not gone but nearly forgotten. *Journal of Educational Psychology, 81*, 392–399.

Green, D. M., & Swets, J. A. (1966). *Signal detection theory and psychophysics.* New York, NY: Wiley.

Han, S., & Dobbins, I. G. (2008). Examining recognition criterion rigidity during testing using a biased-feedback technique: Evidence for adaptive criterion learning. *Memory and Cognition, 36*, 703–715.

Han, S., & Dobbins, I. G. (2009). Regulating recognition decisions through incremental reinforcement learning. *Psychonomic Bulletin & Review, 16*, 469–474.

Healy, A. F., & Kubovy, M. (1978). Probability matching and the formation of conservative decision rules in a numerical analog of signal detection. *Journal of Experimental Psychology. Human Learning and Memory, 7*, 344–354.

Hirshman, E. (1995). Decision processes in recognition memory: Criterion shifts and the list strength paradigm. *Journal of Experimental Psychology. Learning Memory and Cognition, 21*, 302–313.

Holland, M. K., & Lockhead, G. R. (1968). Sequential effects in absolute judgments of loudness. *Perception & Psychophysics, 3*, 409–414.

Izawa, C. (1970). Optimal potentiating effects and forgetting-prevention effects of tests in paired-associate learning. *Journal of Experimental Psychology, 83*(2, Pt.1), 340–344.

Izawa, C. (1971). The test trial potentiating model. *Journal of Mathematical Psychology, 8*(2), 200–224.

Jakab, E., & Raaijmakers, J. G. W. (2009). The role of item strength in retrieval-induced forgetting. *Journal of Experimental Psychology: Learning, Memory, and Cognition, 35*, 607–617.

Jones, T. C., & Roediger, H. L. (1995). The experiential basis of serial position effects. *European Journal of Cognitive Psychology, 7*, 65–80.

Kachergis, G., Cox, G. E., & Shiffrin, R. M. (2013). The effects of repeated sequential context on recognition memory. In *Proceedings of the 35th annual conference of the cognitive science society.*

Karpicke, J. D., Lehman, M., & Aue, W. R. (2014). Retrieval-based learning: An episodic context account. In B. H. Ross (Ed.), *The Psychology of Learning and Motivation*: Vol. 61. (pp. 237–284). San Diego, CA: Elsevier Academic Press.

Keppel, G., & Underwood, B. J. (1962). Proactive inhibition in short term retention of single items. *Journal of Verbal Learning and Verbal Behavior, 1*, 153–161.

Koriat, A., & Bjork, R. A. (2005). Illusions of competence in monitoring one's knowledge during study. *Journal of Experimental Psychology. Learning Memory and Cognition, 31*, 187–194.

Koriat, A., & Bjork, R. A. (2006). Illusions of competence during study can be remedied by manipulations that enhance learners' sensitivity to retrieval conditions at test. *Memory & Cognition, 34*, 959–972.

Lattal, K. M., & Wood, M. A. (2013). Epigenetics and persistent memory: Implications for reconsolidation and silent extinction beyond the zero. *Nature Neuroscience, 16*, 124–129.

Lehman, M., & Malmberg, K. J. (2009). A global theory of remembering and forgetting from multiple lists. *Journal of Experimental Psychology. Learning Memory and Cognition, 35*, 970–988.

Lehman, M., Smith, M. A., & Karpicke, J. D. (in press). Toward an episodic context account of retrieval-based learning: Dissociating retrieval practice and elaboration. *Journal of Experimental Psychology: Learning, Memory, and Cognition.*

Lehman, M., & Malmberg, K. J. (2013). A buffer model of encoding and temporal correlations in retrieval. *Psychological Review, 120*(1), 155–189.

Lockhead, G. R. (2004). Absolute judgments are relative: A reinterpretation of some psychophysical ideas. *Review of General Psychology, 8*, 265–272.

Malmberg, K. J., & Annis, J. (2012). On the relationship between memory and perception: Sequential dependencies in recognition testing. *Journal of Experimental Psychology. General, 141*(2), 233–259.

Malmberg, K. J., Criss, A. H., Gangwani, T. H., & Shiffrin, R. M. (2012). Overcoming the negative consequences of interference that results from recognition memory testing. *Psychological Science, 23*(2), 115–119.

Malmberg, K. J., Holden, J. E., & Shiffrin, R. M. (2004). Modeling the effects of repetitions, similarity, and normative word frequency on judgments of frequency and recognition memory. *Journal of Experimental Psychology. Learning Memory and Cognition, 30*, 319–331.

Malmberg, K. J., & Shiffrin, R. M. (2005). The "one-shot" hypothesis for context storage. *Journal of Experimental Psychology. Learning Memory and Cognition, 31*, 322–336.

Malmberg, K. J., Steyvers, M., Stephens, J. D., & Shiffrin, R. M. (2002). Feature-frequency effects in recognition memory. *Memory & Cognition, 30*(4), 607–613.

Malmberg, K. J., & Xu, J. (2007). On the flexibility and on the fallibility of associative memory. *Memory & Cognition, 35*(3), 545–556.

Malmberg, K. J. (2008). Recognition Memory: A Review of the Critical Findings and an Integrated Theory for Relating Them. *Cognitive Psychology, 57*, 335–384.

Malmberg, K. J., Zeelenberg, R., & Shiffrin, R. M. (2004). Turning up the noise or turning down the volume? on the nature of the impairment of episodic recognition memory by midazolam. *Journal of Experimental Psychology. Learning Memory and Cognition, 30*(2), 540–549.

Mandler, G. (1980). Recognizing: The judgment of previous occurrence. *Psychological Review, 87*, 252–271.

Matthews, W. J., & Stewart, N. (2009). The effect of inter-stimulus interval on sequential effects in absolute identification. *The Quarterly Journal of Experimental Psychology, 62*, 2014–2029.

McGeoch, J. A. (1942). *The psychology of human learning*. New York: Longmans, Green, and Co.

Mensink, G. J. M., & Raaijmakers, J. G. W. (1989). A model for contextual fluctuation. *Journal of Mathematical Psychology, 33*, 172–186.

Miller, G. A. (1956). The magical number seven, plus or minus two: Some limits on our capacity for processing information. *Psychological Review, 63*, 81–97.

Morris, C. D., Bransford, J. D., & Franks, J. J. (1977). Levels of processing versus transfer appropriate processing. *Journal of Verbal Learning and Verbal Behavior, 16*, 519–533.

Murdock, B. B., & Anderson, R. E. (1975). Encoding, storage and retrieval of item information. In R. L. Solso (Ed.), *Theories in cognitive psychology: The Loyola symposium* (pp. 145–194). Hillsdale, NJ: Erlbaum.

Nelson, T. O., & Dunlosky, J. (1991). When people's judgments of learning (JOLs) are extremely accurate at predicting subsequent recall: The "delayed-JOL effect". *Psychological Science, 2*, 267–270.

Nelson, T. O., & Leonesio, R. J. (1988). Allocation of self-paced study time and the "labor-in-vain effect". *Journal of Experimental Psychology. Learning, Memory, and Cognition, 14*, 676–686.

Nelson, A. B., & Shiffrin, R. M. (2013). The co-evolution of knowledge and event memory. *Psychological Review, 120*(2), 356–394.

Palmeri, T. J., & Flanery, M. A. (2002). Memory systems and perceptual categorization. In B. Ross (Ed.), *The psychology of learning and motivation*: Vol. 41. (pp. 141–189). USA: Elsevier.

Peterson, L. R., & Peterson, M. J. (1959). Short-term retention of individual verbal items. *Journal of Experimental Psychology, 58*, 193–198.

Raaijmakers, J. G. W., & Jakab, E. (2013a). Rethinking inhibition theory: On the problematic status of the inhibition theory for forgetting. *Journal of Memory and Language, 68*, 98–122.

Raaijmakers, J. G. W., & Jakab, E. (2013b). Is forgetting caused by inhibition? *Current Directions in Psychological Science, 22*, 205–209.

Raaijmakers, J. G. W., & Shiffrin, R. M. (1980). SAM: A theory of probabilistic search in associative memory. In G. H. Bower (Ed.), *The psychology of learning and motivation: Advances in research and theory: Vol. 14.* (pp. 207–262). New York, NY: Academic Press.

Raaijmakers, J. G. W., & Shiffrin, R. M. (1981). Search of associative memory. *Psychological Review, 88*, 93–134.

Ratcliff, R., Clark, S. E., & Shiffrin, R. M. (1990). List-strength effect: I. Data and discussion. *Journal of Experimental Psychology. Learning Memory and Cognition, 16*, 163–178.

Ratcliff, R., & McKoon, G. (1978). Priming in item recognition, evidence for propositional structure of sentences. *Journal of Verbal Learning and Verbal Behavior, 17*, 403–417.

Ratcliff, R., & McKoon, G. (1988). A retrieval theory of priming in memory. *Psychological Review, 95*, 385–408.

Rodriguez-Ortiz, C. J., & Bermúdez-Rattoni, F. (2007). Memory reconsolidation or updating consolidation? In F. Bermúdez-Rattoni (Ed.), *Neural plasticity and memory: From genes to brain imaging.* Boca Raton, FL: CRC Press, (Chapter 11).

Roediger, H. L., & Karpicke, J. D. (2006). The power of testing memory: Basic research and implications for educational practice. *Perspectives on Psychological Science, 1*, 181–210.

Roediger, H. L., & McDermott, K. B. (1995). Creating false memories: Remembering words not presented in lists. *Journal of Experimental Psychology. Learning Memory and Cognition, 21*, 803–814.

Schiller, D., & Phelps, E. A. (2011). Does reconsolidation occur in humans? *Frontiers in Behavioral Neuroscience, 5*(24), 1–12.

Schwartz, G., Howard, M. W., Jing, B., & Kahana, M. J. (2005). Shadows of the past: Temporal retrieval effects in recognition memory. *Psychological Science, 16*, 898–904.

Shiffrin, R. M., Ratcliff, R., & Clark, S. E. (1990). List-strength effect: II. Theoretical mechanisms. *Journal of Experimental Psychology. Learning Memory and Cognition, 16*, 179–195.

Shiffrin, R. M., & Steyvers, M. (1997). A model for recognition memory: REM—Retrieving effectively from memory. *Psychonomic Bulletin & Review, 4*, 145–166.

Shiffrin, R. M., & Steyvers, M. (1998). The effectiveness of retrieval from memory. In M. Oaksford, & N. Chater (Eds.), *Rational models of cognition* (pp. 73–95). London: Oxford University Press.

Slamecka, N. J. (1968). An examination of trace storage in free recall. *Journal of Experimental Psychology, 76*, 504–513.

Slamecka, N. J. (1969). Testing for associative storage in multitrial free recall. *Journal of Experimental Psychology, 81*, 557–560.

Son, L. K., & Metcalfe, J. (2000). Metacognitive and control strategies in study-time allocation. *Journal of Experimental Psychology. Learning, Memory, and Cognition, 26*, 204–221.

Stretch, V., & Wixted, J. T. (1998). On the difference between strength-based and frequency-based mirror effects in recognition memory. *Journal of Experimental Psychology. Learning, Memory, and Cognition, 24*, 1379–1396.

Treisman, M., & Williams, T. C. (1984). A theory of criterion setting with an application to sequential dependencies. *Psychological Review, 91*, 68–111.

Turner, B. M., Van Zandt, T., & Brown, S. (2011). A dynamic stimulus-driven model of signal detection. *Psychological Review, 118*, 583–613.

Verplanck, W. S., Collier, G. H., & Cotton, J. W. (1952). Nonindependence of successive responses in measurements of the visual threshold. *Journal of Experimental Psychology, 44*, 273–282.

Watkins, O. C., & Watkins, M. J. (1975). Buildup of proactive inhibition as a cue-overload effect. *Journal of Experimental Psychology. Human Learning and Memory, 1*(4), 442–452.

Wickens, D. D. (1970). Encoding categories of words: An empirical approach to meaning. *Psychological Review, 77*, 1–15.

Wickens, D. D., Born, D. G., & Allen, C. K. (1963). Proactive inhibition and item similarity in short-term memory. *Journal of Verbal Learning and Verbal Behavior, 2*, 440–445.

Xu, J., & Malmberg, K. J. (2007). Modeling the effects of verbal- and nonverbal-pair strength on associative recognition. *Memory & Cognition, 35*(3), 526–544.

INDEX

Note: Page numbers followed by "*f*" indicate figures and "*t*" indicate tables.

A

Accounts, masked priming
  Bayesian reader account, 184–185
  memory-recruitment
    demonstrations, subliminal mere-exposure effect, 183
    domain-specific word-recognition, 183
    "episodic resource", 184
    instance-based accounts, cognition, 183
    processing, target, 184
    retrieval account, 183–184
  prospective
    lexical-entry opening account, 182
    representations, 182–183
Attention. *See also* Cognition, attention economy
  aesthetics, 149–151
  creativity, 151–153
  emotion, experience and regulation, 153–156
  safety, 145–149
Automatic and controlled processing
  "action slips", 140
  capture error, 140
  characteristic features, 139
  learning complex skill, 138–139
  systems, thinking, 140–141

B

Bayesian belief revision
  accuracy-based justifications, 77
  average risk estimate, 78–79
  base rate, event, 78
  realistic beliefs, 77–78
Bayesian inference, 28–29
Bias, motivated reasoning and rationality
  description, 42
  implications, 68–69
  measurement
    Bayesian belief revision, 77–79
    motivated reasoning, 85–91
    optimistic belief updating, 80–85
    rationality, 76
    unrealistic comparative optimism, 79–80
    "wishful thinking" theme, 76
  psychology
    conservatism, 45–49
    heuristics and biases, 49–53
    origin, 42–44
    social psychology, 54–59
    Wason's confirmation bias, 44–45, 46*t*
  scope, sources and systematicity
    components, judgment, 72, 73*f*
    "disconfirmation", 71–72
    judgmental distortion, 71
    moderators, 74–76
    "optimistic bias", 74
    "seeking confirmation", 71
    Wason's confirmation bias, 71
    "wishful thinking", 69–70, 73, 74
  statistics
    expected deviation, 59–62
    SDT, 63–68

C

Cognition, attention economy
  attention debt consequences
    aesthetics, 149–151
    creativity, 151–153
    emotion, experience and regulation, 153–156
    safety, 145–149
  automatic and controlled processing
    "action slips", 140
    capture error, 140
    characteristic features, 139
    learning complex skill, 138–139

Cognition, attention economy (*Continued*)
    systems, thinking, 140–141
  cautionary tale, automation, 167–169
  cognitive dissonance, 134
  downplaying risk, 135
  higher order cognitive processes, 135–136
  immediate information value, 158–161
  information processing, 141–145
  mental and behavioral prosthetics
      (*see* Cognitive prosthetics)
  optimal cognition, 170
  resources and bottlenecks
      task coordination "bottlenecks", 138
      "theoretical soup stone" argument, 137
  road conditions, texting behavior,
      134–135, 134*t*
  self-control and willpower, 161–163
  social brain (*see* Social brain)
Cognitive expertise, 228–229, 232–233
Cognitive prosthetics
  academic self-regulatory processes,
      166–167
  "augmented reality", 164–165
  changing a habit, 165–166
  higher education, 166–167
  information technology, 163–164, 165
  MOOCs, 166–167
  older adults, 164
  QuantitativeSelf.com, 165–166
Cognitive reflection test (CRT), 114–117
Conservatism
  Bayes' rule, 45, 47
  belief revision, 45, 47
  Heuristics and Biases program, 49
  inertia effect, 47
  misaggregation and misperception, 48
  probability theory, 47
  source, 49
  undersampling, 47
Creativity
  and ADHD, 152
  default network (DFN), 151–152
  distraction, 151
  exogenous and endogenous inattention,
      152–153, 153*t*
Criterial test, episodic context account
  cumulative recall, 269–270, 271*f*
  distracter task, 269
  free recall tests, 266
  generation effect, 268–269
  inclusion and exclusion tests, 267–268,
      268*f*
  memory tests, 267
  recollection and automatic retrieval,
      267–268
  repeated retrieval practice, 267–268, 268*f*
  semantic elaboration account, 269,
      270*f*
  temporal contextual information, 266
CRT. *See* Cognitive reflection test (CRT)

D

Decision making, 105–106, 116–117
Default network (DFN), 151–153, 153*t*
Distraction
  creativity, 151
  definition, 145–146
  perceptual and cognitive process,
      142–143
  routine activity, 140
  technological, 154–155
  WM, 141–142
Dumb matching
  attribute substitution, 111
  binary prediction task, 109
  characterization, 113
  cups game, 108
  cups task development, 107, 107*f*
  expectation matching, 111
  games condition, 112
  global focus condition, 112–113
  "good enough", 109–110
  intuitive response, 110
  outcome, 107, 108*f*
  prediction sequence, 112–113
Dumb maximizing
  animal literature, 124–125
  binary prediction task, 125–126
  children, 124
  feedback condition, 128
  glucose depletion, 125
  intuitive process, 125
  operant condition, 126–127
  probability matching, 128
  supportive evidence, 128
  system 1 mechanisms, 124
  top-down matching and bottom-up, 126

Index

E

Ease-of-learning (EOL) judgment, 296–297, 297f
Episodic context account, evidence
  constrained recognition test, 273, 274f
  criterial test, 266–271
  discrimination judgment, 273–274, 275f
  distracter task, 273
  elaborative study task, 273
  episodic retrieval mode, 272–273
  free recall, 264, 272–273, 272f
  intentional retrieval, 263–264
  massed retrieval practice, 264
  mnemonic effect, 265
  reinstatement, 263–264
  retrieval practice, 265–266, 266t
  semantic elaboration account, 265
  study-phase retrieval, 263–264
  target items, 272–273
  temporal clustering, 273–274, 275f
Episodic context account, retrieval-based learning
  composite context representation, 261
  decontextualization process, 258–259
  evidence support, 263–275
  memory models, 258–259
  reinstate context, 260–261
  representation and encoding, 259–260
  retention intervals, 259
  search set
    context reinstatement, 262–263
    evidence, 263
    memory performance, 262–263
    representations, 262–263
  spacing effect, 261–262
  temporal context features, 258–259
Evidential inferences
  "essentially faulty widget", 18
  inferential processes, 18
  people and statistics, 20–21
  preschool-aged children, 29–30
  sample and population, 29–30
  similarity-based and theory-based approaches, 17–18
  similarity-based inductive system, 19
Expectation, probability matching
  deliberative system, 110–111
  "dumb" matching, 127
  global focus condition, 112–113
  intuitive process, 113
  mental machinery, 110–111
  sequence-wide, 111
Expert knowledge
  dynamic and natural scenes, integration, 225–226
  experienced and inexperienced drivers
    anticipation ability, 228–229, 228f
    correlations, 229
    forward-shift and backward-shift conditions, 227
    movement-anticipation task, 226
    RM effect, 227–228, 229
    road scenes, onboard camera, 226–227
    standard frame, 226–227, 227f
  expert and novice pilots
    anticipation, 230, 231–232
    distractors, 230–231
    memory, 231–232
    RM effect, 230–231
    visual simulations, 229–230

H

Heuristics and biases program
  "adaptive rationality", 50–51
  base rate neglect, 52–53
  conjunction fallacy, 51–52, 53
  judgment and decision-making, 49–50, 53
  low prior probability, 52–53
  negative assessment, human rationality, 51

I

Inattention
  controlled processing, 148–149
  exogenous vs. endogenous, 152–153, 153t
  fatigue, 167–168
  lack of engagement, 167–168
  and lane keeping, 152
Inductive inference
  absolute frequencies, 24–25
  Bayesian inference, 28–29
  children, 31
  communicative bias, 30–31
  componential analysis, 22–23
  conditional probability, 25–26
  correlations and associations, 22
  global pattern, 25–26

Inductive inference (*Continued*)
  inductive inference (*see* Inductive inference)
  learning causal models, 31–32
  proposals, 27
  psychological mechanisms, 2
  rule-like representations, 26–27
  similarity based
    accounts, 32–33
    "bottom-up", 4
    domain, 4
    statistical inference, 5–6
    unconscious and automatics, 5–6
  statistical inference, 6–9
  statistical learning, 25
  theory based
    accounts, 32–33
    hypothesis testing, 3–4
    rules/criterial feature, 4–5
    scientific theories, 5–6
    "top-down", 4
    young children, 4
  transductive and evidential (*see* Transductive inferences)
  transition probabilities, 23–24
  young children, 26–27
Information processing (IP)
  automatic mode, 144–145
  conversation example, 141–142, 143f
  distraction, 142–144
  stages, 141
  task sharing, 143–144, 144f
  WM, 141–142
Interference
  differentiation and storage, additional information, 301
  long-term memory, 299
  "part-list cuing", 300
  PI, 302
  recognition memory testing, 301
  retrieval-induced forgetting, 299–300
  SAM model, 300
Intuition
  CRT, 114–115
  deliberative system, 106
  dual-system perspective, 125
  Epstein's jelly beans task, 116–117
  prediction task, 106
  probability matching, 110
  substitution process, 106
IP. *See* Information processing (IP)

J
Judgment of frequency (JOF), 302–303, 304

K
Knowledge, motion extrapolation
  cognitive system, 216
  expert knowledge, 225–232
  RM (*see* Representational momentum (RM))

L
Learning and memory, 287–288

M
Masked priming
  accounts
    Bayesian reader, 184–185
    memory-recruitment, 183–184
    prospective, 182–183
  duration, 203–205
  ironies, 181–182
  moving accounts, 208–209
  nonword priming (*see* Nonword priming)
  prime-proportion effects
    accounting, 201–203
    overlap, 197
    repetition-prime-proportion manipulation, 197–198
    stimulus domains, 200–201
    with word stimuli, 198–200
  subliminal primes, 180
  unconscious priming, 180
  visual word recognition, 181
Memory recruitment
  masked priming (*see* Masked priming)
  NCE, 206–207
  redux/denouement, 205–206
Mixed-case nonword priming effect
  ambiguous and unambiguous critical nonword targets, 190
  font/size condition, 189–190
  magnitude, 189
  physical continuity, lowercase letters, 189–190

Motivated reasoning. *See also* Bias, motivated reasoning and rationality
  "biased assimilation", 91
  degree of belief/trust, 90
  motivational influences, 87
  people's inferential processes, 87
  qualitative properties, Bayesian belief revision, 85–86
  "selective exposure", 87–88
  simulation, 91
  wishful thinking, 85

N
Nonword priming
  backward task
    backward lexical-decision task, 190–192, 191*f*
    fluency bias, 193–194
    mixed-case targets, 192
    nonword-based go/no-go task, 193, 194*f*
    positive/default response option, 193
    prime-induced fluency, 193–194
    reversed fluency bias, 193–194
  Bayesian Reader account, 185–186
  Bodner and Masson
    "but see" and "cf." references, 189
    masked repetition priming effect, 187, 187*f*
    naming task, 188–189
    null and positive nonword priming, 188
    pseudohomophone nonword, 188
    target facilitation *vs.* fluency bias, 187–188
    target processing, 188
  fluency bias
    nonword target processing, 197
    word targets, 195–197
    "yes" and "no" response, 195, 196*f*
  frequency attenuation, 186
  lexical account, 185–186
  mixed-case (*see* Mixed-case nonword priming effect)

P
"Phantom vibration syndrome", 157
PI. *See* Proactive interference (PI)

Practice research, retrieval
  best practices, 240
  conditional analyses, 244
  criterial test, 241–243, 242*f*
  generation effect, 243
  measurement, forgetting, 240–241
  methodological issues, 239–240
  mnemonic effect, 244
  recalled target, 241–242
  repeated study condition, 245–246
  restudy condition, 242–243
  retention interval interaction, 245–246
  robust theory, 247
  single recall conditions, 240–241, 241*f*
  study-phase retrieval, 243–244
  success issues, 244–245
  testing effects, 245
  theoretical accounts, 246, 246*t*
Prediction, probability matching
  CRT, 115–116
  "dumb maximizing", 125
  intuitive response, 106
  optimal maximizing strategy, 120–121
  probability matching, 104
  sequence-wide expectation, 112–113
  stochastic dominance, 104–105
Prime-proportion effects, masked priming
  accounting, 201–203
  overlap, 197
  repetition-prime-proportion manipulation, 197–198
  stimulus domains, 200–201
  with word stimuli, 198–200
Proactive interference (PI), 302
Probability learning, 105, 113, 117
Probability-matching
  dumb matching, 107–113
  dumb maximizing, 124–128
  probability matching, 104
  smart matching
    binary prediction task, 120
    dual-systems framework, 119
    glucose, 119–120
    left-hemisphere resource, 119
    misapplication/overgeneralization, 120–121
    outcome sequences, 123–124
    pattern information, 122–123

Probability-matching (*Continued*)
    pattern-search account, 121
    researchers, 121
    tax cognitive resources, 123–124
    testing phase, 122
  smart maximizing
    CRT, 114–115
    deliberative process, 118
    deliberative system, 117
    jelly beans task, 116–117
    mean number, prediction, 115–116, 115*f*
    statistical test, 117–118
  stochastic dominance, 104–105

R

Representational momentum (RM)
  anticipatory character, 232–233
  cognitive expertise, 232–233
  description, 216
  experimental demonstration, 217–218
  expert knowledge
    dynamic and natural scenes, integration, 225–226
    experienced and inexperienced drivers, 226–229, 227*f*, 228*f*
    expert and novice pilots, 229–232
  observers' knowledge, object anticipation, motion, 222
    complex motion "patterns", 221–222
    gravity, 221
    identical visual features, 224–225, 225*f*
    physical principles, 223–224, 223*f*
    rotational movement, 221–222, 222*f*
    target object–inclined plane, 221
  and physical movement
    induced movement, 218
    object's velocity effect, 218
    participants' memory, 219
    physical principles, 220
    real displacement, 220
    target, continuous and rectilinear motion, 219, 219*f*
    vertically moving targets, 219–220
Retrieval-based learning
  active generation, 255
  bifurcation, 250
  concept mapping, 255–256
  criterial test, 256–257, 257*f*

cue overload, 254
elaborative retrieval hypothesis, 252
encoding variability, 251–252
episodic context account (*see* Episodic context account, retrieval-based learning)
forgetting experiments, 255
knowledge accession, 238
memory systems, 238–239
methodological issues, 239
mnemonic effects, 248–249
practice research (*see* Practice research, retrieval)
production effect, 247
psychology, 239
realm, mediated effects, 247
recall test, 254
response times, 248–249
semantic elaboration processes, 248, 253
spacing effect, 257
storage and retrieval strength, 249
transfer appropriate processing, 250–251
variability and study-phase retrieval
  context representation, 277–278
  incidental retrieval, 277–278
  memory trace, 276
  spacing effect, 275
  temporal context, 276
weak cues, 253
RM. *See* Representational momentum (RM)

S

SDT. *See* Signal detection theory (SDT)
Self-control
  description, 161
  "ego depletion", 162–163
  high memory load/low memory load condition, 161–162
  technological distraction, 163
  tempting stimuli, 161–162
Semantic elaboration account, 269, 270*f*
Signal detection theory (SDT)
  base rates and costs and benefits, 67–68
  description, 64
  expected value, response selection, 66–67
  optimal decision criterion, 64, 66–67
  receiver operating curve (ROC), 65–66, 65*f*

unbiased decision criterion, 66
Social brain
  growth, information technology, 156–157
  "phantom vibration syndrome", 157
  sharing process, 157
  social media, 158
Social psychology, bias
  accuracy, 58
  "biased assimilation", 55
  causal attribution, 57–58
  comparative ratings, 56
  description, 54
  dispositional information, 55
  "errors" and "mistakes", 58–59
  motivational and cognitive biases, 56
  "neutral evidence principle", 55
  normative standards, rationality, 57–58
  self-enhancement biases, 58
  social judgment, 54–55
Statistical inference
  children, 6–8
  inductive inference elements, 6, 7f
  psychological theories, 8
  similarity and theory-based approaches, 8–9
Statistical learning
  children, 23–24
  correlated attribution, 22
  people track associations, 21
  statistics, 32–33
  transductive inference, 10–11
Statistics and bias
  accuracy, 60
  "bias/variance dilemma", 62
  description, 59
  feed-forward neural network, 62
  network learning, 62, 63f
  predictor, 60
  variance components and MSE, 60–62, 61f

T

Testing memory
  color-coding items, 307
  harm memory
    advantage high and low performers, 293
    associative recognition task, 290–291
    classes, 297
    criterion task, 291
    deadline effects, 294–295, 295f
    efficiency, 294
    EOL judgment, 296
    information, 298
    item and inter-item information, 290
    learning improvements, 293
    neuroinhibitors, 298
    recognition testing and cued recall, 292
    reconsolidation, 298
    retrieval strategies, 290–291
    self-paced study time, 296, 296t
  learning and memory, 287–288
  output interference, 298–302
  "potentiating" effects, 286
  recognition experiments, 306
  retrieval-induced forgetting, 286–287
  sequential dependencies
    absolute identification trials, 303
    assimilation, 302–303
    JOF, 302–303
    recognition memory and absolute identification, 304
    recollection, 305
    traces and evidence, 305
  signal detection framework, 306, 307
  testing effect
    criterion test, 288
    discrimination performance, 289
    recall and recognition, 288
    recollective processes, 289
    retrieval practice, 286
    source memory task, 289
  WFE, 306–307
Transductive inferences
  conditional probability, 12
  description, 9–10
  descriptive statistics, 14–15
  evidential inference, 15–16
  and evidential inferences (see Evidential inferences)
  inferential features, 15–16
  inferential statistics, 9
  inspector's, 11, 12–13
  machine and statistical learning theory, 10–11, 16
  myopic, 28
  partial information problem, 13–14, 14f

Transductive inferences (*Continued*)
  population and evidential-sample, 11
  "principle of association", 9–10
  psychological models, 15
  sample-population relations, 12
  theory, 16–17

U
Unrealistic comparative optimism, 79–80

W
Wason's confirmation bias, rule induction, 44–45, 46*t*
WFE. *See* Word-frequency mirror effect (WFE)
Willpower, 161–163
WM. *See* Working memory (WM)
Word-frequency mirror effect (WFE), 306–307
Working memory (WM), 141–142

CONTENTS OF PREVIOUS VOLUMES

VOLUME 40

Different Organization of Concepts and Meaning Systems in the Two Cerebral Hemispheres
  Dahlia W. Zaidel
The Causal Status Effect in Categorization: An Overview
  Woo-kyoung Ahn and Nancy S. Kim
Remembering as a Social Process
  Mary Susan Weldon
Neurocognitive Foundations of Human Memory
  Ken A. Paller
Structural Influences on Implicit and Explicit Sequence Learning
  Tim Curran, Michael D. Smith, Joseph M. DiFranco, and Aaron T. Daggy
Recall Processes in Recognition Memory
  Caren M. Rotello
Reward Learning: Reinforcement, Incentives, and Expectations
  Kent C. Berridge
Spatial Diagrams: Key Instruments in the Toolbox for Thought
  Laura R. Novick
Reinforcement and Punishment in the Prisoner's Dilemma Game
  Howard Rachlin, Jay Brown, and Forest Baker
Index

VOLUME 41

Categorization and Reasoning in Relation to Culture and Expertise
  Douglas L. Medin, Norbert Ross, Scott Atran, Russell C. Burnett, and Sergey V. Blok
On the Computational basis of Learning and Cognition: Arguments from LSA
  Thomas K. Landauer

Multimedia Learning
  Richard E. Mayer
Memory Systems and Perceptual Categorization
  Thomas J. Palmeri and Marci A. Flanery
Conscious Intentions in the Control of Skilled Mental Activity
  Richard A. Carlson
Brain Imaging Autobiographical Memory
  Martin A. Conway, Christopher W. Pleydell-Pearce, Sharon Whitecross, and Helen Sharpe
The Continued Influence of Misinformation in Memory: What Makes Corrections Effective?
  Colleen M. Seifert
Making Sense and Nonsense of Experience: Attributions in Memory and Judgment
  Colleen M. Kelley and Matthew G. Rhodes
Real-World Estimation: Estimation Modes and Seeding Effects
  Norman R. Brown
Index

VOLUME 42

Memory and Learning in Figure—Ground Perception
  Mary A. Peterson and Emily Skow-Grant
Spatial and Visual Working Memory: A Mental Workspace
  Robert H. Logie
Scene Perception and Memory
  Marvin M. Chun
Spatial Representations and Spatial Updating
  Ranxiano Frances Wang
Selective Visual Attention and Visual Search: Behavioral and Neural Mechanisms
  Joy J. Geng and Marlene Behrmann
Categorizing and Perceiving Objects: Exploring a Continuum of Information Use
  Philippe G. Schyns

From Vision to Action and Action to Vision: A Convergent Route Approach to Vision, Action, and Attention
Glyn W. Humphreys and M. Jane Riddoch

Eye Movements and Visual Cognitive Suppression
David E. Irwin

What Makes Change Blindness Interesting?
Daniel J. Simons and Daniel T. Levin

Index

VOLUME 43

Ecological Validity and the Study of Concepts
Gregory L. Murphy

Social Embodiment
Lawrence W. Barsalou, Paula M. Niedinthal, Aron K. Barbey, and Jennifer A. Ruppert

The Body's Contribution to Language
Arthur M. Glenberg and Michael P. Kaschak

Using Spatial Language
Laura A. Carlson

In Opposition to Inhibition
Colin M. MacLeod, Michael D. Dodd, Erin D. Sheard, Daryl E. Wilson, and Uri Bibi

Evolution of Human Cognitive Architecture
John Sweller

Cognitive Plasticity and Aging
Arthur F. Kramer and Sherry L. Willis

Index

VOLUME 44

Goal-Based Accessibility of Entities within Situation Models
Mike Rinck and Gordon H. Bower

The Immersed Experiencer: Toward an Embodied Theory of Language Comprehension
Rolf A. Zwaan

Speech Errors and Language Production: Neuropsychological and Connectionist Perspectives
Gary S. Dell and Jason M. Sullivan

Psycholinguistically Speaking: Some Matters of Meaning, Marking, and Morphing
Kathryn Bock

Executive Attention, Working Memory Capacity, and a Two-Factor Theory of Cognitive Control
Randall W. Engle and Michael J. Kane

Relational Perception and Cognition: Implications for Cognitive Architecture and the Perceptual-Cognitive Interface
Collin Green and John E. Hummel

An Exemplar Model for Perceptual Categorization of Events
Koen Lamberts

On the Perception of Consistency
Yaakov Kareev

Causal Invariance in Reasoning and Learning
Steven Sloman and David A. Lagnado

Index

VOLUME 45

Exemplar Models in the Study of Natural Language Concepts
Gert Storms

Semantic Memory: Some Insights From Feature-Based Connectionist Attractor Networks
Ken McRae

On the Continuity of Mind: Toward a Dynamical Account of Cognition
Michael J. Spivey and Rick Dale

Action and Memory
Peter Dixon and Scott Glover

Self-Generation and Memory
Neil W. Mulligan and Jeffrey P. Lozito

Aging, Metacognition, and Cognitive Control
Christopher Hertzog and John Dunlosky

The Psychopharmacology of Memory and Cognition: Promises, Pitfalls, and a Methodological Framework
Elliot Hirshman

Index

VOLUME 46

The Role of the Basal Ganglia in Category Learning
F. Gregory Ashby and John M. Ennis
Knowledge, Development, and Category Learning
Brett K. Hayes
Concepts as Prototypes
James A. Hampton
An Analysis of Prospective Memory
Richard L. Marsh, Gabriel I. Cook, and Jason L. Hicks
Accessing Recent Events
Brian McElree
SIMPLE: Further Applications of a Local Distinctiveness Model of Memory
Ian Neath and Gordon D.A. Brown
What is Musical Prosody?
Caroline Palmer and Sean Hutchins
Index

VOLUME 47

Relations and Categories
Viviana A. Zelizer and Charles Tilly
Learning Linguistic Patterns
Adele E. Goldberg
Understanding the Art of Design: Tools for the Next Edisonian Innovators
Kristin L. Wood and Julie S. Linsey
Categorizing the Social World: Affect, Motivation, and Self-Regulation
Galen V. Bodenhausen, Andrew R. Todd, and Andrew P. Becker
Reconsidering the Role of Structure in Vision
Elan Barenholtz and Michael J. Tarr
Conversation as a Site of Category Learning and Category Use
Dale J. Barr and Edmundo Kronmuller
Using Classification to Understand the Motivation-Learning Interface
W. Todd Maddox, Arthur B. Markman, and Grant C. Baldwin
Index

VOLUME 48

The Strategic Regulation of Memory Accuracy and Informativeness
Morris Goldsmith and Asher Koriat
Response Bias in Recognition Memory
Caren M. Rotello and Neil A. Macmillan
What Constitutes a Model of Item-Based Memory Decisions?
Ian G. Dobbins and Sanghoon Han
Prospective Memory and Metamemory: The Skilled Use of Basic Attentional and Memory Processes
Gilles O. Einstein and Mark A. McDaniel
Memory is More Than Just Remembering: Strategic Control of Encoding, Accessing Memory, and Making Decisions
Aaron S. Benjamin
The Adaptive and Strategic Use of Memory by Older Adults: Evaluative Processing and Value-Directed Remembering
Alan D. Castel
Experience is a Double-Edged Sword: A Computational Model of the Encoding/Retrieval Trade-Off With Familiarity
Lynne M. Reder, Christopher Paynter, Rachel A. Diana, Jiquan Ngiam, and Daniel Dickison
Toward an Understanding of Individual Differences In Episodic Memory: Modeling The Dynamics of Recognition Memory
Kenneth J. Malmberg
Memory as a Fully Integrated Aspect of Skilled and Expert Performance
K. Anders Ericsson and Roy W. Roring
Index

VOLUME 49

Short-term Memory: New Data and a Model
Stephan Lewandowsky and Simon Farrell
Theory and Measurement of Working Memory Capacity Limits
Nelson Cowan, Candice C. Morey, Zhijian Chen, Amanda L. Gilchrist, and J. Scott Saults

What Goes with What? Development of Perceptual Grouping in Infancy
  Paul C. Quinn, Ramesh S. Bhatt, and Angela Hayden
Co-Constructing Conceptual Domains Through Family Conversations and Activities
  Maureen Callanan and Araceli Valle
The Concrete Substrates of Abstract Rule Use
  Bradley C. Love, Marc Tomlinson, and Todd M. Gureckis
Ambiguity, Accessibility, and a Division of Labor for Communicative Success
  Victor S. Ferreira
Lexical Expertise and Reading Skill
  Sally Andrews
Index

VOLUME 50

Causal Models: The Representational Infrastructure for Moral Judgment
  Steven A. Sloman, Philip M. Fernbach, and Scott Ewing
Moral Grammar and Intuitive Jurisprudence: A Formal Model of Unconscious Moral and Legal Knowledge
  John Mikhail
Law, Psychology, and Morality
  Kenworthey Bilz and Janice Nadler
Protected Values and Omission Bias as Deontological Judgments
  Jonathan Baron and Ilana Ritov
Attending to Moral Values
  Rumen Iliev, Sonya Sachdeva, Daniel M. Bartels, Craig Joseph, Satoru Suzuki, and Douglas L. Medin
Noninstrumental Reasoning over Sacred Values: An Indonesian Case Study
  Jeremy Ginges and Scott Atran
Development and Dual Processes in Moral Reasoning: A Fuzzy-trace Theory Approach
  Valerie F. Reyna and Wanda Casillas

Moral Identity, Moral Functioning, and the Development of Moral Character
  Darcia Narvaez and Daniel K. Lapsley
"Fools Rush In": AJDM Perspective on the Role of Emotions in Decisions, Moral and Otherwise
  Terry Connolly and David Hardman
Motivated Moral Reasoning
  Peter H. Ditto, David A. Pizarro, and David Tannenbaum
In the Mind of the Perceiver: Psychological Implications of Moral Conviction
  Christopher W. Bauman and Linda J. Skitka
Index

VOLUME 51

Time for Meaning: Electrophysiology Provides Insights into the Dynamics of Representation and Processing in Semantic Memory
  Kara D. Federmeier and Sarah Laszlo
Design for a Working Memory
  Klaus Oberauer
When Emotion Intensifies Memory Interference
  Mara Mather
Mathematical Cognition and the Problem Size Effect
  Mark H. Ashcraft and Michelle M. Guillaume
Highlighting: A Canonical Experiment
  John K. Kruschke
The Emergence of Intention Attribution in Infancy
  Amanda L. Woodward, Jessica A. Sommerville, Sarah Gerson, Annette M.E. Henderson, and Jennifer Buresh
Reader Participation in the Experience of Narrative
  Richard J. Gerrig and Matthew E. Jacovina
Aging, Self-Regulation, and Learning from Text
  Elizabeth A. L. Stine-Morrow and Lisa M.S. Miller

Toward a Comprehensive Model of Comprehension
Danielle S. McNamara and Joe Magliano

Index

VOLUME 52

Naming Artifacts. Patterns and Processes
Barbara C. Malt

Causal-Based Categorization: A Review
Bob Rehder

The Influence of Verbal and Nonverbal Processing on Category Learning
John Paul Minda and Sarah J. Miles

The Many Roads to Prominence: Understanding Emphasis in Conversation
Duane G. Watson

Defining and Investigating Automaticity in Reading Comprehension
Katherine A. Rawson

Rethinking Scene Perception: A Multisource Model
Helene Intraub

Components of Spatial Intelligence
Mary Hegarty

Toward an Integrative Theory of Hypothesis Generation, Probability Judgment, and Hypothesis Testing
Michael Dougherty, Rick Thomas, and Nicholas Lange

The Self-Organization of Cognitive Structure
James A. Dixon, Damian G. Stephen, Rebecca Boncoddo, and Jason Anastas

Index

VOLUME 53

Adaptive Memory: Evolutionary Constraints on Remembering
James S. Nairne

Digging into Déà Vu: Recent Research on Possible Mechanisms
Alan S. Brown and Elizabeth J. Marsh

Spacing and Testing Effects: A Deeply Critical, Lengthy, and At Times Discursive Review of the Literature
Peter F. Delaney, Peter P. J. L. Verkoeijen, and Arie Spirgel

How One's Hook Is Baited Matters for Catching an Analogy
Jeffrey Loewenstein

Generating Inductive Inferences: Premise Relations and Property Effects
John D. Coley and Nadya Y. Vasilyeva

From Uncertainly Exact to Certainly Vague: Epistemic Uncertainty and Approximation in Science and Engineering Problem Solving
Christian D. Schunn

Event Perception: A Theory and Its Application to Clinical Neuroscience
Jeffrey M. Zacks and Jesse Q. Sargent

Two Minds, One Dialog: Coordinating Speaking and Understanding
Susan E. Brennan, Alexia Galati, and Anna K. Kuhlen

Retrieving Personal Names, Referring Expressions, and Terms of Address
Zenzi M. Griffin

Index

VOLUME 54

Hierarchical Control of Cognitive Processes: The Case for Skilled Typewriting
Gordon D. Logan and Matthew J.C. Crump

Cognitive Distraction While Multitasking in the Automobile
David L. Strayer, Jason M. Watson, and Frank A. Drews

Psychological Research on Joint Action: Theory and Data
Günther Knoblich, Stephen Butterfill, and Natalie Sebanz

Self-Regulated Learning and the Allocation of Study Time
John Dunlosky and Robert Ariel

The Development of Categorization
  Vladimir M. Sloutsky and Anna V. Fisher
Systems of Category Learning: Fact or Fantasy?
  Ben R. Newell, John C. Dunn, and Michael Kalish
Abstract Concepts: Sensory-Motor Grounding, Metaphors, and Beyond
  Diane Pecher, Inge Boo, and Saskia Van Dantzig
Thematic Thinking: The Apprehension and Consequences of Thematic Relations
  Zachary Estes, Sabrina Golonka, and Lara L. Jones
Index

VOLUME 55

Ten Benefits of Testing and Their Applications to Educational Practice
  Henry L. Roediger III, Adam L. Putnam and Megan A. Smith
Cognitive Load Theory
  John Sweller
Applying the Science of Learning to Multimedia Instruction
  Richard E. Mayer
Incorporating Motivation into a Theoretical Framework for Knowledge Transfer
  Timothy J. Nokes and Daniel M. Belenky
On the Interplay of Emotion and Cognitive Control: Implications for Enhancing Academic Achievement
  Sian L. Beilock and Gerardo Ramirez
There Is Nothing So Practical as a Good Theory
  Robert S. Siegler, Lisa K. Fazio, and Aryn Pyke
The Power of Comparison in Learning and Instruction: Learning Outcomes Supported by Different Types of Comparisons
  Bethany Rittle-Johnson and Jon R. Star
The Role of Automatic, Bottom-Up Processes: In the Ubiquitous Patterns of Incorrect Answers to Science Questions
  Andrew F. Heckler

Conceptual Problem Solving in Physics
  Jose P. Mestre, Jennifer L. Docktor, Natalie E. Strand, and Brian H. Ross
Index

VOLUME 56

Distinctive Processing: The Co-action of Similarity and Difference in Memory
  R. Reed Hunt
Retrieval-Induced Forgetting and Inhibition: A Critical Review
  Michael F. Verde
False Recollection: Empirical Findings and Their Theoretical Implications
  Jason Arndt
Reconstruction from Memory in Naturalistic Environments
  Mark Steyvers and Pernille Hemmer
Categorical Discrimination in Humans and Animals: All Different and Yet the Same?
  Edward A. Wasserman and Leyre Castro
How Working Memory Capacity Affects Problem Solving
  Jennifer Wiley and Andrew F. Jarosz
Juggling Two Languages in One Mind: What Bilinguals Tell Us About Language Processing and its Consequences for Cognition
  Judith F. Kroll, Paola E. Dussias, Cari A. Bogulski and Jorge R. Valdes Kroff
Index

VOLUME 57

Meta-Cognitive Myopia and the Dilemmas of Inductive-Statistical Inference
  Klaus Fiedler
Relations Between Memory and Reasoning
  Evan Heit, Caren M. Rotello and Brett K. Hayes
The Visual World in Sight and Mind: How Attention and Memory Interact to Determine Visual Experience
  James R. Brockmole, Christopher C. Davoli and Deborah A. Cronin

Spatial Thinking and STEM Education: When, Why, and How?
David H. Uttal and Cheryl A. Cohen
Emotions During the Learning of Difficult Material
Arthur C. Graesser and Sidney D'Mello
Specificity and Transfer of Learning
Alice F. Healy and Erica L. Wohldmann
What Do Words Do? Toward a Theory of Language-Augmented Thought
Gary Lupyan
Index

VOLUME 58

Learning Along With Others
Robert L. Goldstone, Thomas N. Wisdom, Michael E. Roberts, Seth Frey
Space, Time, and Story
Barbara Tversky, Julie Heiser, Julie Morrison
The Cognition of Spatial Cognition: Domain-General within Domain-specific
Holly A. Taylor, Tad T. Brunyé
Perceptual Learning, Cognition, and Expertise
Philip J. Kellman, Christine M. Massey
Causation, Touch, and the Perception of Force
Phillip Wolff, Jason Shepard
Categorization as Causal Explanation: Discounting and Augmenting in a Bayesian Framework
Daniel M. Oppenheimer, Joshua B. Tenenbaum, Tevye R. Krynski
Individual Differences in Intelligence and Working Memory: A Review of Latent Variable Models
Andrew R.A. Conway, Kristof Kovacs
Index

VOLUME 59

Toward a Unified Theory of Reasoning
P.N. Johnson-Laird, Sangeet S. Khemlani
The Self-Organization of Human Interaction
Rick Dale, Riccardo Fusaroli, Nicholas D. Duran, Daniel C. Richardson

Conceptual Composition: The Role of Relational Competition in the Comprehension of Modifier-Noun Phrases and Noun–Noun Compounds
Christina L. Gagné, Thomas L. Spalding
List-Method Directed Forgetting in Cognitive and Clinical Research: A Theoretical and Methodological Review
Lili Sahakyan, Peter F. Delaney, Nathaniel L. Foster, Branden Abushanab
Recollection is Fast and Easy: Pupillometric Studies of Face Memory
Stephen D. Goldinger, Megan H. Papesh
A Mechanistic Approach to Individual Differences in Spatial Learning, Memory, and Navigation
Amy L. Shelton, Steven A. Marchette, Andrew J. Furman
When Do the Effects of Distractors Provide a Measure of Distractibility?
Alejandro Lleras, Simona Buetti, J. Toby Mordkoff
Index

VOLUME 60

The Middle Way: Finding the Balance between Mindfulness and Mind-Wandering
Jonathan W. Schooler, Michael D. Mrazek, Michael S. Franklin, Benjamin Baird, Benjamin W. Mooneyham, Claire Zedelius, and James M. Broadway
What Intuitions Are... and Are Not
Valerie A. Thompson
The Sense of Recognition during Retrieval Failure: Implications for the Nature of Memory Traces
Anne M. Cleary
About Practice: Repetition, Spacing, and Abstraction
Thomas C. Toppino and Emilie Gerbier
The Rise and Fall of the Recent Past: A Unified Account of Immediate Repetition Paradigms
David E. Huber

Does the Concept of Affordance Add Anything to Explanations of Stimulus–Response Compatibility Effects?
Robert W. Proctor and James D. Miles

The Function, Structure, Form, and Content of Environmental Knowledge
David Waller and Nathan Greenauer

The Control of Visual Attention: Toward a Unified Account
Shaun P. Vecera, Joshua D. Cosman, Daniel B. Vatterott, and Zachary J.J. Roper

Index

CPI Antony Rowe
Eastbourne, UK
May 23, 2014